THE CAMBRIDGE
COMPANION TO

JAMES JOYCE

EDITED BY

DEREK ATTRIDGE

Second edition

PUBLISHED BY THE PRESS SYNDICATE OF THE UNIVERSITY OF CAMBRIDGE
The Pitt Building, Trumpington Street, Cambridge, United Kingdom

CAMBRIDGE UNIVERSITY PRESS
The Edinburgh Building, Cambridge, CB2 2RU, UK
40 West 20th Street, New York, NY 10011–4211, USA
477 Williamstown Road, Port Melbourne, VIC 3207, Australia
Ruiz de Alarcón 13, 28014 Madrid, Spain
Dock House, The Waterfront, Cape Town 8001, South Africa

http://www.cambridge.org

First published 1990, 2004

Printed in the United Kingdom at the University Press, Cambridge

Typeface Sabon 10/13 pt.   *System* LATEX 2$_\varepsilon$ [TB]

A catalogue record for this book is available from the British Library

Library of congress cataloguing in publication data
The Cambridge Companion to James Joyce / [edited by] Derek Attridge. – 2nd edn.
p.   cm. – (Cambridge Companions to Literature)
Includes bibliographical references and index.
ISBN 0 521 83710 3 (hardback) – ISBN 0 521 54553 6 (paperback)
1. Joyce, James, 1882–1941 – Criticism and interpretation – Handbooks, manuals, etc.
2. Ireland – In literature – Handbooks, manuals, etc.   I. Attridge, Derek.   II. Series.
PR6019.09.Z52637   2004   823′.912 – dc22   2003062727

ISBN 0 521 83710 3 hardback
ISBN 0 521 54553 6 paperback

CONTENTS

CONTRIBUTORS

DEREK ATTRIDGE is Professor of English at the University of York. Among his books are *Peculiar Language: Literature as Difference from the Renaissance to James Joyce* (1988), *Joyce Effects: On Language, Theory, and History* (2000), and *The Singularity of Literature* (2004); edited volumes include *Post-Structuralist Joyce: Essays from the French* (1984), *Semicolonial Joyce* (2000), and *James Joyce's 'Ulysses': A Casebook* (2004). He has also published books on poetic rhythm and South African writing.

CHRISTOPHER BUTLER is Professor of English Language and Literature and Student of Christ Church, Oxford. His books include *Early Modernism: Literature, Painting, and Music in Europe, 1900–1916* (1994) and *Postmodernism: A Very Short Introduction* (2002).

SEAMUS DEANE is Keough Professor of Irish Studies at the University of Notre Dame. His publications include the novel *Reading in the Dark* (1996) and *Strange Country: Modernity and Nationhood in Irish Writing since 1790* (1997). He is General Editor of *The Field Day Anthology of Irish Writing*, 3 vols. (1991), the Penguin Joyce (1991–2), and the ongoing series *Critical Conditions: Field Day Essays and Monographs*, 11 vols. (1996–2002).

MARJORIE HOWES is Associate Professor in the Irish Studies Program, Boston College. She is the author of *Yeats's Nations: Gender, Class, and Irishness* (1996), section editor of the *Field Day Anthology of Irish Writing*, volume 4, and co-editor of *Semicolonial Joyce* (2000).

JERI JOHNSON is Senior Tutor, Ashby Fellow, and Tutor in English at Exeter College, Oxford University. She has edited *Ulysses, Dubliners*, and *A Portrait* for Oxford University Press and Virginia Woolf's *The Years* for Penguin, and she is currently editing *The Psychology of Love* for Penguin's newly translated Freud series. She has published essays on Joyce, Woolf, feminist theory, and textual theory.

GARRY LEONARD is Associate Professor of English at the University of Toronto. His two books on James Joyce are *Reading Dubliners Again: A Lacanian Perspective* (1993) and *Advertising and Commodity Culture in Joyce* (1998). He has published numerous articles on Joyce, modernism, and cinema in *Modern Fiction Studies, Novel, American Imago* and other journals.

JENNIFER LEVINE is Senior Lecturer in Literary Studies at the University of Toronto. Her essays on Joyce have appeared in various journals, including *PMLA, JJQ,* and *Novel,* and in collections such as *Joyce in the Hibernian Metropolis* (1996) and *Quare Joyce* (1998).

VICKI MAHAFFEY is Professor of English at the University of Pennsylvania and author of *Reauthorizing Joyce* (1988) and *States of Desire: Wilde, Yeats, Joyce, and the Irish Experiment* (1998), as well as numerous articles on Joyce and Irish writing.

MARGOT NORRIS is Professor of English and Comparative Literature at the University of California, Irvine. She is the author of three books on Joyce – *The Decentered Universe of 'Finnegans Wake'* (1976), *Joyce's Web* (1992), and *Suspicious Readings of Joyce's 'Dubliners'* (2003) – and two other books, *Beasts of the Modern Imagination: Darwin, Nietzsche, Kafka, Ernst, and Lawrence* (1985) and *Writing War in the Twentieth Century* (2000). She assumed the post of President of the International James Joyce Foundation in June 2004.

JEAN-MICHEL RABATÉ, Professor of English and Comparative Literature at the University of Pennsylvania, has authored or edited twenty books on modernist writers, psychoanalysis, and literary theory. Recent titles include *Lacan in America* (2000), *Jacques Lacan: Psychoanalysis and the Subject of Literature* (2001), *James Joyce and the Politics of Egoism* (2001), *The Future of Theory* (2002), the *Cambridge Companion to Lacan* (2003), and the forthcoming *Palgrave Advances in James Joyce Studies*.

JOHN PAUL RIQUELME is Professor of English at Boston University. He is the author of *Teller and Tale in Joyce's Fiction: Oscillating Perspectives* (1983) and *Harmony of Dissonances: T. S. Eliot, Romanticism, and Imagination* (1991), and editor of Fritz Senn's *Joyce's Dislocutions: Essays on Reading as Translation* (1984), as well as editions of *Tess of the d'Urbervilles* (1998), *Dracula* (2002), and *A Portrait of the Artist as a Young Man* (Norton, 2004).

JOSEPH VALENTE is Professor of English and Critical Theory at the University of Illinois. He is the author of *James Joyce and the Problem of Justice:*

Negotiating Sexual and Colonial Difference (1995) and *Dracula's Crypt: Bram Stoker, Irishness and the Question of Blood* (2002). He is also the editor of *Quare Joyce* (1998) and co-editor of *Disciplinarity at the Fin de Siècle* (2002), and his edition of Bram Stoker's *Dracula* appeared in 2003.

JENNIFER WICKE is Professor of English at the University of Virginia. She is the author of *Advertising Fictions: Literature, Advertisement and Social Reading* (1988) and co-editor of *Feminism and Postmodernism* (1992) and the twentieth-century volume of *The Longman Anthology of British Literature* (2002).

A NOTE ON THE SECOND EDITION

In the mid 1980s, I was invited by Cambridge University Press to edit a *Companion to James Joyce*. (Only Chaucer and Shakespeare had been accorded the honour of a *Companion* at that time, and the subsequent blossoming of the Companion series had not a little to do with the success of the Joyce volume.) This was a heady time for Joyce studies: theoretical approaches to literature, indebted primarily to developments in Continental philosophy, had begun to cast new light on Joyce's work, reinterpreting its challenges to the reader in ways that were both illuminating and enjoyable. Joyce's engagement with politics, including Irish nationalism, was being reconsidered. A new 'synoptic' text of *Ulysses*, edited by a team led by Hans Walter Gabler, had just been published, making possible a closer scrutiny of Joyce's working methods. It seemed to me that one of the goals of a *Companion* might be to make available to a wider audience the fruits of that fresh thinking, and I chose, on the whole, younger Joyce scholars who had only recently begun to make their mark.

By the time the volume was published, in 1990, that mark had been well and truly made, and as I write this, thirteen years later, those once young scholars are among the best-known names in the world-wide Joyce community. In the meantime, Joyce studies have not stood still; a series of new approaches to Joyce's writing, developing out of the earlier theoretical innovations and reflecting the successive waves that passed through literary studies more generally, have provided novel interpretations and discovered unsuspected connections. Many of these have involved fuller attention to historical and cultural contexts, especially the Irish context within which and against which Joyce wrote. The labels that have come to be used as short-hand for these approaches don't do justice to their interrelatedness, nor the variety of work that each of them covers, but they do suggest something of the range of new avenues opened up: cultural studies (or, somewhat more narrowly, the study of popular or consumer culture), colonial and post-colonial studies, gay and lesbian studies. Feminist studies, too, went through a transformation, partly in response to these trends. As a result of such developments, the first edition of the *Companion* can no longer be said to reflect the best of current and recent studies of Joyce.

This edition, therefore, includes essays on three new topics by scholars who have made important contributions to Joyce studies since the first edition appeared, 'Joyce and sexuality', by Joseph Valente, 'Joyce and consumer culture', by Jennifer Wicke, and 'Joyce, colonialism, and nationalism', by Marjorie Howes. A new essay on 'Joyce and feminism' has been contributed by Jeri Johnson, and *Dubliners* now has an essay of its own, by Garry Leonard. Regrettably, space considerations have meant the loss of a small number of essays from the first edition, although these will of course continue to be available in libraries. The other essays, and the suggestions for further reading, have been updated.

Although this edition is larger than its predecessor, many fruitful areas of the Joyce terrain have had to be left out. In particular, the study of Joyce's manuscript materials has flourished in the past two decades, and we now have a more particularized knowledge of just how he constructed ('wrote' seems an inappropriate word) his two last books, as well as having more accurate editions of his earlier ones. Anyone who wishes to pursue this dimension of Joyce's creation – which could be thought to extend as much as to underlie his published work – can consult the studies listed in the 'Further Reading' section.

The twenty years during which I have lived with the Joyce *Companion* have been made more enjoyable and fruitful by the cheerful co-operation of my contributors and the sterling efforts of a series of editors at Cambridge University Press: Terry Moore, Kevin Taylor, Josie Dixon, and Ray Ryan. My thanks to them, and to the many other Joyce companions who have travelled with me during this time.

DEREK ATTRIDGE

PREFACE

One might think of *all* the numerous books and articles published about Joyce's work as companions, offering the reader a range of different services: accurate texts, possible interpretations, helpful information, interesting anecdotes about the artist and his models. But few readers have the time – or the desire – to sift through all this material in search of what they most need, and this volume is offered as a first resort for those who wish to deepen and extend their enjoyment and understanding of Joyce's writing. It does not attempt to make Joyce 'easy' (though one of its aims is to remove unnecessary apprehensions about Joyce's 'difficulty'); nor does it present a grand survey of the monuments of Joycean scholarship and criticism. It rests neither on the assumption that all you need in order to enhance your appreciation of a literary text is somebody else's close reading of it, nor on the assumption that the key to comprehension is a mass of inert biographical and historical facts. Joyce's works are approached as verbal artifacts that succeed in exploiting with an extraordinary fullness the potential for human insight and pleasure latent within the verbal and cultural fabric of the twentieth century (which includes its versions of previous centuries); equal attention is given, therefore, to the patterns and peculiarities of Joyce's language and to the threads that weave it into the world's history. Chapters deal with some of the most significant historical contexts within which Joyce's writing takes on its manifold meanings, with the problems and rewards of reading Joyce's texts, and with Joyce's place in the intellectual and political movements of the last and the present centuries. A guide to further reading points the way to more specialized companions.

Joyce is the most international of writers in English. He shares with Shakespeare a global reputation, but, unlike Shakespeare, he crossed many national boundaries in his working career, in his outlook, and in his writing – extending his reach further and further until, in *Finnegans Wake*, he attempted to embrace the languages and cultures of the entire human community. Throughout his career, Dublin remained the other pole of his creative activity, but a Dublin constantly challenged and remade in the light of this internationalist distrust of patriotism and prejudice. A second feature of Joyce's work is the way it has intersected, and continues to intersect, with some of the most important transmutations of Western thought, both during his lifetime (one might include modernism, feminism, psychoanalysis, socialism, pacifism, secularism, and anti-colonialism) and after it (most notably in the movements known broadly as structuralism, post-structuralism, and post-modernism). The contributors to this volume reflect these two features of Joyce's writing: they are of many nationalities, and they all manifest in their different kinds of interest in Joyce an engagement with current intellectual and social changes. The volume as a whole also reflects the remarkable advances made in two areas of Joyce studies over recent decades: the excavations of scholars – textual, biographical, cultural, historical – and the explorations of literary theorists. I believe that the essays which follow demonstrate that the best writing on Joyce today takes advantage of both kinds of advance.

My task as editor has been made considerably lighter by the energy, commitment, and patience of my contributors. I would also like to thank Tom Furniss, Suzanne Hall, Jo Ramsey, and George Kearns for their help, and the students at Southampton, Strathclyde, and Rutgers Universities with whom I learned just how enjoyable reading Joyce can be. We are all, of course, indebted to scores of earlier readers and re-readers of Joyce, most notably James Joyce himself.

DEREK ATTRIDGE

1882   James Augustine Joyce, first child of John Stanislaus Joyce and Mary Jane ('May') Joyce, née Murray, born on 2 February in Rathgar, a suburb of Dublin.

1884   Birth of Stanislaus Joyce, who, of James's nine surviving siblings, was closest to him.

1888   Joyce family moves to Bray, a town south of Dublin. James enrolled in Clongowes Wood College, an élite Jesuit school. Downfall of Parnell (1890) makes a strong impression.

1891   Family financial difficulties cause the withdrawal of James from Clongowes, and a break in his schooling.

1892   Joyce family moves to Blackrock, in suburban Dublin.

1893   Further financial decline and move to the first of a series of more central Dublin addresses. James enrolled as a day student at Belvedere College, another Jesuit school.

1896   Becomes Prefect of the Sodality of the Blessed Virgin Mary.

1897   Wins academic prizes, including prize for best English composition in Ireland in his grade. Catholic faith dwindles.

1898   Enters University College, Dublin.

1899   Attends the riotous opening night of Yeats's *The Countess Cathleen*; supports Yeats.

1900   Publishes article on Ibsen in the *Fortnightly Review*; receives thanks from Ibsen. Reads paper on 'Drama and Life' to the Literary and Historical Society. Writes poems and plays, mostly destroyed.

1901   Writes 'The Day of the Rabblement', which is refused by a college magazine. Joyce publishes it privately.

1902   Graduates from University College; leaves Dublin for Paris, ostensibly to study medicine.

1903   Returns to Dublin in April on receiving news of his mother's illness. She dies on 13 August.

1904   Leaves the family home for a variety of residences, including the Martello Tower at Sandycove. Writes an essay entitled 'A Portrait of the Artist', and poems and stories for magazine publication (later to be included in *Chamber Music* and *Dubliners*). Starts work on *Stephen Hero*. Meets Nora Barnacle on 10 June, and leaves Dublin for the Continent with her on 8 October. Obtains job with Berlitz School in Pola (now Pula, in Croatia), then under Austrian rule.

1905   Obtains job with Berlitz School in Trieste. Son Giorgio born on 27 July. Submits *Chamber Music* and *Dubliners* to London publishers Grant Richards. Stanislaus comes to Trieste to join the family.

1906   Moves to Rome to work as a bank clerk. Writes two more stories for *Dubliners*.

1907   Returns to Trieste. Daughter Lucia born on 26 July. *Chamber Music* published in London. Completes 'The Dead', the last story of *Dubliners*. Gives private English lessons and public lectures, and publishes newspaper articles. Starts rewriting *Stephen Hero* as *A Portrait of the Artist as a Young Man*, radically reducing its length.

1908   Finishes three chapters of *A Portrait*.

1909   Visits Dublin twice, to sign contract with Maunsel and Co. for *Dubliners*, and to set up a cinema. His sister Eva returns with Joyce to live with the family.

1912   Family trip to Galway and Dublin; this is Joyce's last visit to Ireland. Joyce battles with Maunsel editor George Roberts over censorship of *Dubliners*. Printed sheets of the book destroyed by the printer, fearing libel action.

1913   Ezra Pound makes contact with Joyce.

1914   *A Portrait* starts appearing in serial form in the *Egoist*. *Dubliners* published by Grant Richards. Joyce begins work on *Ulysses*. War breaks out, and Joyce faces internment in Trieste.

1915   *Exiles* completed. Joyce and family permitted to leave Trieste for Switzerland; they settle in Zurich.

1916   *A Portrait* published in New York.

1917   Completion of three chapters of *Ulysses*. First of many eye operations. Harriet Shaw Weaver starts supporting Joyce financially.

1918   *Exiles* published in London. *Ulysses* serialization begins in the *Little Review*.

1919   Return to Trieste made possible by ending of war.

1920   At Pound's suggestion, the family moves to Paris, where they will remain for twenty years at a number of addresses. Court case prevents *Little Review* from continuing to serialize *Ulysses*.

1922   *Ulysses* published in Paris by Sylvia Beach's bookshop, Shakespeare and Company.

1923   Begins 'Work in Progress', eventually published as *Finnegans Wake*.

1927   *Pomes Penyeach* published by Shakespeare and Company. 'Work in Progress' begins to appear in sections in *transition*.

1929   Publication of *Our Exagmination round His Factification for Incamination of Work in Progress,* by Samuel Beckett and eleven others.

1931   Marriage of James Joyce and Nora Barnacle in London. Joyce's father dies.

1932   First grandchild, Stephen James Joyce, born to Giorgio and Helen Joyce. Lucia has a mental breakdown.

1933   Court allows publication of *Ulysses* in USA. Lucia enters hospital in Switzerland.

1934   *Ulysses* published by Random House in New York.

1939   *Finnegans Wake* published by Faber and Faber in London and Viking in New York. On the outbreak of war, the Joyces move to southern France.

1940   Permission granted to leave France for Switzerland. Move to Zurich.

1941   Joyce suffers perforated ulcer; dies on 13 January, aged 58. Buried in Fluntern cemetery, Zurich.

1951   Death of Nora Barnacle Joyce in Zurich.

ABBREVIATIONS

Except in the case of the following abbreviations, full details of works referred to are given after each chapter, either in the notes or in a list of works cited.

Archive	*The James Joyce Archive*, ed. Michael Groden, Hans Walter Gabler, David Hayman, A. Walton Litz, and Danis Rose with John O'Hanlon, 63 vols. (New York: Garland, 1977–9)
CH I, II	*James Joyce: The Critical Heritage*, ed. Robert H. Deming, 2 vols. (London: Routledge, 1970)
D	*Dubliners*, ed. Jeri Johnson (World's Classics; Oxford: Oxford University Press, 2000)
E	*Exiles* (New York: Viking, 1951)
FW	*Finnegans Wake* (London: Faber; New York: Viking, 1939). References are to page and line numbers (these are the same in all editions), e.g. *FW* 213.28. Chapters are indicated by book and chapter numbers, e.g. II. 3
GJ	*Giacomo Joyce*, ed. Richard Ellmann (London: Faber; New York: Viking, 1968)
JJ	*James Joyce*, by Richard Ellmann, revised edition (New York: Oxford University Press, 1982)
JJQ	*James Joyce Quarterly*
Letters I, II, III	*Letters of James Joyce*, vol. I, ed. Stuart Gilbert (London: Faber; New York: Viking, 1957; reissued with corrections, 1966); vols. II and III, ed. Richard Ellmann (London: Faber; New York: Viking, 1966)
OCPW	*Occasional, Critical, and Political Writing*, ed. Kevin Barry (World's Classics; Oxford: Oxford University Press, 2000)

P	*A Portrait of the Artist as a Young Man*, ed. Jeri Johnson (World's Classics; Oxford: Oxford University Press, 2000)
PSW	*Poems and Shorter Writings*, ed. Richard Ellmann, A. Walton Litz, and John Whittier Ferguson (London: Faber, 1991)
SH	*Stephen Hero*, ed. Theodore Spencer, rev. John J. Slocum and Herbert Cahoon (London: Jonathan Cape, 1956; Norfolk, CN: New Directions, 1963). References are to page numbers in both these editions.
SL	*Selected Letters of James Joyce*, ed. Richard Ellmann (London: Faber; New York: Viking, 1975)
U	*Ulysses*, ed. Hans Walter Gabler with Wolfhard Steppe and Claus Melchior (New York and London: Garland, 1984; New York: Random House; London: Bodley Head; Harmondsworth: Penguin, 1986). References are to episode and line numbers, which are the same in all these editions, e.g. *U* 10.124.

In quotations, spaced points (. . .) indicate an omission, while unspaced points (...) occur in the original.

I

DEREK ATTRIDGE

Reading Joyce

I

Far more people read Joyce than are aware of it. Such was the impact of his literary revolution that few later novelists of importance in any of the world's languages have escaped its aftershock, even when they attempt to avoid Joycean paradigms and procedures. We are indirectly reading Joyce, therefore, in many of our engagements with the past half century's serious fiction – and the same is true of some not-so-serious fiction, too. Even those who read very few novels encounter the effects of Joyce's revolution every week, if not every day, in television and video, film, popular music, and advertising, all of which are marked as modern genres by the use of Joycean techniques of parody and pastiche, self-referentiality, fragmentation of word and image, open-ended narrative, and multiple point of view. And the unprecedented explicitness with which Joyce introduced the trivial details of ordinary life into the realm of art opened up a rich new territory for writers, painters, and film-makers, while at the same time it revealed the fruitful contradictions at the heart of the realist enterprise itself.

Of course, this momentous cultural shift, which can be said to have altered the way we understand and deploy systems of representation, was not achieved single-handedly and at a stroke by James Joyce. His changing understanding of the way language relates to the world, the work of art to its cultural situation, the commonplace and repetitive in life to the remarkable and the unique, was symptomatic of a wider mutation of thought which had begun before he started writing at the very end of the nineteenth century, and had its complicated roots in the social, economic, and political transformations that occurred before and during his lifetime.[1] But in the field of prose literature, this much broader set of movements found its most potent representative in Joyce, and his own contribution helped to determine the particular form it took in this field.

There is a sense, therefore, in which we can *never* read Joyce 'for the first time'. Because of the ubiquity of his influence, anyone who now picks up a book of Joyce's already has at least some familiarity with the modes of his writing; and in addition the name 'Joyce' – and probably the name of the particular book – are likely to possess in advance a certain aura. This puts today's readers both at an advantage and at a disadvantage compared with Joyce's first readers. We are less likely to be baffled, dismayed, irritated, or intimidated by the strangeness of his writing (unless we have been led to expect something fearsomely difficult). On the other hand, we may miss some of its challenges to our own settled ways of thinking and making sense of the world because we muffle its unique voice: we can all too easily smother the text with our preconceptions about what it does and how it works, failing to perceive the things in it which are resistant to those preconceptions. If we do miss these challenges, we also miss some of the exhilaration, the humour, the pleasurable amazement that Joyce's work has to offer.[2]

I emphasize the pleasures of reading Joyce, because this is where any introduction to his work must begin; an account that loses sight of this fundamental point is in danger of forgetting why we read, or write about, Joyce at all. It is because his work has brought lasting enjoyment to so many people, even through translation into languages other than English or media other than print, that it has played such an important role in the world's cultural history. If we ever succeeded in fully explaining those pleasures, we would no doubt annul them, for they rely on qualities of inexplicability, unpredictability, inexhaustibility. But this is a danger we need not worry about: Joyce's texts are now so woven into the other texts of our culture that they constantly remake themselves as history moves inexorably on, and all our projects of explanation and interpretation get caught up in turn in this changing web, producing yet more transmutations in the very texts which they are trying to pin down.

If we can never read Joyce's works for the first time (though our pleasure may be enhanced if we always do our best to approach them with open minds), we can also never come to the end of our reading of them. We can never say, for example, '*A Portrait* has yielded up all it has to offer me; I can put it down with a satisfying feeling of completion and finality.' As I have suggested, Joyce's texts change as our own cultural surroundings change, which is one reason for their inexhaustibility; another (obviously related) reason is that they are unusually rich texts – and that includes the apparently pared-to-the-bone stories of *Dubliners* – which any single individual, even with the help of a whole library of Joyce criticism, would be unlikely to squeeze dry. Doubtless this inexhaustibility is to some degree characteristic of all the texts we call 'literary', but Joyce's work in particular seems to have a built-in principle of openness to further investigation, further interpretation, further enjoyment. One aspect of this capacity for infinite self-refashioning in Joyce's writing is the way it exposes and plays with the very processes of sense-making that underlie all experiences of fiction, so that the world in which we are invited to participate and find pleasure when we read Joyce includes the world of our acts of reading and comprehension. We cannot help making the attempt to come to the end of a reading, to reach a stable point where it all makes coherent sense, and we should never stop trying to achieve this moment; but it is perfectly possible at the same time to enjoy the prospect of an endlessly repeated failure to do so. Any critical text which claims to tell you (at last) what a work of Joyce's is 'about', or what its structure, or its moral position, or its symbolic force, 'is', has to be mistrusted, therefore; not because it will not be useful to you in a reading of the work in question, adding to your pleasure as you move toward that impossible goal of total understanding, but because it is making a claim that, taken literally, would exclude all other ways of reading the work, now and in the unpredictable future.

II

Reading Joyce is an activity which extends from the small-scale pleasures of appreciating the skilful organization and complex suggestiveness of a single sentence or phrase to the large-scale project of constructing a model that will impart unity (provisionally, at least) to an entire book or the entire *œuvre*, or even the entire *œuvre* together with the history, personal and public, of which it is part. Reading a text of Joyce's can be compared to playing a piece of music – it can be done rapidly, skipping over opaque or repetitious passages to gain a sense of the longer-range patterns and developments, or slowly, savouring the words, puzzling over the conundrums, following up the cross-references. (These two poles move further and further apart in Joyce's work, until in *Finnegans Wake* the ability to jump over a page of apparent gibberish is as important as the ability to spend half-an-hour on a single word.) Other contributors to this book demonstrate ways of reading at many points on this continuum; here I want to exemplify some of the rewards of a reading that focuses on detail, and to touch on a few of the larger issues that arise from such a reading. In order to do this, I have chosen, more or less at random, two passages from the extremities of Joyce's writing career; there is not space to examine any examples in between, but much of the discussion holds good for the rest of Joyce's writing.

The first passage comes from one of Joyce's earliest stories, 'Eveline', written in 1904 for a Dublin magazine, the *Irish Homestead*, and published under the pseudonym 'Stephen Daedalus'. Joyce placed it, in a revised form, as the fourth story in *Dubliners*, and it is from this version that I am quoting. Most of the story is taken up with the twilight thoughts of a young woman who has consented to an elopement in order to escape her impoverished and stultifying life in Dublin. The following passage occurs at the story's halfway point:

> She was about to explore another life with Frank. Frank was very kind, manly, open-hearted. She was to go away with him by the night-boat to be his wife and to live with him in Buenos Ayres where he had a home waiting for her. How well she remembered the first time she had seen him; he was lodging in a house on the main road where she used to visit. It seemed a few weeks ago. He was standing at the gate, his peaked cap pushed back on his head and his hair tumbled forward over a face of bronze. Then they had come to know each other. He used to meet her outside the Stores every evening and see her home. He took her to see *The Bohemian Girl* and she felt elated as she sat in an unaccustomed part of the theatre with him. He was awfully fond of music and sang a little. People knew that they were courting and, when he sang about the lass that loves a sailor, she always felt pleasantly confused.   (D 26–7)

At first sight, what is most remarkable about this writing is its unremark-ableness; it hardly seems to be 'literary' language at all. But that does not mean that it is a mode of writing which is completely transparent, a truth-telling style whose sole aim is to convey as convincingly as possible the actuality of a specific, though presumably imagined, personal experience. There is no obvious reason why we should take pleasure in being exposed to the experience itself; it reveals no glories of the human spirit, and its view of the history and sociology of Dublin is fairly commonplace. Rather, the content (which we are accustomed to thinking of as the *raison d'être* of fiction) serves as a vehicle for the manner of the telling, the slow release of information, the hints and presuppositions that we are invited to elaborate on, the rhythm of mental deliberation that propels the narrative forward, and – our present concern – the controlled language that through its very spareness possesses a hair-trigger suggestiveness. This is not to say that Joyce has reversed the relationship between content and form as it exists in every other story, but rather that he has revealed, by going to an extreme, how unstable that relationship is; and if many readers remain convinced that their pleasure comes from being presented with the actual events of the story, for which the particular mode of writing is merely a skilfully contrived channel, this is probably because our activities as readers are usually more complex than the terms in which we represent those activities to ourselves. (We are less likely to misrepresent to ourselves the way we read, or attempt to read, *Finnegans Wake*, where, as we shall see, 'content' does not offer itself up for immediate apprehension.)

We have no difficulty as readers in identifying the close relationship between the sentences of this passage and the thoughts of the main character. The story's opening sentence has, in fact, introduced us to a narrator with an identifiable style: 'She sat at the window watching the evening invade the avenue.' The lack of any introductory story-teller's formula, the unspecific 'she', the simple past tense of 'sat', the use of a distinctive poetic register sig-nalled by the metaphorical 'invade', the patterned sounds ('evening', 'invade', 'avenue') – all these announce the heightened realism of the dominant tra-dition of late nineteenth-century fiction, and the economical exposition of the conventional short story. But the style of the passage we are examin-ing is markedly different, its rhythms graceless, its metaphors dead, its dic-tion commonplace. We recognize a familiar novelistic device: the narrator's style has given way to one that mimics the speech and thought patterns of the character.[3] Much of the third-person past tense narrative can there-fore be translated into first-person present tense with no difficulty. The third sentence, for instance, easily becomes: 'I am to go away with him by the night-boat to be his wife and to live with him in Buenos Ayres where he has a home waiting for me.' Eveline is rehearsing future events she can scarcely believe in – and the unreality of this future as she recounts it to herself, the strangeness of that name 'Buenos Ayres' surrounded by the ordi-nariness, to her, of Dublin names, is among the hints that she may find it a future that, when it comes to the moment of decision, is impossible to realize.

But this translation, like all translations, changes the text; to read the sen-tence as it actually occurs, in the third person and past tense, is to hover between hearing someone think aloud and hearing someone tell a story about a person's thoughts. If a clearly-identified narrator commenting on Frank were to state that Buenos Ayres is 'where he had a home waiting for her', and we had no reason to think of the narrator as a liar, we would take this as a fact, a given of the story; if a character *thinks* it, however, it has only as much validity as we feel we can ascribe to that thought. Has Eveline found a rescuer, or just another Dublin betrayer? How accurate is her assessment of him – for which the story gives no objective evidence – as 'kind, manly, open-hearted'? There is no way we can give final answers to these questions, and although part of the reading process is trying to reach some tentative conclusion by studying the evidence of the text, of Joyce's writing more widely, and perhaps of the social history of Ireland in this period, the inconclusiveness is something from which we can never escape, because it is built into the story. If a careful reading produces uncertainty, we cannot pluck certainty out of it; Joyce was not so hamfisted a writer as to be unable to make it clear, if he wanted to do so, that Eveline's hopes of a new life are either entirely valid or entirely baseless.[4]

Not all of this passage is equally amenable to translation into first-person thought, however, and we have to pick our way through continually shifting perspectives, relying as best we can on our sensitivity to individual words and turns of phrase. 'He was awfully fond of music': that 'awfully' could only be Eveline. The phrase '*see* her home' followed immediately by 'He took her to *see* . . .' would be clumsy writing in novelistic prose but a natural repetition in thought or speech. And an orthodox narrator would not write 'when he sang about the lass that loves a sailor' but 'when he sang "The Lass that Loves a Sailor"'; for Eveline, however, what is important is not whether this phrase is the title of the song, but what it states and signifies for her relationship with Frank. The reader's enjoyment lies in identifying this language as language normally excluded from literature, but functioning here just as efficiently as the most elaborate of styles to suggest with immense precision a mind, a social milieu, a series of emotions. The pleasure is in the precision, rather than what it is precise about.

There are even more subtle ways in which the illusion of intimacy with the character's own thoughts is created. Look at the repetition of 'Frank' at the beginning of the passage, for example. A narrator would be bound by the rules of English usage to substitute 'he' for the second 'Frank', but the dwelling on the name, the almost ritual quality of the mental state-ment 'Frank is very kind, manly, open-hearted', which is not a discovery but a moment of self-reassurance, belong to the blend of pride, excitement, and anxiety that comprises Eveline's complicated mental state. After that repeated proper name, notice the refrain of *she*'s and *he*'s as subjects of verbs: where a polished writer would introduce some variation, Joyce hov-ers just this side of a banality which would destroy the reader's pleasure altogether.

But reading this text is not entirely a matter of responding to immediately categorizable verbal details. What do we make of 'his hair tumbled forward over a face of bronze'? This is no longer the way Eveline might speak, though its clichés are not characteristic of the narrator either. Perhaps we can read it as the faint echo of a story Eveline has read, and this too might set alarm bells ringing – is she interpreting her experience according to the norms of romantic fiction? What about 'unaccustomed' in 'she felt elated as she sat in an unaccustomed part of the theatre with him'? A slightly posh word going through Eveline's mind to match the rather posh seat? Or a comment from the outside by the narrator, whose voice we might have detected already in the word 'elated'? Then there is 'pleasantly confused'. Our readerly enjoyment here includes some appreciation of the elegant and economical way in which the phrase sums up a complex and contradictory experience – not the kind of enjoyment that Eveline's own style usually offers us. Or is this interpretation just the kind of smug superiority which Eveline finds all too common in her Dublin environment? Joyce's writing – if we read it with sufficient alertness – here raises questions about our own processes of interpretation and judgement.

As readers, we are made hungry for information while traversing this sparse verbal terrain, and we seize on anything concrete, such as proper names – 'Buenos Ayres', *The Bohemian Girl*. We may not recognize the latter name, but its symbolic force is evident: a bohemian girl is exactly what Eveline is not, and the visit to the theatre with Frank obviously stands as a kind of rehearsal of the life she is imagining with him, at once a challenge to conventional mores and – if we take the force of the 'unaccustomed part of the theatre' – an introduction to a new position of affluence and respect. Of course the symbolism of the title may be entirely the author's: Eveline probably reminds herself of the exact name because of its fashionable resonance rather than because of its appropriateness to her situation. But there is nothing unusual, in a literary text, about language that emanates simultaneously from two sources, 'unrealistic' though this may be. Another example is the name 'Frank': within the fictional world and in Eveline's mind it is just a given, but as a word in a literary text it raises a question – is it an appropriate name (as it might have been in an older literary work), or is it ironically inappropriate?

Joyce is engaged in the double task which faces all realistic writers: on the one hand, he is working to produce the convincing effect of a certain kind of mind in a particular emotional state and, on the other, to contrive a narrative progression which gives the reader an active role in piecing together clues and wrestling with uncertainties and puzzles. The demands of naturalism are for a degree of incoherence, a completely nonliterary style, and a minimum of information (since the character has no need to verbalize to herself things she already knows); the demands of the narrative are for clarity, an original and forceful style, and the gradual provision of judiciously organized nuggets of information that will create an onward drive toward revelation and resolution. At a moment like this, Eveline would normally think 'he', not 'Frank'; so Joyce gives us the emphatically repeated 'Frank' both to suggest the character's conscious dwelling on the talismanic word and to furnish the readers with a necessary fact. Eveline has no need to go over the chain of events whereby she and Frank became acquainted, but we are prepared to accept her rehearsal of them as a deliberate basking in the memory of an experience she still cannot quite believe in, as well as part of the mental stock-taking appropriate for a critical moment such as this. At the same time, however, Joyce heightens our awareness of the techniques he so skilfully deploys by raising questions about our strategies of interpretation. And to be aware of how much is going on in this apparently simple style – this is part of Joyce's revolution – is not to puncture the illusion of reality but to enjoy the many-sidedness of language and story-telling, and to relish the readerly activity one is called upon to perform.

If we decide to pursue our craft as readers further than the text itself, we have many contexts to turn to, all of which have the capacity to enrich our experience. The story is part of a collection, and its setting in a specific time and place becomes more important when it is read in this context. Eveline's predicament is understood as a version of a more general problem afflicting Dubliners of a certain class, and this may reduce any tendency to pass judgement on her as an individual. Interconnections between this story and others become evident; for instance, the narrative technique of 'Clay' is a more complicated development of that used here, and Maria, the central figure of that story, might offer a glimpse of what awaits Eveline when she finds, at the end of the story, that she cannot leave Dublin. (Maria, as it happens, sings a song from *The Bohemian Girl*.) Read as part of Joyce's entire *œuvre*, 'Eveline' takes on further resonances. The 'Nausicaa' episode of *Ulysses* presents in Gerty MacDowell an elaboration of Eveline, building fantasies around a stranger whom she interprets in the terms of the romantic world she has read about, while the theme of the mariner whose words need to be treated with caution is comically expanded in the 'Eumaeus' episode. And in *Finnegans Wake* the visiting sailor who offers marriage becomes a Norwegian Captain paying court to a tailor's daughter in a hilariously elaborated anecdote (311.5–332.9).

Other contexts beyond Joyce's *œuvre* beckon as well. There is the social, political, and cultural history of Ireland; further information about *The Bohemian Girl*, for instance, reveals that it is highly relevant to Eveline's romantic hopes. Written by an Irishman, it nevertheless concerns Austrian gypsies, Polish nobility, and a family-romance plot of secret high birth and love triumphant over (apparent) social disadvantage – the very antithesis of what Joyce believed Irish art should be concerned with. And there is the close connection between 'Eveline' and important events and projects in Joyce's life: his intense courtship of a young working woman in Dublin, and his elopement with her to the Continent (less than a month after the publication of 'Eveline'); his fiercely-felt rejection of the narrowness and sterility of Ireland's political, religious, and cultural life; his struggle to forge a progressive European cultural outlook in opposition to the ideological fantasies and fabrications that were to contribute in his lifetime to two world wars. Admittedly, the blandishments of a wooing sailor with stories of a better life on the other side of the globe are a very long way from chauvinist and militarist propaganda, but what can be learned, so pleasurably, from Joyce's critical explorations of the potency of fiction and rhetoric within specific social and economic contexts may help to sharpen the linguistic and conceptual vigilance needed to combat the totalizing and totalitarian manipulations of language and thought still powerful today.

III

Unlike the language of *Dubliners*, that of *Finnegans Wake* casts no spell of realistic illusion. The following is part of a sentence that occurs in II.3:

> . . . our allies winged by duskfoil from Mooreparque, swift sanctuary seeking, after Sunsink gang (Oiboe! Hitherzither! Almost dotty! I must dash!) to pour their peace in partial (floflo floreflorence), sweetishsad lightandgayle, twittwin twosingwoolow. (359.35–360.3)

Here we are not inclined to ignore the medium whereby the content is transmitted; this is language at its least transparent – and this sentence is, for *Finnegans Wake*, relatively free from obscurity. Indeed, it is difficult to talk of a 'content' that is somehow behind these words, pre-existing and predetermining them, as Eveline's mental state might be thought to lie behind the words in the earlier passage: the meanings we discover in a passage like this are clearly the result of an interaction between the text and whatever expectations and knowledge the reader brings to them. This is what happens when we read *Dubliners* too, but there the process is masked by the discreetness and submissiveness of the style.

The newcomer to *Finnegans Wake* may not respond to this unashamed linguistic productivity with delight, however. And if he or she turns to a book about *Finnegans Wake* for help, the result is all too likely to be a sense of intimidation: to make any progress at all, the *Wake* reader, it might appear, needs to be at home in several languages and cultures, to have absorbed huge tracts of esoteric lore and historical fact, and to possess the verbal dexterity of a crossword-puzzle composer as well as the patience of a saint. But there is another way of looking at the *Wake*'s notorious complexity, density, and length: far from demanding exhaustive knowledge, it can be seen as offering every reader, from every background, *some* familiar ground to walk on, precisely because it incorporates so much of the world's linguistic, cultural, and historical knowledge. A wider range of expertise is something the reader can aspire to, if the initial encounter with the book is positive; and then the large number of secondary texts hold out the promise of further pleasures. But the richness of *Finnegans Wake* may be thought of as a comfort, not a threat, to the beginner, since Joyce's work is quite unlike those 'difficult' books which can be understood only if the reader is familiar with a particular body of knowledge. In order to appreciate the *Wake*'s reader-friendliness, however, one has to abandon two assumptions about the act of reading which frequently exist side-by-side (though they are, on the surface at least, contradictory). One is that reading is an act of mastery whereby the text is made to yield up all its secrets and allowed to hold nothing back; the other is that reading is a passive experience whereby the reader receives meanings unambiguously communicated by the text. The *Wake* will never be mastered, never dominated or exhausted by interpretation, nor will it ever offer itself up unproblematically as a single set of meanings; and if a sense of control and singleness of meaning is crucial to a reader's enjoyment, frustration will be the only result. More than this, however: the *Wake* teaches us, in a most delightful way, that *no* text can be mastered, that meaning is not something solid and unchanging beneath the words, attainable once and for all. All reading, the *Wake* insists, is an endless interchange: the reader is affected by the text at the same time as the text is affected by the reader, and neither retains a secure identity upon which the other can depend.

Another Wakean lesson is that different readers find different things in a text, making it impossible to hypothesize a 'typical' reader; and probably more than any other book in existence *Finnegans Wake* responds superbly to group readings. Each member of the group contributes his or her particular insights, which in turn trigger others, in a process which creates a growing network of meanings and patterns. Often a suggestion advanced tentatively by one member ('This seems ridiculous, but I can't help hearing . . .') bears instant fruit as other members offer related perceptions of their own. What I wish to do is to imagine a group of new readers from different backgrounds tackling the book, armed with a minimum of prior knowledge but having available, for use as the discussion progresses, a good dictionary and a good encyclopaedia.

There is no need to begin *Finnegans Wake* at the beginning; let us imagine that our group of readers decides to start with a passage which seems less crammed with multiple meanings than most (I have already quoted part of it), and that one member volunteers to read it aloud:

We are now diffusing among our lovers of this sequence (to you! to you!) the dewfolded song of the naughtingels (Alys! Alysaloe!) from their sheltered positions, in rosescenery haydyng, on the heather side of waldalure, Mount Saint John's, Jinnyland, whither our allies winged by duskfoil from Mooreparque, swift sanctuary seeking, after Sunsink gang (Oiboe! Hitherzither! Almost dotty! I must dash!) to pour their peace in partial (floflo floreflorence), sweetishsad lightandgayle, twittwin twosingwoolow. Let everie sound of a pitch keep still in resonance, jemcrow, jackdaw, prime and secund with their terce that whoe betwides them, now full theorbe, now dulcifair, and when we press of pedal (sof!) pick out and vowelise your name.   (*FW* 359.31–360.6)

The response is a mixture of frowns at the stretches of apparent nonsense and chuckles as gleams of sense – however absurd – shine through. Some sort of purchase on the passage is obtained when the group quickly agrees that there is a syntactic scaffolding which, though interrupted by parentheses and elaborations, is quite firm, presenting a speaker who uses the first person plural to make a statement and to issue a command to a hearer or hearers addressed in the second person: 'We are now diffusing . . . the . . . song of the naughtingels . . . from their sheltered positions . . . whither our allies winged . . . to pour their peace . . . Let everie sound of a pitch keep still . . . and when we press of pedal . . . pick out and vowelise your name.' Syntactic stability is characteristic of the *Wake*, and it often helps in the unpacking of a passage to trace the bare trellis on which the luxuriant verbiage is hung.

The second aspect of the passage on which members of the group quickly begin commenting is the clustering of related terms, some of which are half-concealed in puns and portmanteau words.[5] The most obvious of these clusters concerns birds: everybody hears 'naughtingels' as 'nightingales', and one person who has listened without looking at the text finds the same word in 'lightandgayle'. (When someone else is reading from the *Wake*, it is often helpful to put the book down, as the visual configurations can mask aural echoes.) With this lead to follow, one member of the group who speaks some Italian realizes that the strange word 'twosingwoolow' sounds rather like a badly-pronounced '*usignolo*', which translates into yet another nightingale. No decoding is necessary to add to the cluster the terms 'winged', 'swift', 'sanctuary' (as in 'bird sanctuary'), 'crow', and 'jackdaw'; and someone suggests that 'Hitherzither' could be a description of the hither-and-thither movement of bird flight, perhaps that of the swift. But the group agrees that the main emphasis is on the sounds which birds make, and that a number of the repetitive phrases are reminiscent of conventional representations of birdcalls: 'to you! to you!' echoes 'to whit! to whoo!' (suggesting the additional presence of an owl, another nightbird to join the nightingales), and 'twittwin' suggests a twittering call. Other phrases seem built on similar models: 'Alys! Alysaloe!', 'floflo floreflorence'. Someone points out that the passage contains both 'song' and, buried in 'twosingwoolow', 'sing', while nightingales' song is often said to 'pour'. The syntactic framework is now taking on a body of sense, though that sense is beginning to overflow the rather limited possibilities provided by sequential English grammar. And each time a member of the group finds incomprehensibility suddenly yielding to meaning, or incongruity suddenly revealing a pattern, the discovery seems at once illuminating and ridiculous, satisfying and hilarious.

After a pause, someone notices that 'Florence' leads to another 'Nightingale', and this is picked up by someone else who spots a reference to the famous nineteenth-century soprano Jenny Lind (here apparently transformed into a place, 'Jinnyland'), known in Britain as 'the Swedish Nightingale' (which has become 'sweetishsad lightandgayle'). The next suggestion, by a member with an interest in mythology, produces a discussion but no agreement: is 'terce' a reference to Tereus' rape of Philomela, who was subsequently metamorphosed into a nightingale? The cluster of birdsong references is rapidly expanding, it would seem: to human song, to women, perhaps to physical desire. Are the 'lovers' who are being addressed bird-lovers, lovers of opera and other human song, or lovers in the sexual sense? Again there is no consensus, since all these interpretations can be defended with reference to the passage – yet there is no way of holding the various possibilities together in an organic whole. No subtle tone of voice, no imagined human situation, could make all these meanings valid at the same time: *Finnegans Wake* explodes the belief that language, to be meaningful, must be subservient to a singleness of intention and subjectivity. (So too, we may remember, does 'Eveline'.)

Once the group is on the track of human song a new cluster of terms emerges. One member realizes that the initially puzzling 'rosescenery hay-dyng' introduces two of the most prolific of opera composers, Rossini and Haydn; another suggests that 'twosingwoolow' contains a version of 'sing willow', a refrain associated with songs of lover's grief (she cites Desdemona's 'Willow Song' in *Othello* and – reverting briefly to birds – Ko-Ko's song about a suicidal tom-tit in *The Mikado*); and a third, who is familiar with the traditions of the Western Church, recognizes 'prime' and 'terce' as the names of the first two offices sung each day. He adds that 'vowelise' is close to 'vocalise', which as an English verb can mean to 'sing' and as a French noun is a singing exercise. As the discussion proceeds, human song broadens out to music and sound more generally: 'pitch' and 'resonance' obviously belong to this cluster, and someone who has picked up the dictionary informs the group that 'sequence' can mean 'a composition said or sung in the Western Church' as well as a melodic repetition, and that 'partials' are upper harmonics. Soon the group is picking out the instruments of a somewhat exotic orchestra in the passage too: a gong in 'gang', an oboe in 'Oiboe!', a zither in 'Hitherzither', a theorbo (a kind of lute) in 'theorbe', a dulcimer in 'dulcifair', and, by implication, a piano in 'pedal (sof!)'. And a different kind of organized sound produced by humans emerges from 'Almost dotty! I must dash!': Morse Code.

The proposal is made that the topic of sexuality should be followed up, to see if it also leads to a set of connected meanings. Several members comment together that 'naughtingels' contains not only 'nightingales' but also 'naughty girls' (or 'gels', if we imagine a certain kind of upper-class English accent), and soon other suggestions are forthcoming: 'waldalure' conceals 'allure' (and 'lure', perhaps, if sexual temptation is in the air) and 'twosingwoolow' contains 'woo'. Girls' names are a likely quarry for connotations of glamour and desirability, and the group may well pause on 'Alys! Alysaloe!,' which, backed up by 'allies', implies the presence of an Alice. Someone recalls that the author of *Alice in Wonderland* (the originator of the term 'portmanteau word') liked to entertain and photograph little girls, and an enthusiast of the theatre tells the group about a 1930s stage beauty called Alice Delysio and a French revue artiste named Gaby Delys. At this point, a sceptical participant objects that Joyce could not possibly have put all these meanings into the text, and two answers are forthcoming: one is that we cannot know for certain in any specific case that he did not, and the other is that even if we could, it need not make any difference, since Joyce has deliberately created a text with the power to generate more meanings than he had in mind.

While this discussion has been going on, one member of the group has been noting suggestions of seclusion (especially in natural surroundings) and darkness, which relate both to the nightingale cluster and to the hints of sexual impropriety. 'Dewfolded' implies both night and enclosure; 'sheltered positions' needs no deciphering; 'rosescenery hayding' gives us concealment in a rose-garden in addition to the composers already discovered there; and 'other' is appropriately transformed into 'heather'. A German speaker adds to the list the German word for 'forest' – '*Wald*' – in 'waldalure'; and a French speaker notices that 'duskfoil' combines the fall of darkness with leaves ('*feuilles*'). There is obviously a park in 'Mooreparque', and this is followed by the 'sanctuary' that has already been mentioned; then there is a sunset, or 'Sunsink', with perhaps an echo of the German word for the same phenomenon, '*Sonnenuntergang*', in 'Sunsink gang'. The suggestions of darkness draw the group's attention to words indicative of blackness – 'Moor' (triggering another association with *Othello*), 'pitch', 'crow', 'jackdaw' – as well as an allusion to 'Jim Crow'. The dictionary reveals that this last phrase, although it became associated with racism in this century, was originally the name of a Negro plantation song of the early nineteenth century; and the group considers whether this fact can be related to the presence of the words 'gang', 'pick' and 'hoe' (in 'whoe'). Of course it *can* be related, once the connection has been noted; whether it is a little entertaining dead-end or leads into a new exfoliation of meaning can only be determined by further reading – sometimes a tiny cluster like this can remain dormant for years until one suddenly finds that it is part of a pattern of linked terms running through the chapter or the entire book.

Someone now comments, 'I can't help feeling that the passage is also about battles, though the only example I can point to is the reference to Florence Nightingale, who became famous in the Crimean War.' Others chip in: 'The word "peace" is there'; 'And "allies" suggests a military force'; 'What about the Morse Code we mentioned earlier? – that could go with army signalling.' The group studies the passage for a few minutes, sensitized to this new potential sequence of terms, until light suddenly dawns: 'Of course . . . "waldalure" must be Waterloo!' And a member with some knowledge of that battle picks up the idea: 'Yes, it must be, because "Mount Saint John's" is Mont St Jean, a village near the battlefield whose name the English army used – it's where they built the Waterloo museum. And now I can see an extra reason for the word "allies": on the Continent the battle was often named after another village on the site, La Belle Alliance.' Someone else adds, 'When the passage was read aloud, "sound of a pitch" came over to me as "son of a bitch", but I didn't think it could be relevant – but it *is* the sort of thing you'd be called on an army parade ground. And maybe "pick out and vowelise your name" is an order to speak out and identify yourself.'

A question is now posed by one of the group: 'Is there a specific place where we can situate all this activity?' The answer, the group agrees, must be no, in that the passage traverses a wide range of countries; at the same time, those who have read Joyce's work insist that Ireland, and Dublin in particular, always have a special place in Joyce's writing. Someone who has read *Ulysses* remembers Leopold Bloom's meditations on 'Dunsink Time' – the local Dublin time determined at the Dunsink Observatory – and notices its form adumbrated in 'Sunsink gang'. ('Time', someone notes parenthetically, 'is also there in "secund" and the canonical hours, "prime" and "terce"'.) Another Irish connection is pointed out in 'swift', now not a bird or an adjective of speed, but the Irish writer Jonathan Swift; and the encyclopaedia provides the information that the estate in England where Swift was employed for a time was called 'Moor Park'. Swift, the group also recalls, went 'almost dotty'.

The word 'dewfolded' also arouses comment: although the group has noted the appropriateness of both 'dew' and 'folded' to the thematic concerns of the passage, the portmanteau word they make in combination still has to be explained. It sounds as if 'dew-folded' has been combined with 'twofold', and this provides yet another thread for the group to follow. The exclamations (evocations of birdsong?) always come in pairs: 'to you! to you!'; 'Alys! Alysaloe!'; 'Oiboe! Hitherzither!' 'Almost dotty! I must dash!'; and there is doubling in 'floflo' and 'floreflorence'. 'Twittwin' not only involves doubling, but the word 'twin', and it is immediately followed by 'two'. Two famous women figure in the passage, both Nightingales. However, there is clearly a triple principle at work in 'prime and secund with their terce that whoe betwides them', even if 'betwides' still contains a hint of doubleness in '-twi-' (a prefix we are particularly familiar with in 'twilight') as well as an oscillation between 'between' and 'beside'. This pattern of twos and a three seems to be important, but the group is unable to take it further – until it turns to other passages in the book.

The passage is now glowing with interconnected meanings, but a number of portmanteau words remain unexplained. As long as there is an element in a word unaccounted for there is something more to think about (not that the process would stop if all the deformations could be explained). It is all too easy, having unearthed one or more familiar expressions from a baffling portmanteau, to forget that the distortion itself needs explanation. Having identified 'Moor Park' in 'Mooreparque', for instance, the group still has to ask why it has undergone this transformation. The spelling 'parque' suggests Frenchness to everybody, with an obvious appropriateness to a passage dealing with Waterloo, but the French speaker also proposes that its meaning, 'fate', is connected with the warning 'woe betide them' in 'whoe betwides them'. And the spelling of 'Moore' with an 'e', someone observes, may be a reference to the Irish poet Thomas Moore – a suggestion that is clinched when someone else detects, in 'full theorbe, now dulcifair', the title of one of Moore's songs, 'Fill the Bumper Fair'. (We now have two Irish poets to go with the two Nightingales.) The group still has not come up with an explanation of the spelling of 'Oiboe!' (though the Italian speaker might have a suggestion), 'everie', or 'sof!'; it has not established whether 'in partial' echoes 'impartial' or 'in resonance' 'in residence'; and it remains undecided as to a possible cluster of tools that would include the jemmy and the crowbar of 'jemcrow' and the 'pick' near the end of the passage.

But it is time to pause and recapitulate. The passage presents a voice which describes the song of nightingales from their hiding places in dark vegetation; we, the readers (or listeners) are asked to keep quiet, and then to join in a singing exercise. Clearly this 'content' is of very little interest in itself, like so much of *Dubliners*. But other implications crowd in upon that voice, which we have to treat as only one element in a text that is speaking to us in ways that ordinary speech, with its linear simplicity, cannot achieve. The nightingales (perhaps two of them) are related to other birds associated with dusk, night, or blackness – owls, swifts, crows, jackdaws – and beyond that to women, especially women who sing and women who conventionally represent sexual temptation (though they may, like Desdemona, be innocent). All this takes place within an international context: languages and geographical references take us to Sweden, Germany, Italy, France, Belgium (for Waterloo), England, the American South, the Crimea; and although international co-operation is implied by this free market and by the evocations of many kinds of music, we also detect sounds of battle, hints of slavery, warnings of doom. Sexual difference, it seems, is mapped onto national difference, and sexual encounters onto military ones. (Or vice versa: there is no certainty about what is literal and what figurative in the *Wake*.)

To have got this far is to have transformed an opaque block of language into an almost-too-meaningful complex of ideas and associations; this in itself is a pleasing achievement, and the experience of finding more and more of the obscurity clearing is a fascinating and fulfilling one. In moving through the passage several times, with different thematic clusters in mind, our group has found many of the words and phrases accumulating a number of meanings, like pictures that look different from different perspectives – and this happens not just with portmanteau words and obvious puns, for the *Wake* encourages the reader to scrutinize *every* word for possible openings onto new meanings. From here the group might move to other passages, which would be illuminated by the discoveries made in this one, and on returning to this passage would find yet more in it. Members might also consult some of the secondary material on *Finnegans Wake*, such as the books mentioned in the section in this volume on 'Further Reading', or examine transcriptions and facsimiles of earlier drafts (not that these will furnish 'solutions' to problems of interpretation, but they can suggest fresh pathways to follow), or talk to someone who has spent longer on the *Wake* and has a sense of its recurrent patterns and concerns.

One context that can hardly be ignored is the chapter in which the passage occurs (II.3); like all the *Wake*'s chapters (and like those of *Ulysses*), this has its own distinctive character. It was one of the last major works Joyce completed before his death in 1941: seventy-four pages of Wakean language at its most multi-dimensional and its most comic, bombarding the reader with a constantly proliferating evocation of sounds and sights somewhat uncertainly localized in a Dublin bar-room and featuring both rowdy conversation and broadcasts from a television set and a radio. Armed with this knowledge, the reader will immediately recognize that the passage is based on a radio transmission. The presence of Morse Code hints at this, as does the inclusion of the French term for 'broadcast' – '*diffusion*'. A specific historical framework emerges once we learn that among the BBC's most popular programmes in the 1930s were live transmissions of nightingale songs. (The superior English accent we detected earlier could be that of the early BBC.) Indeed, if our group had started with the secondary material on the *Wake*, it might well have read the passage with the BBC broadcasts dominating its interpretation – a preconception which might have obscured some of the other leads that were followed up. The immediate context of the passage also makes possible a tentative psychological interpretation, since it concerns accusations of a sexual nature levelled against a male figure (usually referred to by the initials HCE): it may be that even the radio broadcast, to HCE's ears, becomes a further accusatory voice.

Ranging more widely, other passages in the book provide a number of constantly repeated motifs, scenarios, and anecdotes which enrich and clarify our reading of this passage. HCE's crime, never given a definitive form but recurring in a multitude of versions, seems to involve two young women committing an indiscretion – perhaps just peeing, perhaps more – in a park, usually Dublin's Phoenix Park (notice its ornithological name), and the whole incident's being observed by three soldiers. The park incident and its ramifications have been developing since the beginning of the book – should we choose to start there. We hear on the first page of 'sesthers wroth with twone nathandjoe' (3.12): these sisters are also Esthers, and Swift had two women-friends who both bore this name. (Unscramble 'nathandjoe' to find 'Jonathan'.) So in our passage Swift and the two girls in the park are not as unconnected as we might have thought, especially if we know that it was at Moor Park that he met one of the Esthers.

Read in this context, our passage seems more obviously concerned with sexual indiscretions than it did on its own; the 'naughtingels', the reiteration of 'two' and the presence of 'three', the emphasis on the bosky seclusion and dewy darkness of the scene, the coexistence of military and sexual imagery, and the fact that the sounds emanating from this hidden place are being publicly broadcast, all resonate with the book's many other versions of a sexual misdemeanour made public, and from there to considerations of transgression, guilt, accusation, and defence. (Other important versions of the incident in the park include the anti-British Phoenix Park murders of 1882, Eve's temptation of Adam in the Garden of Eden, and, as our passage suggests, the Battle of Waterloo – that word functioning as both a proper and a common noun, just as 'Frank' in 'Eveline' is both a name and an adjective.) Knowledge of the indiscreetly urinating girls also enables us to add a further meaning to the phrase 'pour their peace'. And very little that we have found in the passage is not repeated many times, in altered forms, elsewhere in *Finnegans Wake*.

The main point of the communal reading process I have imagined is not, it must be stressed, to demonstrate the complexity of a passage of the *Wake*; it is to show how that complexity holds open numerous entrances to the text, each of which will provide a thread of meaning, together with satisfaction and amusement, and each of which can be traced beyond the passage without the necessity of waiting until every word has been explained. The group I have imagined is obviously a rather exceptional one (though many of the leads I have indicated could have been provided by judicious use of secondary material); but what is important to realize is that it is not essential to an enjoyment of the *Wake* that all these meanings emerge. Since reading the *Wake* is a never-ending activity, it would be quite enough for the time being to register this passage as a radio interlude of birdsong, or as a tranquil evocation of nature, or as a version of the girls' misdemeanour in the park, or as an allusion to the Battle of Waterloo – and it would do no harm to skip it altogether.

If we do choose to linger on the passage, to draw out as many of the threads as we can, we may spend a considerable time, in a group or as individuals, saying the words over and over, listening to their sounds, studying their letters, allowing them to resonate to the furthest reaches of our memory; probably no literary text encourages as full an engagement with all the features of language and all the processes of reading as *Finnegans Wake*. New readers seldom appreciate just how much of the *Wake* remains unaccounted for in spite of the abundance of books and articles that it has generated, and feel that they are stumbling behind what other people have done when they may in fact be breaking completely new ground. One of the pleasures of reading the *Wake* is that it is impossible to predict when an item of apparently useless knowledge will suddenly illuminate a shadowy corner, since each of us is in possession of a somewhat different segment of the cultural treasure-house (or midden-heap, to use one of the *Wake*'s own images) which the text endlessly turns over. We may also want to spend time in the library with guides and reference books, in order to build on the work of others; this is how the individual reader can become the member of a group with a range of specialized knowledges. Some potential readers may question this expenditure of time, so far beyond that demanded by other works. But is not time spent per line of print a crude, because purely quantitative, measure? If we are going to think quantitatively, it might be more appropriate to consider the time Joyce spent in writing the *Wake*: a rough calculation would give us an average of nine days' creative labour per page;

or three days for our passage. An hour or two seems rather little to devote to its interpretation and enjoyment.

Our exercise of reading has also revealed how many of our usual novelistic expectations we have to suspend in reading the *Wake*: expectations that we will find a 'narrative voice', some 'characters', a 'plot', some kind of 'truth'. But it is not that these are absent; rather, they are present in *Finnegans Wake* in much greater abundance than we are used to. Several voices can be heard in this passage; there are a number of 'characters' (including birds, armies, singers, and lovers); plots are thick on the ground (stories of warfare, seduction, exhibitionism); and if there is no truth to be had, there are constant insights into the way language relates to meaning and to itself, the way cultures interconnect, the way history throws up coincidences and repetitions, the way guilt and temptation influence language and thought (and vice versa), the way stories, gossip, reportage, and a hundred other uses of words construct the world in which we live, love, fight, and dream.

All this does not make *Finnegans Wake* utterly unlike any other literary work, however. The kinds of reading to which it responds are only an extreme version of what we do with all literary texts. We have already seen that in 'Eveline', as plain a piece of writing as one could wish for, there are conflicting points of view between which we have to – yet cannot – decide; there is more than one implicit story being played out (the romance with the happy ending, the betrayal of the innocent victim, the escape route blocked by obligations to others); there are words and phrases that resonate in several directions ('face of bronze', '*The Bohemian Girl*', 'pleasantly confused'). Reading *Finnegans Wake* may seem a far cry from reading *Dubliners*, but the same attention to every aspect of every word, the same open-mindedness about possibilities of interpretation, the same curiosity and persistence can produce similar rewards.[6]

By beginning with a short passage in this way, we have avoided what is perhaps the more usual approach to the *Wake*: the application of a simple framework derived from an external source, used as a key to reading. Many readers pick up the book with the expectation that they will be reading about a dream, or about a family called Porter who live above a pub in Dublin, or about a night to complement the day of *Ulysses*; and they are inevitably disappointed when they find that pages go by without any apparent reference to their framework, which was supposed to unlock for them the mysteries of the text. Much more helpful, and derivable from a careful reading of passages rather than from Joyce's remarks to friends or the guesses of early commentators, is an awareness of the interconnected series of patterns, structures, relationships, anecdotes, and myths such as those we discovered at work in our passage. The publican's family is one such structure, but it does not hold the entire book together; the notion that the whole thing is a dream may provide a sense of reassurance when all seems obscure but does not give much assistance when a particular passage has to be elucidated. That Freud's *Interpretation of Dreams* is relevant and illuminating is unquestionable; but it functions like so many other books in the *Wake* – the Egyptian *Book of the Dead*, for instance, or Vico's *New Science* (or Freud's books on jokes and slips of the tongue, for that matter) – as a quarry for ideas, structures, phrases, formulae. Only the reader who spends enough time with the book to grow familiar with all its chapters needs to begin asking questions about total structure; how the coming of darkness depicted at the end of 1.8 relates to the sporadic references to evening in Book II (including those in our passage), night in Book III, and dawn in Book IV; why the seventeen chapters are divided into eight, four, four, and one; whether the 'concluding' monologue offers any kind of vantage point from which to survey the whole text.[7] Here again the *Wake* demands that we suspend our usual practice in reading a literary work. Normally we start constructing a hypothesis about the possible organization and meaning of the whole (whether in terms of plot, symbolic structure, moral lesson, or a combination of these) as we start reading, and as we go on we continuously revise this hypothesis, interpreting each detail in terms of it; the end of the book then comes as the revelation of its true form and thereby of the true meaning of all the details we encountered along the way. The *Wake* helps us to see that this is not the only way to read a novel; that the details may undermine or be in excess of any overall structuring principle, and that the structure may be something we create out of rather than derive from the elements offered by the text.

At the same time, the *Wake* makes it evident that we cannot read *without* creating structures, sequences, and relationships; that is what interpretation is. One reader will trace through the book all the references to night and the sleeping body, another will become hyper-alert to family and gender roles, a third will mine the text for impulses of desire and guilt on the model of psychoanalysis. All will produce valid and valuable readings, capable of enhancing the text for other readers; all will leave most of the *Wake*'s resources untapped. No single mind could give all the possible meanings of the *Wake* equal and simultaneous weight, and there is no need to assume that Joyce, brilliant verbal artist though he was, ever did. To create a text as full of interconnections as *Finnegans Wake* is, connections within itself and with the weave of human culture of which it is both simulacrum and constituent part, is willingly to lay aside the reins of intentionality and let the text's meanings work in the world to which it belongs.[8] The willingness to relinquish authorial control is an evident property of *Ulysses* as well; and is it not also true, to some degree at least, of 'Eveline', and, for that matter, of any literary work that engages with the texts, cultural, historical, political, commercial, psychological, or technical, of its time and ours? Reading Joyce is only one of many ways to pursue an interest in the unceasing traffic – in both directions – between words and the world, but it is one that can throw light on all the others, and offer as it does so the pleasures of an undogmatic and regenerative comic awareness.

IV

Reading Joyce's *œuvre* is, as an ever-renewed activity, more than a lifetime's work (or play); and when we take into account the massive heap of books written about that *œuvre* towering around it – and growing larger at an ever-increasing rate – the task of even beginning to feel at home with Joyce may make the newcomer quail. But there is no need for alarm: none of those books is essential to the reader of Joyce in search of pleasure and understanding, and at the same time all of them are potential allies. Although complaints about the overproduction of secondary commentary on Joyce (as with Shakespeare) will always be heard, it is a real problem only for the diligent librarian or the obsessive scholar. It is possible to think of the growing pile of books 'on Joyce' as neither a threatening rampart casting deeper and deeper shadows over the original brightness of Joyce's genius nor a heroic monument to the task of total elucidation whose final moment draws nearer and nearer. This metatextual mountain is not in any simple way *outside* Joyce's own writing at all: it could be seen as continuous with the text it surrounds, extending that text to something much larger and richer than it was when Joyce first wrote it; and there is also a sense in which it is *inside* Joyce's original text, interleaving and interlineating it, dilating it to many times its original size. Take the library shelves which hold a hundred books containing interpretations of Joyce: they also hold, inside those same books, much of Joyce's text itself, quoted, paraphrased, fragmented, dispersed, rearranged, expanded. In reading through those books you are reading, and rereading, the Joycean text itself, seen from constantly-changing viewpoints and enhanced by ever new juxtapositions.

However, there is no need to move beyond the original work at all to experience its special rewards. Help in reading Joyce is not confined to the books that surround his own; his texts themselves teach us how to read them, provoking laughter at our *naïveté* when we fall into the trap of thinking of the world they create as a world that existed before they brought it into being, encouraging us to do without our need for singleness of meaning or certainty of position, showing us how our language is a powerful, and powerfully funny, determiner – but also underminer – of our thoughts and acts. Many of the most influential literary theorists of the past forty years, whose views have percolated into thousands of classrooms, have testified to the importance of reading Joyce in the development of their ideas.[9]

So Joyce's work has actually been growing over the years, and the number of ways of reading it has also been growing, all of them of some value, none of them final or definitive. There could not possibly be a 'correct' way of reading, or even starting to read, the textual mass that consists of Joyce's texts themselves, all the texts of which *they* are readings (and we are only just beginning to appreciate how many of Joyce's words come not freshly-minted from his brain but copied out from other books),[10] all the works of Joycean criticism and biography which read *them*, all the transcripts and facsimiles of manuscript material, and all the other texts which have a potential bearing on Joyce. At one extreme are the readers who will read one or two of Joyce's books, relying entirely on the general familiarity I have already mentioned to help them find enjoyment and stimulation; at the other extreme are the professionals and the monomaniacs, who may attempt to read not only the Joycean texts themselves several times but, impossibly, all the other works with which they interrelate. In between are a multitude of options, all of them valid and valuable; there is no justification for saying that a reading of *Ulysses* by a Dubliner born towards the end of the nineteenth century is 'better' or 'truer' than one by a reader born in 1970 who has never set foot in Ireland, and the same applies to readers who have and who have not read the rest of Joyce's work, or biographies of Joyce, or the available manuscripts, or a pile of critical books, or a cross-section of early twentieth-century fiction, or the history of Europe. But what is undoubtedly the case is that all these encounters with Joyce are different, and to keep coming back to Joyce after detours through these and other readings (whether readings of books or of the world outside books) is to keep on engaging with recreated texts and thereby discovering new pleasures. If there *is* a way of reading Joyce that could be thought of as less than fully worthwhile, as something of a waste of human energy, it would be one that fails to bring together an active and curious attention to the words on the page with whatever store of knowledge and experience the individual reader has accumulated.

What I have been saying about the relation between Joyce's texts and the texts that surround them holds true for the different parts of Joyce's *œuvre* as well. The reader returning to a work of Joyce's after having read, or reread, another one finds it a different work (or, to put it another way, finds that he or she has become a different reader). Several of the essays in this volume discuss the interconnectedness of all Joyce's productions: not just the way the early texts prefigure the later texts, but the way the later texts rewrite the early texts, and in so doing proffer readings of those texts that would not otherwise emerge – and that Joyce himself, when he wrote those early texts, may not have been in a position to appreciate. To take one example: the beginning of *Ulysses* both continues and retroactively transforms the ending of *A Portrait*, exposing Stephen Dedalus's heroic ambitions as an artist at the close of the earlier text to the possible accusation of self-deceived posturing when we learn in the later text of their unimpressive outcome.

Something similar happens *within* the covers of Joyce's books, too: 'The Dead' can be regarded as a reading of all the stories of *Dubliners* that come before it, and thus offers the reader a fresh perspective on them; the later chapters of *Ulysses* reread and thereby remake the earlier chapters. And even the boundaries between works become porous; in some ways the first three chapters of *Ulysses* belong more with *A Portrait* than they do with the last three chapters of *Ulysses* – which in turn might be said to be a prelude to *Finnegans Wake*. To begin a work of Joyce's at the beginning and to read to the end is therefore to exercise only one of many options. New readers of *Ulysses* may find their first reading less arduous if they begin at chapter 4 (the opening of the second part of the book), then move from the end of chapter 6 to chapters 1 to 3 before proceeding to chapter 7. There will be some losses in doing this, but some gains as well; and we need not fear that the irate ghost of Joyce will come to haunt us with an insistence on linear integrity, since his texts themselves undo such a notion. One of the great pleasures of being a lifetime reader of *Ulysses* or *Finnegans Wake* is singling out one episode and treating it as a relatively independent work; many of these chapters are, after all, as long as a medium-sized novel. As a way of freeing oneself from too rigid a notion of the organic and self-sufficient work of art (a notion that Joyce expounds but also ironically exposes in *A Portrait*), it is sometimes worth trying to think of Joyce as the author of around sixty distinct works – with interesting interconnections – that happen to have been bound together as the chapters of a number of differently-titled volumes.

Equally, the unpublished and the published texts of Joyce interlock in ways which make the separation between these categories somewhat artificial (and render the notion of a 'definitive' edition an impossible one). Thus, for example, a kind of 'Greater *Finnegans Wake*' is emerging, consisting of the final text and the mass of notebooks from which it was drawn, carefully preserved by Joyce so that they could be read by posterity and now widely available in the facsimile edition of the *James Joyce Archive* and in the transcriptions of *The 'Finnegans Wake' Notebooks at Buffalo*. To give another example, the reader who reads *A Portrait* together with *Stephen Hero*, the

surviving fragment of its predecessor which Joyce abandoned, has a complex experience that cannot simply be described in terms of 'preliminary'
and 'final' versions of the same text. One way of approaching *Stephen Hero*,
in fact, is as an addendum to *A Portrait* exemplifying the type of novel that
the Stephen of the end of *A Portrait* would have written – and then, by the
time of *Ulysses*, abandoned.

As this example might suggest, there is a similar fluidity at the borderline
between fiction and biography; the various Stephens of *Stephen Hero, A
Portrait*, and *Ulysses*, together with the Shem of *Finnegans Wake*, are related
in interesting (and ultimately unspecifiable) ways not only to one another,
but also to the consciousness we perceive – with increasing difficulty – as the
'author' in each of these books, as well as to the individual named 'James
Joyce' whom we meet in the biographical accounts by, say, Stanislaus Joyce or
Richard Ellmann. (We might recall that Joyce's early pen-name was Stephen
Daedalus.) And the Dublin in which most of Joyce's fictions are set is neither
wholly identifiable with nor wholly distinguishable from the real city, just as
the 16 June 1904 we encounter in *Ulysses* is and is not a day in history of
which the newspapers bearing that date provide some record.

Yet another permeable boundary is that between the works as published
and the commentary which Joyce deliberately circulated to guide early interpreters. For instance, *Ulysses* carries no chapter-titles, but the reader who
is aware of the titles which Joyce gave to friends, knowing they would be
made public, and which have become standard in commentaries on Joyce,
will have a different experience from the reader who has not come across
them. We cannot say whether or not these 'are' the titles of the episodes,
however; all they offer us is a possible way of reading the book, one which is
based on a decision to ignore the striking blankness at the top of the initial
page of each chapter. (Accepting the titles does not lead automatically to a
single interpretation of the chapters that follow, however.)

As readers, then, we cannot divide up the Joycean text into absolutely
leakproof boxes: original/quotation, *Dubliners/A Portrait/Ulysses/Finnegans
Wake*, published/unpublished, fictional/historical, internal/external, and so
on. Part of Joyce's revolutionary achievement in literature, and in the understanding of literature and other cultural forms, was his demonstration of
the interrelations and interpenetrations of such categories. And we cannot
come to the end of making sense of the Joycean text, finding patterns and
structures in it, following tracks through it, and – by the same token –
deriving pleasures from it. It entices us into repeated acts of interpretation by proffering us keys and promising us conclusions, but it proffers
and promises with such teeming generosity that no single key or conclusion can stand for very long. In one sense, this makes it an extraordinary

œuvre, pushing to the limits all the traditional features of the novel as a genre such as characterization, narrative voice, plot, symbolization, and ethical or political significance; but at the same time this is what makes it such a *typical* literary *œuvre*, revealing just what a self-contradictory institution literature is, and just how much pleasure is generated by those contradictions in the ordinary act of reading. One result is that reading Joyce can make a difference to all one's reading, enriching, complicating, and perhaps even undermining it (at least until it becomes possible to substitute a fuller sense of what reading is for the narrow one that often prevails in educational establishments).

The number of entrances to the Joycean mansion, therefore, is potentially infinite; the main requisites for a visit are a sharp eye and ear, a willingness to be surprised, and of course a sense of humour. The chapters of this book provide introductions to some of these ways in, and will suggest many more in passing. Different readers will, of course, find some approaches more congenial than others: if you like crossword puzzles you may enjoy piecing together the scraps of information about the characters' lives scattered through *Ulysses* or constructing a plausible plot that might undergird the linguistic extravagances of *Finnegans Wake*; if you value the textures of language that poets have traditionally exploited you can relish the carefully modulated patterns of Joyce's sounds and syntax; if you find coincidences, human oddities, and unexpected incongruities funny, Joyce will provide endless amusement; if you enjoy the novelist's capacity to convey the motions of thought and feeling or the sensory experiences of the body, there will be mimetic pleasures in abundance for you; if you have an interest in history, in culture, in politics, in the problems of the artist, in literary theory, you will find that any of these will open doors in Joyce's works. But these are only ways in: Joyce's writing can reveal sources of fascination and exhilaration which you were not expecting to find, and if you feel at times that Joyce is laughing at you just as much as you are laughing at him, you have begun to appreciate the delightfully unsettling energies of his art.

NOTES

1 Other chapters of this book trace some of the ways in which Joyce's achievement was both shaped by and helped to shape a wider complex of cultural movements.
2 Joyce's shorter published works – his collections of poetry and the play *Exiles* – are, at least on the surface, more obviously conventional than his four major works, *Dubliners, A Portrait of the Artist as a Young Man, Ulysses,* and *Finnegans Wake*; but some of the texts which remained unpublished during his lifetime, notably *Giacomo Joyce*, also demand unusual strategies of reading (see Vicki Mahaffey's contribution to this volume).

3 This device goes by many names – free indirect discourse, narrated monologue, empathetic narrative, *style indirect libre, erlebte Rede* – and is perhaps best regarded as a cluster of techniques ranging from precisely recoverable thoughts to a slight colouring of the narrator's style by that of the character. (A related device, in which specific thoughts are not implied, goes by the name of 'The Uncle Charles Principle': see Hugh Kenner, *Joyce's Voices* (Berkeley: University of California Press, 1978), ch. 2.) Earlier examples, such as those in Jane Austen's fiction, usually involve the thoughts of more highly educated and sophisticated characters than Joyce chooses. Joyce's revisions of 'Eveline' for *Dubliners* involved many substitutions of words and phrases more appropriate to Eveline's limited mental world than the ones he first used (see *Dubliners*, Viking Critical Library edition, ed. Robert Scholes and A. Walton Litz (New York: Viking, 1969), pp. 238–40).

4 The most vigorous proponent of the view that Frank is a liar has been Hugh Kenner; for a discussion of Kenner's various accounts of the story, and a counter-argument, see Sidney Feschbach, '"Fallen on His Feet in Buenos Ayres": Frank in "Eveline"', *JJQ* 20 (1983), 223–7. In a traditional narrative, of course, the truth would be revealed in the denouement. Katherine Mullin, in her chapter on 'Eveline' in *James Joyce, Sexuality and Social Purity* (Cambridge: Cambridge University Press, 2003), shows how complex were the associations of Buenos Aires as a destination for Irish women in the late nineteenth century.

5 The portmanteau words of *Finnegans Wake* – Joycean inventions which fuse two or more words, sometimes in different languages – probably constitute the most alarming feature of the book for new readers; they are also central to its operation and the pleasures to be had from it. For further discussion, see Derek Attridge, *Peculiar Language: Literature as Difference from the Renaissance to James Joyce* (Ithaca: Cornell University Press, 1988), ch. 7.

6 There are, of course, many passages in *Dubliners* with more elaborately contrived subtleties than the relatively simple example we have examined. See also Garry Leonard's discussion of the language of *Dubliners* in ch. 5.

7 For an interpretation of the *Wake*'s structure which discusses these matters, as well as making valuable use of Freudian dream theory, see Margot Norris's contribution to this volume.

8 It is worth pondering why *Finnegans Wake* is as long as it is – could not Joyce have achieved the same results in a much shorter work? One answer would be that only a work of massive proportions could produce such rich and overdetermined inter-connections that it escapes any possibility of interpretative mastery, and achieves an openness to all possible futures akin to that of the human brain itself.

9 Jacques Derrida discusses his indebtedness to Joyce in 'Two words for Joyce', in Derek Attridge and Daniel Ferrer, eds., *Post-Structuralist Joyce: Essays from the French* (Cambridge: Cambridge University Press, 1984), pp. 145–59; Hélène Cixous wrote her doctoral dissertation – and many later essays – on Joyce; Julia Kristeva has paid special attention to Joyce in her theoretical writtings on literature; and Jacques Lacan devoted one of his famous seminars to Joyce. Northrop Frye, Wolfgang Iser, Umberto Eco, Fredric Jameson, Stephen Heath, Raymond Williams, and Colin MacCabe have all written important texts on Joyce. Even those who

have reacted vigorously against Joyce – like Georg Lukács and Carl Gustav Jung – have recognized his importance.

10 The study of manuscript materials is currently revealing how much of Joyce's writing is built up from jottings made in notebooks while he went through other books; see Margot Norris's discussion of the genesis of *Finnegans Wake* (pp. 157–9 below), and the works listed in Further Reading.

2

SEAMUS DEANE

Joyce the Irishman

In *Stephen Hero*, the abandoned forerunner to *A Portrait of the Artist as a Young Man*, the undergraduate artist-hero attacks the Irish educational system and gives promise of his rebellion against it and the culture it represents:

> The deadly chill of the atmosphere of the college paralysed Stephen's heart. In a stupor of powerlessness he reviewed the plague of Catholicism . . . The spectacle of the world in thrall filled him with the fire of courage. He, at least, though living at the farthest remove from the centre of European culture, marooned on an island in the ocean, though inheriting a will broken by doubt and a soul the steadfastness of whose hate became as weak as water in siren arms, would lead his own life according to what he recognised as the voice of a new humanity, active, unafraid and unashamed. (SH 198–9/194)

Joyce's repudiation of Catholic Ireland and his countering declaration of artistic independence are well-known and integral features of his life-long dedication to writing. Yet he was formed by the Ireland he repudiated and his quest for artistic freedom was itself shaped by the exemplary instances of earlier Irish writers who had, in his view, failed to achieve that independence which he sought for himself, an independence which was at once the precondition and the goal of writing.

When we survey his achievement in retrospect, it seems surprising that the uncertain and fragmented accomplishment of nineteenth-century Irish literature should have reached a culmination in his fiction and in the poetry of Yeats. It seems quite inexplicable that an oppressed and turbulent country, which had lost half its population and its native language only thirty-five years before Joyce was born, could have begun to produce literature of world importance as he reached his early teens. But some explanations are forthcoming when we look more closely at Irish literary culture in the nineteenth century. Most importantly, an understanding of some of the stresses and strains of that literature help us to understand why Joyce produced works like *Ulysses* and *Finnegans Wake* in his maturity. The deformations of the

English language and of the traditional form of the novel which we encounter in these are anticipated in the conflict between Irish, Hiberno-English and standard English which is a feature of the Irish writing Joyce knew.

The most important of Joyce's Irish predecessors was the poet James Clarence Mangan (1803–49), whose tragic and miserable life was represented by Joyce as an emblem of the characteristic alienation of the true artist. More significantly, Joyce exaggerated the extent to which Mangan had been ignored by his countrymen after his death. For, as Joyce saw it, Mangan also represented the artist who was spurned by his countrymen in a typically treacherous fashion, largely because he had identified his own multifarious woes with those of his suffering country. Joyce's obsession with betrayal manifests itself in unmistakable fashion in the lectures he delivered on Mangan, in Dublin in 1902 and in Trieste in 1907. Wherever he looked, in Irish political or literary history, he found that the master-theme was betrayal. The great political crisis which dominated his early life – the fall of Parnell – probably governed this reading of his country's past and helped to define for him the nature of the embattled future relationship between him and his Irish audience. Parnell was, in Joyce's view, a heroic spirit brought low by his own people, who sold him 'to the pharisaical conscience of the English non-conformists' (*OCPW* 144) or, in a more famous formulation, listened to Parnell's plea that they should not throw him to the English wolves. 'They did not throw him to the English wolves: they tore him apart themselves' (*OCPW* 196).

It may be that betrayal was a Joycean obsession; certainly it provided him with a way of reading the Irish past as a series of narratives which led to the same, monotonous denouement. But betrayal implies a preceding solidarity, a communion between the victim and his treacherous countrymen. The most appealing and dangerously seductive form of solidarity in Irish conditions was that offered by Irish nationalism, in all its variant forms, from the United Irishmen of 1798 to the Young Ireland movement of the 1840s and the more recent Fenian and Home Rule movements. It was Mangan's downfall as an artist that he could not free himself from the tragic history of his nation. 'The history of his country encloses him so straitly that even in his moments of high passion he can but barely breach its walls' (*OCPW* 135). Mangan's art is, therefore, caught in the toils of a political crisis from which it can never be freed until that crisis has been resolved. So 'the most distinguished poet of the modern Celtic world' (*OCPW* 131) has suffered oblivion in his own land because he is, on the one hand, not national enough, and, on the other hand, too national ever to be appreciated for his own individual and remarkable qualities as a poet. This paradox leads to Joyce's declaration that if Mangan is to achieve the posthumous recognition he deserves, it will be without the help of his countrymen; and if he is ever accepted by the Irish as their national poet it will only be when the conflicts between Ireland and the foreign powers ('the Anglo-Saxon and the Roman Catholic') are settled. This settlement 'will give rise to a new civilization, either indigenous or purely foreign. Until that time, . . . he will be forgotten' (OCPW 130). The history of Mangan, his miserable life and the oblivion Joyce claimed had descended upon him after his death, was a carefully construed cautionary tale for the Irish artist who wished to elude the fickle acclaim of his treacherous countrymen. The portrait of Mangan is one of Joyce's early fictions. It is his portrait of the artist as a Young Ireland man.

But the portrait reduces the importance of other aspects of Mangan's career which have a direct bearing on Joyce. We are told how competent a linguist Mangan was, how he knew the languages and literatures of Italy, Spain, France, Germany, England and, of course, Ireland. In addition, he had some Sanskrit and Arabic. In a passage which could be a description of Joyce himself, we are told:

> The learning of many lands goes with him always, eastern tales and the memory of curiously printed medieval books which have rapt him out of his time – gathered together day by day and embroidered as in a web. He has acquaintance with a score of languages, of which, upon occasion, he makes a liberal parade, and has read in many literatures, crossing how many seas, and even penetrating into Peristan, which is not to be found in any atlas. (OCPW 132)

This is Mangan disguised as Joyce. Mangan's linguistic competence was not of this order at all. But the central fact about Mangan's poetry is that so much of it is offered to us as translation, often from exotic sources, Turkish, Coptic, Arabic, which were beyond his reach. Mangan is a characteristic nineteenth-century Irish author in his fascination with translation as an act of repossession. He betrays other languages into English, the better to possess both them and the English in which he writes; but his ultimate 'betrayal' is that of his own authorship. He is not the original author, merely a secondary, intermediate author. He is an artist whose relationship to his material is oblique, regarding it as something rare and strange which passes over into language that cannot but be secondary, insufficient. In this respect, he is indeed a central figure in the literature of the period in Ireland. For the role of translation in Irish letters had, at least from the beginning of the nineteenth century, become crucial in a country in which the riches of the native literature were being made accessible in the English language as part of the effort of the new cultural nationalism which had emerged after the Act of Union in 1800. This movement was led by Sir Samuel Ferguson

(1810–86) and others in the pages of the *Dublin University Magazine*, founded in 1833, and then by Thomas Davis and his allies in the pages of the *Nation*, the newspaper which spoke for the nationalist Young Ireland movement. Mangan's poems appeared in both these publications. Moreover, he was for a time employed in the Ordnance Survey Office in Dublin, from which the 're-mapping' of Ireland was being carried out. In this remapping, Irish place-names, of every description, were to be re-rendered in English equivalents.[1] Mangan was, in other words, centrally involved in a series of movements in which translation played an important part, the translation of ancient literature and names into an English which would be, simultaneously, an estrangement from the original and also a means of repossessing that which had been lost.

Joyce's own career as a writer is dominated by the same linguistic anxieties. He could write the spiritual history of his own country, but only when he found that mode of English appropriate to Irish experience, through which the Irish could repossess their experience in an English which was unmistakably an Irish English. In that light, Mangan was bound to be as important to him as was William Carleton to Yeats.[2] Yet Mangan's essential alienation from the nationalist cause, to which he had been recruited by the Fenian rebel John Mitchel (see the latter's introduction to the *Poems of James Clarence Mangan* (1859), reprinted with the centenary edition of the *Poems* in 1903), had great appeal for Joyce. Although he shared the general view that Mangan was a nationalist poet, he also recognized that the poetry would not be seen for what it truly was as long as the two imperialisms, British and Roman Catholic, prevailed. Nor did he believe that nationalism was anything other than an extension of those imperialisms, despite its apparent antagonism to them. Like Mangan, he could find no alternative to imperialisms and nationalism other than an attitude of fierce repudiation.[3] In his disaffection, he sought to show that the theme of betrayal, which dominated the political narrative of nationalism, also characterized translation, its preferred method of cultural repossession.

Thus, in Ireland, the problem of being a writer was in a very specific sense a linguistic problem. But it was also a political problem. The possibility of maintaining one's integrity as an artist while being involved with a community's enterprise was, initially at least, looked upon with scepticism by Joyce. Yet the achievement of that integrity could only be complete when it was expressed as an indication of communal and not merely personal possibility. In that respect, Joyce's project went beyond what Mangan represented.

The essential loneliness and apartness of the artist was tragically epitomized by other writers, and in other conditions. If Mangan served as the primary Irish example in Irish conditions, Oscar Wilde was the most notorious

Irish example in English conditions. Joyce does not give particular stress to Wilde's Irishness, although it is an element in his interpretation of Wilde's fate. Instead, he chooses to read the life and work of Wilde in a religious, specifically Catholic, light. Wilde died a Roman Catholic – he 'closed the chapter of the rebellion of his spirit with an act of spiritual devotion' (*OCPW* 150). For Joyce, there is a peculiar fitness in this last act of the life. For it was in accord with

> the vital centre of Wilde's art: sin. He deceived himself by thinking that he was the harbinger of the good news of neo-paganism to the suffering people. All his characteristic qualities, the qualities (perhaps) of his race: wit, the generous impulse, the asexual intellect were put to the service of a theory of beauty which should, he thought, have brought back the Golden Age and the joy of youth to the world. But deep down, if any truth is to be educed from his subjective interpretation of Aristotle, his restless thought which proceeds by sophisms rather than syllogisms, his assimilations of other natures alien to his own, such as those of the delinquent and the humble, it is the truth inherent in the spirit of Catholicism: that man cannot reach the divine heart except across that sense of separation and loss that is called sin. (*OCPW* 151)

Once more, we see Joyce translating an author into his own image, or, at least, into the image of his own protagonist, Stephen Dedalus. Wilde is a type of the heroic artist brought down, like Parnell, by the mob. But his life, like Mangan's, contains within itself a spiritual truth which has been obscured by the public version of his career. In Wilde's case, the secret of that truth was best represented in his novel *Dorian Gray*. Wilde is, as an artist, no more the preacher of the new paganism to an enslaved people than was Mangan the preacher of freedom to an oppressed community. In each case, the truth is more fundamental than that. In each case, the truth is to be found in the apartness, the separateness of the artist, a separateness which is experienced only because it was preceded by a repudiation of fake solidarity. Wilde's mother, Lady Wilde, was a fierce Irish nationalist who wrote for the *Nation* newspaper under the pen-name 'Speranza'. Little trace of that nationalism remains in Wilde's writings. His rejection of middle-class culture is even more complete. His peculiar blend of socialism and dandyism and his assiduous attempts to create a myth of himself have their affinities with Mangan's careful creation of an adversarial and tragic version of his own life. Mangan's 'translations' from the Arabic, indeed his re-siting of his poetry within the frame of the Orient, are analogous to Wilde's revision of the bourgeois society in terms of classical Greece and the 'new paganism' which he derived from it. Like Mangan, Wilde assimilates natures foreign to his own, producing the fiction of a new and revolutionary community both as an alternative to existing social and political forms and as an antidote to and an assertion of separateness. Once more, we are involved in an act of translation. An original state of belonging is exchanged for a secondary state of separateness which then, by assimilation and translation of 'foreign' materials, tries to reconstitute a more genuine communality.

For Joyce too, this is a central problem. He returns to it in the opening chapter of *Ulysses*, in which Buck Mulligan, the poor man's Wilde, mouths the doctrine of Wilde's 'new paganism' (*U* 1.176). Mulligan, Wilde's 'Irish imitator' (*Letters II* 150) is, of course, a betrayer, the 'Usurper' (*U* 1.744), the quoter of Wilde's prefatory aphorism to *Dorian Gray*, translated into the new emblem of Irish art. He refers to Caliban's rage at not seeing his face in a mirror and exclaims to Stephen, 'If only Wilde were alive to see you', which evokes Stephen's bitter retort that the mirror is a symbol of Irish art, 'The cracked lookingglass of a servant' (*U* 1.143–7). In Irish conditions, mimesis is a double problem. The mirror that is held up to nature is cracked and it belongs to a servile race, a race of imitators, a people that cannot bear to see its own sorry reflection in the glass, nor bear to see that its authentic nature is not reflected in the glass. It is either a distorted image or it is no image. Joyce, therefore, gives an extra twist to Wilde's dicta in the Preface to *Dorian Gray*:

> The nineteenth century dislike of Realism is the rage of Caliban seeing his own face in a glass.
>
> The nineteenth century dislike of Romanticism is the rage of Caliban not seeing his own face in a glass.

Joyce, in his reading of Wilde, recognizes that the issue of representation is critical for the Irish artist. Mangan's art was recognizable to the extent that it seemed to represent nationalism in art; Wilde's to the extent that it represented the 'new paganism'. But these representations are merely analogues for what each was trying to represent. Someone like Buck Mulligan intensifies the problem by being himself a false representation, an imitator, of Wilde. He embodies the servility of the Irish imagination. Joyce himself, on the other hand, sees his role as that of the artist who will not, like Mangan, be distorted in the glass of communal desire. He will be the true artist. He will escape false representation and, in doing so, come to terms with the medium in which this representation has been made – the vexed medium of a language which carries within itself the idea of the re-presentation in one form of a culture which initially existed in another, earlier form. In a newspaper article of 1907, 'Ireland at the Bar', Joyce protested at the misrepresentation of Ireland to the world and chose, as an illustration of his theme, the story of a namesake, Myles Joyce, who was executed for a murder he did not commit. Myles Joyce was tried in an English-speaking court, but knew no English. His language was Irish. For James Joyce, he is a symbol, one he will revert to again in *Finnegans Wake*. 'The figure of this bewildered old man, left over from a culture which is not ours, a deaf-mute before his judge, is a symbol of the Irish nation at the bar of public opinion' (*OCPW* 146). Representation is a language problem; but it is also a problem to decide what is to be represented. The civilization of Myles Joyce is not that of James Joyce. What civilization, then, does James Joyce possess?

In *The Decay of Lying* (1891), one of Wilde's personae had confronted the inversion of the belief that Art imitates Life.

> I can quite understand your objection to art being treated as a mirror. You think it would reduce genius to the position of a cracked looking-glass. But you don't mean to say that you seriously believe that Life imitates Art, that Life in fact is the mirror, and Art the reality?

In bending forward to see himself in the cracked mirror which Mulligan has taken from the maid's room at his aunt's house, Stephen sees himself as others see him. Genius is thus reduced. What looks at him from the servant's mirror is 'Life'; the consciousness that surveys this reflection is 'Art'. The mirror is offered by the mock-Wildean, the fake artist who steals from the servile the emblem of reality. This, of course, is part of Joyce's objection to the Irish Literary Revival, expounded with considerable force and bitterness in his pamphlet of 1901, 'The Day of the Rabblement'.

The artist who 'courts the favour of the multitude' (*OCPW* 51) becomes a slave to it. In words similar to those he used in the passage from *Stephen Hero* (quoted above), Joyce goes on to say that such an artist's 'true servitude is that he inherits a will broken by doubt and a soul that yields up all its hate to a caress; and the most seeming-independent are those who are the first to reassume their bonds' (*OCPW* 52). Enslavement to the 'rabblement' is the governing condition of representation. This truth had made itself evident in Mangan and had been seen by Wilde; both had been cruelly victimized by it. Now, in 1901, it was manifesting itself again in the work of the Irish National Theatre and its concession to folk-art, a sorry collapse after a promising beginning. Once more, truth was betrayed.

Although Joyce was opposed to the folkish, even folksy, elements of the Irish Revival, he is himself a dominant figure in that movement. Officially, he stands apart, as ever. Yeats, George Moore, Edward Martyn, Lady Gregory, Synge, Padraic Colum and their supporters seemed to him to be dangerously close to committing themselves to a version of the pseudo-Irishness which had once been the preserve of the stage-Irishman of nineteenth-century England and was, by the last decade of the century, becoming the property of the Celtic Irishman of the day. Yet, despite his difference, Joyce had much in common with these writers. In the work of all of them, Ireland, or an idea of Ireland, played a special role. For the revivalists, who were intent on turning nationalist political energies into cultural channels, the idea of Ireland was an invigorating and positive force. It embodied vitality and the possibility of a new kind of community, radically different from the aggregate crowds of the industrialized democracies. The distinction was enhanced by the predominantly rural character of Irish society, transformed by the writers into something very different from its harsh reality. For instance, Synge, in *The Playboy of the Western World*, could make Mayo, the home of the Land League and the Agrarian War of the 1880s, into the site of the self-realization through language of the 'stuttering lout', Christy Mahon. However, Joyce, like Wilde and Shaw, was a Dublin writer. For him, as for them, Ireland was a negative idea, a place which threatened the artist's freedom and integrity, in which gifts were wasted and language was used as a deadly weapon. All three of them came from families that had been broken by various forms of fecklessness, alcoholism and squalor. They too transformed that bitter reality. Wilde became a dandy, Shaw became GBS, and Joyce became the professional exile from a home he never, imaginatively speaking, left. Yet these three cosmopolitan writers, like the cultural nationalists of the Revival, produced work of a self-conscious linguistic virtuosity in which English was manipulated to the point at which mastery over it began to sound like the mastery that can be achieved over a foreign language. Like Mangan, Joyce and his contemporaries wore their linguistic rue with a difference. Their language did not represent an identifiable world beyond itself. It represented the ways in which the idea of Ireland represented the reality of Ireland. It was, in effect, an exercise in translation.

Joyce made it clear that, in his opinion, the Revival was conceding to public pressure by allowing the caricatured, but popular, version of Ireland to become the abiding image of the Abbey Theatre. This was wrong on a number of grounds. It deprived the artist of his independence; it nurtured provincialism; and it did this in the guise of a return to the 'natural'. Exile safeguarded independence; cosmopolitanism helped to avoid provincialism; and the return to the natural was to be achieved, not by a romanticizing of rural and peasant life, or of the idea of the Celt and his lost language, but by an unflinching realism which, like that of Ibsen, stripped the mask from the pharisaic middle-class society of urban Europe and exposed its spiritual hypocrisy and impoverishment. In that respect, Ireland was indeed a special country. It lived under the political domination of England and the religious domination of Rome while it espoused a rhetoric of freedom, uniqueness, especial privilege. Ireland was, in fact, especially underprivileged and was, on that account, more susceptible to and more in need of an exemplary art than any other European country. It was in Joyce's art that the interior history of his country could be, for the first time, written. Joyce set himself up as the anatomist of Irish illusions, but this did not in any sense inhibit him from believing that, under the 'lancet of my art', 'the cold steel pen' (*U* 1.152–3), the soul of the country would be revealed. He medicalized the condition of his culture and subjected it to a surgical analysis. But the surgeon in Joyce attended upon the corpse of a dead or moribund country; the priest in Joyce attended upon the soul that was released from its terminal condition.

> Just as ancient Egypt is dead, so is ancient Ireland. Its dirge has been sung and the seal set upon its gravestone. The ancient national spirit that spoke throughout the centuries through the mouths of fabulous seers, wandering minstrels, and Jacobin poets has vanished from the world with the death of James Clarence Mangan. With his death the long tradition of the triple order of the ancient bards also died. Today other bards, inspired by other ideals, have their turn.   (*OCPW* 125)

If Ireland was to be seen, it would be in the full light of an Ibsenite dawn, not in the glimmer of a Celtic twilight. The Revival was, from its inception, an anachronism. It was a bogus attempt to revive the old Gaelic culture which lay beyond the pale of the modern consciousness.

Joyce's civilization was not, therefore, that of Myles Joyce, of Yeats and Lady Gregory and the Abbey Theatre, or of Mangan. Equally, it was not that of the comic dramatists, Sheridan, Goldsmith, Wilde, and Shaw, all of whom performed the role of 'court jester to the English' (*OCPW* 149). It was the civilization of Catholic Dublin, related to but distinct from that of Catholic Ireland. Joyce tried to persuade the publisher, Grant Richards, that his collection of stories, *Dubliners*, was about a city that still had not been presented, or represented, to the world. He insists, on many occasions, on the emptiness that preceded his own writings about that city. It is an historical but not yet an imaginative reality. Although Dublin has been a capital for 'thousands of years' and is said to be the second city of the British Empire, Joyce claims that no writer has yet 'presented Dublin to the world'. Furthermore, 'the expression "Dubliner" seems to me to have some meaning and I doubt that the same can be said for such words as "Londoner" and "Parisian"' (*Letters II* 122). In the following year, 1906, the same publisher received from Joyce a sequence of famous letters, defending his text from charges of indecency and suggestions for changes, and declaring the importance of this 'chapter of moral history' as 'the first step towards the spiritual liberation of my country'. Richards is asked to 'Reflect for a moment on the history of the literature of Ireland as it stands at present written in the English language before you condemn this genial illusion of mine . . .' (*Letters I* 63). 'It is not my fault', he writes a month later, 'that the odour of ashpits and old weeds and offal hangs round my stories. I seriously believe that you will retard the course of civilization in Ireland by preventing the Irish people from having one good look at themselves in my nicely polished looking-glass' (*Letters I* 63–4). The mirror held up to Culture was going to reflect a reality no-one had presented before. Dublin would find it an unwelcome sight, but Dublin and Ireland would be liberated by it. Joyce is an author without native predecessors; he is an artist who intends to have the effect of a missionary.

By insisting that Dublin had not been represented before in literature, Joyce was intensifying the problem of representation for himself. He abjured the possibility of being influenced by any other Irish writer, because there was, in effect, none who belonged to his specific and peculiar version of his civilization. He was bound, therefore, to find a mode of representation that was, as far as Irish literature was concerned, unique. But the literature of Europe did offer possible models, and Joyce repeatedly spoke of Dublin – as in the letter to Grant Richards – as a European city. Indeed, he saw it as a city that inhabited three spheres of civilization. The first was that of the British Empire; the second that of Roman Catholicism; the third that of the ancient Europe to which Ireland had made such an important contribution. All three of these co-existed in Dublin, the only major European city which had not yet been commemorated in art.

So Dublin was the second city of the Empire, the seventh city of Christendom, the first city of Ireland; rich in history, it was now to become famous in art. The art would have to be similarly hospitable in its range; it could not be provincial, but it could have provincialism as one of its themes. To be truly European, the art would have to represent the city as an inheritor of the Judaeo-Greek civilization, in a language which would be as diversified and varied as the city's dense and intricate past.

First, provincialism had to be exposed and explained as a disease, a paralysis of the will. In one sense, the clinical and 'scrupulous meanness' (*Letters II* 134) of the style of *Dubliners* is perfectly competent 'to betray the soul of that hemiplegia or paralysis which many consider a city' (*Letters I* 55). But Joyce's enterprise was founded on a paradox. Dublin was an absence, a nowhere, a place that was not really a city or a civilization at all. It was a Cave of the Winds, like the 'Aeolus' chapter in *Ulysses*, the home of the cosmetic phrase, the Dublin rouge on the faded cheek of the English language. Joyce wanted to dismantle its provincialism and its pretensions; yet he also sought to envision it as the archetypal modern city, as the single place in which all human history was rehearsed. It had to be both nowhere and everywhere, absence and presence. Somehow, he had to find the language which would register both aspects of the city. He had to scorn it for its peripherality and praise it for its centrality. Between these two possibilities, his strange language vacillates and develops.

Like the other Irish writers of the turn of the century, Joyce learned the advantages of incorporating into his writing the various dialects or versions of English spoken in Ireland. This was not simply a matter of enlivening a pallid literary language with colloquialisms. He went much further than that. He incorporated into his writing several modes of language and, in doing so, exploited the complex linguistic situation in Ireland to serve his goal. The chief features of that situation included a still-living oral tradition which had begun to influence the writing of fiction in Ireland more than sixty years before Joyce was born, in the work of novelists like Gerald Griffin, the Banim brothers and, above all, William Carleton. The English spoken by the mass of the Irish people and partly recorded in the works of these writers was oral-formulaic in its compositional principle and closely related to Irish. Much misunderstanding of this language and its supposed misconstructions was created by the application to it of the conventions of a literate print-culture. Certainly, the English language, as spoken in nineteenth- and early twentieth-century Ireland, was profoundly altered in its syntax, grammar and vocabulary by the migration of Irish speakers from a predominantly oral culture. The linguistic collisions and confusions which were an inevitable consequence were often taken to be characteristic of a particularly 'Irish' cast of mind. This could lead, especially in times of political crisis, to a malign stereotyping of the Irish; equally, it often led to a benign view of Irish 'eloquence', quick-wittedness and linguistic self-consciousness.[4] Joyce would have felt the impact of this linguistic interchange in the standard clichés of the stage Irishman, but he would also have known its more sophisticated variations, in the work of Wilde and Shaw and in the Revival's declared objective of reinvigorating the English language with the energetic speech of the Irish peasantry. His own work is itself part of the history of Ireland's complicated linguistic condition.

Dublin was a strange mix of the oral and the literate cultures. It prided itself on its reputation for wit, good conversation, malicious gossip, oratory, drama, and journalism. Joyce's work reflects this aspect of the city's culture. It is a mosaic of set pieces – sermons, speeches, stories, witticisms, rhetorical extravaganzas, and mimicries. The culture of print is also reproduced and parodied. The 'Nausicaa' and 'Oxen of the Sun' episodes in *Ulysses* are among the best-known examples. Pulp-literature and 'high' literature are equally subject to this form of mimicry; language is always being proffered as a species of performance. In fact, the histrionic nature of Joyce's achievement aids and abets his peculiar combination of pedantry and humour. The weighty and arcane learning of a Stephen Dedalus has to be worn lightly if he is to keep his local reputation on the Dublin stage as 'the loveliest mummer of them all' (*U* 1.97–8). Moreover, it is one of the most important of all the Joycean performances that a character should take possession of the language of others, the public language, and render it as his inimitable own. This is one of the several functions of quotation in Joyce's work. The ability to incorporate the words of others into one's own particular language-system is a sign of a 'character', a presence on the Dublin scene. In the first few pages of *Ulysses*, Buck Mulligan quotes Latin, Greek, Wilde, Swinburne, and Yeats, besides singing a song and blending all of this into his 'hyperborean' (*U* 1.92) conversational assault on Stephen. Quotation is one of the structural principles of *A Portrait of the Artist as a Young Man*. Stephen collects words and quotations with increasing eagerness until the novel finally becomes a quotation from Stephen's own writings. We are to presume that the world which gave itself to him in words has now become junior to his own word-world. To make the world conform to words is a characteristic aspiration of a culture which has found it for so long impossible to make its words conform to the world. The speaker of Irish-English in the world of increasingly Standard English finds it too difficult to conform to the imperial way. He takes as his script the advice: 'When in Rome, do as the Greeks do.' There is a certain scandal in such behaviour. It is a linguistic way of subverting a political conquest.

Subversion is part of the Joycean enterprise. However, the bitterness attendant upon it is accompanied by the joy of renovation. There is nothing of political or social significance which Joyce does not undermine and restructure. Dublin and Ireland are dissected and yet both are revitalized; the English language is dismembered and yet reinvigorated; Catholic hegemony is both destroyed and reinstated; the narrowness of Irish nationalism is satirized and yet its basic impulse is ratified. Even the most deadening features of his culture yield priority to its enlivening, creative aspects. He is one of the few authors who legitimizes the modern world, seeing its apparent randomness and alienation as instances of an underlying diversity and communion. If Dublin offered him nothing else, it at least provided him with the experience of a modern city which was also a knowable community. That sense of community, city-wide and country-wide, was possibly more alive and more widespread in his generation than in any since. His interest in Irish politics confirmed his sense that the Irish community was susceptible to a reformulation of the idea of its essential and enduring coherence.

One of Joyce's undergraduate friends, Constantine Curran, has described how effectively Joyce suppressed in his fiction the intellectually vital aspects of life at University College, Dublin, and how carefully nurtured was the fable of his refusal to sign the student protest against Yeats's play *The Countess Cathleen* in 1899.[5] Similarly, it has been demonstrated how Joyce concentrated on the more derelict areas of Dublin in his effort to portray the city as the centre of paralysis and squalor.[6] In fact, despite the impression given by Joyce's early fiction, Dublin was experiencing a revival of energies which outmatched anything known since the Act of Union in 1800. He was not, of course, unaware of this. When he spoke or wrote of it, he tended to concentrate on its political manifestations. In various articles he wrote on Irish political matters, Joyce shows himself to be a supporter of the Sinn Fein movement, which had been founded by Arthur Griffith, and a rather uncritical admirer of Fenianism and its formidable influence. The most notable of these are the 1907 essays, 'Fenianism', 'Home Rule Comes of Age' and 'Ireland at the Bar', the 1910 article, 'The Home Rule Comet' and the 1912 piece, 'The Shade of Parnell'. The collaboration between old Fenianism and the new Sinn Fein had, he believed, 'once again remoulded the character of the Irish' (*OCPW* 140). But the Irish parliamentary party which sat at Westminster and which had overthrown its great leader Parnell in 1890 seemed incapable of recognizing that this remodelling had happened at home; instead they naively believed that the transformation of Ireland's fortunes would come from legislative changes in the English system – like the breaking of the veto of the House of Lords. The Irish national character had indeed altered; but the English were their old, unreconstructed selves and would never willingly yield to any separatist doctrine preached in Ireland. Yet the Irish themselves had their own, irredeemably fatal flaw. They could not be faithful to anything. Ireland's willingness to make common cause with British democracy, Joyce claims, should neither surprise nor persuade anyone: 'For seven centuries it has never been a faithful subject of England. Nor, on the other hand, has it been faithful to itself' (*OCPW* 159). Ireland has entered into the British domain but has never really been part of it; the conqueror's language has been adopted but his culture never assimilated; the Irish 'spiritual creators' have been exiled, only then to be boasted about back home. The governing motif of betrayal and the association between Ireland's treatment of its political and artistic heroes, although significant, is perhaps less important than the implied reason for Ireland's traditional unfaithfulness. Having exiled her spiritual creators, she has no 'soul', no mode of existence in which faithfulness is a meaningful category. Instead of her true soul, she has surrendered all to the authority of the Church, a foreign institution which operates as a political system, disguised as a spiritual one. Ireland has remained faithful to that faithless master only because she has been incapable of remaining faithful to her true self. That self, created by the artist, has no existence. Now it must be invented. Its invention demands that a certain view of Dublin, of University College, of Joyce's parents, of Mangan, Wilde, Yeats and all the others must be accepted as an authentic version of the inner spiritual void in which the Irish artist – James Joyce – must function, creating out of nothing, fascinated by stories which recount the intricacies of betrayal, of the self and of others, as well as opposing stories of fidelity and solidarity. Treachery and fidelity are the terms which determine the development of Joyce's fiction, as they determine his reading of Ireland's past and present. The remodelling of the national character, undertaken by groups like Sinn Fein and the Irish Revival, is indeed a heroic enterprise, but it is a futile one unless it accepts that the remodelling has to begin with the problem of fidelity to Rome rather than with the problem of fidelity or infidelity towards the British system. It is Rome, not London, which rules the Irish mind. London will readily use Rome for its purposes. But the Roman imperium is the more subtle and pervasive because it encroaches on the territory which should be ruled by the artist.

If proof were needed, the developments in Irish political history seemed to provide it. Once Ireland had shaken off the shackles of British rule, Church rule became ever more dominant. 'The Church has made inroads everywhere, so that we are in fact becoming a bourgeois nation, with the Church supplying our aristocracy . . . and I do not see much hope for us intellectually.'[7] Yet Joyce's views on the spiritual thraldom of Catholicism are a good deal less interesting than the methods he employed in his fiction to dramatize the profound conflicts which the pressure of Catholicism could generate in those brought up in its all-encompassing ambience. The hostility of the Church towards almost all movements for Irish liberation, from the United Irishmen to the Fenians, Parnell and beyond, is only the most superficial manifestation of these conflicts. At a deeper level, the challenge of Catholicism is to individual liberation, and Joyce, well-trained by the Jesuits and compelled by an attraction for the faith he wished to repudiate, envisaged that particular struggle in terms of the revolt of the artist heretic against official doctrine. Sometimes he modified this into a struggle between an aesthete-heretic against a provincial and philistine Church which had taken possession of the mob mind. But, at root, the conflict was even more painful. It was a conflict between a son and his parents – cultural, religious, biological – and a desperate attempt to go beyond the terms set by such a conflict by producing a theory of the self as its own parent, or, less desperately, a desire of the self for alternative, surrogate parents who would permit the imagination to live its necessarily vicarious existence. This is the plight of Stephen Dedalus in *Ulysses*.

There are two forms of Catholicism in Joyce's work. One is European, the other Irish. European Catholicism, as he has Stephen speak of it in *Ulysses*, is based on the doctrine of the Trinity; Irish Catholicism, influenced in this respect by the Italians, is a more sentimental faith, based on the idea of the Holy Family, the vulgar version of the Trinity. For all his undergraduate extravagance, Stephen is enacting a central Joycean dilemma. Catholicism provides him with two versions of parenthood and of community, Trinity and Holy Family. Literature provides, in the life of Shakespeare, matching versions. The Trinitarian version is that whereby Shakespeare is the author of the play *Hamlet* which contains Hamlet the Father and Hamlet the Son; but it also contains Gertrude who is the mark in the play of Ann Hathaway's infidelity to Shakespeare. With Claudius and young Hamlet, she helps to create a grotesque version of the Holy Family. Equally, Trinity and Family can be replaced by Greek and Jew, and the relation between these can veer from much nodding in the direction of the Wildean attempt to preach a new Hellenistic paganism to Judaic-Biblical England, to the prurience of Bloom, staring at a Greek statue in the National Museum, observed and described by the pseudo-Greek, fake Wildean, Buck Mulligan, who turns to Stephen and says, 'He knows you . . . O, I fear me, he is Greeker than the Greeks' (*U* 9.613–15). In this ninth episode, the obsession with betrayal merges with the anxiety to find a basis within oneself for origin. The association between homosexuality and cuckoldry, clearly indicated in this and subsequent passages, includes the association between Greeks and Jews (via Wilde and Swinburne as modern Greeks, and Bloom as modern St Joseph). Further, the 'Greek' homosexuality is the 'Love that dare not speak its name' (*U* 9.659), while the 'Jewish' love is linked to the Holy Family, itself a betrayal of the doctrine of the Trinity and carrying within it the inevitable heterosexual betrayal which leaves Joseph a cuckold. In the true beginning, of which Christ's birth is the duplication, was 'the Word'. All through the 'Scylla and Charybdis' episode, the motif of naming, of losing or hiding the name of the father or of the origin, recurs as Stephen weaves his extraordinary theories. Yet for all the Greek and Jewish references, the ultimate reference is to Stephen himself and to Ireland, to Wilde and to Mangan (one of whose best-known poems is 'The Nameless One'), and even, by insinuation (in *U* 9.660–1), to Thomas Moore, who notoriously 'loved a lord' in the sense that he loved English society, and wrote a song, 'O Breathe Not His Name', about Robert Emmet, the rebel, who pleaded that his epitaph not be written until his country took her place among the nations of the earth (see *U* 11.1274–94). All these sexual references finally achieve their full political dimension as Bloom enters Barney Kiernan's pub to confront the Citizen in episode 12, 'Cyclops'.

The notion of self-authorship, creation of the self by becoming one's own father, is entertained by Stephen in a series of reflections which begin with the invocation of a parent – God the Father, Shakespeare – and move to the notion of the father betrayed – King Hamlet, Saint Joseph – to the repudiation of the betraying woman, thence to the idea of homosexual, all-male love, and finally to the 'economy of heaven' where, as Stephen says, with a flourish, 'there are no more marriages, glorified man, an androgynous angel, being a wife unto himself' (*U* 9.1051–2). The four participants in this conversation, Mulligan, Best, Eglinton and Stephen, are all bachelors. When Bloom leaves, passing between Mulligan and Stephen, Mulligan whispers: 'Did you see his eye? He looked upon you to lust after you' (*U* 9.1209–10). The role of Wilde (and Swinburne) has a clear function in the series of homosexual and literary allusions which punctuate the discussion. Homosexual love, of which he and Swinburne and the Shakespeare of the sonnets are representatives, is here presented as the Greek alternative to the heterosexual love, celebrated in marriage, to which the Jews are more given than any others. 'Jews . . . are of all races the most given to intermarriage' (*U* 9.783–4). As the conversation breaks up, it is the shadow of the cuckold, Bloom, which passes between the two young bachelors. If betrayal is to be avoided, parenthood, origin, must be removed from others to oneself. It is an impossible position, but then Stephen is, as Mulligan says, 'an impossible person' (*U* 1.223).

Every heretic mentioned in the text (Sabellius, Photius, Arius, Valentine), every author, every contrasting opposition, signals parenthood, priority, origin. The point is that Stephen is caught in a dream of origin which can never be realized. There is no ultimate beginning, there is only the desire for it, for a total independence from all and everyone else. This desire is itself generated by fear of betrayal which, in turn, is associated with sexual infidelity. Ireland has betrayed itself over and over again, most recently and memorably in the sexual scandal of the Parnell affair; the Catholic Church betrayed its founding mystery, the Trinity, by substituting for it the story of the Holy Family, in which Joseph is betrayed into the position of the merely nominal father of God. Stephen and Bloom are both involved in parental and marital betrayals which are, in their turn, closely associated with religious affiliation, Christian and Jewish, while the 'Greek' Mulligan is the ultimate betrayer who cannot even recognize his own treachery towards Stephen. Just as he reads the Irish political tradition in the light of this theme, Joyce, through Stephen, reads Shakespeare and the English literary tradition in the same way. Church, State and Culture are the betrayed remnants of an originary purity towards which Stephen, as artist, dedicates himself. In such a situation, only art is beyond betrayal. It is the only activity to which Stephen can give his fidelity because it is a form of production in which his own authorship is secure. The problem is, of course, that Stephen is always about to be an artist. He has his theory complete, but it does not fit with the circumstances of flawed paternity which surround Bloom.

Ulysses is as concerned as is *Dubliners* with failure. The form of the failure is more brilliant, because it is the result of sophisticated, exotic, ingenious readings of the past and of the present which are finally disabling for the readers – Stephen and Bloom in particular. The semiotic systems of Dublin, Irish history, literature, are all read under the sign of a betrayal which, while it exposes, does not reveal. That is to say, failure is exposed but the way to success is not revealed. Stephen, remembering his meeting in Paris with the exiled Fenian, Kevin Egan, and the stories of the Fenian escapades and associated Irish political enterprises, thinks of them all as phantasmal, failed and fading attempts. 'Of lost leaders, the betrayed, wild escapes. Disguises, clutched at, gone, not here' (*U* 3.243–4). In his 1907 lecture, 'Ireland, Island of Saints and Sages', Joyce declared, 'It is high time Ireland finished once and for all with failures' (*OCPW* 125). Yet much of his own work is precisely on this theme. He analyses the psychology of subjection in his people by showing the paralysis which has overtaken them in their endless, futile quest for an origin which will provide them with an identity securely their own. Such an origin is always beyond history, since history, as we have seen, is for him a sequence of betrayals, the effect of which is to leave the Irish people leaderless, subjected to an authoritarian Church, bereft of that spiritual life which only the artist, in his quest for origin, can provide.

Characteristically, when Joyce does find the originary story, it involves a betrayal. The legend of the Fall of Man is an extra-historical narrative, a kind of metacommentary, which is repeated in endlessly diverse forms throughout human history, which both derives from and returns to it. At the centre of this mass of historical material is Irish historical experience. It has the fall of man deeply inscribed upon it, from the story of the fall of the High King Rory O'Connor, to the execution of the radical Republican Rory O'Connor in 1923. It moves from the era of Saints and Scholars to the Devil Era of the great modern leader, De Valera. Repetition is the law of this universe; in every event, the originary event reappears. Origin is always with us. Yet the origin is visible only when the story is told in the language which contains all languages, in the Ur-speech which is the language of the dreaming or subconscious mind of HCE, Everyman, who Haveth Childers Everywhere. *Finnegans Wake* is Joyce's Irish answer to an Irish problem. It is written in a ghost language about phantasmal figures; history is haunted by them and embodies them over and over again in specific people, places and tongues. If Ireland could not be herself, then, by way of compensation, the world would become Ireland. Thus is the problem of identity solved. Irish history is world history *in parvo*. The mutilated sequences of war, failure, disaster, lost language, broken culture, are brought under the governance of a single, mastering story which renders everything thought to be unique as typical.

Yet just as *Ulysses* had made real order out of apparent chaos, *Finnegans Wake* sustains individuality within the frame of the archetypal. The Earwicker family, for instance, is a version of Joyce's family; yet the figures within it are always coalescing 'through the labyrinth of their samilikes and the alteregoases of their pseudoselves' (*FW* 576.32–3). The events of the Irish War of Independence against the British, the signing of the Treaty, the civil war which followed, and the subsequent entry of De Valera into parliamentary politics are all presented in fractured form as specific happenings in themselves and also as representative events. We can see here, a little more clearly, how Joyce grappled with the problem of representation. Individual items, which by themselves might be meaningless, gain significance when seen as part of an overall pattern. Therefore, if the pattern is sufficiently hospitable, everything can be represented within a system and everything therefore has whatever meanings the system is able to produce. Nevertheless, the governing pattern has, in itself, an originary meaning which is replicated throughout all subsequent variations. We have seen that, for Joyce, in his readings of Mangan, Wilde, Irish politics, and so forth, the theme of betrayal was the repeated meaning which linked all the aspects of Irish experience together. His task was, in part, to demonstrate that this was indeed a given, originary pattern rather than a retrospective, enforced one. In *Finnegans Wake*, the linking theme of transgression and betrayal is legitimized by the nature of language itself. Repetition, puns, homonyms, resemblances, echoes, carefully arranged, reveal or are proposed as revealing a cousinship between the events which these sounds describe. Alliance between word-sounds reveals an alliance between those things which the word-sounds represent. Joyce is involving himself and us in a stupendous act of retrospective translation, whereby the distinctions and differences between words and languages are collapsed into a basic, originary speech native to the subconscious, not the conscious, mind. This is his version of the lost language of Ireland; it is also the lost language of the Irish soul, that entity which had not been articulated into existence before Joyce. In effect, what this lost language tells is the story of the transgression which led to its loss, the story of the life of the soul lost to the life of the conscious mind, the narrative of an Edenic Ireland which, through sin, became postlapsarian and British.

Here we have the Mangan position transfigured. Where he made all his texts 'secondary' by positing a real or imaginary 'original' from which they derived, Joyce makes all other texts secondary by actually producing the original language of which they are the later derivations. Thus the divine thunder which inaugurates civilization, according to the theory of Vico, who plays a role in *Finnegans Wake* similar to that of Homer in *Ulysses*, can be translated, so to say, into the gunfire of an ambush in the Irish War of Independence or the boom of the guns at the Battle of Waterloo. The reader must go forward to the individual instance and back to the originating example. This is, after all, a dream which we are interpreting, and the language of dreams must, as Freud had shown, go through a series of readings before they can yield a meaning we can recognize, even though the meaning was already there in the original 'language'. This is what Joyce himself had done in reading the careers of Mangan, Parnell, Wilde, the Fenians. The Irish had dreamt in their own language and then betrayed the dream into the English language in such a manner that the original meaning had been lost, misread; as a consequence, for this transgression, they had been punished. English did not translate the dream because the Irish did not possess, had, indeed, refused to accept, the culture which English represented. So Joyce, following in the steps of all of those who had been busily translating Irish material – especially legendary material – into English, went very much further than the second-hand Carlylese of Standish O'Grady, or the Kiltartan dialect of Lady Gregory, or the peasant speech of Synge, who takes a drubbing, chiefly from Mulligan, in the 'Scylla and Charybdis' episode.

Joyce translated in the other direction. He brought English and as many other languages as he could manage – including Irish – back to the literary equivalent of the Indo-European from which they had all sprung. In doing this, he confronts the problem of parenthood, as well as the problem of translation and betrayal, on the level of language itself, not merely on the level of language-as-narrative.

Given this, Joyce can indulge as freely as he likes in detail. The minutiae of Dublin life, ever-present throughout *Ulysses*, now undergo a second transformation. The geography of the city and the history of the country were readable there in specific, if generous, contexts. Dublin could be the Mediterranean, Irish history could be a version of episodes from the Greek legends or from Biblical history. But in *Finnegans Wake*, Dublin's Phoenix Park can be anything from the Garden of Eden to the field of Waterloo, including the site of a phallic rebirth represented by the Wellington monument, the '*duc de Fer*'s overgrown milestone' (*FW* 36.18). In the hands of 'Maistre Sheames de la Plume' (*FW* 177.30), the poor old Iron Duke and his obelisk can take on almost any meaning. The strangest effect of this titanic effort of translation is that the text is never revealed; rather, it is produced by the reader. There is no question any longer of a skeleton key which will turn in all the locks. This translation does not translate. The thousands of proper names in the text are so interwoven that even the minutest knowledge of Irish affairs (and the more minute the better, given that so many of the names are of Irish provenance) does not legitimize, say, a reading of the text as a version of Irish history in a Babylonian dialect. Names specify, but these are names that also typify. Even in *Dubliners*, the anorexic opposite to this Rabelaisian carnival, Joyce kept offering specifications that seemed treacherous. Is there any significance in the fact that the miching episode in the story 'An Encounter' culminates at three o'clock on a Friday afternoon? Perhaps there is a reference to the Crucifixion, perhaps not. Support can be gathered from all sorts of details. But is that a possible reading, or a deliberately implanted possible misreading? The bareness of the short stories is a challenge to elaborate interpretation; the richness of *Finnegans Wake* is a challenge to a reading that might be too basic, a reading that says everything here is the same but different, that all we see are multiple, fused versions of the Fall of Man. The treachery which obsessed Joyce is fundamental to his practice of writing. For he leaves us to wonder if the text that he offers is one which has been so fully articulated that it can go no further; or if it is a text which is so blurred that it awaits and invites full articulation. This was not only a problem for him. He saw it as the problem of his culture. Dublin had never been represented in literature before. Perhaps he was the first to represent it; or perhaps he was the first to show that it was not representable.

For all that, Joyce was, and knew himself to be, part of the Irish Revival. A remodelling of the idea of Ireland was under way and, although his sense of the problem of finding a new representation for what had not yet come into existence was more acute than that of his contemporaries, he could see that people as diverse as Yeats, Pearse, De Valera, and Synge were extending the process which had been made most manifest in the earlier generations by writers like Mangan and Wilde, and by political figures like Thomas Davis and John O'Leary. That sense of renewal is clear throughout *Finnegans Wake*. The country and culture he repudiated was also the country and culture he re-imagined. The absence could become a presence. Time and again in his writing Joyce characteristically salutes and bids farewell to the Ireland he had left and to the Ireland he created in his absence from it and its absence from him.

NOTES

1 See Frank O'Connor, *The Backward Look: A Survey of Irish Literature* (London: Macmillan, 1967), pp. 150 ff.; Seamus Deane, *A Short History of Irish Literature* (London: Hutchinson, 1986); J. H. Andrews, *A Paper Landscape: The Ordnance Survey in Nineteenth Century Ireland* (London: Oxford University Press, 1975). See also Brian Friel's play *Translations* (London: Faber, 1982), for a contemporary treatment of this theme.

2 William Carleton (1794–1869) published his *Traits and Stories of the Irish Peasantry* between 1830 and 1833. He is renowned as the first writer in English to provide an authentic account of the life and speech of the Irish peasantry. Yeats wrote an introduction to his own selection, *Stories from Carleton* (London: W. Scott, 1889).

3 See David Lloyd, *Nationalism and Minor Literature: James Clarence Mangan and the Emergence of Irish Cultural Nationalism* (Berkeley, Los Angeles, London: University of California Press, 1987), p. 209.

4 See Alan Bliss, *Spoken English in Ireland, 1600–1740* (Dublin: Dolmen Press, 1979).

5 C. P. Curran, *Under the Receding Wave* (Dublin and London: Gill and Macmillan, 1970), pp. 96–110. See also his *James Joyce Remembered* (London: Oxford University Press, 1968).

6 J. C. C. Mays, 'Some Comments on the Dublin of *Ulysses*', in Louis Bonnerot, ed., *Ulysses: Cinquante ans après* (Paris: Didier, 1974), pp. 83–98.

7 Arthur Power, *Conversations with James Joyce* (London: Millington, 1974), p. 65.

3

JEAN-MICHEL RABATÉ

Joyce the Parisian

'*Trieste – Zurich – Paris*, 1914–1921'; 'PARIS, 1922–1939'. Anyone who has read Joyce will recognize the famous dates and place names which link the writing of *Ulysses* and *Finnegans Wake* to a particular context, to circumstances whose importance is not merely anecdotal but, if only to judge from the recurrence of these very names in Joyce's last book, structural. Joyce's exile, recaptured by the three cities which, each in its turn, saw the inception of new developments in the writing of *Ulysses*, was to end in Paris. Does this make him a 'Parisian'? If we speak of Joyce as a 'Parisian', two images, two contrasting clichés, immediately come to mind: Joyce as part of the Bohemian crowd of the 'Expatriates', the Irish genius adding his own tenor voice to the hoarse chorus of drunken American 'Pilgrims' wandering between Odeonia and the cafés of Montparnasse; or the secretive writer, living only with his family and a small group of devotees, pent up in an ivory tower, completely indifferent to his surroundings, absorbed by the drawn out *tour de force* of having to finish his universal history before the real apocalypse of the century comes... If both clichés indeed contain an element of truth, I shall try to show first that they correspond to different phases of Joyce's Parisian life, and then, that they misconstrue the very organic relationship he had established with his elected Ithaca. Neither, say, Hemingway's version, nor Arthur Power's,[1] can manage to convey the specific role of Paris for Joyce, who may well be called, as *Finnegans Wake* coins it, a 'paleoparisien' (*FW* 151.9) – that is, first of all, an 'arch-parisian'.

'Arch-parisian' Joyce was bound to be, and in two senses; in the historical sense of his feeling very early an attraction to Paris – called by Paris, almost a 'calling', which receives momentous mythological overtones in *Ulysses*; and in the transcendental sense of a 'principle' underlying the anarchic tendencies implied by the nomadism of perpetual exile. It is true that Joyce's early and brief stay in Paris was not to prove entirely satisfactory. His surprising decision to register there as a medical student for the academic year

1902–3 was soon turning all his energies to the practical strategies of survival; he experienced hunger and solitude much more than the lively atmosphere of the *carabins* of the Latin Quarter. The Bibliothèque Sainte Geneviève saw him poring over the dusty pages of Aristotle's works more than on the newest publications of the post-Symbolist avant-garde. And when he discovered *Les Lauriers sont coupés* by Dujardin in a station kiosk, it was because he remembered that George Moore had mentioned him, not because of any awareness of the literary trends in Paris.[2] Yet, when the moment came for a second departure which he knew would be a final exile from Dublin, his mind was still fixed on Paris. When planning the great 'adventure' of eloping with Nora Barnacle, he writes to her on Michaelmas Day 1904: 'I do not like the notion of London and I am sure you won't like it either but at the same time it is on the road to Paris and it is perhaps better than Amsterdam . . . It amuses me to think of the effect the news of it [our adventure] will cause in my circle. However, when we are once safely settled in the Latin quarter they can talk as much as they like' (*Letters II* 57). As it turned out, the Berlitz school had only a position in Pola, in present-day Croatia, to offer, which Joyce accepted; but his adolescent dream – to be able to live with Nora as a 'man' – was realized sixteen years later when Pound suggested that he should come to Paris in order to finish writing *Ulysses*. Although his acceptance of Pound's suggestion seemed reluctant, he was in fact making good what he had failed to experience when a poor Irish student in Paris, soon called back by the news of his mother's fatal illness.

Paris therefore immediately provides a myth, aptly evoked by the phrase 'the Latin Quarter'; however, this does not imply that it is the artistic or intellectual glamour of Paris that attracts the young Joyce. From the very start, Paris has been identified with 'life', a mystical force which ought to be perceived in Dublin but remains thwarted by the general air of Irish corruption or paralysis. In another letter of the same crucial period preceding his departure with Nora in 1904, and following shortly after the day later to be commemorated as 'Bloomsday', Joyce writes about Paris. He starts with a meditation on Grafton Street by night:

> The street was full of a life which I have poured a stream of my youth upon. While I stood there I thought of a few sentences I wrote some years ago when I lived in Paris – these sentences which follow – 'They pass in twos and threes amid the life of the boulevard, walking like people who have leisure in a place lit up for them. They are in the pastry cook's chattering, crushing little fabrics

of pastry, or seated silently at tables by the café door, or descending from carriages with a busy stir of garments soft as the voice of the adulterer. They pass in an air of perfumes. Under the perfumes their bodies have a warm humid smell' –

While I was repeating this to myself I knew that life was still waiting for me if I chose to enter it.   (*Letters II* 49)

The sensuous pleasure taken in a contemplation of the night crowds on Grafton Street has to be relayed by an even more sensual awareness of these Parisian prostitutes, in what was first written as a Paris epiphany, later included in *Giacomo Joyce*, finally to be reworked as part of Stephen's memories of his student days and of his strolls on the Boulevard Saint Michel in *Ulysses*. The sexual 'entering' this letter calls up is a first step away from Dublin, a preparation for the proud flight away from the Irish nets, and it also provides a new superimposition of several cities: the glitter of Dublin's most fashionable area is transformed into a more salacious Parisian evocation, which later encompasses Trieste. The following vignette occurs in *Giacomo Joyce*: 'Trieste is waking rawly: raw sunlight over its huddled browntiled roofs, testudoform; a multitude of prostrate bugs await a national deliverance. Belluomo rises from the bed of his wife's lover's wife: the busy housewife is astir, sloe-eyed, a saucer of acetic acid in her hand . . .' (*GJ* 8). It is followed two pages later by another Parisian motif: 'In the raw veiled spring morning faint odours float of morning Paris: aniseed, damp sawdust, hot dough of bread: and as I cross the Pont Saint Michel the steelblue waking waters chill my heart. They creep and lap about the island whereon men have lived since the stone age . . .' No wonder all these carefully remembered scenes contain hints of a mystical 'stream of life' and even adumbrations of a 'wake' – especially as the second vignette alludes to a service in Notre-Dame, the gothic cathedral to which Joyce at a later stage compares his writings.

When the same motifs reappear in *Ulysses* ('Paris rawly waking, crude sunlight on her lemon streets . . . Belluomo rises from the bed of his wife's lover's wife . . . Faces of Paris men go by, their wellpleased pleasers, curled *conquistadores*' (*U* 3.209–15)), the connection between the clichés of 'raw' naturalism and subtle mythical overlayering is clinched in an apotropaic image evoking at the same time the judgement of Paris – his choice of Aphrodite leading to the rape of Helen and the Trojan war – and the fall of Icarus: 'seadeath, mildest of all deaths known to man. Old Father Ocean. *Prix de Paris*: beware of imitations. Just you give it a fair trial. We enjoyed ourselves immensely' (*U* 3.482–4). (The 'Prix de Paris' is a horserace still famous today.) But, even if there was some enjoyment in the Paris Joyce knew, the 'Prix de Paris' turned out to be a certain price he had to pay for – precisely – staying in Paris: the price of fame, of pure innovation and radical experimentation, may indeed have been high, and Joyce could wonder whether, in a derisive echo of Henri IV's boast that Paris was worth his conversion to Catholicism, 'was Parish worth thette mess' (*FW* 199.8–9).

Of course, when Joyce arrived in Paris in 1920 for what was to be a stay of two decades, it was a far different place from the Latin Quarter he had glimpsed as a student in 1902–3. It was a city which had taken the lead in artistic experimentation in an unprecedented fashion, and as a number of young Americans had stayed on after the war, attracted as much by the rate of exchange which enabled them to live very cheaply as by the more exciting night life it provided (by contrast with a Puritan America carried away by Prohibition), it had also become the capital of the English-speaking community abroad. The names of Hemingway, Stein, Scott Fitzgerald, McAlmon, Antheil, Pound, to name but a few celebrities, are among those who made Paris into a paradise for all expatriates. Joyce, who had known, if only tangentially, the artistic avant-garde in Zurich during the war, whilst refusing to be included in any group, probably missed the intellectual stimulation this had provided when he returned to Trieste in 1919. Besides, Joyce would not have come to Paris without Ezra Pound's insistence. Much more than Joyce, Pound was in search of a 'capital' from which he could launch new schools and movements and create the new 'Renaissance' he attempted to bring about almost single-handedly. Just as Joyce was increasingly dissatisfied with a post-war Trieste in which a nationalist crisis was brewing, Pound had only felt growing rancour and anger against the still-Victorian London he had inhabited since 1908. Pound signalled his break with London in two poems, *Homage to Sextus Propertius*, in which he used the mask of the Latin poet to rail at British Imperialism, and, more decisively, *Hugh Selwyn Mauberley*, which marks his abandonment of the aesthetic pose he had kept for a few years among the Georgian poets. Pound was a foreign correspondent of *The Dial*, and his visit to Paris in June 1920 was to provide the material for his 'Island of Paris' reports, in which he argued that the only place that was intellectually and artistically alive in Europe was Paris.

It was also in the same month of June 1920 that Pound and Joyce finally met in Italy. Joyce, disgusted with Trieste, even thought of leaving for Ireland (as he writes, in order to buy cheaper clothes!); Pound was unsure of where he would go next, even contemplating a return to the United States. Thus Pound could suggest that Joyce should stop in Paris on his way to London, promising to pave the way for him, inculcating all his acquaintances with the idea that they would soon have to do everything to help a very needy family of Irish people, a family which also contained his latest discovery. For a long time, Joyce thought his stay in Paris would be temporary, hesitating between London and Rome as his next destination. A letter Valery Larbaud sent to a friend in May 1921 (that is about eight months after Joyce had come to Paris) still stresses the provisional nature of his Paris settlement: '*Ulysses* is not finished yet. Joyce is working on the last two episodes, Eumaeus (sic) and Penelope. He thinks he will be through in May and will then leave for Rome with his family.'[3] It is interesting to see Rome vying with Paris for pre-eminence in Joyce's mind, since the common point of the two capitals, besides being important ideological centres, is that they had been the places of unpleasant short stays (1902–3 being in many ways parallel to 1906–7, when Joyce worked as a bank clerk in Rome). Perhaps he hoped to redeem these unrewarding experiences. Paris, at any rate, was more central than Rome, since Joyce could see himself roughly situated mid-way between Trieste and Dublin, Zurich and London, which were the main cities where his European correspondents lived.

Another irony of these crossed exiles is that Pound duplicated with Joyce what he had done with Eliot, who was to reap the benefits of the literary revolution they had brought about in London by just remaining there: having installed Joyce in Paris and introduced him to all his friends, Pound soon grew as dissatisfied with Paris as with London, and then decided to settle in Rapallo in order to be a closer witness to what he took for a Fascist Renaissance in Italy. On the other hand, during the twenty years or so of their French stay, the Joyces remained faithful to the deep imprint of their Trieste sojourn by speaking only the Triestine dialect of Italian in the family, a fact which astounded new Italian friends living in Paris, like Nino Frank.

However, although they lived in one city, a list of the Paris addresses of the Joyces will give a sense of their deliberately perpetuated exile. This has been described by friends such as Louis Gillet, who explains that one cannot say that Joyce 'settled' in Paris 'for he continued wandering between Passy and the Gros-Caillou, Montparnasse and Grenelle, not counting the escapades, the eclipses, the letters which without warning showed him to be in London, Folkestone, Basel, Copenhagen. His page in my address-book is filled with numerous erasures. I never saw him in the same lodgings for more than six months.'[4] Louis Gillet exaggerates slightly there, for Joyce did stay more than six months in a few places, as the following list of moves to new addresses shows:

1920 July	9, rue de l'Université (VIIe)
July	5, rue de l'Assomption (XVIe)
November	9, rue de l'Université (VIIe)
December	5, Boulevard Raspail (VIe)
1921 June	71, rue du Cardinal Lemoine (Ve)
October	9, rue de l'Université (VIIe)
1922 November	26, Avenue Charles Floquet (VIIe)
1923 August	Victoria Palace Hotel, 6 rue Blaise Desgoffe (VIIe)
1924 October	8, Avenue Charles Floquet (VIIe)
1925 June	2, Square Robiac (192, rue de Grenelle) (VIIe)
1931 April	Hotel Powers, 62 rue François Ier (VIIIe)
September	'La Résidence', 41 Avenue Pierre Ier de Serbie (VIIIe)
October	2, Avenue Saint Philibert (XVIe)
1932 April	Hotel Belmont et de Bassano, 28–30 rue de Bassano (VIIIe)
October	Hotel Lord Byron, Champs Elysées (VIIIe)
November	42, rue Galilée (VIIIe)
1934 September	7, rue Edmond Valentin (VIIe)
1939 April	34, rue des Vignes (XVIe)
October	Hotel Lutetia, Boulevard Raspail (VIe)[5]

The second address (rue de l'Assomption) and the fifth (rue du Cardinal Lemoine) are the two flats which were offered rent-free, for a short period, to Joyce, the first by Madame Bloch-Savistsky, a friend of Pound's who was to translate *A Portrait*, the second by Larbaud, on whose friendship I shall comment later. All these addresses indicate a preference for the left bank, but always in its most fashionable areas, plus a few incursions into Passy and the sixteenth arrondissement. 'Reeve Gootch was right and Reeve Drughad was sinistrous!', as *Finnegans Wake* confirms (*FW* 197.1). Yet, even if they are mostly located around the 'lootin quarter' (*FW* 205.27), these were not the kind of addresses one would associate with a writer 'down and up in Bohemian Paris'. Two addresses stand out as having been kept much longer than the others, the one in Square Robiac used from 1925 to 1931, and the rue Edmond Valentin one (almost five years). Although Nora was prone to abuse her husband and reproach him for his heavy tipping and drinking at night, the general lack of stability became a fact of their lives and she learnt to put up with it. But the decisions to leave these two addresses, in 1931 and in 1939, determine specific periods marked by their own crises.

Joyce had come to Paris with one main wish: to be able to complete *Ulysses* in a relative quiet which he could not find in Trieste. Thanks to the almost unlimited generosity of Harriet Weaver, he had no further money problems and could spend all his time writing. While finishing *Ulysses* (which took him longer than he had expected), he had to arrange for its publication and see to the French translations of *Exiles* and *A Portrait*; and then he had to deal with the translation of *Ulysses*. This corresponds to a relatively frantic period in Paris which lasted until the late twenties, the moment when Joyce really enjoyed his '*vie parisienne*'... Meanwhile he had to concentrate again on the writing of 'Work in Progress', which was initially published in instalments, first in the *transatlantic review* in 1924, then in various places (*Contact Collection of Contemporary Writers, Criterion, Navire d'Argent, This Quarter*) in 1925, until the appearance of *transition* provided a steady outlet for the serial publication (seventeen instalments from April 1927 to the end of 1938) of a work which baffled the editors of other, less experimental magazines. The publication of *Anna Livia Plurabelle* by Faber and Faber in 1930 signals the end of this first period; Joyce had produced a text which could justify the claims of his new work, stand on its own and be appreciated as a new type of prose-poetry. Furthermore, doubts over his writing, renewed eye troubles, the increasing strangeness of Lucia, capped by the death of his father (29 December 1931), led to a crisis in 1931–2 during which Joyce wrote very little or with great difficulty.

Such a crisis found direct expression in a desire to leave Paris. In a very dejected mood, Joyce wrote to Harriet Weaver in March 1931:

> I understand that both Miss Monnier and Miss Beach have written to you to come over for the séance on the twenty-sixth which for all I know may celebrate the close of my Paris career, just as that of the 7th of December, 1921, opened it . . . So to conclude I shall probably go into a small furnished flat in London and then perhaps go to Zurich and then perhaps go back to London and then perhaps go somewhere else and then perhaps come back to Paris.
>
> (*Letters I* 302–3)

But along with the despair and the incertitude, there appeared a few encouraging elements; Joyce adds this revealing remark: 'The second good point is that I think if the séance of the twentysixth is successful it will probably break the back of the english resistance to Work in Progress as they usually follow a Paris lead over there' (303). The séance alluded to was a reading of *Anna Livia* on 26 March 1931, in French by Adrienne Monnier and in English by Joyce. In his typically superstitious way, Joyce was once more attempting to give a definitive pattern to his life by splitting it into decades, and he had decided that his Parisian decade had come to an end.

Joyce rightly surmised that this decade of almost steady successes leading to worldwide recognition had to be linked for himself and for posterity with the efforts of Sylvia Beach and Adrienne Monnier on his behalf. Adrienne Monnier had started her own lending library and bookshop in 1915, during the war, and her American friend Sylvia Beach had in 1919 opened a bookshop which was primarily an English-speaking lending library close by. Beach's need to sacrifice herself for a good cause and her devotional approach to her job were to find in Joyce an idol whom she 'worshipped' (as she admitted herself), and to whom she was to devote more and more of her time, until Joyce's callousness provoked Adrienne's resentment. At one point, Sylvia Beach jokingly referred to Shakespeare and Co. as the 'Left Bank', implying that she had become Joyce's (and other artists') personal banker...[6]

One of the high moments in the crusade led by these two sincere and enthusiastic women in favour of *Ulysses* was the lecture referred to in Joyce's letter; given to more than two hundred people by Larbaud in Adrienne Monnier's bookshop on 7 December 1921, this event launched the reputation of the book in France. Joyce had responded to the pressure put on him by the lecture and the accompanying translations by hurrying to finish the novel, so that he and his friends were also able to celebrate the forthcoming publication undertaken by Sylvia Beach,[7] with the help of Maurice Darantiere, the Dijon printer. Subscriptions began to pour in, and when the book was published in 1922, it was almost immediately a best-seller in Sylvia Beach's bookshop. 'Bloomsday' very soon became the pretext for festivities and commemorations among the little group of friends of both bookshops.

Thus Joyce was right to recollect the date of 1921 as a turning-point in his life. But during the crisis of 1931, what was really at stake was his wish to inscribe himself in a symbolic legitimacy at last, by renouncing the still Luciferian stance that had been his until then. This he hoped to achieve through a departure from Paris and a step by step return to Dublin. The first step was the embarrassingly belated marriage with Nora, which took place in London in July 1931. Along with the planned marriage went the concept of a 'fifth hegira' (*Letters III* 217) to London – an idea which Beach, for instance, did not approve of: 'It is useless to discuss my present condition with Miss Beach. As she does not know what my motive is . . . she naturally regards my acts in a wrong light' (*Letters III* 215). It is therefore time to consider more carefully the 'fourth hegira', the move to Paris in 1920, in order to understand the milieu Joyce found when he arrived there and the way in which it sustained his work for nineteen years.

The first happy coincidence noticed by Joyce after his arrival in Paris was the fact that everyone seemed interested in Homeric parallels: 'Odyssey very much in the air here. Anatole France is writing *Le Cyclope*, G. Fauré the musician an opera *Pénélope*. Giraudoux has written Elpenor (Paddy Dignam). Guillaume Apollinaire *Les Mammelles de Tirésias*' (*Letters III* 10). He himself felt enthralled by 'Circe', an episode which he insisted he had to write in Paris. After he had rewritten 'Circe' for the sixth or seventh time (Larbaud told him that this episode alone would suffice to establish the reputation of a French writer), he stayed on until the book was finished. However, my main contention is that Joyce was not so deeply absorbed in his own Odyssey that he could not perceive the main literary trends in Paris. And if he did finally stay in Paris till the last moment, until, that is, the German threat in 1940 forced him to leave, it was because he felt in Paris a unique blend of respect for tradition and playful love of experimentation. Moreover, he kept a very keen eye on what was written around him; once he had been made aware of Giraudoux's parallel Homeric attempts, he had to know more about him, and in this particular case his verdict was extremely negative. 'Giraudoux belongs to the school of poets whose day has passed, the so-called rhetoricians, and waits in vain for his Du Bellay and his Ronsard to come to life again. Never have I come upon a writer who was such a brilliant bore', he told Jan Parandowski in 1937.[8]

However, it seems indubitable that Joyce had first access to the French literary circles thanks to the network of friends gathered by Adrienne Monnier, and that he eventually shared her tastes: she had an instinctive dislike of surrealism, more precisely of André Breton whom she immediately rejected, while she and Sylvia Beach remained on good terms with Aragon, whose excellent command of English enabled him to be a staunch customer of Beach's bookshop. Beach herself stresses the fact that her French friends were the first and the last supporters of her venture. The main enthusiasm of Monnier and Beach (for they made a point of selling only books which they liked, often becoming personally acquainted with their authors) were Valery Larbaud, who called himself the bookshop's godfather, Léon-Paul Fargue, whose obscene wit was peerless, and the more established Valéry, Gide, and Claudel.

Joyce's relationship with Larbaud unhappily remained somewhat instrumental; as with Pound, Joyce seemed to have little interest in his writings, and to consider Larbaud primarily as an excellent translator. Larbaud is now thought of as a good modernist poet, but at the time he was above all interested in translation (an art on which he has written some of the most intelligent statements to date). Joyce did not have to court Larbaud as he later did Gillet; Larbaud came to him of his own will, and was immediately 'raving' about *Ulysses*. Larbaud's support opened the door of the *Nouvelle Revue Française* to Joyce, in spite of the reservations of the editor, Jacques Rivière (who would be similarly hostile to a publication of Artaud's poems in 1923). Thus, Larbaud's lecture was published in 1922 in what was the best literary magazine in France, and was soon translated into English in Eliot's *Criterion*. This triggered a series of translations and articles, so that the year 1922 can be called a 'Joyce year' in Paris: the *Ecrits Nouveaux* published 'Arabie' a few days after the publication of *Ulysses*, while the

March issue of *La Revue de Genève* contained 'Un incident regrettable' ('A Painful Case'). The critical acclaim of Joyce, largely due to the atmosphere of scandal surrounding his recent book, was kept up by the translation of *A Portrait of the Artist as a Young Man* as *Dedalus* in March 1924, followed by the first issue of the new magazine *Commerce* (with Valéry, Larbaud, and Fargue as the editors), which in the summer of 1924 offered the initial publication of passages from *Ulysses* in translation. And to crown it all, the university was made aware of the Joyce phenomenon by a bilingual essay written by one of the leading professors of the period, Louis Cazamian, who wrote *L'Oeuvre de James Joyce* in 1924.[9] This extremely rapid recognition contrasted strongly with the reluctance of the literary milieux in England and Ireland.

Besides, help was to come from an unexpected quarter: the staunchly conservative *Revue des Deux Mondes*. The first article on Joyce to be published there, dated 1 August 1925, was 'Du côté de Joyce', stressing the link between Proust and Joyce, a point later reiterated to satiety. The article was rather hostile, but nevertheless showed an understanding of Joyce's techniques which was then quite remarkable. Joyce on the whole was happy with the article, knowing that such hostile criticism brought excellent publicity. What he could not imagine was that the author, Louis Gillet, subtly coached by Sylvia Beach, was slowly to change his mind, becoming within five years one of Joyce's most ardent advocates, and a very close personal friend. The total surrender of 'our review of the two mounds' (*FW* 12.19–20) indicated a major recognition, and it is necessary to read the whole of Gillet's *Stèle pour James Joyce* in order to appreciate the depth of such a critical reversal.[10] This occurred precisely at the time of Larbaud's disaffection with Joyce's 'Work in Progress', which he called a 'divertissement philologique'.[11]

It is clear that in the strategy employed by Joyce to convert Gillet to his side he attempted to become more French than the French, declaring for instance about *Ulysses*: 'In the wooden horse borrowed from Dujardin I put the warriors I stole from Victor Bérard.'[12] Joyce has been accused by his brother Stanislaus and by Mary Colum of using Dujardin as a decoy to hide more relevant borrowings from Freud or Dostoevsky; but if he systematically publicized his debt to *Les Lauriers sont coupés* (an undistinguished piece of prose revery, even if it indeed 'invents' a continuous stream-of-consciousness technique), to the point of sparking off a revival for an older and forgotten writer whom everyone associated with fin-de-siècle symbolism, it was his way of inscribing his cultural roots in France. No doubt Joyce could have acknowledged an 'Ich stamm aus Flaubert', as Pound would have it; he even saw in Larbaud another heir to Flaubert and to his own novels: 'Larbaud result of JJ. and GF.' (Notebook VI.B.8–88.) But the French heritage he modestly claimed for himself had also to be proudly invented; this went as far as his name: he confided to Gillet that 'the name of Joyce is an old French word, in which one finds the name of M. de Joyeuse'.[13] Joyce could also have commented on the way French people called him 'Monsieur Joasse' (a pronunciation of his name not too far from that of 'Jolas', and one which would make him synonymous with 'very happy' ('*joice*' or '*jouasse*' or '*joasse*') in French slang). Joyce was not only trying to look as French as possible in order to win over a conservative French critic, by a trick exposed in *Finnegans Wake* ('Parysis, *tu sais*, crucycrooks, belongs to him who parises himself' (*FW* 155.16–17)), he was busy finding confirmations of his decision to become a Parisian by organizing a system of felicitous coincidences and mystical prophecies. This implied that his new identity should be more than a mask, since it entailed an awareness of a rich and ancient tradition. It is the image of this culture which should occupy us.

Joyce may have surprised Parandowski when referring to Giraudoux as a 'poet', but this was consistent with his view of French culture as a whole. Louis Gillet was no less surprised when he heard Joyce explain that the French language was not, as English-speaking people are prone to say, primarily the language of analytic prose, but the language of poetry: 'Contrary to all expectations, the musical language *par excellence* for him was French, because of the softness of intervals and the quantity of silent syllables that gave to it something airy and diaphanous, which Claude Debussy felt so well, something *soluble dans l'air* as the delightful Lelian says.'[14] This is a far cry from what the young Joyce had had to say about French poetry during his first stay in Paris: 'Paris amuses me very much but I quite understand why there is no poetry in French literature' (*Letters II* 24). It is not that French poetry was something Joyce discovered when he came to Paris for the second time; his encounter with Valéry, whom he admired, probably had little to do with his preference for a purely French musicality. It seems that he had studied French poets systematically when still in Trieste: a large notebook with his Trieste address contains poems in French by Samain and Rimbaud, and prose excerpts of Mallarmé's 'Divagations'.[15] Joyce professed an unbounded admiration for the softest and most musical French poet, Verlaine, and knew many of his texts by heart. Wyndham Lewis told Richard Ellmann how they had drinks with prostitutes in local Paris cafés, and how Joyce was called '*le poète*' because he would quote Dante and Verlaine to their astounded ears. One night, Joyce had only had to quote Verlaine in French to the bartender to be recognized and allowed in after closing time (*JJ* 515–16).

Among the contemporaries, Joyce enjoyed the poems of Valéry, Fargue and Soupault, and he could recite the famous opening of 'Ebauche d'un serpent'[16] (with its characteristic mute 'e's) although he deplored Valéry's inability to read his own verse musically. Only an Irish tenor could do justice to the music of French poetry! One of the earliest *Finnegans Wake* notebooks (VI.B.5, composed in 1924) bears the traces of this fascination for the 'serpent', thirty-four lines of which are copied in a neat handwriting. Valéry represented for Joyce the Mallarmean line of descent, a heritage that had been intellectualized in an effort to bridge the gap between poetry and science. But his poetics did not preclude rich clusters of images close to the unconscious. The neo-Platonic meditation of Valéry's 'Ebauche d'un serpent' on the 'error' or 'sin' (*faute*) of a creation which masks the sun of absolute truth has lent a few overtones to the cosmogony of the Fall in the *Wake*, and precipitated the association of S (the Serpent as devilish tempter) and Sistersen among the *Wake* sigla.

Joyce's knowledge of French poetry was not limited to the writers he usually met in the rue de l'Odéon; he was able to comment on the mistake of omitting Maurice Scève's 'Poèmes à Délie' from a Danish translation of French love poems before 1800. This evinces not only excellent taste, but also a familiarity with the French hermetic tradition which culminates with Mallarmé (*JJ* 693). Joyce's relation to the French language as a whole is surprisingly similar to his relation to music: in both cases he shows relatively classical tastes and a love of the spoken voice which are nevertheless buttressed by an understanding of a tradition which reaches back to the Renaissance and the mediaeval period. This mixture of sophisticated historical knowledge and lack of sophistication in the direct enjoyment of the medium's materiality is typical of the effect *Finnegans Wake* was meant to achieve. And it is not a coincidence if the musicality of the last pages of the *Wake* is meant to climax on an almost silently whispered 'the'...

Thus it is no surprise to see that Joyce was generally impatient with the surrealists, who, unlike Valéry, could not intellectually justify every word, every letter in their collages packed with wild images. He was much more indulgent towards contemporary French novelists, especially Gide and Proust. He told Power and other friends that he admired Gide, not for the experimental novelistic technique of *mise en abyme* with which he is generally associated, but for the purity of his style. (Joyce always had a priggish grammarian's awareness of stylistic correction in French, as his slightly sophomoric comments on Flaubert reveal (*JJ* 492).) He offered *La Symphonie pastorale* to Power, with the words 'Let it be your model'; he praised *La Porte étroite* for being 'a little masterpiece', 'as fine as a spire on Notre Dame' (*CJJ* 76–7). The one book he could not abide was *Corydon*, a kind of Platonic dialogue in which Gide attempted to give biological grounds for pederasty.[17] Hence, Gide appears as 'Gidding up' (*FW* 347.27) in the Butt and Taff episode of the *Wake*, in which he is turned into a French counterpart of Oscar Wilde.

Joyce's reverence for Proust (whose funeral he attended in 1922 after a missed opportunity for a direct conversation (*JJ* 508–9)) could be hedged by reservations, but at times could find a less guarded expression, as with Power, precisely because the latter did not like *La Recherche*: 'He is the best of the modern French writers, and certainly no one has taken modern psychology so far, or to such a fine point' (*CJJ* 78). And he refused to acknowledge that Proust had indulged in mere 'experimentation', explaining that his stylistic 'innovations were necessary to express modern life as he saw it . . . Proust's style conveys that almost imperceptible but relentless erosion of time which . . . is the motive of his work' (*CJJ* 79). Unoriginal as these remarks are, they testify to the sympathy Joyce felt for the French writer, since the terms he uses for him are taken up almost verbatim in a defence of his own artistic ambitions (*CJJ* 95).

Joyce could have found an echo or some support among the French writers who were promoting a revival of Catholic literature in the late twenties, as suggested by François Mauriac's fervid reaction to the reading of the translation of *A Portrait of the Artist*. Mauriac writes to the translator in May 1924: 'With what emotion have I finished *Dedalus*! Madame, perhaps you have read some of my pages, and thus were able to guess that this frightening book [*ce livre terrible*] was meant for me . . .'[18] But support was unavailable from this side, essentially because of Claudel's fierce opposition. Though he remained a friend of Gide (in the steady hope of converting him!) and of Adrienne Monnier, Claudel always expressed the most vehement rejection of Joyce, and when Monnier sent him a copy of the French translation of *Ulysses* while he was in the diplomatic service in Washington, he sent it back. It was a book which to him did not 'offer the least interest', but smacked of heresy. In his diary and letters Claudel gives a harsh description of Joyce, who, he says, 'inspired a true revulsion' in him: *'Joyce was a man eaten up by insects* ['*un homme en proie à l'insecte*', an astonishing phrase with hints of 'incest']. He made me think of arboraceous plants devoured from the inside by bostrychidae . . . A man who separates himself from the source of life and who only lives on himself, as they say, is *autophagous*! The last phase was this second book in which I read a few passages, the verb turned back upon itself, feeding and burning itself.'[19] No-one else was as violent, but a few testimonies left by other Parisian literary figures such as André Suarès, who took Joyce to task for his uneducated arrogance and his middle-class mind,[20] show that negative impressions were not peculiar to English people like Wyndham Lewis. It is important to remember this fact, which justifies Joyce's exaggerated politeness and painful silences: such strategies were not only symptomatic of a withdrawal from life, but defence tactics in the mandarin world of French letters.

On the other hand, one needs only to read Adrienne Monnier's essay on Joyce's *Ulysses* to realize that the French intellectual circles also had first-hand introductions to Joyce's works, and intelligent, informed, and sympathetic accounts of Joyce's major novel. As if to answer Claudel's accusations of 'blasphemies' uttered by a 'renegade',[21] she stresses Joyce's 'charity', his mysticism of the human, and his fundamental humility: 'The overwhelming task that [Joyce] imposed upon himself, that invention of the sensible world – an inventory that supposes, that calls for a classification – no doubt has nothing to do with traditional saintliness, but it nevertheless has something saintly about it, even in the Christian sense, which distinguishes it from the ordinary enterprises of philosophy or literature.'[22] One of the young intellectuals who used to frequent her bookshop no doubt followed the hint: Jacques Lacan probably met Joyce in Adrienne Monnier's bookshop, and, when just twenty, heard Larbaud's 1921 lecture on *Ulysses*. Lacan's title for the long seminar he devoted to Joyce in 1975–6 memorializes him as 'Joyce the Symptom' ('Joyce le Sinthome'), which, along with a pun on Aquinas ('saint Thomas'), also means 'Joyce the Saintly Man' of literature.[23] But if Lacan was able to pay off an old debt by such a masterly reading, the debt perhaps derives from the fact that, from very early on, the founder of the Paris Freudian School may have owed to Joyce a central concept, that of the capitalized Other – just as he found it nicely formulated in Louis Gillet's commentary on the Shakespeare theories developed by Stephen Dedalus: 'In *Hamlet*, Joyce would argue that the main character, the character who dominates everything, who is the real hero, is not Hamlet but the Ghost; it is not the living one, it is the Other [*c'est l'Autre*]; not the mortal but the immortal presence.'[24]

At any rate, even if Joyce is not the father's ghost looming large behind Lacan's Paris School, he himself took some pains to prove the 'Catholic' nature of his works, commissioning McGreevy to write an essay on the theme for the collection on *Finnegans Wake* published in 1929.[25] Some of his efforts must have seemed amply rewarded when, in 1940, he discovered a favourable review of the *Wake* in the *Osservatore Romano* (*JJ* 739). By this time he had found a *cénacle*, a set of apostles, and two authorized commentators: Eugène Jolas and Jacques Mercanton.[26] Jolas had an intense, mystical relationship to literature; he was basically a Romantic and a Jungian, all of which may have been foreign to Joyce's linguistic and historic preoccupations. But Jolas had a keen eye for any kind of verbal experimentation, he had no political bias, and he was ready to open his magazine not only to sections from 'Work in Progress' (they were published in almost every issue of *transition* for ten years, from the first number in 1927), but also to commentaries, discussions, and tireless defences and illustrations of the new synthetic polyglossary invented by Joyce. Jolas soon became a kind of prophet, heralding the death of the King's English, thus showing himself to be the first critic to act out the implications of the parodic Bible contained in *Finnegans Wake*. Even if Joyce did not endorse the most extreme statements or the manifestos announcing the 'Revolution of the Word' in *transition*, there were enough points of contact to let the main contributors to the magazine stand as the official interpreters of the *Wake*, and to give Joyce a renewed sense of rootedness in Paris. But if Jolas was very quickly entrusted with a general plan of the work, it was Mercanton, the Swiss writer, who was deemed the appropriate successor to Stuart Gilbert as the authorized commentator on *Finnegans Wake*. However, this last development belongs to Joyce's sixth hegira in 1939, to a final exile which took him back to Switzerland, but alas, did not last very long...

Even before these last troubled years, in which all his energies were devoted to the completion of the *Wake*, Joyce could note the bleak changes affecting Paris: 'Paris is frightfully dear and has become, they say, the ugly duckling of the great capitals. Most of the foreign colony has fled', he wrote in 1935 (*Letters I* 362). In spite of what has been said about Joyce's lack of political commitment (belied by the active help tendered to Jewish friends), his political sense was extremely acute, as witnessed by the remark he made to Mercanton in 1938: 'In a year France will be Fascist. But there is reason to believe that she will not have to call in fascism from the outside; it will come to her from within.'[27] It is perhaps as well that Joyce did not live long enough to see his prediction come true.

With a sad blindness as to the real cause of her husband's organic disease, Nora complained during one of the last summers which they spent in Paris that her husband had 'fits' and nervous 'pains' in his belly whenever she managed to drag him away from Paris (*JJ* 710); it was clearly an undiagnosed stomach ulcer which killed Joyce, and not his being taken from Paris for too long – but being away from Paris meant above all not being able to write his final testamentary opus, *Finnegans Wake*, which had become Joyce's sole obsession. By the same token, when the book was finished, Joyce did not show the same desperate wish to survive which had borne him through terrible personal tragedies. Besides, thirteen years earlier, in a letter to his father written in 1923, Joyce blames on Nora the fact that they cannot leave Paris and go to a sunnier and cheaper city: 'If I had my way I should live in a quiet place near Nice on the Mediterranean Sea but Nora dislikes it and she has some friends here and so has Giorgio and so has Lucia.' But then he immediately connects their immobility to the positive influence of Parisian intellectual circles: 'Moreover it cannot be denied that the greater part of my reputation is due to the generous admiration of French writers here' (*JJ* 541).

The question that now remains unavoidable is whether the admiration that was lavished on Joyce in Paris – which at times seemed singularly unfounded when it came from people who could not understand his aesthetics or even his language – spoilt him. Stanislaus Joyce seemed to believe that the pernicious influence of Parisian coteries had prompted his brother to emulate Gertrude Stein in obscurity and daring. The answer to such a question depends on how far one is willing to follow Joyce to the end, to accept that the *Wake* is the logical development of *Ulysses*. I do not mean, of course, that one should re-open the old debate concerning Joyce's opacity or hermeticism. Even if he is shown by certain Parisian accounts as awkward or scheming, regally isolated in a close circle of prejudiced friends, taking shelter in silence and exaggerated politeness – in certain cases to the point of prudishness – it must be said that his monstrous work could not have been produced in any other milieu; the word 'milieu' does not simply refer to exceptional private circumstances, but also maps out a whole intellectual history which Joyce traversed with an extremely far-seeing gaze.

Joyce told Arthur Power, in a meaningful understatement on which he refused to comment further, that Paris was 'a very convenient city' (*CJJ* 50). Power was wrong to conclude that 'the surrounding French life with all its brilliance and attraction seemed to pass over him': if it is true that Joyce was not interested in the erotic glamour of *la vie parisienne* which so mystified his Irish friend, he had had more than his share of vital nourishment among the Parisians. He declared to George Moore: 'Paris has played an equal part in our lives' (*JJ* 617), but was still more to the point when he said: 'In my heart Paris is the second city after Dublin.'[28] If he had written *Ulysses* while still a Dubliner at heart, describing Dublin so accurately, as he claimed, that one could reconstruct it a thousand years after some all too imaginable catastrophe, who else but the last Irish Parisian of *l'entre-deux-guerres* might have had the courage and the dedication to reconstruct universal history for all the generations to come? Paris may well have been 'the last of the human cities' (*JJ* 508) for him, the last conch in which one could hear the murmur and prattle of all the languages of man.

NOTES

1 For a popular account of the life of American 'Pilgrims' in Paris during the twenties, see Ernest Hemingway, *A Moveable Feast* (London: Jonathan Cape, 1964). Arthur Power's recollections of James Joyce in the twenties make it plain that Joyce did not want to have anything to do with the crowd of hard-drinking aesthetes, to the point of determinedly avoiding their favourite cafés and of sticking to his own three

restaurants, Les Trianons, Fouquet's and Chez Francis. See Arthur Power, *Conversations with James Joyce*, ed. Clive Hart (London: Millington, 1974); hereafter referred to as *CJJ*.

2 See Richard Ellmann's invaluable biography in its revised edition, *JJ* 126.

3 Valery Larbaud – Marcel Ray, *Correspondance 1899–1937*, III (1921–37), ed. Françoise Lioure (Paris: Gallimard, 1980), p. 15.

4 Louis Gillet, 'Farewell to Joyce', trans. G. Markow-Totevy, in Willard Potts, ed., *Portraits of the Artist in Exile: Recollections of James Joyce by Europeans* (Portmarnock: Wolfhound Press, 1979), p. 167.

5 I have slightly modified the list established by Bernard Gheerbrant in the exhibition shown during the 5th Symposium Joyce in Paris, in Jacques Aubert and Maria Jolas, eds., *Joyce and Paris 1902...1920–1940...1975*, I (Lille: CNRS and Université de Lille III, 1979), p. 135.

6 Noel Riley Fitch, *Sylvia Beach and the Lost Generation: A History of Literary Paris in the Twenties and Thirties* (London: Souvenir Press, 1984), p. 88. See also Shari Benstock, *Women of the Left Bank: Paris 1900–1940* (Austin: University of Texas Press, 1986), pp. 194–229.

7 As Noel Fitch has proved it had been at Joyce's instigation, not at Beach's. See *Sylvia Beach and the Lost Generation*, p. 78.

8 Jan Parandowski, 'Meeting with Joyce', in Potts, *Portraits of the Artist*, p. 156.

9 See the whole recapitulation given by Francine Lenne in 'James Joyce et Louis Gillet', in Jacques Aubert and Fritz Senn, eds., *Cahier de l'Herne James Joyce* (Paris: L'Herne, 1986), pp. 151–75.

10 Louis Gillet, *Stèle pour James Joyce* (Marseille: Editions du Sagittaire, 1941).

11 Quoted by Dougald McMillan in *Transition 1927–38: The History of a Literary Era* (New York: George Braziller, 1976), p. 180.

12 Joyce's Letter to Louis Gillet, 20 November 1931, quoted in *Cahier de l'Herne James Joyce*, p. 161.

13 *Stèle pour James Joyce*, p. 101.

14 Louis Gillet, 'The Living Joyce', in Potts, *Portraits of the Artist in Exile*, pp. 196–7.

15 *Archive 2, Notes, Criticism, Translations, and Miscellaneous Writings*, prefaced and arranged by Hans Walter Gabler, pp. 375–83.

16 Paul Valéry, *Oeuvres* I, Pléiade edn (Paris: Gallimard, 1957), p. 138.

17 Jacques Mercanton, 'The Hours of James Joyce', in Potts, *Portraits of the Artist in Exile*, p. 223.

18 Letter to Ludmila Savitzky shown in Gheerbrant's 1975 exhibition 'James Joyce et Paris'. See Aubert and Jolas, *Joyce and Paris* I, p. 121.

19 *Cahier de l'Herne James Joyce*, p. 91. This comes from a letter written to Louis Gillet and never sent by Claudel. See the complete text in Paul Claudel, *Oeuvres en prose*, Pléiade edn (Paris: Gallimard, 1965), pp. 1485–6. Claudel, by an ironic twist of fate, was to take Louis Gillet's seat at the Académie Française (see *Oeuvres en prose*, pp. 634–58).

20 See the introduction by Jacques Aubert and the unpublished diary by André Suarès in *Cahier de l'Herne James Joyce*, pp. 139–50.

21 *Cahier de l'Herne James Joyce*, p. 129.

22 Adrienne Monnier, 'Joyce's *Ulysses* and the French Public', in Richard McDougall, *The Very Rich Hours of Adrienne Monnier: Translations and Commentaries* (New York: Charles Scribner's Sons, 1976), p. 124.

23 Jacques Lacan's original opening lecture for the Paris James Joyce Symposium, in which he gives these biographical indications, has been published in *L'Ane* 6 (Fall, 1982), 3–5. See *Joyce avec Lacan*, ed. Jacques Aubert (Paris: Navarin, 1987). For an account of Lacan's literary interests, see Elisabeth Roudinesco, *La Bataille de cent ans, Histoire de la psychanalyse en France* II, 1925–85 (Paris: Seuil), 1986.

24 *Stèle pour James Joyce*, p. 151.

25 Thomas McGreevy, 'The Catholic Element in *Work in Progress*', in Samuel Beckett *et al., Our Exagmination Round his Factification for Incamination of Work in Progress* (1929) (London: Faber, 1972), pp. 119–27. See also Beryl Schlossman's excellent book, *Joyce's Catholic Comedy of Language* (Madison: University of Wisconsin Press, 1985).

26 Mercanton's complete essays on Joyce are in print as *Ecrits sur James Joyce* (Vevey: L'Aire, 2002).

27 Jacques Mercanton, 'The Hours of James Joyce', in Potts, *Portraits of the Artist in Exile*, p. 241.

28 Jan Parandowski, 'A Meeting with James Joyce', in Potts, *Portraits of the Artist in Exile*, p. 159.

4

CHRISTOPHER BUTLER

Joyce the modernist

I

There are many kinds of modernism – one has only to think of the differences between Picasso and Kandinsky, Schoenberg and Stravinsky, or Joyce
and Kafka to appreciate this. The number of books and articles devoted to
attempts at defining the term is huge.[1] In what follows I wish to see Joyce's
relationship to what is often loosely called the 'modernist movement' in a
fairly simple way. First of all I look at his becoming 'modernist' in the most
obvious sense – that is, by moving beyond his nineteenth-century predecessors. I then sketch his relationships to others who had diversely managed the
same feat, and thus opened up an extraordinary avant-garde market-place
of competing styles. Joyce made a contribution to this critical moment so
great that he posed an acute problem to his successors: after *Ulysses* and
Finnegans Wake, what types of expression in writing could possibly remain
undiscovered?

Modernist artists at the beginning of the century were to a large degree
moved to this unprecedented freedom and confidence in stylistic experiment
by what they saw as radically new ideas, current in that period, concerning
consciousness, time, and the nature of knowledge, which were to be found in
the work of Nietzsche, Bergson, Freud, Einstein, Croce, Weber, and others.
And these ideas contested in a dramatic manner the beliefs of the older
generation.[2]

This revolt focused on a 'transvaluation of all values'; and those who
were most self-conscious about it tended to be followers of Nietzsche. Thus
although he was generally sceptical about this sort of enthusiasm, Joyce
thought of himself as a Nietzschean in 1904, when as 'James Overman' he
was all for neopaganism, licentiousness, and pitilessness (*JJ* 142, 162, 172;
Letters I 23).[3] Thinkers like Nietzsche helped to sustain his opposition to
those totalizing religious and philosophical frameworks characteristic of the
nineteenth-century bourgeoisie. 'My mind rejects the whole present social

order and Christianity' he tells Nora (*Letters II* 48), and his Stephen Daedalus is 'fond of saying that the Absolute is dead' (*SH* 211/206). Thus Joyce and many like him at this time (particularly Eliot) seem to have favoured that relativist opposition to the beliefs of the past which is one of the chief legacies of Pater and William James. Its symptoms were pragmatism, pluralism, and that most typical of modernist strategies, a sceptical irony. And so when the protagonist of *Stephen Hero* wishes to express feelings of love,

> he found himself compelled to use what he called the feudal terminology and as he could not use it with the same faith and purpose as animated the feudal poets themselves he was compelled to express his love a little ironically. This suggestion of relativity, he said, mingling itself with so immune a passion is a modern note.
>
> (*SH* 174/174: the 'feudal terminology' derives from Dante's *Vita nuova*.)

It is this scepticism concerning received ideas that Georg Brandes's *Men of the Modern Breakthrough* (1880), Ibsen, Björnson, Jacobsen, Drachmann, Flaubert, Renan, and J. S. Mill, all had in common. Joyce revered Brandes and was certainly influenced by Ibsen, Flaubert, and Renan. He documents his version of this intellectual revolt, amongst students 'who regarded art as a continental vice' (*SH* 38/34), most explicitly in *Stephen Hero* and *A Portrait*, which show how he extricated himself from the prevailing faiths of his contemporaries. But this rejection of religion and nationalism is not I think the most important part of the story concerning Joyce's turn-of-the-century scepticism. For it also resides, paradoxically enough, in his extraordinary attachment to fact. The 'scrupulous meanness' of *Dubliners* is his way of following Arnold in seeing things as they really are: and it is his realism which perpetually combats larger ideological commitments. A remark he made to Arthur Power is extremely significant from this point of view, and expresses an attitude which underlies his work through to the completion of *Ulysses*:

> In realism you get down to facts on which the world is based; that sudden reality which smashes romanticism into a pulp. What makes most people's lives unhappy is some disappointed romanticism, some unrealisable misconceived ideal. In fact you may say that idealism is the ruin of man, and if we lived down to fact, as primitive man had to do, we would be better off. That is what we were made for. Nature is quite unromantic. It is we who put romance into her, which is a false attitude, an egotism, absurd like all egotism. In *Ulysses* I tried to keep close to fact. (Power, p. 98)

This Ibsenic destruction of illusions, and the charitable and humorous attitude Joyce brings to it, is of course implicit rather than overt in much of his work, and it led to obvious bafflement in a number of critics who did not attempt to describe Joyce's attitudes to the doctrines or ideologies (other than Catholicism and nationalism) that were popular among his contemporaries. Honourable exceptions were Richard Brown and Dominic Manganiello, and more recently there has been a considerable amount of work along these lines, including books by Robert Spoo, Vincent J. Cheng, Joseph Valente, and Andrew Gibson.

Joyce's attitude to the modernist climate of ideas thus has largely to be inferred from his essentially solitary (and egotistical) experimentalism, and from our sense of the ideological risks it ran. For by the time he is writing *Ulysses* he has set himself the 'task' 'of writing a book from eighteen different points of view and in as many styles, all apparently unknown or undiscovered by my fellow tradesmen' (*Letters I* 167), and this stylistic diversity enshrines an essentially relativist attitude towards the 'truthful' depiction of reality. It makes an implicit stand against the ideological authority of the nineteenth-century novel, and of those other incorporative ideas which threatened him (as for example in the sermon of the *Portrait*). He thus uses modernist techniques, as Karen Lawrence argues, to adopt a 'series of rhetorical masks' which make us 'doubt the authority of any particular style'. The various methods of narrative in *Ulysses* are thus 'different but not definitive ways of filtering and ordering experience' (p. 9). For although Joyce obeys the underlying causal necessities of narrative, and is as obsessively concerned with accuracy as Proust, he also makes us see his history of a day within a number of stylistic frameworks, which are all relative to one another, and which often disrupt the conventions of word formation and syntax. This is the beginning of Joyce's 'revolution of the word', which is completed in *Finnegans Wake*.

II

Joyce's revolution towards this kind of sceptical relativism has its roots in the nineteenth century. Matthew Arnold makes a remark in his essay on Heine of 1863 which is distinctively echoed in Joyce:

> Modern times find themselves with an immense system of institutions, established facts, accredited dogmas, customs, rules, which have come to them from times not modern. In this system their life has to be carried forward, yet they have a sense that this system is not of their own creation, that it by no means corresponds exactly with the wants of their actual life, that for them, it is customary not rational. The awakening of this sense is the awakening of the modern spirit.   (p. 109)

This confrontation with the customary is engaged with enthusiasm by modern writers like Nietzsche, Ibsen, Shaw, Marinetti, Kraus, Tzara, and others, in the name of a very different kind of rationality. But in allying himself with this movement of ideas, Joyce goes beyond Arnold in rejecting any desire for an overall metaphysical order, however tinkered with, in which 'culture' takes on the responsibilities of religion. He would probably have agreed with Wilde's comment: 'It is enough that our fathers believed. They have exhausted the faith-faculty of the species. Their legacy to us is the scepticism of which they were afraid' (pp. 1039–40). For Arnold's was always a confused and confusing demand, as T. S. Eliot pointed out: 'The total effect of Arnold's philosophy is to set up culture in the place of Religion, and to leave Religion to be laid waste by an anarchy of feeling' (p. 387). Through Stephen Daedalus in *Stephen Hero*, Joyce the Catholic confronts this loss of faith head on, while retaining, and secularizing, much of the vocabulary of religion, as, for example, his perplexing notion of 'epiphany' shows.

The tradition of thought descending from Arnold through Wilde and others was equally significant in legitimizing feelings of distance and alienation from a social and intellectual context. In displaying this tension in a young man Joyce was at one with many of his contemporaries, like Frank Wedekind in *Spring Awakening* (1891–2), Robert Musil in *Young Törless* (1906), André Gide in *L'Immoraliste* (1902), and Thomas Mann in *Tristan* and *Tonio Kröger* (1903), the latter of whom argues at one point as follows:

> Literature is not a calling, it is a curse, believe me! When does one begin to feel the curse? Early, horribly early. At a time when one ought by rights still to be living in peace and harmony with God and the world. It begins by your feeling yourself set apart, in a curious sort of opposition to the nice, regular people; there is a gulf of ironic sensibility, of knowledge, scepticism, disagreement, between you and the others; it grows deeper and deeper, you realise that you are alone; and from then on any rapprochement is simply hopeless! What a fate!
>
> (pp. 153–4)

The young Daedalus of *Stephen Hero* (1904–6) has very similar characteristics, and has also the highly Arnoldian awareness 'that though he was nominally in amity with the order of society into which he had been born, he would not be able to continue so' (*SH* 184/179). He defines his sense of the modern to his friend Cranly as an anti-traditional seeing of things as they really are, whose inspiration lies in science. But it is not perhaps the science one might expect:

> The modern spirit is vivisective. Vivisection itself is the most modern process one can conceive. The ancient spirit accepted phenomena with a bad grace. The ancient method investigated law with the lantern of justice, morality with the

lantern of revelation, art with the lantern of tradition. But all these lanterns have magical properties: they transform and disfigure. The modern method examines its territory by the light of day.　　　　　　　　　　(SH 190/186)

Here is the Ibsenite Stephen, who has been told (admittedly by a priest) that his paper devoted to Ibsen on 'Art and Life' 'represents the sum of modern unrest and modern freethinking' (SH 96/91).[4]

Joyce and Stephen stand here at pretty well the same point of evolution, in 1906, just before the extraordinary stylistic transformation of *Stephen Hero* into *A Portrait of the Artist* (rather as Pound reduced a conventional thirty-line poem into the experimental and imagist two-line 'In a Station of the Metro'). But before this commitment to experiment of a recognizably modernist kind in the opening of *A Portrait*, Joyce manages what the other major modernists of the period also achieved: the complete recreative and parodic mastery of previous traditions.

It is this mastery which reveals the strongly conservative approach to art of the early modernists (as opposed for example to the futurists and dadaists who succeeded them). I am thinking here of Matisse's Impressionist and Picasso's Symbolist paintings; of Pound's recreation of the forms of the late nineteenth-century tradition, including the Browningesque monologue; of Stravinsky's neo-Debussyan impressionism in *The Firebird* (1909–10) and *King of the Stars* (1911–12), and of Schoenberg's writing of the symphonic poem *Pelléas and Mélisande* (1902–3) in a manner that deliberately exceeded in complexity the work of all his predecessors. All these early modernists thus work through Symbolism and its derivatives; and then go significantly beyond it, by inventing radically new languages for art. What they do not do is ally themselves to an avant-garde which expresses its revolutionary intentions in manifestos. In his work up to *Ulysses* Joyce makes this assimilation of tradition in a very similar manner, first producing a distinctly Chekhovian set of short stories, the last of which, 'The Dead', is profoundly Symbolist and Ibsenic at the same time; then manifesting in *A Portrait* the early modern metamorphosis of previous styles, by weaving the mental worlds and the verbal characteristics of Pater, Newman, and others into Stephen's consciousness. Here, as Lodge puts it,

> Joyce varied his style to imitate various phases of his hero's narrative, . . . declared his secession from the fully readerly mode of narrative, and began his career as a fully-fledged modernist writer.　　　　　　　　　　(p. 130)

An ironic gap is thus opened up between Stephen's self-emancipating thoughts as an arrogant young man and his poetic mimicry of his predecessors. This demands from the reader that awareness of allusion and split level of response that Eliot's 'Prufrock' before him and Pound's 'Hugh Selwyn Mauberley' after him also demand. It was indeed this stylistic self-consciousness and range of reference that Pound himself was so quick to notice in 1915:

> His style has the hard clarity of a Stendhal or Flaubert . . . He has also the richness of erudition which differentiates him from certain able and vigorous but rather overloaded impressionist writers. He is able, in the course of a novel, to introduce a serious conversation, or even a stray conversation on style or philosophy without being ridiculous. (*Letters II* 359)

This display reflects the reading of a well-informed and up-to-date young man; and it parallels Joyce's own. For he too had questioned conventional morality with the help of Ibsen and Shaw, and was in a position to judge D'Annunzio (temporarily) better than Flaubert by 1900. Between 1900 and 1902 he also read Zola, Hauptmann, Verlaine, Huysmans, and Tolstoy, and was guided through the Symbolist movement by Arthur Symons. He was thus familiar with the most challenging of realist writing, as well as with French Symbolism and its influence. Indeed he kept his devotion to early Yeats, especially *The Wind among the Reeds*, and the feebleness of his own (and Stephen's) poetic efforts shows that he did not get much beyond this late Symbolist aesthetic in verse. Most significantly by the time he comes to write *A Portrait* he sees his work as going beyond that of writers in the realist tradition, like Hardy, Gissing, and Moore.

Nevertheless Joyce's *resistance* to certain contemporary ideas is of equal importance. His philosophical allegiances are to the pre-moderns, for example to Aquinas, for even when he is subverting Catholic dogma, one can feel that so far as Stephen's aesthetic theories go, he believes that the Scholastics have at least correctly formulated the categories with which we have to think (*SH* 81ff./77ff.). And although Joyce may have welcomed 'beauty' in Yeats and others (an old-fashioned Paterian aesthetic category to which he seems to have remained pretty loyal) and seen the advantages, in terms of extending the subject matter of literature, of the moral liberalism of Flaubert, Tolstoy, Hauptmann, and Ibsen, he was not going to fall entirely for those Schopenhauerian or Nietzschean or occultist ideas which intoxicated others of his generation in Europe. Thus as Stephen walks to the University (*P* 147ff.) he is attended by the ghosts of writers not very different from those available to Hardy's Jude in Christminster meadow: Hauptmann, Newman, Guido Cavalcanti, Ibsen, Ben Jonson, Aristotle, Aquinas.

Joyce's extraordinary fidelity to past time thus means that the *ideas* he presents in his books are not those of the modernist avant-garde. It is through his style that modernism is implied. And so it is the stylistic innovations of the opening and closing pages of *A Portrait* which launch Joyce into an original modernist experimentalism which is almost wholly unpredictable in terms of these earlier influences. A novelist deeply indebted to Joyce, Anthony Burgess, describes the montage of the book's opening pages as follows:

> Prose and subject-matter have become one and inseparable; it is the first big technical breakthrough of twentieth-century prose-writing and, inevitably, it looks as if anybody could have thought of it. The roots of *Ulysses* are here – to every phase of the soul its own special language; *Finnegans Wake* must seem, not a wilful aberration from sense, but a logical conclusion from that premise. (p. 50)

Faced with this sort of thing, the reviewer in the *Manchester Guardian* (March 1917) thought that 'there are ellipses . . . that go beyond the pardonable . . . [and] obscure allusions. One has to be of the family, so to speak, to "catch on"' (*CH I* 93). And the reviewer in *The New Age* had similar difficulties, commenting that '. . . his wilful cleverness, his determination to produce Kinematographic effects instead of a literary portrait, are due entirely to a lack of clarity'. For him, *A Portrait* seemed to be 'a mere catalogue of unrelated states' (*CH I* 110). It is precisely this initially baffling associativeness which is a central symptom of modernist writing. Joyce poses the same sorts of problems as we find in the poetry of Guillaume Apollinaire, Blaise Cendrars, Eliot, and Pound.

III

Joyce thus enters the experimental mainstream of modernism by an extraordinary display of technique, and not by any anterior commitment to some avant-gardist doctrine. Nevertheless, by the time he had published the earlier episodes of *Ulysses*, he could at the very least claim to have bequeathed to his successors new resources which were not simply matters of style. He had managed a distinctive reinvention of Symbolist experience through the 'epiphanic' moments of *A Portrait* and its aesthetic theory (*P* 174–81; epiphany is discussed explicitly in *SH* 216ff./211ff.), and he had revived and immeasurably extended the presentation of the 'stream of consciousness', which was previously to be found in Edouard Dujardin, whom he acknowledges, and in Arthur Schnitzler's *Lieutenant Gustl* (1901), of which he possessed a copy. By 1922 he had challenged all who wished to write after him by producing a designedly encyclopaedic epic, whose sustained mythical parallelism raised in an acute form the post-Nietzschean and post-Jungian questions of the nature of history as repetition. He thus vastly extended the experimental repertoire available to the novelist; and also, paradoxically enough, influenced the general movement of the nineteen-twenties back towards a conservative neo-classicism. We see Eliot attempting this assimilation of his work when he emphasizes Joyce's control and order and form, in his influential account of the Yeatsian 'mythical method' of the book (*CH I* 269–70).[5]

These aspects of his work immediately influenced the Anglo-American modernist movement in general, including Eliot, as Ronald Bush and others have shown. Joyce's use of allusion to different cultural periods, which yet have an underlying coherence, leads to Eliot's 'Sweeney Among the Nightingales'; and similar considerations affect Pound's *Cantos* IV to VII (see Bush, pp. 207–43, and Sultan, *passim*). For by 1919 both Eliot and Pound had read the manuscript of 'Sirens', and their discussion of *Ulysses* must have had a considerable influence upon the former's 'Tradition and the individual talent', which is virtually a manifesto for a method which others might follow. Bush also discerns the influence of the 'Nestor' episode of *Ulysses* on Pound's *Cantos* V and VI, and on Eliot's 'Gerontion', which seems to respond to Stephen's remark, 'History . . . is a nightmare from which I am trying to awake' (*U* 2.377). Pound had wanted 'Gerontion' to resemble his own work more closely in its fragmentation, but Eliot happily seems to have defended its underlying Joycean coherence.

Pound had had doubts concerning 'Sirens' and so did not see anything more of Joyce's work till the 'Circe' episode came to him in April 1921. He and Eliot thought it magnificent. It is thus Joyce's *Ulysses* which may well have been the crucial impetus to the major work of Pound and Eliot in this period, and have provided some of the central aesthetic principles governing their work and their interaction at this time.

The influence of *Ulysses* as an experimental achievement seems to have been undoubted from the beginning; and its influence on writers like Virginia Woolf, William Faulkner, John Dos Passos, Alfred Döblin, Hermann Broch, Vladimir Nabokov, and others has been ably demonstrated by R. M. Adams. But its relationship to the modernist movements which surrounded its making is much more doubtful. Of course it is an obvious fact of literary history that Joyce's critical reputation partly stood or fell with that of his early modernist supporters, like Pound and Eliot, and his later surrealist ones, like Eugène Jolas and Philippe Soupault. And even his detractors, like Wyndham Lewis, managed to focus upon central issues in his writing (to judge by the strong response to *Time and Western Man* in *Finnegans Wake*). Joyce seems nevertheless to have been extremely reticent in his critical judgements on his modernist contemporaries. Ellmann records positive judgements on André

Gide's *Caves du Vatican*, Wyndham Lewis's *Tarr*, and little else. Joyce seems to have been interested enough in Eliot to parody him (see *JJ* 572, 495), but he does not seem to have much liked Pound's work beyond the relatively conservative *Cathay* (*JJ* 661).

I suspect that although Joyce knew about other types of modernist experimental activity, he was not going to be drawn on them, as his silence at the end of the following exchange with Budgen shows:

> 'Does this episode ['Cyclops'] strike you as futuristic?' said Joyce.
> 'Rather cubist than futurist', I said, 'every event is a many-sided object. You first state one view of it and then you draw it from another angle to another scale, and both aspects lie side by side in the same picture.'
>
> (Budgen, pp. 156–7)

The contents of his library in 1920, as reported by Ellmann (*Consciousness*, pp. 97ff.), are consistent with the restriction of his interest to those ideas which could have influenced his characters at that point in the moral history of his country at which he chose to place them. Thus, for example, his chief sources for the interpretation of Homer are Butler and Bérard, rather than Frazer and the Cambridge School, whose use of comparative anthropology and construction of a 'primitive mentality' was becoming so influential. Eliot was far more self-consciously up to date in his view of myth as a cultural phenomenon. We only find Gide, Jens Peter Jacobsen, Lawrence, Lewis, Heinrich Mann, Woolf, Bergson, and Nietzsche (and, as we shall see, Freud) amongst those of his books which could be thought to have been of much interest to the avant-garde of his time. The one truly avant-gardist text he possessed, Marinetti's *Enquête internationale sur le vers libre et Manifeste du Futurisme* (1909), does not seem to have inspired him. This sort of evidence is hardly conclusive, however, for Joyce was very likely far more aware of what was 'going on' than the extant evidence would suggest, and it will be up to future critics to advance parallels to contemporary art more convincing than those in the current literature (see, for instance, Loss, *Joyce's Visible Art*). Indeed, I suspect that he was very well-informed when he needed to be for his own purposes; his remark to Stanislaus in a letter of 15 July 1920 is significant, for he is well able to support his assertion that the 'Odyssey is very much in the air here' [Paris] by references to Anatole France, to Fauré's *Pénélope*, to Giraudoux, and to Apollinaire's *Les Mamelles de Tirésias* (*Letters III* 10). It seems, then, that so far as his experimental techniques were concerned Joyce was very good at disguising the sources of his inspiration. As Budgen remarks,

There are hints of all practices in *Ulysses* – cubism, futurism, simultaneism, dadaism and the rest – and this is the clearest proof that he was attached to none of the various schools that followed them. At one time in Zürich . . . I quoted to him one full-sounding phrase I had learned: 'Noi futuristi italiani siamo senza passato.' 'E senza avvenire', said Joyce. Any other doctrine would have called forth the same comment. ['We futurists are without a past.' 'And without a future.'] (p. 198)

It is the *ideology* of avant-garde movements which Joyce finds irrelevant to his purposes; and my judgement is that he quickly appropriated all available modernist techniques, while keeping himself well clear of the often inflated claims for 'simultaneity', the 'destruction of the past', and so on, of the manifestos. Although his earlier readers thought they could discern such influences upon him (so that in 1923 Ernest Boyd, for example, compares his work to that of Romains and the Unanimists, while maintaining that 'its form is more akin to the German Expressionists' (*CH I* 304)), there are no obvious modernist *sources* for the leading candidates, such as the Night-town episode, which indeed makes use of what seem to be the techniques of stage presentation, and on occasion the abbreviated 'telegraphic' language, of much German expressionist drama.

Joyce's work thus has to be placed within the modernist tradition by critical comparison rather than through the study of its direct influence. The presentation of the city as subject in *Ulysses*, for example, fits into just such a sequence, descending in the twentieth century through Jules Romains' *La Vie unanime* (1907), Biely's *Petersburg* (1913), and many other works. Joyce celebrates the city as they do, rather than seeing it as alienating, in the manner of sociologists like Ferdinand Tönnies and Georg Simmel at the turn of the century, and more pessimistic writers than he, from Gissing and Conrad through to Döblin's *Alexanderplatz*. The poets' treatment of the city similarly divides between optimistic celebrants like Apollinaire and Cendrars, and pessimists like Rilke, Heym, and Benn. In their light however Stephen Dedalus strikes us as a Baudelairean flâneur from a less troubled age. This designedly retrospective tone is sustained by Joyce to prevent too facile an accommodation of his work to artistic activity contemporary with its writing. Thus the 'Aeolus' episode is clearly 'modernist' in its interest in the newspaper and its use of headlines, an interest affirmed by Apollinaire, Cendrars and, most noisily, by Marinetti, who sees the city as a site for new modern materials which are juxtaposed to one another like 'the great newspaper (synthesis of a day in the world's life)' (Apollonio, *Futurist Manifestos*, p. 96). But Joyce's use of this topos is also deeply traditional, as the episode explores the art of rhetoric back to the Greeks (see Vickers, *In Defence of*

Rhetoric, pp. 387–404). It is this synthesis of past and present, rather than a merely ironic or satirical juxtaposition of the 'classical' and the modern (as in Eliot), that seems to me to be one of Joyce's most distinctive achievements.

His presentation of many events taking place simultaneously within a single time-span, or presented in different parts of the text and then unified in the mind of the reader (through an apprehension of 'spatial form') as he or she grasps the interactive life of a great city, also seems to have obvious affinities with the unanimism of Romains, the 'dramatism' of Barzun, and the much vaunted 'simultaneism' of Cendrars's *Prose du Transsibérien*, all of which emphasized the rhythmical and cinematic techniques of montage to express city life. Cendrars summarizes these tendencies in his 'A.B.C. du Cinéma' (1919), when he asks for a

> Remue-ménage d'images. L'unité tragique se déplace. Nous apprenons. Nous buvons. Ivresse. Le réel n'a plus aucun sens. Aucune signification. Tout est rhythme, parole, vie. Il n'y a plus de démonstration. On communie.[6]

The simultaneism of 'Wandering Rocks' seems to be as virtuosic a treatment of this sort of theme as could be imagined, and Joyce's ambition with respect to it immense: 'If I can get to the heart of Dublin I can get to the heart of all the cities in the world' (*JJ* 505). But his inspiration may also have been directly cinematic, and influenced by concepts of montage as we find them in Eisenstein (with whom he discussed the possibility of turning *Ulysses* into a film, *JJ* 654) and others. Indeed the *Evening News* pointed out in 1922 that 'his style is in the new fashionable kinematographic vein, very jerky and elliptical' (*CH I* 192), and Carola Giedion-Welcker compares *Ulysses* to 'the cinematic-technical transmission' of futurism (*CH II* 442). This judgement is hardly surprising, for the language of *Ulysses* can be at least as 'poetic', and fragmented in its presentation of the isolated or juxtaposed image, as that of avant-garde poets like Marinetti, who used a 'simultaneist' and juxtapository technique. Joyce's work thus parallels that of Apollinaire (in 'Zones' and 'Vendémiaire') and Cendrars (in his *Pâques à New York* (1912) and *Prose du Transsibérien* (1913)), or German city poets like van Hoddis, Lichtenstein, and Stadler.

After Joyce, in the work of writers like Dos Passos, Döblin, and Musil, these techniques are variously adapted to the theme of city life, often enough in the light of Eliot's judgement that Joyce had given order to what he called, with inappropriate pessimism, 'the immense panorama of futility and anarchy which is contemporary history' (*CH I* 270). Eliot wholly fails to appreciate the progressive and optimistic elements in Joyce's thinking, and his view is surely more applicable to his own *Waste Land* or (minus the myth) to a work like Dos Passos's *Manhattan Transfer* (1925).

CHRISTOPHER BUTLER

IV

As my frequent references to contemporary critics have already shown, it is to the history of Joyce's reception that we have to turn in order to appreciate how he was located with respect to the modernism of his contemporaries. For Joyce never made avant-gardist propaganda for his own work; though he was willing (as in *Our Exagmination*) to leave that to others. So far as the critical understanding of *Ulysses* is concerned, the prime documents to emerge after these initial critical reactions are Budgen's memoir, *James Joyce and the Making of 'Ulysses'*, and Gilbert's *James Joyce's Ulysses*, but the latter at least is more a work of exegesis than an apology for *Ulysses'* position within the modern movement. They are nevertheless the main sources for the establishment of *Ulysses* as a central text within the high modernist period after the First World War.

The criticism of the reviews is by and large disappointing in its lack of sophistication; moral shock rationalized by reference to Freud seems to have formed the staple of many early attempts to relate Joyce to contemporary goings-on. He is thus 'completely anarchic' and 'in rebellion against the social morality of civilisation' according to Middleton Murry (*CH I* 196); and he 'deliberately ignores moral codes and conventions' according to Holbrook Jackson (*CH I* 198). Gosse thought that Joyce was 'a sort of Marquis de Sade, but he does not write so well' (*CH I* 313).

Objections like this last to the 'poetic' juxtapositions and alogicalities of Joyce's prose miss the point. For the reader is expected to rationalize Joyce's use of language by reference to the great change in assumptions concerning our mental life which was proclaimed (though not invented) by the modernists. This is the essentially post-Freudian assumption that there is an intelligible, and revelatory, *rationale* for the association of apparently disjunct ideas. This was much attacked at the time, for example by Max Eastman, as a mere 'cult of unintelligibility', of which he also accuses Hart Crane, e. e. cummings, and Gertrude Stein (*CH II* 489).

There seems nevertheless to have been considerable agreement with Edmund Wilson's claim (in the *New Republic*, 1922) that *Ulysses* was the 'most faithful X-ray ever taken of the ordinary human consciousness' (*CH I* 228). Wilson develops this claim in his account of the modern movement (as essentially post-Symbolist) in *Axel's Castle*:

> Joyce is indeed really the great poet of a new phase of human conscious-
> ness. Like Proust's or Whitman's or Einstein's world, Joyce's world is always
> changing as it is perceived by different observers and by them at different times.
>
> (p. 221)

78

This rather obvious reaction gets on to much more controversial ground with the assumption that Joyce's work was somehow designedly Freudian. Thus an early approving review by Joseph Collins claimed that *Ulysses* 'would seem to substantiate some of Freud's contentions' (*CH I* 223), and the *Daily Express* in 1922 perhaps articulated the ordinary reader's sense of what Freud stood for by pointing out that it displayed 'all our most secret and unsavoury private thoughts' (*CH I* 191). Mary Colum even more confidently proclaimed that it was a 'book written on the subconscious method' (*CH I* 234), and the *Sporting Times* review reported that 'Nausicaa' had been defended in New York as 'the unveiling of the subconscious in the Freudian manner' and thus as un-aphrodisiac (*CH I* 194).[7] In this context perhaps the judgement of Holbrook Jackson, that 'every action and reaction of his [Bloom's] psychology is laid bare with Freudian nastiness', and that 'much of the action of *Ulysses* is subconscious' (*CH I* 199), and of Ford Madox Ford that it was 'a volume of dream interpretations by Freud' (*CH I* 277), might have struck the contemporary literate reader as authoritative.

There are of course two aspects of this type of judgement: clearly Joyce would have known that he had provided excellent examples for psychoanalytic interpretation, which claims to interpret all sorts of neurotic behaviour. But it is a separate question to decide on the nature of any Freudian influence on him. It was not until he was living in Trieste that Joyce read Vico (*JJ* 340), Freud on Leonardo, Ernest Jones's Freudian study, *Hamlet and his Problems*, and Jung's 'The significance of the father in the destiny of the individual', and he probably learnt more about psychoanalysis from Ettore Schmitz, the author of *La coscienza di Zeno*, whom he came to know there. But he concluded that Freud was in any case anticipated by Vico, and claimed, in a peculiar return to the Catholicism he had rejected, to prefer the confessional as a mode of self-revelation.[8]

Thus although Stephen refers to the 'new Viennese school' in the library scene, and the 'Circe' episode could certainly be said to incorporate, as Freud said dreams would, the events of the previous day, and to reveal various complexes and fears in the main characters (see Hoffmann, pp. 137 ff.), Joyce's *moral* attitude to psychoanalysis (like that of D. H. Lawrence) seems to have been very hostile, at least in the period of *Ulysses*. For although he admitted, in attacking the notion that there was a moral to be found in *Ulysses*, that he had 'recorded . . . what you Freudians call the subconscious', he went on to say 'but as for psychoanalysis it's neither more nor less than blackmail' (*JJ* 524; and compare Ellmann, *Consciousness*, pp. 54ff.). *Finnegans Wake* on the other hand is clearly indebted to psychoanalysis, to which it frequently alludes. A Freudian interpretation of its language, and a Jungian one of its myths and symbols, seems inevitable.[9]

V

As our brief discussion of the psychology of Joyce's characters shows, it is one of the most obvious features of his work from *A Portrait* on that he withdraws the presence of the omniscient author who stage-manages the reader's judgement, in favour of a focus upon a particular consciousness. Joyce of course found this move from the external to the psychologically inward in the novel as mediated by James, Meredith, and Butler, and it was already part of the continental tradition in Chekhov, Maupassant, Huysmans, Jacobsen, D'Annunzio, Bourget, and Turgenev. And in developing it in modernist terms he extends a tradition which runs through Conrad, Mann, Proust, and Gide. As Quinones points out, Bloom like Marcel in *A la recherche du temps perdu*, Hans Castorp in *The Magic Mountain*, Tiresias in *The Waste Land*, Birkin in *Women in Love*, Jacob in *Jacob's Room*, and Clarissa Dalloway in *Mrs Dalloway*, is a 'reflective, passive, selfless and tolerant witness'. And 'the creation of these complex central consciousness constitutes one of the major achievements of modernism' (pp. 95ff.).

These developments entailed a fundamental change in the traditional conjunction between author and (realist) literary text.[10] For Joyce the authority of the text, as an 'omniscient' documentary work in a 'transparent' relationship to its subject matter, is displaced to various rhetorics or styles which are nominally independent of the author as a reliable source of knowledge. This relationship is at its most extreme in *Finnegans Wake*. Like James, Mann, Conrad, and Gide, Joyce displaces that critical relation to society, which had previously been expressed by the author as narrator, to the evocation of a particular consciousness within the text.

It is this concentration on the subjective which, paradoxically enough, freed modernists like Joyce to achieve another aim, not obviously compatible with it: that of the aesthetic autonomy of the experimental work. For it is not simply the nature of passing states of consciousness of the world that become interesting to modernists under the influence of thinkers like William James, Bergson, Freud, and Ernst Mach, but also the way in which the hidden consciousness of the artist *behind* the text may *implicitly or indirectly* display his or her own formal procedures. It is this hidden thematic patterning that is so completely missed by Wyndham Lewis in his polemic concerning the Bergsonian treatment of time in relation to consciousness in modernism, and makes ridiculous his accusation that Bloom and Stephen are 'overwhelmed in the torrent of matter, of *nature morte*. This torrent of matter is the Einsteinian flux. Or (equally well) it is the duration flux of Bergson' (*CH I* 362).

The first and essential step towards this state of affairs for the modernists involved a confrontation with the techniques of the realist text, a confrontation which is at its most extreme in *Finnegans Wake*. It entailed a radical withdrawal from established modes of representation; for nearly all the major experimental works of the early modernist canon deviate from a previous consensual language, and often enough also from common sense. Music abandons the natural 'Pythagorean' language of tonality, cubism abandons the naturalist methods of Renaissance perspective and the facts of vision of the Impressionists. The alogical poetry of Apollinaire, Gottfried Benn, and others, and the stream of consciousness writing of Joyce, Dorothy Richardson, Woolf, and the surrealists, abandons that language of rational control which had been so heroically exercised in the introspections of the protagonists of the nineteenth-century novel. Hence the deep contrast (which is not simply a matter of the earlier censoring of sexual material) which we find if we compare Isobel Archer in James's *Portrait of a Lady* and Dorothea Brooke in George Eliot's *Middlemarch* with Molly Bloom, let alone Anna Livia Plurabelle.

The exploration of consciousness from this point of view forced literary modernists further and further, through Dada and surrealism, into that 'crisis of language' which derives from the work of Hölderlin and Mallarmé, and Rimbaud's *Lettres du voyant* (1871): 'Trouver une langue; du reste, toute parole étant idée, le temps d'un langage universel reviendra!'[11] As George Steiner remarks, this does no less than proclaim a new programme for language and literature (p. 117). And in *Finnegans Wake* Joyce simply bypasses Dada and surrealism in rising to Rimbaud's challenge. He presents us with a universal accretion of *all* languages, and of the underlying myths inherent in their metaphorical structures.

This revolution was prepared by the simple rejection in *Ulysses* of those consensual metadescriptions, emerging from a narrator, which are typical of the realist mode. It is thus hardly surprising that Colin MacCabe and others who write within a post-structuralist framework have made 'the experience of language' central to their interpretation of Joyce, early and late. Thus in 'Sirens' 'the nature of language becomes the concern of the text'; 'Cyclops' is a 'montage of discourses'; and *Finnegans Wake* 'turns around the connexion between writing and sexuality' (MacCabe, pp. 54, 64, 79ff., 90, 133). Joyce's night book, founded in the philosophy of Vico, nevertheless met with resolute opposition from its early readers, and most hurtfully from his brother Stanislaus, who called it 'drivelling rigmarole', 'unspeakably wearisome', and 'the witless wandering of literature before its final extinction' (*Letters*

III 102–3). In his attempt to promote it through *transition* and through the apostolic twelve critics of the *Exagmination*, Joyce was forced into a rare alliance with the avant-garde and its doctrines.[12]

The *Wake* was conceived at the climax of the high modernist revival of formally extremely complicated works. These often aim at a kind of formal self-containment which facilitates the expression of an autonomous world, and thus revert to the Symbolist notion of the Mallarméan 'Grand Livre', the culminating encyclopaedic masterpiece. Thus Beckett tells us that 'His writing is not *about* something; *it is that something itself*' (Beckett *et al.*, p. 14), and Jolas proclaims:

> The new artist of the word has recognised the autonomy of language and, aware of the twentieth century current towards universality, attempts to hammer out a verbal vision that destroys time and space. (Beckett *et al.*, p. 79)

This claim that the experimental work can emancipate itself from the substructure of experience itself, and hence from the causal structures that underwrite all realism, is echoed by Marcel Brion, who argues that *Ulysses* is 'one of the Einsteinian miracles of the relativity of time', leading inexorably to the *Wake*, which he says is 'essentially a time work' (Beckett *et al.*, pp. 30–1).

Joyce's project thus resembles that of works like Berg's *Wozzeck* (1922), Schoenberg's *Moses and Aaron* (1930–2), Duchamp's *The Bride Stripped Bare by her Bachelors, Even* (1915–23), and ultimately of even so conservative a work as Eliot's *Four Quartets* (1943), all of which thrive on occult hidden orders, which are independent of the usual mimetic aims associated with a particular content. What his book also has in common with music, rather than with the language of his predecessors and successors, is the aim of reinventing the basic elements of the language of his art, in what McAlmon called 'an esperanto of the subconscious' (Beckett *et al.*, p. 110). He thus superimposes the languages and stories of many races, under which are supposed to lie the simplest of (Viconian) mythical narratives. For rather as pitches freed from traditional tonal relationships manage to enter into hitherto prohibited relationships with one another, and so to require the invention of wholly new principles for their ordering (which may also involve the revival of neo-classical forms as underlying structure, as in Berg), so Joyce invents a vocabulary which allows the words of different languages to interact.

This analogy with music is one that Joyce himself was inclined to exploit (*JJ* 703), and McAlmon tells us that 'he wishes to believe that anybody reading his work gets a sensation of understanding, which is the understanding which music is allowed without too much explanation' (Beckett *et al.*, pp. 110–11). Indeed this parallel is turned to with relief by nearly all the early commentators on the *Wake*, who are not so much concerned to situate it in the context of the (declining) modernist culture of its time, as to attempt baffled exegesis and to defend its language. Even Beckett says that it is 'not only to be read. It is to be looked at and listened to' (Beckett *et al.*, p. 14). This procedure realizes for Joyce an 'aesthetic of the dream' wholly independent of everyday experience, in which 'the forms prolong and multiply themselves, where the visions pass from the trivial to the apocalyptic, where the brain uses the roots of vocables to make others from them which will be capable of naming its phantasms, its allegories, its allusions', as he put it to Edmond Jaloux (*JJ* 559).

Joyce's work perpetually challenges us to appreciate and bring to light the formal manoeuvres of the hidden hand, of the parodist of past styles in *A Portrait*, of the inventor and arranger of eighteen new ones in *Ulysses*, and of the celebrant of the occult orders hidden within that most subjective of experiences, the dream, in the *Wake*. He is adamant that all of his methods can be explained and justified: 'If you take a characteristic obscure passage of one of these people [modern writers] and asked him what it meant, he couldn't tell you; whereas I can justify every line of my book' (*JJ* 702). This challenge is always a joy to meet. For some, he always plays fair and preserves consistency, as those proponents of the realistic novel, or of the reconstruction of a lost Dublin underlying *Ulysses*, or of the coherent plot underlying *Finnegans Wake*, would be the first to affirm. For others, and more recently, his inconsistencies are of equal interpretive importance.

Joyce indeed wanted to be interpreted; in this he follows one of the central aims of early modernism, which was to attract an audience which was willing to attempt to decode the relationships between stylistic medium and message. His works, from *Stephen Hero* to *Finnegans Wake*, mark in this respect the essential steps in the evolution of literature from the Symbolist epoch to the post-modern; and it should be added, that whatever our mode of interpretation may be, in reading Joyce we are perpetually entertained by the most humorous and charitable of all twentieth-century writers.

NOTES

1 Some relevant distinctions are attempted in Chefdor, Quinones, and Wachtel, pp. 1–15.
2 See, for example, Hughes, pp. 63ff. The classic account of modernist tendencies as Oedipal revolt is to be found in Schorske's *Fin de Siècle Vienna*; this generational

model has appealed to many historians of the period, for example Wohl in Chefdor, Quinones, and Wachtel, pp. 66–79.

3 There is also a mixture of Zarathustra and Marx in Joyce's 'A Portrait of the Artist', a short autobiographical piece written in 1904 and submitted to *Dana*. See Scholes and Kain, *The Workshop of Daedalus*, pp. 56–74. It is discussed in Manganiello, *Joyce's Politics*, pp. 67–72.

4 The paper corresponds to Joyce's own on 'Drama and Life' of October 1899, delivered in January 1900 (see *JJ* 71–2). It is according to Manganiello the work of a 'socialist artist' (pp. 44–5).

5 Of course Joyce favoured classicism on his own definition from the start. See *SH* 83, and Goldberg, *The Classical Temper*.

6 'Swirling jumble of images. Tragic unity is displaced. We learn. We drink. Drunkenness. The real no longer has any sense. No meaning. Everything is rhythm, speech, life. There are no more proofs. We're all in communion' (Cendrars, *Aujourd'hui*, p. 254). See also Kern, pp. 67–88.

7 This was broadly correct; see *JJ* 502ff., esp. 503. The 'pink 'un' concluded nevertheless that *Ulysses* was 'sordidly pornographic' and 'immensely dull' (*CH I* 194).

8 He discusses the *Five Lectures on Psychoanalysis* and Freud's doctrines concerning slips of the tongue with a friend – which emerge, for example, in Bloom's saying 'the wife's admirers' rather than 'the wife's advisers' in *Ulysses* (12.767) – as early as 1913 (*JJ* 340), and he recorded Nora's dreams and his own interpretations of them (*JJ* 436ff.). But he refused analysis by Jung (though later accepted it for his own daughter) (*JJ* 466, 676).

9 See Hoffman, *Freudianism and the Literary Mind*, pp. 122ff. and 139ff., Norris on dream in *The Decentered Universe*, pp. 98–119, and, most impressively, Bishop, *Joyce's Book of the Dark*, pp. 15–18 and 179ff. Bishop emphasizes the comparison with, and prior indebtedness to, Vico.

10 See Butler, 'Joyce and the Displaced Author', and Mahaffey, *Reauthorizing Joyce*.

11 'Find a language; for the rest, since all speech is idea, the time of a universal language will return!'

12 Thus many of the points made in Jolas's *Manifesto of the Word*, heavily reliant as it is on Blake and Rimbaud, could be applied to the *Wake*, especially the declarations numbered 3 to 6. See *JJ* 588.

WORKS CITED

Adams, Robert M. *After Joyce*. New York: Oxford University Press, 1977

Apollonio, Umbro, ed. *Futurist Manifestos*. London: Thames and Hudson, 1973

Arnold, Matthew. 'Heinrich Heine'. In *Lectures and Essays in Criticism*, ed. R. H. Super. Ann Arbor: University of Michigan Press, 1962

Beckett, Samuel, *et al. Our Exagmination Round His Factification for Incamination of Work in Progress* (1929). London: Faber, 1972

Brown, Richard. *James Joyce and Sexuality*. Cambridge: Cambridge University Press, 1985

Budgen, Frank. *James Joyce and the Making of 'Ulysses'* (1934). London: Oxford University Press, 1972

Burgess, Anthony. *Here Comes Everybody: An Introduction to James Joyce for the Ordinary Reader*. London: Faber, 1965
Bush, Ronald. *The Genesis of Pound's Early Cantos*. Princeton: Princeton University Press, 1976
Butler, Christopher. 'Joyce and the Displaced Author'. In W. J. McCormack and Alistair Stead, eds., *James Joyce and Modern Literature*. London: Routledge, 1982, pp. 54–74
Cendrars, Blaise. *Aujourd'hui*. Paris, 1931
Chefdor, Monique, Ricardo Quinones, and Albert Wachtel, eds. *Modernism*. Urbana: University of Illinois Press, 1986
Cheng, Vincent J. *Joyce, Race, and Empire*. Cambridge: Cambridge University Press, 1995
Eliot, T. S. *Selected Essays*. London: Faber, 1951
Ellmann, Richard. *The Consciousness of Joyce*. London: Faber, 1977
Gibson, Andrew. *Joyce's Revenge: History, Politics, and Aesthetics in 'Ulysses'*. Oxford: Oxford University Press, 2002
Gilbert, Stuart. *James Joyce's Ulysses* (1930). New York: Random House, 1955
Goldberg, S. L. *The Classical Temper: A Study of James Joyce's 'Ulysses'*. London: Chatto and Windus, 1961
Hoffman, Frederick J. *Freudianism and the Literary Mind*. 2nd edn, Baton Rouge: Louisiana State University Press, 1957
Hughes, H. S. *Consciousness and Society: The Reorientation of European Social Thought, 1890–1930*. London: McGibbon and Kee, 1967
Kern, Stephen. *The Culture of Time and Space, 1880–1918*. London: Weidenfeld and Nicolson, 1983
Lawrence, Karen. *The Odyssey of Style in 'Ulysses'*. Princeton: Princeton University Press, 1981
Lodge, David. *Modes of Modern Writing*. London: Arnold, 1977
Loss, Archie K. *Joyce's Visible Art: The Work of Joyce and the Visual Arts*. Ann Arbor: UMI Research Press, 1984
MacCabe, Colin. *James Joyce and the Revolution of the Word*. London: Macmillan, 1979
Mahaffey, Vicki. *Reauthorizing Joyce*. Cambridge: Cambridge University Press, 1988
Manganiello, Dominic. *Joyce's Politics*. London, Routledge, 1980
Mann, Thomas. *Tonio Kröger*. In *Death in Venice, Tristan, Tonio Kröger*. Trans. H. T. Lowe-Porter. Harmondsworth: Penguin, 1955
Power, Arthur. *Conversations with James Joyce*, ed. Clive Hart. London: Millington, 1974
Quinones, Ricardo. *Mapping Literary Modernism: Time and Development*. Princeton: Princeton University Press, 1985
Scholes, Robert, and Richard M. Kain. *The Workshop of Daedalus: James Joyce and the Raw Materials for 'A Portrait of the Artist as a Young Man'*. Evanston: Northwestern University Press, 1965
Schorske, Carl Emil. *Fin de Siècle Vienna: Politics and Culture*. London: Weidenfeld and Nicolson, 1980
Spoo, Robert. *James Joyce and the Language of History: Dedalus's Nightmare*. New York: Oxford University Press, 1994

Steiner, George. *After Babel: Aspects of Language and Translation*. London: Oxford University Press, 1975

Sultan, Stanley. *Eliot, Joyce and Company*. New York: Oxford University Press, 1988

Joseph, Valente. *James Joyce and the Problem of Justice: Negotiating Sexual and Colonial Difference*. Cambridge: Cambridge University Press, 1995

Vickers, Brian. *In Defence of Rhetoric*. Oxford: Oxford University Press, 1988

Wilde, Oscar. *Complete Works*. London: Collins, 1966

Wilson, Edmund. *Axel's Castle*. New York: Charles Scribner's Sons, 1931

5

GARRY LEONARD

Dubliners

Like a great play, *Dubliners* exists as written, and yet also awaits performance. We read the stories, determined to ferret out what they mean, only to end up wondering about ourselves. Paradoxically, the protean quality of these stories – the way they seem to have something to say about everything – makes them appear, to the first time reader, to be about nothing at all. They begin in the middle of something and stop unexpectedly with what may or may not be a new beginning. Or to describe this a different way, the stories read as if someone has made a two-hour film by putting the camera on a tripod and letting it run, and then brought the result directly to the screen, with no editing. Upon first reading, there seem to be no obvious clues to the strategy behind Joyce's selection of a bewildering array of obscure street names, stray thoughts, lost corkscrews, gold coins, lost plumcakes, confiscated adventure books, and forgotten novels of a dead priest. Never before, it seems, has a writer used so much detail to explain so little.

At the same time, there is an undeniable drive in the stories, an urgency many readers feel, but cannot account for: what does Father Flynn wish to confess in 'The Sisters'? What has happened to make Lily behave so strangely in 'The Dead'? The stories appear to be taking the reader toward a moral dilemma, or a climax, or a revelation, or at least a conclusion, and then they stop, but without appearing to have ended. I can sympathize with this frustration. When I first read 'The Sisters', I was not troubled by its abrupt ending because I thought there was something wrong with my edition, and that the 'end' of the story had somehow failed to be printed in my text: 'So then, of course, when they saw that, that made them think that there was something gone wrong with him....' (*D* 10). And then the story is over! It not only ends in the middle of something, it doesn't even conclude with a full sentence. I was also puzzled that a writer I had been told was a master of the English language had to use the word 'that' three times in this strangely uncommunicative sentence.

Although I had figured out for myself that there was something wrong with Father Flynn, I was waiting for the story to tell me what. To merely have it repeated that something was amiss, without having it specified – 'of course' there was 'something wrong' – was frustrating in the extreme. How is it these people manage to talk and talk without actually saying anything? And yet they were saying 'something' because I couldn't seem to let the story alone. Maybe Father Flynn sinned when he taught the boy how to say the Catholic Mass. Maybe the sisters could have saved his life, but refused (why else draw attention to them so much by calling the story 'The Sisters'?). Maybe there was something wrong with the narrator, who, after all, has nightmares of the dead priest trying to confess to him, and in general, has become so self-conscious in the wake of Father Flynn's death he declines to eat any crackers for fear of embarrassment: 'I would make too much noise eating them' (D 7). I read over the story again and again, but, still, it seemed more gaps than substance. Every clue upon closer inspection turns out to be another riddle. The boy's dream for instance: 'I felt that I had been very far away, in some land where the customs were strange – in Persia, I thought.... but I could not remember the end of the dream' (D 6). What does it mean to not remember the end of a dream, and yet to remember there was an end, but one which you have forgotten? How could Joyce expect this dream to be any use at all in discerning the point of his story?

And what of the three words the boy loves and fears: *gnomon, simony, paralysis*? A 'gnomon' is actually a term for a riddle, or the bar on a sundial that casts a shadow indicating the time, or a geometric figure of a parallelogram with a corner missing (which is where he originally saw the word – in his mathematics book). The multiple definitions of this word seem to offer a clue of some sort, at least to me if not to the boy. Adding to this, 'simony' is the selling of something of spiritual value for material gain, though the boy may not know that, either. But this connects to something that *is* disturbing the boy: how much of what he does not know is nonetheless affecting him? The adults seem anxious about Father Flynn, although they are not able to give their reason, and don't even finish their sentences. Old Cotter says 'My idea is: let a young lad run about and play with young lads of his own age and not be... Am I right, Jack?' (D 4). And yet on a daily basis he has been sent to bring the priest his snuff, and has stayed hours longer to be told about the bewildering intricacies of church law. And what about the geometric figure? Is the narrator the missing corner, feeling, as he does, alone and apart from his family. His uncle claims to always tell him to 'box his corner' (D 4) and, indeed, he is sitting in the corner, literally, when he refuses Eliza's offer to have some crackers.

Slowly, on my third or fourth reading, I began to sense, reluctantly, and with some alarm, my affinity with the boy who narrates the story. He doesn't understand what's going on, and neither do I. He struggles to form a coherent narrative out of apparently unrelated details, and so do I. Joyce refuses to be an omniscient narrator because the twentieth century is anything but an Age of Faith. It is a time of deep incertitude, with an accompanying deep suspicion of all meta-narratives (that is, theories which purport to explain everything). No wonder the boy notices, when viewing the dead Father Flynn in his coffin, the 'idle chalice on his breast'; this is the same chalice, perhaps, Eliza refers to when she tells the story of what seemed to begin Father Flynn's decline: '– It was that chalice he broke.... That was the beginning of it. Of course, they say it was all right, that it contained nothing, I mean' (D 9).

Or is Eliza right in a way she does not intend? Father Flynn's loss of faith, the discovery that his chalice 'contained nothing' – is this crisis in faith something he passed on to the boy without ever identifying it as such?: 'Sometimes he had amused himself by putting difficult questions to me' (D 6). In one of Joyce's earliest publications, before the writing of *Dubliners*, he expressed his pleasure in the works of the great Norwegian dramatist Henrik Ibsen by praising Ibsen's genius for presenting the life of a character in a way that does not preach about the meaning of his life, but invites the reader to observe closely and speculate: 'By degrees the whole scroll of his life is unrolled before us, and we have the pleasure not of hearing it read out to us, but of reading it for ourselves, piecing the various parts, and going closer to see wherever the writing on the parchment is fainter or less legible' (*OCPW* 32). This desire to 'go closer' and see not what is clear, but what is 'fainter or less legible' seems sound advice for approaching the many gaps in 'The Sisters' where sentences never get finished, voices tail off, silence retakes the room again and again.

Indeed, in the opening paragraph of the story, the narrator is a 'reader' of sorts, passing Father Flynn's window 'night after night' hoping to interpret for himself what has happened: 'If he was dead, I thought, I would see the reflection of candles on the darkened blind for I knew that two candles must be set at the head of a corpse' (D 3). But this anticipated clarity is immediately replaced by a vague dread about, but also a fascination with, the parts of his relationship with Flynn that are fainter and less legible: 'It filled me with fear, and yet *I longed to be nearer to it and to look* upon its deadly work' (D 3, italics mine). Here is the invitation and the warning of *Dubliners*: come closer, look for where it fades, where it is illegible, but know that what remains unsaid is often what we fear to say, or even think, and yet, at the same time, might wish to hear shouted aloud – the longing and the fear that accompanies genuine insight unadulterated by self-delusion or wishful thinking: deadly work, indeed, but perhaps an antidote to the 'moral paralysis' Joyce identifies as one of the subjects of this work.

The writing project that became *Dubliners* began simply enough. George Russell, an older man of letters, wishing to bring the obviously precocious but as yet unpublished Joyce a little bit of spending money, proposed that his young friend write something for *The Irish Homestead*, an agricultural journal where Russell served as an editorial adviser. Could he write, Russell asked, 'something simple, rural?, livemaking?' which readers would not be shocked by (*JJ* 163). The short answer to this question would appear to be 'no'. The longer answer – going on at least since 1914 when the collection first appeared – is that Joyce does not seem to have been capable of writing anything simple. Indeed, one of the dynamics of what would become his style of composition consists of adding, altering, and amending what he initially wrote, seeking a greater and greater degree of subtlety and finesse. Sometimes the stories seem simple – what could be simpler, after all, than the clichéd, whimsical remarks of the adults in 'The Sisters'? But it is the very simplicity of Old Cotter's remarks that keep the boy awake later in the evening: 'I puzzled my head to extract meaning from his unfinished sentences' (*D* 4). Readers of Joyce know how the boy feels. We, too, have puzzled to extract meaning over his sentences – finished and unfinished – in these works.

I, for example, have taught *Dubliners* for many years, but every time I present it to first time readers I learn something new. For me, these stories remain, by turns, fascinating, puzzling, enigmatic, and deceptively simple. One minute I am in the grip of some new way of talking about the story, excited by how I am helping it come alive for the students, and then, later, I am dismayed at how I have bullied some aspects of the story into supporting my reading of it. So a 'guideline' to reading *Dubliners* needs to acknowledge the multi-faceted quality of the stories. The stories are interested in issues of identity and the self, but they are equally involved with issues of politics and what it feels like to be a part of Ireland as a nation with a particular history and a particular place within the British Empire. Then again, they also present subtle interrogations of gender construction and the relationship between desire and the external circumstances that help shape it. Family and religion – in Joyce's case Catholicism – might complete a preliminary list of the issues and tensions Joyce puts into play in these stories.

Of course, what a list cannot do justice to is precisely what is Joyce's greatest accomplishment: he develops a style that puts all these various factors into play virtually at the same time. When characters appear paralysed by indecision, or overwhelmed with unwelcome insight, or resolutely oblivious to the significance of various events in their lives, we are invited to see these moments as a complex convergence of all the issues I have named so far.

Joyce himself telegraphs a fascination with such moments of overdetermined convergence when he privileges the notion of an 'epiphany' as the primary aesthetic building block of his stories. His character Stephen Daedalus (presented in an unfinished manuscript, *Stephen Hero*, that became *A Portrait of the Artist as a Young Man*) outlines the basic idea: 'By an epiphany he meant a sudden spiritual transformation, whether in the vulgarity of speech or of gesture or in a memorable phase of the mind itself' (*SH* 216/211). This is not so much a moment of insight as a point where hitherto disparate observations, thoughts, and desires rearrange themselves into an unsuspected pattern that shatters often long held ideas about one's self and one's surroundings.

In the famous conclusion of 'Araby', for example, the boy, on the simplest level, realizes, as the Bazaar is closing down around him, that he doesn't have enough money to buy a present for Mangan's sister. What makes such a moment a literary and stylistic masterstroke is Joyce's careful preparation for this moment, so that the reader can tease out for himself or herself the convergence of the political, the personal, the familial, the textual, and the religious. In the case of the political, the shop girl is English, implying the goods themselves are yet another way for England to profit from the chronically dissatisfied citizens of colonial Ireland. In terms of the personal, the boy realizes upon seeing the shop-girl flirt with two admirers that he has done nothing at all similar, and so he has fantasized a relationship with a girl who, in fact, thinks nothing about him at all. In terms of the family, the reason for his lateness is his uncle's late appearance – and the abrupt way he hung up his coat upon arriving home, his insistence on singing a song, and his wife's bad temper, all show the tangled web of animosity and alcohol the boy seeks to escape, if only for one night. In terms of the textual, while the boy may not be aware of the extent to which he has patterned his journey on the search for the Holy Grail in King Arthur, the reader is invited to see the parallels, and to note that the boy's savagely felt disillusionment is partly the result of his fairytale script smashing unexpectedly into the very reality it was meant to dissolve: he is no Sir Lancelot, nor was he meant to be. Finally, in terms of the religious, the Bazaar is presented as a sort of profit-driven and indifferent Church. As the boy's sense of despair mounts, the 'Church' is described as gradually dimming its lights.

In other words, the Joycean epiphany does not so much confirm a truth as disrupt what one has grown comfortable accepting as true. But hunting for the epiphany in each story is not a simple matter. Little Chandler, in the story 'A Little Cloud', returns home after his conversation with Gallaher, only to find he hates his furniture, his wife, his marriage, and even his infant son, for robbing him of the chance to be an acknowledged poet. But is this even true?

One could argue that the reason he has never written any poetry (despite writing favourable reviews of the unwritten poetry in his head) is that this allows him to continue fantasizing that he one day might. And yet the price he is paying for this treasured fantasy is the growing unhappiness in his marriage to a woman who is increasingly hostile toward him because she resents his resentment of her. Even Gallaher, whose forceful stories of unending success have set in motion Little Chandler's attack of disillusionment, is not what he appears. His stories of loose women, wild times, and unlimited choices ('I've only to say the word and to-morrow I can have the woman and the cash' (D 62)) are so over the top we are free to suspect he is back in Dublin trying to make himself feel more important than he actually is.

He has, after all, contacted Little Chandler for this purpose alone, and not out of any sense of continuing, or deepening, a friendship, despite Little Chandler's strenuous efforts to see it that way. Realizing this about Gallaher allows us to make more sense both of his refusal to visit Little Chandler's home, and his insulting dismissal of marital sex as something that 'must get a bit stale' (D 62). Significantly, he offers this putdown only after Little Chandler has begun trying to ease out of the role of fawning friend to become someone on more equal footing. So why is Little Chandler even having a drink with this man who does not bother to hide his disdain? If we glance at the opening of the story we see Little Chandler preoccupied with the upcoming rendezvous with Gallaher, reflecting, 'it was something to have a friend like that' (D 53). Like the narrator of 'Araby', or Maria in 'Clay', Little Chandler uses almost constant fantasy to insulate himself from the reality of his life as he is living it. This misreading of reality for the sake of shoring up a fragile self-esteem leaves him chronically exposed to abrupt disillusionment and frequent panic.

If I am allowed to judge by my students, almost all first time readers of Joyce will be intrigued by the complexity of my interpretation of one of these stories, but will ask, 'Do you really think Joyce meant all that?' In the case of Joyce, we can say 'very likely', because starting from the point shortly before he began writing *Dubliners*, through the ten-year period where he fought to see it published, Joyce wrote letters to his brother and his potential publisher arguing at length for the purpose of the collection, clearly seeing it as a project with its own serious agenda. When his publisher wanted deletions and changes to the manuscript, for fear of libel, Joyce elevated his rhetoric to the nearly Evangelical: 'I seriously believe that you will retard the course of civilization in Ireland by preventing the Irish people from having one good look in my nicely polished looking-glass' (*Letters I* 63–4). On a somewhat calmer note, he talks about intending 'to write a chapter of the moral history of my country' (*Letters II* 134).

The course of civilization, the moral history of my country – Joyce may have lacked a publishing record at this point in his career, but there was no shortage of ambition. Further evidence that Joyce regarded *Dubliners* as a multi-faceted project can be seen in the extensive revisions he made to the 1904 version of 'The Sisters' published in *The Irish Homestead* when in 1906 he prepared it for the published collection. Virtually everything I have quoted above was added. The original opening – 'Three nights in succession I had found myself in Great Britain-street at that hour, as if by Providence' (*D* 190) – is replaced by the much more striking 'There was no hope for him this time: it was the third stroke' (*D* 3). The vague reference to 'Providence' is dropped, as is any reference to an 'I', or a specific locale, or a time. As a result, what is distilled from the original sentence is the pure affect of the narrator, delivered to us with a narrative style contoured to fit the precise arc of the narrator's mood – what Joyce elsewhere would describe as 'the curve of an emotion'.[1]

At the very least, in his rewriting of 'The Sisters', Joyce continues to take his story a long way from Russell's quaint request that he write 'something simple'. But, actually, Russell and Joyce are not as far apart as they seem. Both Irishmen were keenly aware their country needed to 'have one good look' in a looking-glass – however differently it might be polished. The relationship with Imperial Britain was slowly devolving, and with it came an increasing urgency for Ireland to understand itself as Irish, whether that meant reviving the Gaelic language, or Gaelic sport, or collecting and publishing whatever could be found of Irish mythology. *The Irish Homestead* itself, the journal Russell drew Joyce's attention to, was intended to appeal to dairy farmers (an ad for an electric milking machine shares the page with Joyce's first version of 'The Sisters'), hence Russell's specific instructions to Joyce that the story be 'rural'. As Katherine Mullin has pointed out, most of the stories in *The Irish Homestead* extolled the virtue of the Irish countryside and its presumed ability to supply all the material and spiritual solace any man or woman of Ireland might require.[2]

But if this were so, why the fierce rate of emigration? The 'simple' stories in *The Irish Homestead* were in fact propaganda: a mass-produced fantasy insisting that the rural life in Ireland was the only source of true salvation and anyone who turned their back and left would regret it for the rest of their life – if they even lived that long in the hostile world beyond Ireland's shores. In many of the stories, characters about to emigrate suddenly realize, just in the nick of time, all their happiness is in Ireland, and only heartache and despair abroad. In this context, the story 'Eveline', Joyce's second contribution after 'The Sisters', as Mullin points out, 'masquerades as a simple anti-emigration propagandist fiction' but 'in fact interrogates the terms and functions of the nationalist propaganda it supposedly embodies' (191). What this means is that Joyce's project in *Dubliners* was both local – that is to say, in conscious dialogue with the stories of a little agricultural journal, *and* national – interested in placing Dublin on the world map, writing a moral history of a people, and furthering the course of civilization in Ireland.

Eveline, in the end, cannot leave Ireland – so far, so good, this is, after all, the endpoint of all the anti-emigration stores. But to what, and to whom, is she returning? Nothing more or less than: an increasingly violent alcoholic father who has no one but her to beat, since her oft-beaten brothers have already fled, and a thankless exhausting job where even her salary is not her own. But then why is she unable to leave? Her mother, dying exhausted and half-mad at a young age, has extracted from her a promise she would not go. Likewise, her boyfriend 'Frank' would seem to more or less fit the profile of the stock seducer in the anti-emigration tales, although Joyce leaves that uninterrogated in order to atomize all the ways the reality of life in Dublin entraps and paralyses Eveline. As Mullin suggests, no doubt what Eveline longs for when 'amid the seas she sent a cry of anguish' is the sort of correctional vision of a pastoral, restorative Ireland patiently waiting to fold her into its embrace and heal her, but far from any reassuring vision she is frozen into a consciousness-obliterating panic: 'She set her white face to him, passive, like a helpless animal' (D 29).

If readers use *The Irish Homestead* as a looking-glass they see the whole-some simple face of someone who need only accept the idea of a pure and nurturing homeland to be happy. If they pick up the looking-glass of *Dubliners*, however, their own frightened faces stare back at them. But what makes 'Eveline' so apparently simple, and yet so wondrously complex, is the way Joyce works within the formula of the anti-emigration story and uses it to show that people stay where they are in Dublin not because they discover the wisdom of doing so, but because they are trapped – and one of the ways they are trapped is the ideology of a pure and lovely Ireland presented by the sort of stories that, as Russell puts it when inviting Joyce to write one, 'play to the common understanding for once in a way'. Now we can understand that Joyce's notion of the epiphany – the rearrangement of a fantasized reality into an actual one – may well be intended as a specific antidote to moments such as those in *The Irish Homestead* where all the difficult realities of life in Ireland are ignored and replaced by a pleasant image of an Irish lass waving from her cottage window at her man happily tilling the ground with his hoe, only pausing to acknowledge her adoring gaze.

Such a story is not a looking-glass at all, but a magic mirror converting a hard reality into a compensatory fantasy. No wonder Joyce reacted so strongly to his publisher's suggestion that it should not matter much to him if he should be asked to alter this or that. His whole purpose was to polish the mirror of *Dubliners* until it could give nothing but an accurate reflection of what was there, to present life as it appeared to him, and not as how he had been told it was: 'It is not my fault that the odour of ashpits and old weeds and offal hangs around my stories' (*Letters I* 63–4). Joyce's almost complete refusal to alter anything in the text of *Dubliners* might seem obstinate unless it is read against what I have tried to outline here: his urgently felt desire to tell the truth as he saw it (and even how he smelled it!) and thus stand against the tide of sentimentalized Irish nationalism he blamed for distorting the reality everywhere before their eyes. Joyce's point can now be clear to us, if it wasn't to his publisher: he will not aid and abet the distorted mirror of *The Irish Homestead* and its like, deforming reality into unreal scenarios that lead people into despair over conditions of life about which they are, and remain, inarticulate because nowhere is their actual life accurately presented or interrogated in the fictions that they read. In fact, nothing seems to enrage Joyce quite as much as writings about his country that romanticize and sentimentalize reality into what it might be pleasant to imagine, rather than present and reflect what actually is: 'I am nauseated by their lying drivel about pure men and pure women and spiritual love forever: blatant lying in the face of truth' (*Letters II* 191–2).

So we know Joyce had an urgent and ambitious project in mind when he began *Dubliners*. But that alone could not account for the fascination the stories still hold today and will, I am sure, continue to hold, for readers tomorrow. We are a long way from Joyce's various parochial concerns, however deeply felt and influential they may have been at the time. Certainly Joyce went on to write even more ambitious works, but *Dubliners* is not merely the promising beginning of a great writer's career; it would remain a great work in its own right had Joyce never written anything else. Why do the stories continue to live and breathe in atmospheres far removed from what Joyce liked to refer to as 'dear, dirty, Dublin'? The answer, in a word, is 'style'. In order to present reality as he saw it, Joyce had to figure out a way to show how much of what we think of as is real is in fact the result of influences upon us we may not be aware of. He had to develop a method of telling stories that would show the belief systems of his various characters while at the same time delineating all the various sources for these beliefs, whether they be found in religion, popular culture, family, or political propaganda.

In the same way that alternative meanings vie for our attention in the stories, we see the characters within the stories privileging one version of 'reality' by ignoring or denying some of the significance of their surroundings. In the short story 'Clay,' a game is recounted where three saucers are placed on a table and the blindfolded player lowers her hand into one of the three saucers. One holds water, the other a prayer-book, the third a ring. It is a sort of fortune-telling game where water might signify a sea voyage, the prayer-book entrance into a convent, and the ring a forthcoming marriage. But as Maria takes her turn, confusion overtakes her:

> She felt a soft wet substance with her fingers and was surprised that nobody spoke or took off her bandage. There was a pause for a few seconds; and then a great deal of scuffling and whispering. Somebody said something about the garden, and at last Mrs Donnelly said something very cross to one of the next-door girls and told her to throw it out at once: that was no play. Maria understood that it was wrong that time and so she had to do it over again: and this time she got the prayer-book. (*D* 80)

How does Joyce choose to narrate this event, and why?

We might notice first how there is no authoritative dimension to the narrative voice. Events are related in a matter-of-fact way with no hint of their wider significance. But the narrative is not simply impartial; rather, it is partial in relation to what Maria can and cannot see. We are not given the expressions on people's faces, we are not told what is in the saucer, or even what it looks like, and all this *because Maria is blindfolded* and the apparently impartial narrative accommodates itself to the peculiarities and limitations of her own point of view. This is one of Joyce's great stylistic achievements: an 'objective' narrative that, at the same time, appears unable to exceed the character's perspective. But there is an additional problem. Though Maria is blindfolded, she is not deaf, and yet all we learn of the conversation conducted right in front of her is 'somebody said something about the garden' and 'Mrs Donnelly said something very cross to one of the next-door girls' (*D* 80). And then, as if the sound has been turned up again, she suddenly hears, perfectly clearly, Mrs Donnelly saying 'throw it out at once' and 'that was no play'. We are then told only what Maria has allowed herself to realize: 'Maria understood that it was wrong that time and she had to do it over again.'

Maria, in other words, has only heard what allows her to understand as little as possible. Derek Attridge points out that her lack of response, her 'non-epiphany', dictates the actions of the other characters, who move quickly to minimize the trick; presumably one or more of the girls added a saucer of dirt to show their dislike for Maria.[3] The narrative does not comment on Maria's perspective because it participates in it. Maria cannot bear to understand the extent to which she is disliked, and so the narrative is powerless to record what she refuses to register. This is not parody, or satire or social commentary, but what I might call compassionate irony. Joyce himself described his style as 'scrupulous meanness', and certainly we can see the careful attention to ordinary detail and unrelenting accuracy about Maria's constricted reaction, but by constricting the scope of the narration in exactly the same way Maria constricts her point of view, we are able to sympathize with Maria in this moment.

All of us, I would imagine, have felt moments of dissociation when suddenly confronted with a situation that contradicts our preferred view of ourselves. The trick played on Maria threatens to undermine the only remaining solace in her difficult life: that she is well-liked wherever she goes, and that she is 'a veritable peacemaker'. It threatens to destroy the first illusion, and Maria's thought to 'put in a good word for Alphy' with Joe, his brother, excites another moment of disharmony and nearly destroys the second: 'But Joe cried that God might strike him stone dead if ever he spoke a word to his brother again and Maria said she was sorry she had mentioned the matter . . . and there was nearly being a row . . .' (D 80). Because the narrative establishes no separate point of view from Maria's, it is the reader who finds himself or herself with enough distance to reflect on the wider significance of the passage. It is also the reader, and only the reader, who can set this incident against other incidents and see a pattern Maria herself cannot bear to see.

When an 'elderly gentleman' makes room for her on the bus, she sees him as 'a colonel-looking gentleman' (again, we are offered no competing description by the narrator) and we 'see' what happens between them through the prism of Maria's unacknowledged disappointment that she never got married, and now must spend whatever days are left to her working for her keep in a laundry for ex-prostitutes. But in this moment, with this particular gentleman, Maria is about to be courted and she knows her part perfectly: 'Maria . . . favoured him with demure nods and hems . . . she thanked him and bowed, and he bowed to her and raised his hat' (D 79). Suddenly we are back in the world favoured by *The Irish Homestead*, with the sort of 'pure men and pure women' and 'spiritual love forever' Joyce denounced as 'blatant lying in the face of truth', but truth can only seep in from the edges given Joyce's narrative style of compassionate irony, so the sole clue we get that the 'colonel-looking gentleman' might be a drunk looking for a bit to eat (he does make a point of asking what is in the bag) is Maria's declaration after she leaves the bus, 'how easy it was to know a gentleman even when he has a drop taken' (D 79).

This, coupled with her later discovery her plumcake is missing, completes the nowhere narrated story of Maria as a sad woman daily regretting her unmarried state: 'Maria, remembering how confused the gentleman with the greyish moustache had made her, coloured with shame and vexation and disappointment' (*D* 79). Disappointment and vexation, perhaps, but why shame? This is the second time Maria has blushed. The first, more pleasant, occasion was the actual buying of the plumcake when the 'stylish young lady behind the counter, who was evidently a little annoyed by her, asked her was it wedding-cake she wanted to buy. That made Maria blush . . .' (*D* 78). Maria blushes and becomes 'confused' any time circumstances beyond the reality she has constructed for herself threaten to intrude. Her third and final blush occurs when asked to sing. She sings the first verse of the song twice, 'but no one tried to show her her mistake' (*D* 81). The second, unsung, verse of the song, 'lurking beyond the text', to use Attridge's phrase (*Joyce Effects*, 48), involves a man offering a marriage proposal to his beloved.

In the same way that Maria cannot 'hear' a discussion about the trick played on her, she cannot see the shenanigans of an inebriated old man, or sing her most devoutly disavowed fantasy: a man on bended knee proposing marriage. But more devastating still, Joyce makes it clear that every person in the room, without talking to anyone, works to preserve her delusions: 'no one tried to show her her mistake'. As with the hasty removal of the fourth saucer, everyone present conspires to keep Maria from 'having one good look in [a] nicely polished looking-glass'. And yet, at the same time, helping Maria preserve her delusions causes Joe to scramble to reach for another bottle and preserve his own: 'his eyes filled up so much with tears that he could not find what he was looking for and in the end he had to ask his wife to tell him where the corkscrew was' (*D* 81).

I do not have the space to bring this kind of attention to all the other stories of *Dubliners*, so I have chosen to offer this detailed analysis of a paragraph in 'Clay' as an investigative model, and assure the reader it will yield dividends for every story in the collection, whether the story involves James Duffy's self-satisfied sense of superiority in 'A Painful Case', or Corley's misguided sense of himself as knowing and cunning in 'Two Gallants', or Bob Doran's befuddled sense that it must somehow be he who has brought about the necessity of a marriage proposal to Polly in 'The Boarding House'. The final example in the collection is Gabriel, in 'The Dead', a more sophisticated Maria, who chases his own ideal self-image all night long at a Christmas party that, we are told, 'had gone off in splendid style as long as anyone could remember' (an *Irish Homestead* phrase if ever there was one!).

The final overlay in *Dubliners* I would like to present concerns its depiction of modernity and the commodity culture it has brought into being. Looking at the stories from this perspective also demands that we look at the history of modernity as a history, and not just as something that happened. We know about the history of the Industrial Revolution, which is also the history of machines and their effect on labour and society, but we know a great deal less about the history of the things these machines produced, and their effect on modern configurations of subjectivity as demonstrated through specific constructions of identity, gender, desire, and pleasure. Even a glance in our bathroom cabinets – do we use Brut deodorant or Secret – makes the point that we use 'things' to designate our gender, our personality, our aspirations and our anxieties; the aggregate of all these things becomes our 'lifestyle' whereby our conception of ourselves becomes visible to others: in the twenty-first century, in an era that has been described as 'the age of spectacle', to be is to be seen.

As part of his project, Joyce declared: 'I do not think that any writer has yet presented Dublin to the world' (*Letters II* 122). To present Dublin is to present an emerging city, complete with newspapers, trams, electric lights, advertising, music halls, pubs, offices, and the kind of modern home life that attempts to serve as an oasis of calm in the jostling life of an urban centre.[4] The city itself can serve as a source of exhilaration or disappointment, compensation, or deprivation. Hynes's public rendition of a nostalgic poem in 'Ivy Day in the Committee Room' seems part of an older, oral tradition of consolation in the face of futility, but Joyce was aware that mass media might provide more popular forms. After all, the Araby Bazaar is described as a magical land of electrical lights where goods are brought indoors and made to look oracular, a prototype of the modern shopping mall. The description of the hypnotizing force of the Bazaar is deliberately opposed to an earlier description in the story of a more traditional street market where unexciting items are haphazardly displayed in the undifferentiated light of daytime. Whereas the street market jostles and disturbs the boy ('I imagined that I bore my chalice safely through a throng of foes' (*D* 20)), the Araby Bazaar, at least at first, unexpectedly activates a dream of potential fulfilment and contentment that overtakes his every waking thought ('I wished to annihilate the tedious intervening days' (*D* 21)). The subsequent deflation when he is unable to find the commodity that would complete him, and cause Mangan's sister to love him, is perhaps a feeling not so unknown to those of us today – nearly a hundred years later – who have set out on a shopping expedition full of delight about some unspecified joy ever more about to be ('– If I go, I said, I will bring you something' (*D* 21)), only to be unsettled by the price of our dream ('I lingered before her stall, though I knew my stay was useless . . .' (*D* 24)). The transition Joyce depicts in 'Araby' is the move from undifferentiated 'street' goods to commodities: articles made to appear magical, even salvational, through advertising, packaging, and presentation.

Joyce is fascinated with the trivia of life, and invests it with epic resonance, because he searches for reality within what I call 'the history of now': the unrecorded yet quintessential facts of everyday lived experience.

When Stephen Dedalus, in Joyce's novel *Ulysses*, dismisses Irish art as 'the cracked lookingglass of a servant' (*U* 1.146), he is hinting at the danger of staring back into an idealized past in order to obscure the pain of an oppressed present and an apparently intractable future. Such a view will bring on poignant laments such as Hynes's poem about Parnell, but they will forbid more practical remedies, whatever they might be. But what Joyce may not have understood is that, in his obsession to present the Dubliners he knew, and not the Irish heroes he was told to read about, he crafted a style of story telling that allowed the apparently trivial world of everyday living to become the stuff of comedy, pathos, and tragedy in a way every bit as resonant as the works of Shakespeare. It is this narrative technique, Joyce's 'style of scrupulous meanness', that presents the perspective of his characters as they themselves experience the world, self-delusions and all. In addition to this perspective, however, he places them in a world of detail, presented in a tone of indifference, that nonetheless suggests how their perspective came to take the shape it has.

To return to 'Eveline', for example, we know the shop-girl is torn between honouring the promise to her mother to keep the house together, and her own barely developed sense that she may have a right to be happy. As a backdrop to this, the house is described through her memory of her having dusted it, day in and day out, for years. The inventory of what she has dusted would seem to have no more motivation than the fact that, well, it's just what she dusted. But the promises to Margaret Mary Alacoque, hung so prominently on the wall, speak of the need for a woman to sacrifice herself for the good of the home and the family. More subtly, the photograph of a priest she does not know, a photograph routinely handed about by her father to his friends with the cryptic comment 'He is in Melbourne now' (*D* 25), speaks to how excluded she is from the events of her father's life, and how she has been taught to keep her place and show no curiosity, as though she were his servant and not his daughter (which, of course, is how he treats her). This, in turn, establishes as credible his remarkable indifference to her feelings as he takes from her a hard-earned salary and returns it to her in bits and pieces just before the weekend markets are due to close, with the unfair taunt: 'had she any intention of buying Sunday's dinner?' (*D* 26).

So Eveline may be merely cataloguing the things she has dusted as she wonders how much she will miss home, but we are invited to see what a psychological prison home has become and realize, as well, and at the same time, that Eveline's incomprehension of the pattern revealed by these objects silently demonstrates how subtly and imperceptibly she has been put in a situation where potential insight is systematically reconfigured into panic and paralysis. To offer a similar example in an entirely different register, 'A

Painful Case' opens with a lengthy paragraph recording, also with dispassionate intensity, the set-up of Duffy's room. The fact that Duffy's books are arranged according to size betrays the life-denying passion for order that will cause him, as he himself puts it, to 'sentence [Mrs. Sinico] to death' (*D* 89). The moral isometrics of his journal entries ('Love between man and man is impossible because there must not be sexual intercourse and friendship between man and woman is impossible because there must be sexual intercourse' (*D* 86)) suggest that a pun is intended, as he has also 'sentenced' himself into a lonely place where any meaningful relationship between himself and others is forbidden by his austere, self-condemning fantasy that he has saved himself from the paralysis of Dublin life by refusing to participate in it.

What I have outlined so far offers a way to notice how the stories communicate significance through what the characters know or wish to know, but also what they are unable to see, or are afraid to feel. But this may suggest that the stories are an elaborate crossword puzzle, one where we use the clues we are given to 'fill in' the information we lack. Indeed, the history of the critical reception of *Dubliners* up until the last decade or so has largely been a debate on how best to fill in gaps. Early commentators such as Magalaner and Tindall concentrated almost exclusively on symbolism: the ordinary objects had symbolic resonance – usually related to Catholicism – and if the symbolic pattern generated by chalices, or references to various saints, could be laid over the apparently realistic story, we would see the 'hidden meaning'.[5] Later commentators in the seventies, such as Ghiselin and Hart, became fascinated with the complex interrelationships between and among the stories.[6] In the past twenty years, and in the wake of post-structuralist theory, there has been a productive debate on whether or not 'filling in the gaps' should be the whole point; perhaps the fact of gaps, silences, elisions, displacements, and moments where meaning falters, should be examined in their own right, rather than eliminated by the (overly?) ingenious critic.

Richard Ellmann once remarked 'we are still learning to be Joyce's contemporaries', and the stories of *Dubliners*, so apparently strange and persistently cryptic, present a prototype of our contemporary world. In a similar vein, Attridge has remarked 'far more people read Joyce than are aware of it', by which he means to draw attention to how much modern communication and interpretation borrows from the model set out by Joyce nearly a century ago. Joyce makes the familiar strange, waiting for us to see that often in the modern world it is the trivial that is profound and that a traditional understanding of life as 'historical' is no longer the way we experience our life. Instead, the ordinary is elevated to the level of the epic. The chalice is empty, but the commodity is sacred. The most profound epiphanies of all occur not in the stories we read in *Dubliners*, but in us as we read them. So perhaps, in the end, Joyce completed the assignment given to him by Russell all those years ago, and really has written something that can 'play to the common understanding for once in a way', although that 'way' could not, as it turned out, be 'something simple'.

NOTES

1 From Joyce's essay 'A Portrait of the Artist' (*PSW* 211).
2 Katherine Mullin, 'Don't Cry for Me, Argentina: "Eveline" and the Seductions of Emigration Propaganda', in Derek Attridge and Marjorie Howes, eds., *Semicolonial Joyce* (Cambridge: Cambridge University Press, 2000), pp. 172–201.
3 Derek Attridge, *Joyce Effects: On Literature, Theory, and History* (Cambridge: Cambridge University Press, 2000), pp. 49–50.
4 For a more in-depth analysis see: Garry Leonard, *Advertising and Commodity Culture in Joyce* (University Press of Florida, 1998).
5 William York Tindall, *A Reader's Guide to James Joyce* (New York: Noonday, 1959); Magalaner, Marvin, ed., *A James Joyce Miscellany* (New York: The James Joyce Society, 1957).
6 Brewster Ghiselin, 'The Unity of Dubliners' (1956), in Morris Beja, ed., *James Joyce's 'Dubliners' and 'A Portrait of the Artist as a Young Man': A Casebook* (London: Macmillan, 1973), pp. 100–16; Clive Hart, ed., *James Joyce's 'Dubliners': Critical Essays* (London: Faber, 1969).

6

JOHN PAUL RIQUELME

Stephen Hero and *A Portrait of the Artist as a Young Man*: transforming the nightmare of history

The fates of Irish Artists: Wilde, Joyce, aestheticism, and nationalism

Early readers of *A Portrait of the Artist as a Young Man* (1916) aware of the recent history of Irish writing would probably have heard an echo of Oscar Wilde (1856–1900) in Joyce's title. Wilde's *The Picture of Dorian Gray* (1891) concerns an artist, the painter Basil Hallward, who produces a portrait of the young Dorian Gray that, like Joyce's work, portrays and reveals the artist himself. Hallward's painting of a young man is 'a portrait of the artist', as Hallward declares in the first chapter of Wilde's book.[1] The Greek names given to the central characters in both works invite the association, which yields a difference: Stephen Dedalus's story of intended escape from Ireland's limitations contrasts with Dorian Gray's self-destruction in England. Dorian murders the artist and kills himself, while Stephen tries to bring himself into being as an artist. Wilde is never mentioned in *A Portrait*, as he is in *Ulysses* (1922), perhaps because Joyce was more at ease later in his career about acknowledging his precursor's place in his work. He may also have felt that the similarity of the titles was sufficiently evident to conjure Wilde's book and his life as important contexts for reading *A Portrait*.[2]

Joyce's essay, 'Oscar Wilde: The Poet of "Salomé"', confirms that he was thinking about Wilde and *Dorian Gray* while he was writing *A Portrait*. The occasion for the essay, published in an Italian newspaper, was the 1909 performance in Trieste of Richard Strauss's opera, *Salomé*, whose libretto was inspired by Wilde's play of the same name. 1909 was the mid-point of the decade, noted at the end of *A Portrait*, that it took Joyce to transform his manuscript of *Stephen Hero* (begun in 1904) into *A Portrait* (published serially beginning in 1914). The article indicates that Joyce knew Wilde's works well, that he recognized Wilde's deeply Irish qualities, and that he blamed the English for Wilde's downfall. Joyce also mentions the influential English writer, Walter Pater (1839–94), who taught at Oxford when Wilde studied there. The important role Pater plays in Wilde's novel and in Joyce's essay arises from his praise of both beauty and the wisdom to be gained through art. Pater's writings were central to English aestheticism of the 1880s and 1890s, a movement whose attitudes were identified in the public mind with the slogan 'art for art's sake'. Wilde and Pater, a maligned Irish writer and an influential English writer, both associated with aestheticism, provide contexts and significant details for Joyce's writing. Although influenced by Pater's aestheticism, mediated primarily by Wilde and the Irish poet, W. B. Yeats (1865–1939), Joyce and his young artist character encounter difficulties and project goals that require a different engagement with history and material reality than the Paterian worship of beauty enables.

After his imprisonment in England for unlawful acts of 'gross indecency', Wilde, the most brilliant playwright of the English theatre in the 1890s, died in poverty in France in 1900 during Joyce's second year of university studies in Dublin. Joyce's antipathy for the English with regard to Wilde's case, particularly his sense that Wilde was their victim, is clear when he asserts that Wilde shared the fate of his namesake, Oscar, only son of Ossian in Celtic myth, 'tragically killed by the hand of his host while sitting at table' (OCPW 148). Joyce takes exception to the idea that Wilde was 'a monster of perversion' who emerged inexplicably from 'the modern civilization of England', describing him instead as 'the logical and inevitable product of the Anglo-Saxon college and university system, a system of seclusion and secrecy' (OCPW 150). The 'English authorities' punished him, in Joyce's view, not for committing a crime but rather for provoking a 'scandal' (OCPW 150), that is, for bringing into the public eye acts that many others had committed as well. In this regard, Wilde resembles the Irish parliamentary leader, Charles Stewart Parnell (1846–1891), an advocate of Irish Home Rule, or limited autonomy, who is mentioned prominently in parts I, II, and V of A Portrait. Like Wilde, Parnell was hounded by the English press, who made sensational news out of sexual scandals. By leaving out of the narrative of A Portrait the death of Stephen's sister, harrowingly described in Stephen Hero, and the death of his mother, mentioned emphatically in Ulysses, Joyce heightens the impact of Parnell's death on his young character and on readers early in A Portrait. That impact is not primarily personal, as are the deaths of his sister and mother, but political in ways that affect our response to the rest of Stephen's story. Instead of Oscar Wilde's death, we are invited to consider the fate of a mythic figure, Icarus, who, like Wilde, flew dangerously high. Unable to fulfil their promise of achievement, the political leader, the artistic precursor, and the mythic youth combine to colour from the outset our sense of the issues and the risks for Stephen.

Considering Wilde's fate, it is understandable that, rather than following his path to England, Stephen Dedalus chooses the Continent to make a writing career, as did Joyce. The decision is one step toward changing a history of disappointments by avoiding a repetition. As critics have frequently noted, Stephen's resentment toward the English is clear in the lengthy scene in part v (*P* 154–60) in which he talks with the English priest who is the dean of studies at University College, Dublin, where Stephen is a student. The scene's mixture of styles is also significant. Because the priest is an English convert to Roman Catholicism, he represents two foreign presences within Irish culture. Just before the encounter, Stephen asks himself if the College, as a Jesuit building, is 'extraterritorial', a place where he is 'walking among aliens' (*P* 155). Stephen and the priest are at odds over the English language, specifically the words *tundish* and *funnel*, both part of the English lexicon, though *tundish* is rarer. When Stephen thinks to himself 'How different are the words *home, Christ, ale, master* on his lips and on mine', he has in view differences in pronunciation and in meaning. Especially because Parnell's Home Rule initiative for Ireland had not succeeded, the Irish as a nation did not think of *home* with the same sense of autonomy and security as could the English. Despite the fact that the priest is 'a countryman of Ben Jonson' (*P* 159), whose songs please Stephen (*P* 148), he misunderstands Stephen's figurative use of the word 'lamp' (*P* 157) during their conversation. The divergences are multiple.

In his critical probing of English attitudes, Joyce follows Wilde in *Dorian Gray* by echoing Pater's writings. The echoing occurs as an embedded joke in the language and action of the scene involving the English priest. The Englishman is presented as intellectually flatfooted in the act of trying to teach Stephen 'an art', one of 'the useful arts', 'lighting a fire' (*P* 155). The priest's action and speech embody mundanely and ironically one of Walter Pater's best-known assertions, from the 'Conclusion' to *The Renaissance*, concerning art's ability to stimulate impressions with an intensity like fire: 'To burn always with this hard, gem-like flame, to maintain this ecstasy, is success in life.'[3] Pater teaches not the lighting of a literal fire but the kindling and maintaining of an internal flame. Further, in the long passages of thought, Stephen responds critically to the priest with language that derives from Pater. Just after the priest reveals 'one of the secrets' of building a fire, 'Not too much coal', Stephen thinks about the man's lack of 'beauty', despite a history of 'tending . . . , bearing . . . , waiting . . . , striking' (*P* 155). Stephen's rhetoric of beauty and his present participles evoke Pater, whose formulations frequently include them. This Irish student has internalized the techniques of an English writer for use against another Englishman whose act of flame tending is itself a bathetic embodiment of the English writer's own statements. He mimics in order to undermine. The ironic framing and multiple implications of the language representing scene and thinking keep the style from being reducible to any single perspective. Rather than being univocal, the style tends toward a polyphony that challenges the literal without abandoning it.

Like Wilde in *Dorian Gray*, Joyce uses Paterian language without providing explicit indications in the narrative that we should accept or reject it. The lack of overt guidance leaves the reader to consider how to measure the irony, which in Wilde's case is arguably deep and directed with a vengeance against English attitudes that he links to aestheticism.[4] Joyce's strategy is to provide a mixture of styles as the context for challenging and measuring the adequacy of aesthetic tendencies, whose rhetoric he turns against itself. Although still under the influence of Pater at the end of *A Portrait*, Stephen has come a long distance toward breaking away, in part by means of a countervailing, grittier style of thinking that is reflected in the writing. Joyce responds ironically and sceptically to Pater when he has the English priest tend a flame and when he juxtaposes in Stephen's experiences Paterian aesthetic moments with contrary realistic ones. In turning away from Pater toward writing that takes the body and history into account, Joyce's artist resists a siren call from England. He hears but does not obey, heading instead for other shores on which the Irish writer is less likely to meet the fate of Oscar Wilde.

The mixture of styles that begins developing in *A Portrait* renders memory in ways that engage readers in a process of looking back critically and also looking forward. The engaged and engaging mix takes advantage of the diverse, contradictory Irish situation that Stephen faces in order to displace more single-minded styles that might tend to perpetuate the way things have been. The shift is from aestheticism, which appears apolitical in its emphasis on beauty, toward an aesthetic politics, an art that recognizes its embodiment and its responsibilities within history. *A Portrait* develops toward the more extravagantly diverse writing of *Ulysses*, toward a hybrid style that, through mimicry, amalgamation, and transformation, allows us to occupy multiple perspectives virtually simultaneously. The tendency is toward self-correction. Conceptually and politically, the mixed style corresponds to the 'zone of occult instability' and 'fluctuating movement' that Frantz Fanon identified as the third stage in generating a national consciousness within a culture that has been dominated from the outside, as Ireland had been by England.[5] Joyce was not in sympathy with the Irish tendencies that correspond with Fanon's first two stages: assimilation to the values and customs of the dominant culture, followed by aggressive rejection of that culture through advocating indigenous practices. Joyce was neither a 'West Briton' (*D* 149, *SH* 69/64), that is, a British sympathizer who behaved as though Ireland were a western province of England, nor a supporter of Irish nationalism as an uncritical return to cultural roots.[6]

Stephen's critical attitude toward the English priest is matched by his determination in his conversation with his Irish nationalist friend Davin a few pages later (*P* 169–71) not to accede to Irish pressures to conform. Asserting that 'a man's country comes first', that it has priority over being 'a poet or mystic' (*P* 171), Davin advises Stephen to 'Try to be one of us' (*P* 170). Stephen responds that, although Davin thinks him 'a monster', 'This race and this country and this life produced me' (*P* 170). His statement echoes Joyce's assertion that Wilde was the product of cultural institutions, not a 'monster of perversion'.

Stephen's insight about himself and how he is mistakenly viewed is cognate with an insight about Wilde that may be true of the artist in general, with these Irish artists as central instances. In Stephen's case, however, the threat to his freedom is not primarily England but Ireland, whom he calls 'the old sow that eats her farrow' (*P* 171). Stephen identifies the 'nets flung at' the soul in Ireland 'to hold it back from flight', including 'nationality, language, and religion'. Rather than trying to be 'one of us', he will 'try to fly by those nets' (*P* 171). His statements here are double. By flight he means both leaving the earth with the equivalent of wings and a more practical, but necessary, flight, literal escape from the pressures to conform in Ireland. 'Fly by' suggests avoiding the nets, but it can also mean flying by means of them, that is, turning them to advantage selectively and strategically. Stephen's Paterian rhetoric directed against the English priest is one example of transforming a potentially entangling net, though not an Irish one. Joyce's mixing of distinctly Irish elements of scene, behaviour, thinking, and speech in a composite style also turns nets, those that Stephen mentions, to other purposes. By contrast with more single-minded, monological styles, Joyce's diverse style remembers rather than forgets as part of a dialogical process that resists instead of accepting. A critical style of recollection that collects and transforms diverse elements is not, however, available to Joyce or to Stephen from the start. Joyce earns it over time. Whether his artist character will do so is an open question.

Transformations of style and history: from *Stephen Hero* to *Ulysses*

We can begin measuring the distance Stephen and his creator travel away from aestheticism by comparing the central character of *Stephen Hero*, called Stephen Daedalus, with Stephen Dedalus in *Ulysses*. Near the end of what has survived of *Stephen Hero*, Stephen claims that one function of writing is 'to record . . . epiphanies', 'the most delicate and evanescent of moments' (*SH* 216/211). By epiphany he means 'a sudden spiritual manifestation, whether in the vulgarity of speech or of gesture or in a memorable phase of the mind itself'. Stephen's interest in writing evocative prose vignettes, of the sort Joyce himself wrote, is aesthetic, but 'vulgarity' invites a realistic style. Joyce moved beyond Pater's influence when he produced the realism of *Dubliners* (written 1904–7), which is antithetical to Pater's lush, late-Romantic writing. Stephen has yet to take that step in *A Portrait*, where he thinks admiringly in part IV of 'a lucid supple periodic prose' (*P* 140) that derives from Pater. His thoughts include a diction of 'ecstasy' and 'trembling' (*P* 145) that also evokes Pater. The continuing or lingering influence of aestheticism on Stephen Daedalus and his counterpart in *A Portrait* and *Ulysses* complicates the impression that he may be moving toward the kind of writing that Joyce himself produced.

The evidence concerning Stephen's artistic potential, including his readiness to face and affect historical realities, is mixed, and the problem of judging him is difficult for several reasons.[7] Prior to *Ulysses*, we may be dealing with two characters, both named Stephen, about whom different judgements can be made, since the narratives of *Stephen Hero* and *A Portrait* differ in more significant ways than the spelling of the character's surname. Although these characters resemble each other, only provisional identification is warranted. Later, in *Ulysses*, Stephen's experiences and views from *A Portrait* carry over but not with any great force or frequency. Joyce complicates our response to the artist character(s) by assigning many details from his own life to Stephen. In his own publishing career, he adopted the pseudonym 'Stephen Daedalus' (*JJ* 164) when he published early versions of three *Dubliners* stories. Joyce's frequent intimate renderings of Stephen's thinking in *A Portrait* and *Ulysses* further contribute to blurring the boundary between narrator and character, despite the third-person narration. Since Joyce is writing fiction and not pure autobiography, it is important not to identify the real author in any absolute way with the young artist character; nevertheless, the texts frequently encourage us to consider the alignment.

In presenting Stephen prior to *Ulysses*, Joyce employs the two epiphanic modes of stark realism – 'the vulgarity of speech or of gesture' – and visionary fantasy – 'a memorable phase of the mind itself' – as delimiting extremes in his character. In both *Stephen Hero* and *A Portrait*, Stephen alternates between visionary and material, internal and external. He continues to feel attracted by visionary possibilities until the end of *A Portrait* and is influenced by them when he writes both his villanelle and his journal. But the evocations of Stephen's competing allegiances differ substantially in the two narratives that focus primarily on him. In *Stephen Hero* Stephen is both ruthlessly analytical and visionary. At a crucial moment in his development, his encounter with the disturbing reality of death intensifies both his critical bent and his visionary yearnings. In *A Portrait*, by contrast, Joyce presents the two perspectives of realism and fantasy not primarily as aspects of character but fundamentally as aspects of style. Having emerged as mutually modifying and mutually challenging attitudes, these styles of Stephen's thinking overlap and evoke each other. In *A Portrait* realistic and visionary are complexly intertwined elements in a style emphasizing memory. The double temporal orientation points toward Joyce's more allusive initial style in *Ulysses*.

Memory is not just personal in *A Portrait* and *Ulysses*. It is also cultural and historical. Joyce's writings recognize equally the cultural memory of myth and the historical realities of contemporary life, as well as the process by which those present realities have come into being. One of Joyce's achievements that eludes Stephen even in *Ulysses* is the merging of these kinds of memory in styles that also acknowledge the personal and the aesthetic. In *Ulysses* Stephen says that he is 'trying to awake' from the nightmare that is history (*U* 3.377). Instead of treating history as a bad dream from which we might wake up and escape, Joyce engages with history, using a realistic style strategically in a mixture of styles that interprets and transforms history and realistic detail by merging them with myth. When Joyce attributes mythic aspects to characters in styles that both recognize and challenge the ostensible limits of realism and history, he actualizes a potential that Stephen has yet to grasp. In his dialogue on art, 'The Critic as Artist' (1891), Wilde has Gilbert say that 'The one duty we owe to history is to rewrite it.'[8] Joyce accepts this duty but understands that when we make history we cannot do so just as we please. By calling his artist character 'Dedalus', a name simultaneously passed on from Stephen's Irish father and bestowed by the Irish writer of the narrative, Joyce realizes a cultural memory that invites a forward direction toward what 'has not yet come into the world' (*P* 212). Dedalus is simultaneously the artist character's heritage and a name that he can live up to only by influencing the history of the future. In *A Portrait*, it is not obvious that Stephen is ready to take a step that neither repeats the past nor escapes from history. The dates at the close of the book, 1904 and 1914, however, point forward from the narrative's end to a future a decade later in which Stephen is more likely to take such a step.

In *Ulysses* Stephen remembers his former commitment to an art that captures spiritual manifestations and transcends history. During the recollection, which occurs in the third episode, Stephen is again on the beach and may remember his former allegiance to a spiritual, Paterian notion of art because the surroundings remind him of the earlier beach scene reported in *A Portrait*. An important event has intervened between these two scenes.

Stephen's mother has died during the unnarrated period following the end of *A Portrait* and preceding the beginning of *Ulysses*. During the day of *Ulysses*, the fact of her death almost exactly one year earlier is the often unstated background for Stephen's thinking, including this memory. Joyce turns to an encounter with death, like the one involving Stephen's sister in *Stephen Hero*, as he composes an alternative for both realism and fantasy. Those earlier styles are being complicated and displaced by a mixed style that involves a recognition of death, that is, a hybrid style that evokes our mortality and the mortality of the artist.

Stephen's remembrance, in which he addresses himself, focuses on his epiphanies:

> I was young . . . Books you were going to write with letters for titles. Have you read his F? O yes, but I prefer Q. Yes, but W is wonderful. O yes, W. Remember your epiphanies written on green oval leaves, deeply deep, copies to be sent if you died to all the great libraries of the world, including Alexandria? Someone was to read them there after a few thousand years, a mahamanvantara. Pico della Mirandola like. Ay, very like a whale. When one reads these strange pages of one long gone one feels that one is at one with one who once . . .
>
> (U 3.136–46)

The passage provides stylistically the position Joyce reaches soon after *A Portrait*. There is nothing quite like this allusive, parodic, internal dialogue in either *Stephen Hero* or *Dubliners*. The style of *A Portrait* comes closer to it, prepares the way for it, but does not fully reach it. The language reflects on and reinterprets the past. In this self-mocking moment, Stephen retrospectively places his epiphanies among his grandiose, youthful projects, as adolescent fantasies. He has turned mystical traditions to ironic purposes.

With its exaggerated use of the impersonal pronoun, 'one', and its evocation of art's timeless quality, the passage makes fun of Pater's essays, in particular his 'Pico della Mirandola'.[9] This is not the first time Stephen has turned away from enthusiasms. The turning away is always only partial because an effect remains. The most obvious example of the pattern is Stephen's commitment to the Catholic Church. As many critics have pointed out, his religious upbringing, including especially his education by the Jesuits, continues to inform the way he thinks. The mixture of intimate knowledge and scepticism in the Ulyssean Stephen's thoughts, his former attraction but present aversion to the aesthetic reverence that inspired the epiphanies, points to one of Joyce's major stylistic achievements. Joyce develops this double temporal perspective, the perspective of memory, in the works written before *Ulysses*, especially in *A Portrait* and 'The Dead'. By means of it we can experience simultaneously both scepticism and the deeply-felt impact of thoughts and events in the central character's changing sensibility. Joyce's inherently double, or multiple, interiorized style renders the ambivalence and dissonance of Stephen's mental life, especially the interplay of self-scrutiny with recollection. As Joyce complexly presents them, ambivalence, dissonance, and interplay inform the mental process of creativity. They also embody what Wilde called 'the truth of masks', that is 'a truth in art', an insight whose 'contradictory is also true'.[10]

Joyce's early fiction moves from the episodic fragments of *Stephen Hero*, through the realistic stories of *Dubliners*, to the discontinuous narrative and flamboyant narration of *A Portrait*. The shift is from either fantasies or seemingly objective, realistic presentations to recollections or other moments of mental activity, structured like memories, that mingle the imaginative and the ostensibly objective in ways that enable a judgement and movement forward. The mediation announces itself stylistically, often through obscure allusions and personal references that hinder as well as enhance our understanding; this style is opaque rather than transparent. Because of the differences from the earlier narratives, including stylistic ones, the passage from *Ulysses* gives us a version of Stephen's development, through and away from mystical aestheticism, against which we can gauge the earlier versions. Although his trajectory is toward allusive mental play and self-mockery, the frame for Stephen's sometimes carnivalized thinking in *Ulysses* and earlier is his situation as Irish and an artist. He is able, literally at times, to close his eyes to his surroundings, but the reader recognizes, as Stephen also must, that he faces pressure from both his Irish friends and the English: Davin and the English priest and, in *Ulysses*, Buck Mulligan and the Englishman, Haines.

Stephen Hero: from restraint to extravagant defiance

The fragments of *Stephen Hero* present Stephen's interest in the occult, not in relation to Pater, as in *Ulysses*, but through his reverence for Yeats's mystical short stories. In chapter 23, during Stephen's second year at the university, he devotes himself to his literary enthusiasms, including Yeats's stories from *The Tables of the Law* concerning Owen Aherne, Michael Robartes, and mystical excess. At the same time, he pursues whimsical research into Renaissance Italian writings at a little-used Dublin library. His recollection in *Ulysses* of reading 'the fading prophecies of Joachim Abbas' 'in the stagnant bay of Marsh's library' (*U* 3.107–8), which occurs just before the memory of the epiphanies, refers to this period. In *A Portrait* Yeats's characters are barely mentioned, and in *Ulysses* Stephen distances himself from other artists with mystical tendencies. In *Stephen Hero*, however, he can 'believe in the reality of their existence' (*SH* 183/178). Identifying with these 'outlaws' (*SH* 183/178) who possess secret wisdom, Stephen can take a stand against the restrictive conventions of Irish culture. His writing of epiphanies reflects the same attitude.

In this work, Yeats's writing provides a turning point for Stephen that is rendered largely in terms of his character rather than through style. After reading Yeats's stories, he protests extravagantly against the restrictions of Irish culture. As had many English and Irish artists of the 1890s, including Oscar Wilde, Stephen chooses the road of excess to protest middle-class conventions. Around the time that he recites publicly from memory Yeats's story, 'The Tables of the Law', 'A certain extravagance began to tinge his life' (*SH* 184/179). His uninhibited behaviour reaches a memorable climax at the end of the next chapter when he interrupts his Italian tutorial and runs after Emma Clery to propose a night of lovemaking.

'The Tables of the Law' and the spiritual aestheticism it represents contribute to Stephen's change in behaviour by providing an artistic focus for his intense anger against Irish culture. That anger emerges in the aftermath of his sister's illness and death, for which there are no equivalents in *A Portrait*. Despite unconventional views, eccentricities, frustrations, isolation, and arrogance, Stephen's public conduct before her death remains largely within the bounds of convention. Even though he baits Father Butt with a question about unseemly passages in *Twelfth Night* (*SH* 34/28), Stephen tolerates for a time the contradictions in his culture, which he reacts to with amusement (*SH* 35/29). Later, when the paper he delivers at the Debating Society is attacked, he still responds in a restrained way, then decides gradually to withdraw without clamour from groups and activities. Prudence and tolerance serve Stephen well until he realizes that the issues demand a less restrained response.

In presenting the death of Isabel due to a serious illness in Stephen's presence at the beginning of chapter 23, Joyce draws on his realistic epiphany concerning the decline toward death of his younger brother Georgie (*PSW* 179). Besides Stephen's brother Maurice, Isabel is his only appreciative auditor. By this point in the narrative, he has largely given up not only on the Debating Society but also on the young people who gather regularly at the Daniels' household, for whom he would sometimes play the piano and sing. Stephen's playing for Isabel is obviously motivated by neither desire, which he feels for Emma, nor rebellious, intellectual comradeship, which he shares with Maurice. There is desperation and determination, as well as pathos, in Stephen's pretence that Isabel is not near death. Stephen cannot save her, but they achieve a special kind of understanding when 'once or twice he could have assured himself that the eyes that looked at him from the bed had guessed his meaning' (*SH* 166/161). In these scenes we witness Stephen putting on his mask of seriousness for a more humane purpose than self-protection. It enables him to undertake a work of kindness and establish communication with an audience that matters to him. Like Isabel, the success is short-lived, and Stephen's moods of selfish indulgence recur, at times in a style that is the precursor for the Paterian ending of part iv of *A Portrait*: 'in his soul the one bright insistent star of joy trembling at her wane' (*SH* 167/162).

Rather than disappearing after Isabel's death, Stephen's reveries and his commitment to the kind of spiritualized art he finds in Yeats intensify. But the situation has changed. In a way that is exceptional in *Stephen Hero*, Joyce renders the change briefly through style by describing the funeral in chapter 23 realistically: 'Standing beside the closed piano on the morning of the funeral Stephen heard the coffin bumping down the crooked staircase' (*SH* 171/167). Given the piano's regular appearance and its importance in the previous chapter, the closed instrument reiterates the shift indicated stylistically by the disturbing news that Stephen's mother has reported: 'There's some matter coming away from the hole in Isabel's . . . stomach' (*SH* 168/163). After the funeral, Stephen finally breaks significantly with decorum by choosing to drink a pint with the carriage drivers rather than having a more genteel drink with the middle-class mourners. The gesture marks a permanent shift in his conduct, his relationships within the family, and his attitude toward the family's Irish social context.

By juxtaposing in *Stephen Hero* a Paterian style and a realistic style, though briefly, Joyce presents Stephen's difficult, contradictory situation and the opposing extremes of his attitudes in a way that anticipates his extended use of those styles in *A Portrait*. But neither style is suitable for capturing the energy with which Stephen sometimes thinks and reacts in *Stephen Hero* and in the later books. That energy emerges as clowning and laughter in numerous scenes both preceding and following Isabel's death. In response to a self-deprecating story Maurice tells him, for example, he 'exploded in laughter' (*SH* 64/59). He has to resist the impulse to express his antic disposition to the President when they discuss the censoring of his paper (*SH* 99–103/94–7). During a Good Friday sermon, he indulges 'his gambling instinct' by trying to outpace the priest's various translations of *Consummatum est*, running quickly through a list of possibilities, wagering 'with himself as to what word the preacher would select' (*SH* 125/120). Much later, well after Isabel's death, Stephen and Lynch have a funny conversation about love and sex (*SH* 195–7/191–2), and he parodies the mechanical catechism of his Italian lessons by composing his own humorous alternative (*SH* 197/192–3).

Joyce moves in such passages toward presenting Stephen not only as serious but as energetically engaged in the way he sometimes is in parts IV and V of *A Portrait* and in *Ulysses*. When Stephen deceptively wears a serious mask to cover a mocking interior response, he has already begun practising the 'silence, exile, and cunning' (*P* 208), announced near the end of *A Portrait*, by which he will refuse to serve home, fatherland, and church. But Joyce has yet to find an adequate style for presenting at length Stephen's 'scornful mind scampering' (*SH* 102/97) in active dialogue with itself and its surroundings. By contrast with the condensed, allusive internal dialogue we have already seen in the early part of *Ulysses*, Stephen's thoughts in *Stephen Hero* have a ponderous, awkward quality that does not capture the energy he sometimes humorously expresses.

His self-reflections regularly take the form of self-doubts in which Stephen recognizes that he, like his culture, is full of inconsistencies. He thinks about or experiences vacillations at various times, including a moment near the end of chapter 22. The contradictions emerge in Stephen's doubts about himself: 'Even the value of his own life came into doubt with him. He laid a finger upon every falsehood it contained' (*SH* 167/162). Such misgivings are presented more extensively shortly after the culminating episode with Emma in a segment (*SH* 208–11/204–6) that is stylistically unusual in *Stephen Hero* because it seems to present at length, though awkwardly, an internal colloquy. 'An embassy of nimble pleaders' from the Church state their positions (*SH* 208/204), but these 'ambassadors' must be internal ones, since Stephen is involved in 'reflections'. The implications for Stephen's character are clear. He is criticizing and testing himself, motivated by residual fear and insecurity about continuing temptations to conform in order to succeed. In short, he has yet to move entirely beyond the crisis of his break with the Church.

Because he knows he may be self-deceived, Stephen's self-doubt involves ambivalences that are different in kind from the ones he despises in his culture, which is oblivious to them. After Isabel's death, Stephen's encounters with the cultural contradictions elicit some new responses. He realizes, for instance, that the members of the Debating Society 'revered' the 'memory of Terence MacManus', a revolutionary patriot, 'not less . . . than the memory of Cardinal Cullen', an ultra-conservative clergyman who spoke out against the nationalists (*SH* 178/173). Earlier, Stephen might have responded with restrained amusement, but his response now is total withdrawal and sarcasm. Stephen's sensitivity to contradictions leads him to literary projects, such as love verses and epiphanies, that allow him to resist his society by working with opposing elements in combination. We hear first about the love poetry, on which Stephen labours instead of pursuing his academic studies, between the death of Isabel and his infatuation with Yeats's stories. Inspired by Dante's *Vita Nuova*, he expresses his love in 'feudal terminology', but also 'a little ironically': 'This suggestion of relativity, he said, mingling itself with so immune a passion is a modern note: we cannot swear or expect eternal fealty because we recognise too accurately the limits of every human energy' (*SH* 179/174). In his typically ambivalent fashion, Stephen sees both loss and gain in transforming the idealizing language of love. What it loses in 'fierceness' it gains in 'amiableness'. Stephen humanizes his poetry by tempering exaggeration with a sense of human limitations. That Stephen takes this direction just before he discovers Yeats's mystical stories suggests that he will not follow the path of ahistorical, visionary fantasies for long. In his retrospective response to his verses, Stephen recognizes his own excesses. In chapter 26, he tells Maurice he has burned them because 'they were romantic' (*SH* 232/226). This judgement about his earlier efforts anticipates Stephen's thinking about his epiphanies in *Ulysses*.

Introduced late in *Stephen Hero*, the epiphanies enable Stephen to proceed by means of contradiction. In writing them, he can employ both stark realism and visionary experience in a mode that, like his love poetry, has the potential for being internally differential. In the representing of a vacuous reality, the artist recognizes and rejects its defects; in the evocation of visionary experience, the artist displaces debased, ordinary reality with a spiritual alternative. In *Stephen Hero*, however, Stephen never transforms his dual epiphanic procedure into anything more than a double gesture of defiance. An exaggerated swerving between extremes could become the vertigo of madness, as Stephen himself senses. Despite their excessive, narcissistic qualities, the epiphanies hold out distantly the possibility of juxtaposing and merging opposites stylistically to present the oscillations of thought and to generate alternatives for the future. The stylistic mingling can realize Fanon's 'fluctuating movement' as the dialogical interaction of discourses in an internally divided culture that, by simultaneously looking forward and looking back, begins to take on new, unpredictable forms. Joyce moves toward such stylistic and conceptual possibilities only after abandoning *Stephen Hero*.

A Portrait of the Artist as a Young Man: contraries and the name of a question

Despite the self-indulgent qualities of the epiphanies, Stephen's working by contraries is a step toward achieving the fluctuation of perspectives that we encounter in his thinking and his life in Joyce's later works. The putting into practice of Blake's precept that 'Without Contraries is no progression' and

Wilde's 'truth of masks' has only just begun in *Stephen Hero*. Eventually, the alternation tending toward a process of extremes merging and modifying one another becomes an important structural principle for Joyce, one that responds to divisions within his artist character and within Irish society. His contrasting styles in *A Portrait* present a character whose experiences regularly involve opposing forces that seem irreconcilable, such as the violent political and religious antagonisms that Stephen witnesses during the Christmas dinner in part I. The strongly divergent aspects of the book's language pertain simultaneously, though in different ways, to the writer who has learned to work with contrasts and to the character whose life and social context are filled with them. Various judgements about Stephen become possible in the frame of a new complexity that arises from Joyce's differential style for capturing the shifting qualities of conflict and memory. The complexity arises as well from a narrative structure that emphasizes repetition rather than continuous, chronological development and from the merging of the personal with myth and with history.

In *A Portrait* we see the swerving in Stephen's life more clearly and regularly than in *Stephen Hero*.[11] At the end of each of *A Portrait*'s five parts, Joyce uses elevated language to suggest that Stephen achieves a momentary insight and intensity through a transforming experience: his communion with nature and his fellow students after complaining to the Rector at the end of part I; his sexual initiation in the encounter with a prostitute at the end of part II; his post-confession, pre-communion peace at the end of part III; his commitment to art climactically presented as an encounter with an idealized woman at the end of part IV; and the exclamations about hopes for the future in mythic and racial terms at the end of Stephen's journal. At the start of each succeeding part, Joyce counters ironically the intensity of the preceding conclusion by switching immediately and unexpectedly to a realistic style and realistic details: the bad smell of Uncle Charles's tobacco in part II; the craving of Stephen's belly for food in part III; the mechanical, dehumanized character of Stephen's religious discipline in part IV; and in part V the dreary homelife that is the daily context and one frame of reference for Stephen's aesthetic ambitions. The pattern of contrasts is also repeated at various minor junctures in the narrative, for instance, at the end of the first section and the beginning of the second section of part II, when Stephen's revery about Mercedes is followed by the 'great yellow caravans' (*P* 54) arriving to remove the family's belongings. By juxtaposing extremes, Joyce arranges the events of Stephen's life without relying primarily on continuous action. Like *Stephen Hero*, *A Portrait* is episodic, with little or no transition from one situation to another, but the later work provides an orienting sequence of rises and falls for Stephen's development. Joyce emphasizes the pattern by abandoning narrative continuity to make moments that are separated in time contiguous in the narration.

Even within the individual, juxtaposed moments of elevated, climactic insight and countering, realistic perception, a pattern of contrast and possible merger sometimes appears. When this happens, a highly complex process of reading can ensue that may mimic Stephen's process of recollection. The possibilities for this kind of reading are most evident late in the narrative, once the reader knows Stephen's thinking and its language well. Stephen seems to remember at some level his earlier elevated experiences in a way that connects them. The situation is complicated because he apparently remembers and connects elevated moments not just as a group but in relation to the realistic moments that follow them. And he remembers and links other experiences as well. Rather than presenting Stephen explicitly recollecting opposing moments, Joyce depends on the reader's remembering, connecting, and anticipating. And he presents Stephen's thoughts in language that, through repetitions from earlier scenes, suggests that a remembering and crossing-over may be taking place. In addition, we encounter regular reminders of the mythic details that Stephen's story embodies in transformed ways.

A feedback is created whereby Stephen's later experiences, which in some ways repeat earlier ones, repeat with a difference because they occur against the background of what has gone before. The reader has access to this feedback through the increasingly mixed language that leads back to earlier scenes of different kinds. Because the language is complexly layered, the reader comes to every scene with frames of reference derived from earlier elements of the narrative, but each scene in turn results in new retrospective framings of what has gone before and new prospective framings of what is to come, and so on until the various frames overlap or nest within one another. The unusual effect mimics the process of Stephen's remembering his complicated, differential past as he encounters each new experience, but the effect depends on the reader's active recollection of earlier passages.

In the closing pages of part IV, for example, Stephen has an intense experience on the beach, reported in Paterian language, after which he naps in a nest-like, sandy nook. Having decided to lie down, he feels the heavens above him 'and the earth beneath him' (*P* 145). When he wakes, 'recalling the rapture of his sleep' (*P* 145), Stephen holds these oppositions together briefly. He imagines a merging of two realms in his image of the moon embedded in the earth: 'He climbed to the crest of the sandhill and gazed about him. Evening had fallen. A rim of the young moon cleft the pale waste of the sky like the rim of a silver hoop embedded in grey sand; and the tide was flowing in fast to the land with a low whisper of her waves, islanding a few last figures in distant pools' (*P* 173). Visionary and material, heaven and earth, sea and land, process and stasis merge and interact in a vivid promise of harmonious union. Not only do heaven and earth merge as silver blends with grey, but the tide, though flowing fast, has been humanized: her waves whisper.

The conjoining of opposites extends and momentarily fulfils Stephen's intense experience on the beach, which, like the earlier elevated moments, is quickly followed by its opposite. At the beginning of part v, Stephen drinks 'watery tea', chews 'the crusts of fried bread that were scattered near him', stares 'into the dark pool of the jar' of tea, remembers 'the dark turfcoloured water of the bath in Clongowes', and rifles idly with 'greasy fingers' through a box of pawntickets, whose lid is 'speckled with lousemarks' (P 146). As at the beginning of the three preceding parts, a debunking takes place through style. But the situation is more complicated now, because the language closing part IV already anticipates details of the realistic passage to come. Those details include pools of liquid and past participles ('fallen', 'embedded') that are displaced by the numerous past participles at the start of part v ('fried', 'scattered', 'scooped', 'rifled', 'scrawled and sanded and creased'). The pool of tea enables an ironic recollection of the pools of seawater for Stephen and the reader, but the additional recollection of Clongowes embeds these later pools in memories that make any simple contrast of two isolated moments impossible. The overlap between the two scenes creates a stylistic double helix, in which visionary intensity with its elevated language and a grimy reality with its material details mutually frame one another. They have become styles of memory that engage with each other and evoke the unlikely bridging of contrary views. We begin to see each through the lens of the other, as Stephen may have begun seeing them. One effect of the specific combination at this crucial juncture in the story is to invite a judgement about the Paterian aesthetic impulse from the perspective of an impoverished, specifically Irish, social and economic situation.

Joyce enables us to recognize a crossover and not just a contrast in the styles that close and follow the beach scene, because he has given us only a few pages earlier a kitchen scene as a prelude for both later moments. The 'knife with a broken ivory handle . . . stuck through the pith of a ravaged turnover' (P 137) that Stephen sees in that earlier scene anticipates the later scattered breadcrusts, but it also anticipates the moon embedded in the sand. Stephen on the beach may himself be recalling the earlier image as he half-perceives and half-creates the later one. If so, he is reaffirming what took place in the kitchen on his return home after having decided not to become a priest, when, perhaps to his own surprise, he joined his ragamuffin brothers and sisters in their singing. When Stephen rejects a religious vocation and chooses art, he allies himself with the sobering but communal realities represented by the family situation and not just with heightened, aesthetic experience.

Because the embedded moon carries a memory of the broken knife and the family along with it, the family situation nests within the visionary scene rather than simply debunking it. The relation between these portions of the narrative parallels the relation between modern events and myths in Joyce's writing; those relations are not simply ironic. The two kitchen scenes frame and implicitly comment on the beach scene that comes between them, but since the framed and framing scenes overlap, the implications are multiple. They open possibilities for the artist character and the reader rather than pre-scribing a single perspective. We carry the mutually-framing recollections of these earlier related scenes into the second section of part v. Stephen writes his villanelle in a room in which a soupplate from the previous night's sup-per remains on the table as a link to the descriptions of the kitchen (*P* 184). Although Stephen is intent on 'shrinking from' the ordinary world, his mem-ories and his surroundings keep thrusting that world into his thoughts. In this section, the two apparently antagonistic styles of aesthetic intensity and objective realism merge, though they continue to alternate. In creativity, as Joyce here presents it, fantasy, perception, and memory mingle as imaginative production. Rather than serving a common purpose of protesting conven-tion, as in the epiphanies, or of mutually debunking one another, fantasy and realism converge in a style that renders the attempt to produce something new. The convergence occurs under the auspices of memory, both explicitly presented and inscribed in phrases repeated from earlier sections. With this convergence, the style of Stephen's thinking not only in *A Portrait* but also in *Ulysses* becomes possible. The flame Stephen attempts to keep burning as he writes is both the visionary intensity of his dream and the emotion he feels for a real woman. His flame-tending proceeds next to a table on which, in the midst of composing, he notices a real, burnt-out candle, 'its tendrils of tallow and its paper socket, singed by the last flame'; he must write out his poem as best he can on the back of a torn 'cigarette packet' (*P* 184). The two styles have been conjoined and transformed to represent writing proceeding not just as it pleases but against and by means of the limits of circumstance. Stephen retains the intensity of Pater's aestheticism, but his candle is a material object.

The interacting styles of *A Portrait* begin actualizing a potential in Stephen for self-correction that is only hinted at in *Stephen Hero*. But the combination of self-criticism with intense commitment in his journal suggests goals that are largely over the horizon. Stephen explicitly distances himself there, for instance, from his earlier enthusiasm for Yeats's visionary heroes: 'Michael Robartes remembers forgotten beauty and, when his arms wrap her round, he presses in his arms the loveliness which has long faded from the world. Not this. Not at all. I desire to press in my arms the loveliness which has not yet come into the world' (P 212). Although Stephen rejects nostalgia about a delusory past, he does not present convincingly the beauty to come. Stephen can laugh at some of his own tendencies in ways that anticipate *Ulysses*, but he accepts, as most readers probably also do, the truth of his mother's remark that he still has much to learn about the heart (P 213). Stephen's emotional potential and his artistic talent remain to be developed when he writes the last, hopeful entries in his journal. The question remains whether Stephen can take advantage of the disparate conflicting perspectives and experiences that inform his tale and its telling to forge as the voice of his race the hybrid style of writing that Joyce constructs as one vehicle for Stephen's story. Like Fanon's 'zone of occult instability', Stephen's portrait turns out to be the name of a question about the future and its relations to the past, about our duty not to escape from history but to rewrite it and reinvent ourselves.

NOTES

I wish to thank Derek Attridge and Jonathan Mulrooney for their responses to a late version of this essay.

1 Oscar Wilde, *The Picture of Dorian Gray*, ed. Isobel Murray (Oxford and New York: Oxford University Press, 1981), p. 5.

2 For commentaries on the relation of Joyce's narrative to Wilde's that focus on homosocial and homoerotic elements, see the following essays in Joseph Valente, ed., *Quare Joyce* (Ann Arbor: University of Michigan Press, 1998): Joseph Valente, 'Thrilled by His Touch: The Aestheticizing of Homosexual Panic in *A Portrait of the Artist as a Young Man*', pp. 47–75; Vicki Mahaffey, 'Père-version and Im-mère-sion: Idealized Corruption in *A Portrait of the Artist as a Young Man* and *The Picture of Dorian Gray*', pp. 121–36.

3 Walter Pater, *The Renaissance: Studies in Art and Poetry* (1893), 4th edn, ed. Adam Phillips (Oxford: Oxford University Press, 1986), p. 152.

4 I argue for Wilde's ironic relation to Pater in 'Oscar Wilde's Aesthetic Gothic: Walter Pater, Dark Enlightenment, and *The Picture of Dorian Gray*', *Modern Fiction Studies* 46 (2000), 609–31.

5 Frantz Fanon, 'On National Culture', in *The Wretched of the Earth*, trans. Constance Farrington (New York: Grove Press, 1965), p. 227.

6 Critical discussion of *Stephen Hero* and *A Portrait* focusing on Joyce's complicated relationship to nationalism include: Emer Nolan, *James Joyce and Nationalism* (London and New York: Routledge, 1995), pp. 36–47; Vincent J. Cheng, *Joyce, Race, and Empire* (Cambridge: Cambridge University Press, 1995), pp. 57–75; Marian Eide, 'The Woman of the Ballyhoura Hills: James Joyce and the Politics of Creativity', *Twentieth Century Literature* 44: 4 (Winter 1998), 377–91; Pericles Lewis, *Modernism, Nationalism, and the Novel* (Cambridge: Cambridge University Press, 2000), pp. 1–51; and Gregory Castle, *Modernism and the Celtic Revival* (Cambridge: Cambridge University Press, 2001), pp. 188–207.

7 Wayne Booth discusses the difficulty the reader faces in judging Stephen without explicit guidance from the narrator in a widely reprinted essay, 'The Problem of Distance in *A Portrait of the Artist as a Young Man*', in *The Rhetoric of Fiction* (Chicago: University of Chicago Press, 1961), pp. 323–36. Robert Scholes also discusses the difficulty in 'Stephen Dedalus, Poet or Esthete?' *PMLA* 89 (1964), 484–9. Hugh Kenner, whose negative judgement of Stephen has been influential, discusses Stephen in 'The Portrait in Perspective', in *Dublin's Joyce* (London: Chatto and Windus, 1955), pp. 109–33, which has also been widely reprinted. He extends his argument in a more convincing later essay, 'The Cubist Portrait', in *Approaches to Joyce's 'Portrait': Ten Essays*, ed. Thomas F. Staley and Bernard Benstock (Pittsburgh: University of Pittsburgh Press, 1976), pp. 171–84. S. L. Goldberg provides a more sympathetic judgement of Stephen in his *James Joyce* (Edinburgh: Oliver and Boyd, 1962). I argue for a positive judgement of Stephen in *Teller and Tale in Joyce's Fiction: Oscillating Perspectives* (Baltimore: The Johns Hopkins University Press, 1983).

8 Oscar Wilde, 'The Critic as Artist', in *The Artist as Critic: Critical Writings of Oscar Wilde* (1969), ed. Richard Ellmann (Chicago: University of Chicago Press, 1982), p. 359.

9 Pater, *The Renaissance*, pp. 20–32.

10 Oscar Wilde, 'The Truth of Masks', in *The Artist as Critic*, ed. Ellmann, p. 432.

11 Hugh Kenner was probably the first critic to discuss the pattern of triumph and undermining in the five parts of *A Portrait* in 'The Portrait in Perspective', in *Dublin's Joyce* (London: Chatto and Windus, 1955), pp. 109–33.

7

JENNIFER LEVINE

Ulysses

What do we need to know in order to read *Ulysses* properly? An intimidating question, perhaps, by which to introduce a notoriously intimidating book. But reading of any kind, whether of *Ulysses* or of *Goldilocks and the Three Bears*, never takes place in an entirely blank or virgin mind. Other discourses are always implicated. Unlike *Goldilocks*, however, *Ulysses* poses the question of prior knowledge with some urgency because it can make us feel so unknowing, and with such devastating speed, and because sometimes a small bit of information available outside the novel, or inside it but hundreds of pages further on, can just as quickly unravel pages of confusion. One of the questions raised by such difficulties is central to literary studies in general: what is inside the literary object? What lies outside it? Can the border lines be drawn with any certainty? My intention is not to proclaim boundaries, nor to choose between right or proper readings and wrong ones, but only to indicate the kinds of knowledge that *Ulysses* seems to require. My survey is brief, and hardly exhaustive. It is a preface to the major focus of this essay: what is *Ulysses* 'about', and how can it be read?

When T. S. Eliot wrote about Joyce's work soon after its publication in 1922 he argued that its use of *The Odyssey* as both subtext and pretext 'made the modern world possible for art'.[1] He might also have said that *The Odyssey* has a similarly enabling function for Joyce's readers: that it makes *Ulysses* possible for a modern audience. For us, now, familiarity has naturalized the title. Wrenched out of its original Homeric context (it is the Roman version of 'Odysseus'), the name 'Ulysses' seems entirely Joycean. But that title is a provocation. Imagine for a moment that this seven-hundred-page novel is called *Hamlet* and you will regain a sense of it as a text brought into deliberate collision with a powerful predecessor. Leaving aside the question of whether that meeting is heroic or satirical it is obvious that even the initial decision to give each episode a name sets a whole interpretive machinery into play. Readers of *Ulysses* – however much they might disagree about what it means or what it is worth – have agreed to refer to the episodes by Homeric titles (the ones Joyce used in correspondence after 1918 as parts came out serially) in *The Little Review*, but which he omitted, substituting numbers, when *Ulysses* appeared in book form in 1922). Thus the first episode is known as 'Telemachus', the second is 'Nestor', the third 'Proteus', the fourth 'Calypso', and so on: 'Lotus Eaters', 'Hades', 'Aeolus', 'Lestrygonians', 'Scylla and Charybdis', 'Wandering Rocks', 'Sirens', 'Cyclops', 'Nausicaa', 'Oxen of the Sun', 'Circe', 'Eumaeus', 'Ithaca', and 'Penelope'. Further, again by common consent, section I (the first three episodes, focusing on Stephen Dedalus) is known as the Telemachiad, section III (the last three); as the Nostos, or return. Section II (the twelve middle episodes) is the Odyssey proper, displaced in time and space to the streets of Dublin at the beginning of the last century: 16 June 1904, to be precise.

The Homeric parallels are irresistible. Granted, we do not need the *Odyssey* to tell us that Stephen is a young man troubled by the fact that he is a son, and has a father, nor that Bloom is haunted by memories of the son who never really was – his second child, Rudy, having died only days after his birth. But it sharpens our sense of the potentially filial relationship between them to see them also as Telemachus and Odysseus. (They are not simply that, of course. Stephen may be cast as Telemachus, but he thinks he is playing Hamlet.[2] One might argue that he never does find out he is emoting on the wrong stage.) Similarly, it is obvious enough that Bloom is odd man out in Dublin: he does not drink; he does not buy drinks for others; he does not bet (though he is suspected of doing so); he is a Jew (and doubly alien from his Jewishness, for he has chosen to become both Catholic and Protestant). In the effusive round of greetings that punctuate the Dublin day, Bloom is pointedly unacknowledged. Yet when we recall that Odysseus' name may be punningly linked to *outis*, nobody, and that he draws on that facelessness for his own tactical advantage, we recast Bloom's uncomfortable place in society and invest him with a certain power – the power, for example, to escape the blinkered and bullish nationalist in the 'Cyclops' episode, just as Odysseus outwitted the bloodthirsty Cyclops. Like Odysseus, Bloom seeks after knowledge, though the scale of his curiosity is endearingly domestic. 'Wonder what I look like to her', he thinks as he feeds the cat. 'Height of a tower? No, she can jump me' (4.28–9). If we know even the bare bones of the Odyssean plot, the texture of *Ulysses* thickens. Certainly Molly Bloom's assignation with Blazes Boylan resonates against Penelope's legendary faithfulness. The more detailed our knowledge of Homer's epic, the stronger the echoes with *Ulysses*. The more precise, too, our sense of difference.

Caveat lector, therefore. In resorting to Homer, even by calling a chapter 'Penelope' or 'Nestor', we are insisting on something that Joyce himself took care to tone down by excluding chapter headings – though certainly, allusions to the *Odyssey* remain scattered throughout the work. The reader of *Ulysses* should not insist on parallels – Homeric or other – with too much vehemence. Bloom, after all, does not kill his wife's suitor(s). In fact he is careful to stay away during the hour of assignation. The nearest thing to a confrontation between him and Boylan is the one dramatized in 'Circe' where Bloom, as flunky and voyeur, is instructed to apply his eye to the keyhole and play with himself while his rival offhandedly announces his intention to 'just go through her a few times' (15.3789). Abjectly, Bloom offers 'Vaseline, sir? Orangeflower . . .? Lukewarm water . . .?' (15.3792–3) and asks 'May I bring two men chums to witness the deed and take a snapshot?' (15.3791–2). For 'Circe's' Bloom, there is intense erotic pleasure in betrayal: '(*his eyes wildly dilated, clasps himself*) Show! Hide! Show! Plough her! More! Shoot!' (15.3815–16). The passion here is very different from the avenging fury of Homer's world, and defines the role of the patriarch/husband in ways for which the epic poet would probably feel contempt. It might even be argued that the task of killing off the suitors is not so much neglected as given over to Molly, who picks them off one by one with dismissive wit in the closing episode.

The first generation of Joyce's readers affirmed his standing as an artist by insisting on the heroic premeditation of the Homeric allusions (a scenario by which Joyce becomes the epic hero of his own literary Odyssey). Stuart Gilbert's pathbreaking study, for instance, is based on a set of correspondences which Joyce himself had provided.[3] Each episode is assigned its own precise time, place, symbol, colour, body part, literary technique, and Odyssean subtext. But readers tempted by symmetries like these should know that Joyce gave another commentator/friend, Carlo Linati, a rather different outline, and with a similar authorial 'guarantee'.[4] More recently, with Joyce's legitimacy no longer in question, critics have been less anxious to reveal hidden correspondences, and more interested in the way *Ulysses* flirts with disconnection. There is a certain point at which the tactful reader holds back, wary of saying that this or that will unlock *Ulysses*'s secrets.

Homer offers the most obvious 'key' to *Ulysses*, but Shakespeare and Dante are similarly between the lines.[5] Although it does so with some irony (particularly in 'Oxen of the Sun'), *Ulysses* makes it clear that it places itself within – perhaps at the end of – a long line of literary history, and that this is one of the contexts in which it is to be read. It follows that the ideal reader would be extraordinarily well versed in the Western literary tradition. But few of us can claim that kind of knowledge: education demands both more and less of us in the twenty-first century than at the beginning of the twentieth. Happily for us now, a number of specialized guides to *Ulysses* have been produced in the interim and the flurry of information available electronically can put even a beginning reader in the know with astonishing speed.[6] Still, each reader has to decide how often, and when, to consult such materials. This is a strategic choice since the knowledge gained by stopping to find a reference or establish an allusion must be balanced against the urge to read on. The narrative impetus also offers solutions, though of a different kind. One of the interesting things about *Ulysses* is that it can be read at two speeds, fast or slow, and at every possible combination of the two. The institutionalization of Joyce's work, the fact that *Ulysses* has become a 'great book', more often than not encountered as a set text at the university level, means that there is considerable pressure to opt for the fixed (and often delayed) moment of knowledge. The danger is that *Ulysses* begins to be read as an elaborate conundrum, a literary jigsaw puzzle that can only be addressed if every piece is put in place in consecutive order, left to right, top to bottom. Sometimes the need to know what everything 'means' in *Ulysses* should be resisted.

Joyce's own earlier writing is very much a part of the intertextual network that *Ulysses* draws on. Readers coming to *Ulysses* with a knowledge of *A Portrait of the Artist as a Young Man* and *Dubliners* are at a considerable advantage. When Bloom steps into the carriage at the very beginning of 'Hades' they too will recognize and acknowledge his fellow-mourners: Martin Cunningham and Arthur Power from the short story 'Grace' and Simon Dedalus, still on the long slide down begun in *A Portrait*. In 'Cyclops' there will be another recognition. On its own, the episode hardly draws attention to the drunk blubbering in the corner and trying to ingratiate himself with the Citizen's dog (12.486–97). But this drunk has a name – Bob Doran – and readers of 'The Boarding House' will recognize in him the grey little man set up by his formidable landlady and her daughter Polly (who might, or might not, also be a victim). That story of entrapment, now given a new, more bitter closure, foregrounds Doran's brief appearance. He is totally befuddled by both drink and marriage. And yet, though the judgements in this episode are not to be taken at face value, there is also the intriguing possibility that mild Mr Doran was always potentially as low as the Mooneys: 'lowest blackguard in Dublin when he's under the influence' (12.384–5) – and that *Ulysses* rewrites *Dubliners*.

The earlier texts are most significant in the case of Stephen Dedalus for they project a history onto a character who is now back in Dublin, utterly penniless, recalled by his father's telegram to a dying mother. He was last seen (at the end of *A Portrait*) in rather different circumstances: setting out on his heroic journey to forge the uncreated conscience of his race. (Clearly, *Ulysses* picks up on the less savoury implications of 'forging': the artist's making is inherently a kind of deceiving, an idea that *Finnegans Wake* will develop extensively.) Readers familiar with *A Portrait* will also know, in spite of the opening pages' attention to Mulligan, that the one to watch is Dedalus: quite flat and undramatic in comparison, but potentially explosive. It is worth considering here the dramatic parallel with *Hamlet*. In the court scene that introduces both Hamlet and Claudius, it is Claudius who hogs the show. He wears brilliant royal robes, stands centre stage, and holds the full attention of his court while he speaks, and speaks, and speaks. Hamlet meanwhile, dressed all in black, stands to the side, and says very little that is not private and for his own ears only. In 'Telemachus' every gesture and utterance of Mulligan's is emphasized with an adjective, an adverb, or a richly descriptive verb. Stephen, in contrast, 'displeased and sleepy', looks 'coldly' at him, merely steps up, follows him 'wearily', and asks 'quietly'. Mulligan, in the first two pages, 'intones', calls out 'coarsely', gurgles 'in his throat', adds 'in a preacher's tone', gives 'a long slow whistle', and laughs 'with delight'. He says a great number of things, by turn 'sternly', 'briskly', 'gaily', 'frankly', 'thickly', and, at last, 'quietly'. Stephen is silent for almost fifty lines until he finally 'says': first 'quietly', then 'with energy and growing fear'. In between, he merely 'says'. Like Hamlet, however, he will soon gather all eyes and ears to himself – at least until Bloom's entry in 'Calypso'.

The kinds of knowledge I have discussed so far are essentially literary. But there are other worlds, beyond the literary, by which readers have set their course through *Ulysses*. Broadly speaking, the most interesting and important critical work on Joyce of the past decade has focused on the social text, reconstructing a rich body of cultural, political, and material life. As is demonstrated in this volume by Marjorie Howes, Joseph Valente, Jennifer Wicke, and Jeri Johnson, the turn to a theorized but carefully specific history has made it possible to rethink Joyce's relationship to a whole set of issues that had previously been considered mere 'background' – if at all. The range of languages and codes within which the novel is inscribed has a great deal to do with Joyce's sense of himself as a citizen – and not only as a Dubliner, but as a European. Most pointedly, however, Irish history and politics, Catholicism, the Celtic Revival, popular culture, Dublin geography, and a certain slice of middle-class Dublin life in the years before and after the turn of the century all play their part.[7] Real Dubliners are written into *Ulysses*, not always with the benefit of a new name. Nor does Joyce spare himself: details of his own life (many of them less than flattering) are drawn into the portrait of Stephen Dedalus. A great deal of what you might consider safely inside the fictional frame only makes sense if you can go outside it. For instance, if you know that the ancestor whose parliamentary record Mr Deasy quotes in 'Nestor' to prop up his claim to being a 'true' Irishman and a patriot actually voted in precisely the opposite way (2.278–80), you see that Deasy is convicting himself out of his own mouth, and you begin to discern the broader themes of deluded and indulgent self-representation that Joyce plays on in *Ulysses*. Later, in 'Sirens', where only fragments from 'The Croppy Boy' sung by Ben Dollard (11.991–1141) are given in the narrative, it helps to hear the whole song in your head, and to understand the historical context out of which it comes, in order to catch the subtle ironies by which national and marital betrayal are linked together. Regret, disguise, double identity, sudden discovery, avenging judgement: these attend Bloom as well as he sits and listens in the adjoining restaurant of the Ormond Hotel, knowing that Boylan is at 7 Eccles St with Molly.[8]

When Joyce was asked, after many years of exile in Europe, whether he would ever go back to Ireland, his answer was a question: 'Have I ever left it?' (*JJ* 292). Ambivalent as it was, Joyce's tie to his native land, to its history and culture, is everywhere in his work. Dublin was perhaps the deepest point of contact, and throughout the writing of *Ulysses*, hundreds of miles away on the Continent, Joyce depended on his aunt Josephine Murray to supply him with vital local trivia. He asked her to check, for instance, 'whether there are trees (and of what kind) behind the Star of the Sea Church in Sandymount visible from the shore and also whether there are steps leading down at the side of it from Leahy's Terrace'.[9] To a certain extent a 1904 map of Dublin is as good a guide through *Ulysses* as Homer's *Odyssey*. It will at least decode, for the non-native reader, the insistent placing of characters at named streets, buildings, and monuments.[10] *Ulysses* describes a quintessentially urban world (though not an industrial one). Most of the action takes place in a public space, and most of the action is talk – the kind of talk that happens when men hang out together at street corners or in public bars. If a Dublin city map would be useful, so too would a Dublin voice, whose cadences are threaded into *Ulysses*' elastic English. The temptation is always there, in spite of one's mid-Atlantic (or other) blunders, at least to try to sound Irish.[11] Perhaps this is why the marathon 1982 Irish radio broadcast of the entire book, read by Irish actors, can be yet another useful entryway into *Ulysses*. However, by voicing a reading it forces choices that print (Joycean print more than most) allows you to suspend.

I have spoken, so far, of the bodies of knowledge that you can bring to *Ulysses*: Homer's epic, the Western literary tradition, Joyce's earlier work, the Catholic and Irish cultural milieu, details of Dublin life, the sound of Dublin speech. The list goes on and on. But I have not yet considered the larger interpretive gestures by which that knowledge may be read into place, and by which *Ulysses* has been given shape. Or rather, shapes – for, Proteus-like, it has no single canonic identity. The current proliferation of critical languages allows us to see more clearly than was possible under a single dominant mode of criticism the extent to which a literary work's status and meaning are determined at least as much by communities of readers as by the intentions of writers. This is even more markedly so with *Ulysses*, which – among all the other things it does – undertakes an exploration and critique of reading. At many points it predicts the insights of current literary theory – though usually with far more wit and humour.

What I intend here is not to describe the various schools of criticism *vis à vis Ulysses*, but to provide something more general and schematic. I will propose that the initial moment in any reading is a decision about genre. What kind of a literary object is *Ulysses*? Three implicit answers have been offered: that it is primarily a poem; that it is really, still, a novel; and, most recently, that it is a 'text'. I shall use these general rubrics to introduce and to distinguish among lines of approach that continue to lead us into the work in interesting ways.

What would be entailed in a poetic reading of *Ulysses* and why would it be proposed in the first place? Of course, there are poems and there are poems. There is *The Odyssey*, and then there is Blake's 'London' – or Stephen's little lyric in 'Aeolus' (7.522–5). Each requires a different kind of reading. But some things may still be commonly assumed about the genre. To read a piece as a poem is to assume, first of all, that it uses language in special ways and is not to be taken literally (in contrast to the putative transparency of 'scientific', 'objective', or 'ordinary' language). These distinctions are by no means unproblematic. They have been disputed with considerable force on the grounds that all language is figurative, and that no utterance is free of intentions. For my purposes here, however, I will allow poetry its metaphorical privilege in order to highlight what many readers of *Ulysses* have found so striking: the liberties it takes with ordinary syntax and ordinary diction, its intense play with language, its metaphorical rather than narrative logic, its symbolism, its dense allusiveness.

Consider the opening paragraphs of *Ulysses*, with their unexpected images ('the light untonsured hair, grained and hued like pale oak'), their laconic yet symbolically portentous details ('a bowl of lather on which a mirror and a razor lay crossed'), and perhaps most notably, their quirky syntax: a way of arranging words within a sentence that keeps you pleasurably on edge, the way a poetic line does – though for different reasons since Joyce is not compelled by the poet's metrical clock (the one that often beats against the grain of prose-time). He is writing prose, undoubtedly, but a prose that takes unusual liberties: 'Halted, he peered down the dark winding stairs and called out coarsely . . . He faced about and blessed gravely thrice the tower, the surrounding land and the awaking mountains' (1.6–11).

The initial 'halted', the strangely delayed 'gravely', and the ambivalent 'thrice' (does Mulligan bless each place three times?) are just a little 'off'. They make the sentences sound not wrong so much as foreign. One might argue that for Joyce, as for Stephen Dedalus in *A Portrait*, and indeed for any Irishman, English was both familiar and foreign, always an acquired speech. This complicated relationship allowed him a special insight into the fact that we are never at home in language, not even in our mother tongue. In spite of all our efforts to make the link between words and things seem irresistibly natural, language is profoundly artificial. The paradoxical force of poetry is that it is the most contrived and conventional of discourses, and yet it achieves an effect of perfect (i.e. perfectly appropriate, perfectly natural) utterance. Joyce's 'poetry' exposes that paradox to our gaze.

Consider the beginning of 'Calypso', the chapter in which Leopold Bloom makes his entrance. 'Mkgnao!' cries the cat, and then 'Mrkgnao!', and then again, loudly, 'Mrkrgnao!' (4.16, 25, 32). 'Miaow!' says Bloom later, answering back in standard English (4.462). A certain position is being staked out here. The writer of *Ulysses* makes it clear that, unlike Bloom, he has an obligation to the truth of that cat's talk, and the ability to transcribe it. With the idiosyncratic 'Mkgnao' and its variants Joyce claims the poet's prerogative to mint new words as necessary. He also identifies the essential conventionality of language: 'Miaow' will never be quite the same again.

Since poetic language is taken to be densely and even cryptically allusive, another reaction to 'Mrkrgnao' is worth noting here as well. The Italian translator of *Ulysses* has seen in it a covert version of Mrkr, the Greek spelling of Mercury, and thus a signal to the Homeric Hermes which imbues it with epic significance.[12] Perhaps he too carries a message to Bloom from the gods. Or maybe it is just a reminder of how far Bloom's Dublin has fallen from the epic scale set by Homer. Or, alternatively, 'Mrkrgnao' may be read as a reference back to the first episode and to the explicitly mercurial Malachi, Buck Mulligan. Thus Bloom's early-morning interlocutor is made analogous to Stephen's, and inexorably a thread is drawn between the two protagonists. Note that Stephen and Bloom do not really engage with each other until later at night, in the 'Circe' chapter. And yet by the time they do so they will already have been brought together, as here, by a long series of rhetorical connections.

Here you begin to see the real force of the poetic model for *Ulysses*, which is its vision of the work as a vast symbolic project whose logic is metaphorical and allusive rather than narrative. Indeed, on the strictly narrative evidence – that is, how often Stephen and Bloom meet, and what happens when they do – their relationship is marginal.

In its overwhelming desire for connections the poetic model simultaneously simplifies and complicates the reading project. It allows you to organize and construe the work, but only if, first, you recognize it as a series of organizable terms. In this sense poetic readings are radically suspicious for they assume that things are not as they seem and that the truth lies under the surface. Everything must be raised up to the same level of significance. (One repercussion is that the laughs in *Ulysses*, and sometimes the gentle humour, tend to get translated out. How seriously, after all, should you take the interchange between Bloom/Ulysses and the feline Hermes?) This engenders a paradox. On the one hand, poems are notoriously untranslatable – and *Ulysses* certainly proves the rule. At every turn it places difficulties in its translator's path, for every word, it seems, is linked to other words across pages and episodes in an intricate allusive network.[13] On the other hand, such language can never simply be taken literally. It does not so much resist translation as demand it. Thus to read *Ulysses* as a poem can be a long process of exegesis, or intralinguistic translation on the model A 'really is' B. A great many codes can make that equation possible: most notably the Homeric (as we have seen), the Jungian (by which *Ulysses*' particulars are given archetypal force and Stephen, Bloom, and Molly emerge as the essential psychic triad), and the theological. Take the fact that Molly's period starts some time at night after the events of 16 June. If you are persuaded that Joyce's Catholicism is deeply implicated in his work, then Molly does not simply begin to menstruate. The blood that threatens to stain the sheets ('O Jesus wait yes that thing has come on me . . . O patience above its pouring out of me like the sea' (18.1104–5, 1122–3)) will be 'intimately allied to the various consecrations throughout Dublin of Christ's blood and body'.[14] This coincidence (along with others) elevates Molly into the missing term in the trinity of Father (Bloom), Son (Stephen), and Holy Spirit, and it is most significant that, just when Father and Son come as close together as they will get ('Silent, each contemplating the other in both mirrors of the reciprocal flesh of theirhisnothis fellowfaces' (17.1183–4)), one of them is elucidating 'the mystery of an invisible attractive person, his wife Marion (Molly) Bloom, denoted by a visible splendid sign, a lamp' (17.1177–8).

The details fall into place, sometimes, with uncanny precision. It can be very satisfying to pattern *Ulysses* in this way. But to do so requires a continuous effort of translation and a willingness to bypass the more prosaic levels of signification. Or, to be more prosaic myself, to forget that Bloom and Stephen are standing in the back garden at Eccles Street, about to take a companionable pee together. They look up at a second floor window and see 'the light of a paraffin oil lamp with oblique shade projected on a screen of roller blind supplied by Frank O'Hara, window blind, curtain pole and revolving shutter manufacturer, 16 Aungier street' (17.1173–6). Note that here the specificity of description is commercial, not religious. Note, too, that the moment of 'perfect unity' between Bloom and Stephen recalls an earlier mirroring in 'Circe' just after Boylan and Molly's voices are heard 'sweetly, hoarsely', and in lascivious union, and Bloom – 'eyes wildly dilated' – calls out: 'Show! Hide! Show! Plough her!' (15.3815). Bloom and Stephen then gaze into the mirror at Bella Cohen's. What they both see reflected back at them is '*The face of William Shakespeare, beardless . . . rigid in facial paralysis, crowned by the reflection of the reindeer antlered hatrack in the hall*' (15.3821–4): not so much Holy Father and Holy Son, as fellow cuckolds – and perhaps fellow artists too – in a less than holy trinity. And yet, even in this counter-reading, elements from across the work are picked out and pulled together to construct a paradigm – in this case rather more earth-bound than spiritual, and certainly more attuned to scepticism than to faith – but a paradigm, nonetheless, feeding into a broadly poetic sense of the work.

In this version of *Ulysses*, sequence is less important than a synchronic and spatial mapping based on repetition: allusions, echoes, symbols, and archetypal patterns all being, essentially, modes of repetition that forestall the onward moving logic of narrative. But then, reading *Ulysses* is often a case of moving backward through the pages (to check a detail, note an echo, revise an interpretation) as much as forward. Like the verbal icons or the well-wrought urns of the New Criticism (which imaged poetry in this way for an entire generation) Joyce's 'poem' is to be taken whole, apprehended as a complex unity whose intricacy matches that of a vital organism and whose parts all coexist in a single, ideal, moment of time.

To read *Ulysses* as a poem, finally, is to assume that it will reward scrupulous attention and that the intensity with which you focus on a short lyric may – no, must – equally be given to every page of this very long work. Nothing is contingent or insignificant. Bloom's comment on Molly's joke about Ben Dollard (that he has a 'bass barreltone' voice, punning on the fact that he has become fat as a barrel on Bass beer) holds for *Ulysses* as well: 'See, it all works out' (8.122). This offers both a daunting and a liberating prospect. How can you ever hope to master its densely interlocking verbal networks? But then, you can start anywhere, because everything matters equally, and meaning can exfoliate from any centre. On the whole, the first generation of Joyce's readers adopted the poetic model, and I suspect that most first readings of *Ulysses* will do so too, for it privileges the rage for order that motivates us when we first encounter a new work. It also gives us a strategy for beginning. While long sections of surrounding text may remain opaque, a single page, or paragraph, or even a few lines can generate enough of a sense that it does all work out – at least here – to keep us going.

Of all the genres, the novel is most resistant to definition – perhaps because it is always 'novel', or new, always a challenge to canonic forms. In this sense, *Ulysses* may be the most typical novel in world literature. However, it is also possible to speak of it as novelistic in a more conventional sense, as the kind of writing Virginia Woolf celebrates in 'Mr Bennett and Mrs Brown'. 'All novels', she says, 'deal with character, and . . . it is to express character . . . that the form of the novels, so clumsy, verbose, and undramatic, so rich, elastic, and alive, has been evolved.'[15] Indeed, it would be impossible to speak of *Ulysses* without referring to its characters, to what they do, and to the densely described society they inhabit.

The presence of a human figure in a landscape is irresistible. The viewer's eyes swerve toward it and make contact there, first. Similarly for readers of *Ulysses*, the force of character is compelling, though *Ulysses* does not 'give' them to us in quite the straightforward way we might expect. Helpful formulations like 'he said' or 'she thought' are usually absent. Oblique and even confusing attributions abound. At the same time, it tells us a great deal more than we are used to hearing. It does not avert its gaze when Bloom picks his toes and smells his fingers (17.1480–91). It follows him into the toilet and tracks the motions of his body and his mind with unembarrassed ease. 'Something new and easy. No great hurry. Keep it a bit' (4.501–2). The phrases apply three ways, it seems: to the story Bloom reads while sitting on the 'cuckstool', to Bloom's own sense of his bodily functions, and also to the narrative's languid pleasure in letting the words themselves come out. My point here is not merely that *Ulysses* breaches the borders of propriety. More than that: it can give the internal life of characters with an extraordinary sense of intimacy. Indeed, if any literary catch-phrase still clings to *Ulysses* it is 'stream of consciousness'. However, you do not need to privilege that technique (which, in any case, is better termed 'interior monologue') to see that reading character is a potent method for reading *Ulysses*. In the opening episodes, for instance, once you realize that much of what happens is happening inside Stephen's head (like the Oxford scene (1.165–75), or the visit to Aunt Sara's (3.70–104)), whole chunks of the novel become available. Instead of unnerving and frustrating shifts from one kind of language to another, even from one story to another, you recognize that you are tracking a mind in action and respond accordingly.

'Aeolus' is an interesting section to look at in this light. If you think of the six preceding chapters as conduits to character – to Stephen Dedalus and

Leopold Bloom in particular – 'Aeolus' is immediately striking because it seems to turn its back on both of them. To a great extent the progressive filling in of Bloom's and Stephen's perspectives is what makes the early sections of *Ulysses* intelligible. You hang on to them; you listen for their voices and they lead you through the thicket of language. In 'Aeolus' that thicket is specifically foregrounded. Set largely in a newspaper office, and filled with talk about talk, the chapter is saturated with the languages of rhetoric and of wind – an ironical gloss on Dublin's hot air. The sounds of 'Aeolus' are insistent too, as the machinery of urban life drowns out individual voices. The episode begins:

IN THE HEART OF THE HIBERNIAN
METROPOLIS

Before Nelson's pillar trams slowed, shunted, changed trolley, started for Blackrock, Kingstown and Dalkey, Clonskea, Rathgar and Terenure, Palmerston Park and upper Rathmines, Sandymount Green, Rathmines, Ringsend and Sandymount Tower, Harold's Cross. The hoarse Dublin United Tramway Company's timekeeper bawled them off:
– Rathgar and Terenure!
– Come on, Sandymount Green!
    Right and left parallel clanging ringing a doubledecker and a singledeck moved from their railheads, swerved to the down line, glided parallel.
– Start, Palmerston Park!   (7.1–13)

To come upon such an opening, especially after the intimacy of 'Hades', is as unnerving as suddenly discovering in the midst of a noisy foreign city that you have lost your guide, that there is no one to speak for you and no one whose language you understand. Bloom does turn up again (by the third short section (7.26–7)), and Stephen somewhat later (7.506), but as the talk in the newspaper office swirls around them, and as the capitalized headlines repeatedly intrude, neither is allowed his old status as *the* figure in the landscape. However, even though Bloom and Stephen keep fading from view (and in subsequent chapters they will do so even more), the novelistic lure of character remains. If Bloom is absent for a good half of the episode (7.450–961), and Stephen does not come in until half-way through (7.506), we begin to pay attention to other voices in 'Aeolus', to other entries and exits, to other bursts of talk, and to other silences. Later chapters of *Ulysses* will provide more sustained access to minor characters by speaking in their own language (for example, Gerty MacDowell in 'Nausicaa' and the sourly loquacious 'I' of 'Cyclops'). In 'Aeolus' the presentation is still dramatic and external, but the construction of character it makes possible is remarkably subtle. One of the effects of rereading *Ulysses* is that the noisy foreign city ceases to be quite so foreign and the talk that swirls about separates out into distinctly heard and comprehended sentences.

One of the voices heard in 'Aeolus' is J. J. O'Molloy's. He is by no means central to *Ulysses* – nor to this episode. Nevertheless, if you track him through this chapter you will have a good sense of the investment in character that moves *Ulysses* along. The minute he enters the scene Bloom provides a running commentary on his past and present situation. (And, of course, in a typically novelistic complication, the mere fact that Bloom does so, as if compelled to notice and to understand, adds to our construction of his character as well. He is not unlike a certain kind of novelist, for whom the smallest detail of dress or gesture can summon up a whole life story.) 'Cleverest fellow at the junior bar he used to be. Decline, poor chap. That hectic flush spells finis . . . What's in the wind, I wonder. Money worry' (7.292–4). When we use Bloom's mini-story as the magnet that picks up subsequent references to O'Molloy, the drama being played out emerges. J. J. O'Molloy has come to the newspaper offices with a single purpose in mind: to ask Myles Crawford for a loan. Characteristically for *Ulysses*, the actual request is not directly rendered nor is the motive stated. It can only be inferred from Crawford's negative, but not particularly explicit, answer, and from O'Molloy's carefully orchestrated silences. '– *Nulla bona*, Jack', says Crawford, 'I'm up to here. I've been through the hoop myself . . . Sorry, Jack.' (7.996–8). Crawford's embarrassment at being asked and at intending to say no may well explain his histrionic reaction to Bloom, who interrupts the tête à tête by making his own request – or rather, Mr Keyes's: the tea merchant wants 'just a little puff' in exchange for renewing his advertisement. Crawford's rejection is loudly colourful, and in sharp contrast to his careful treatment of O'Molloy:' . . . he can kiss my arse . . . He can kiss my royal Irish arse . . . Any time he likes, tell him' (7.981, 991–2).

Once this scene of request and rejection is played out, O'Molloy's previous invisibility becomes perceptible. Consider his entry into the scene. He will not be drawn into conversation, even by the warm welcome of his fellow citizens (7.280–90). After minimal courtesies he responds with a silent shake of the head to Dedalus's greeting (7.290), fails to react to someone's 'You're looking extra', except perversely, by 'looking [instead] towards the inner door' and asking 'Is the editor [Myles Crawford] to be seen?' (7.296–8). Learning that Crawford is in his 'inner sanctum' he strolls to a desk and begins to look through a file. In effect he lapses into silence and invisibility until the editor reappears. Even then, he does not deign to respond to Ned Lambert's whispered remark (7.366), and only breaks into speech and motion after a direct greeting from Crawford:

– . . . Hello Jack . . .
– God day, Myles, J. J. O'Molloy said, letting the pages he held slip limply
back on the file. (7.381–3)

He comes to life with Crawford's entrance, like an actor who steals the scene
(otherwise full of noisy bombast) by the sheer quietness of his gestures – but
like an actor for whom only part of the audience matters. He plays very deliberately to Stephen and Crawford, and to them only. He murmurs, he offers
his cigarettes 'silently', he speaks 'gently', he murmurs again, he says 'quietly'
and then again, 'in quiet mockery', 'smiling palely'. For a moment he speaks
'eagerly', but otherwise he keeps a cool control over himself, 'moulding his
words' as he performs his role. He is poised, alert for the moment when he
must call Crawford aside and pose the question. Even then, he throws it off
as if an afterthought, turning first to Stephen, who has handed Mr Deasy's
letter to the editor:

– I hope you will live to see it published. Myles, one moment.
He went into the inner office, closing the door behind him. (7.907–8)

When he comes out the question will have been asked. We hear only the
answer, which is fulsome but negative, and O'Molloy wastes no time upon
it. 'J. J. O'Molloy pulled a long face and walked on silently' (7.1000). As
before, others attempt to draw him in, but he will have none of it.

– I see [says Professor McHugh after Stephen's parable of the plums] . . . Moses
and the promised land. We gave him the idea, he added to J. J. O'Molloy.
. . .
J. J. O'Molloy sent a weary sidelong glance towards the statue and held his
peace. (7.1061–5)

The construction of a world in which characters 'really' live is so dense
in *Ulysses* that even a marginal character like O'Molloy has his own complicated set of motives and gestures to move through – a kind of ballet that
we can reconstruct and dance along with, even without the revealing inner
speech that characterizes Bloom or Stephen. If, on first reading, 'Aeolus'
seems to pull the rug out from under the novelistic table so carefully set
in the preceding chapters, every rereading intensifies your sense of 'being
there', and of that voyeuristic pleasure in overheard conversation that typ-
ifies the novel. No coincidence, perhaps, that the little drama being played
out between J. J. O'Molloy and his fellow Dubliners repeats the larger drama
of social mobility, of class and money, that animates the genre as a whole,
and that certainly entangles Stephen in its logic. The interesting thing about
16 June 1904 is that for Stephen at least things might still go either way. He
might yet become the artist – even the author of *Ulysses*, as some have argued.

But O'Molloy's pointed recognition of him equally suggests that he has seen a fellow loser, and that his own artful, even elegant, performance prefigures what Stephen will become: a stylish cadger, and not particularly successful. Dramatically, too, O'Molloy's relative silence in 'Aeolus' echoes Stephen's in the opening pages of *Ulysses* and draws yet another thread between them. The paradigm thickens: a timely reminder that while poetic and novelistic readings are separable in theory, they are not necessarily so in practice.

Current literary study is anything but homogeneous. One of the most widespread tendencies, affecting many different approaches to literature, might be described under the rubric 'textuality'. In a major interpretative shift, it 'thinks' the work in question as text, thus stressing its paradoxical identity as a web, a tissue, a signifying field, or even a process of signification, rather than a self-contained entity.[16] To speak of text is also to transgress generic and even literary distinctions. Advertising copy, novels, epic poems, and historical or philosophical writing are all, inherently, textual: *Ulysses'* plunder of a vast range of discourses – many of them flamboyantly extra-literary – comes immediately to mind. The text is Penelope's web: constantly made and unmade, an impossible weaving with ravelled selvedges. And Penelope too is made and unmade by such a text, for 'textuality' calls the reading subject into question.

The dictionary defines 'text' in a number of ways, not all of which are appropriate here. Indeed, the distinction between text (as authoritative, original writing) and commentary (secondary and presumably parasitical) is precisely what – for a textual reading – *Ulysses* undermines with such inventiveness. The various intertextual networks at play in 'Aeolus' gesture toward this blurring of borders. The 'Oxen of the Sun', to which I shall turn shortly, offers an even more elaborate example. You may also recall Bloom's cat in 'Calypso', whose 'Mrkrgnao' seemed to announce an essentially poetic project. But consider the complications. 'Mrkrgnao': a Greek version (Mrkr) of a Roman version (Mercurius) of a Greek name (Hermes). Translation upon translation, and curiously circular: the pure place of origins from which the poetic allusion draws its force is not quite as stable as one might think – nor as pure. Instead what we have is a web of reference points none of which is clearly privileged, and a putative text (Mrkr) which is itself a commentary. This perspective on 'Mrkrgnao' announces a rather different project.

A text is a 'theme or subject on which one speaks', a 'statement on which one dilates' (*OED*): never autonomous, never fully complete in itself, but always awaiting a reader/speaker who will call it out into life. It is most markedly at this point of symbiosis with a reader that *Ulysses* takes on its contemporary form as text. Without ever naming you directly *Ulysses* is constantly addressing you as its reader. There is no grand opening to an 'Idle reader . . .', as in *Don Quixote*. There is no 'Reader, I married him', as in *Jane Eyre*. But just as you tend to forget you have a body until some part of it malfunctions (what could possibly make a nose more obvious to its owner than a cold?), *Ulysses*, so full of moments of congestion and unease, foregrounds you as the reader in the text.

If the reading activity appropriate to poems and novels – indeed, to writing of all kinds – has been knowing or understanding, the one currently attached to texts is 'play'. The choice is telling. First of all, it invokes a particular kind of freedom within constraints, as when you might speak of the play of a hinge or of cogs in a wheel, the focus being on the inter-relationship between moving parts in a machine rather than on the stable and separate identity of any one part. It makes a great deal of sense to think of *Ulysses* in motion, its elements knowable only in relation to each other. One of the most relentless and yet exhilarating effects of the book is the way the verbal ground keeps shifting under you. Many readers have argued that *Ulysses* makes a major break with itself in the middle episode, 'Wandering Rocks'. It could also be argued that the experiments with style of the second half – powerfully antimimetic – are present from the beginning. And vice versa: that even the most obviously subversive episodes (like 'Oxen of the Sun') sustain the commitment to point of view, character, and painstaking mimesis begun with 'Telemachus'. Either way, however, there is an acknowledgement that this play-full text is constantly differing from itself.

To speak of play in this sense, with all its attendant notions of machinery and construction, is clearly a provocation to any sense of the literary work as an organic entity, and in particular to the notion that like a natural organism a work like *Ulysses* will evince in each of its parts the same inevitable logic that motivates it as a whole. (These assumptions are central to the poetic model of *Ulysses*.) Instead the relationship of parts to whole, of microcosm to macrocosm, is understood as asymmetrical and contradictory. This is most strikingly the case in the extraordinary shifts that take place between (and sometimes within) episodes. There are certainly elements that hold the whole thing together: the reiteration of allusions, themes, motifs; the persistence of named characters; the chronological sequence of episodes that record events in Dublin, hour by hour, from the morning of 16 June 1904 until the early hours of the next day. But 'play' responds to the countervailing sense that the episodes do not so much share a common life as work together in contradiction. You might note here that textual readings tend to place the difficulties of *Ulysses* at the centre of their accounts, and to make them part of the solution rather than the problem to be explained (away).

Play is not merely *in* the text-system. The text must *be* played, like a musical score. Without the performance it is only black marks on a white page. But then, one might also ask: 'What are you playing at?' Play is never entirely faithful. Potentially at least, it is a kind of trifling with or fingering of the text – not paying it due respect. Certainly the notion of play is subversive, particularly to the authority of intentions and meaning. If the text is not a natural organism, or like one, then its author loses his old status as God-like creator. Play is anarchic, however. Its impulse is not imperialist. It does not simply seek to dethrone the writer in order to put the reader in his place.

To play is not only to perform but also to enjoy, to take ludic pleasure in the text, and with it. (I cannot stress enough how sheerly funny *Ulysses* can be.) At the same time, as anyone who knows children will confirm, play is intensely serious work. What is at stake is nothing less than the desire to honour, to pay homage to the gods by imitating them, whatever form they might take: Cowboys and Indians, Superman, or Mother. Indeed, there is more than that at stake, for the other side of imitation is subversive parody: the need to kill the gods. You play 'Mother' in order to steal her power and thus dethrone her. Or, at least, to see what it would be like if only that were possible.

The 'Oxen of the Sun' episode can be read in this light. Joyce, now a reader of the literary tradition, is playing at writing: doing and being Shakespeare, Milton, Pepys, Swift, Carlyle, Newman. At the same time, by overdoing them, he is in effect undoing them. The chapter's reader too is enmeshed in the play of making and unmaking, for a whole set of recognitions is required. At the very least you must recognize that the styles keep changing, and that they follow each other in chronological order. The joke falls flat if you do not play your part. The game becomes an absurd solitaire. A close look at the episode and at some of the readings it has elicited will give a more precise sense of how, and why, *Ulysses* and notions of textuality have gravitated towards each other.

Dublin's Maternity Hospital: ten p.m. Stephen has been drinking with his cronies for most of the afternoon and is now mired in a boozy debate with a group of medical students on the subjects of conception, contraception, and abortion. He is reminded at various points of his own struggle to engender a new literary life. Soon after the chapter begins, Bloom comes in. He has survived the hour of assignation between Molly and Boylan (four o'clock), but he has not returned home. Most recently ('Nausicaa'), in imitation of the fireworks display at Sandymount Strand, he has relieved some of his feelings. Gerty MacDowell – a young woman he does not know – has conveniently arranged herself so that he can look up her skirt, and with this encouragement he masturbates. By the time he reaches the hospital he is spent and makes few incursions into the rowdy talk around him. In another room in the hospital

Mrs Purefoy labours hard and long to bring her child into the world. His birth is finally announced and soon afterwards Stephen and company go off to Burke's pub to prolong their drinking. Bloom hovers, paternal, close behind.

This sequence of events is simultaneously revealed and hidden by a series of narrative disguises that mimic English Literary History. The styles move forward in a chronological sequence leaving no identity stable in their wake. Bloom for instance is first gestured at as 'Some man that wayfaring was ... Of Israel's folk' (14.71–2), 'that man mildhearted' (14.80), 'The man that was come in to the house' (14.111), then named as 'the traveller Leopold' (14.126), 'childe Leopold' (14.160), 'Sir Leopold' (14.169–70), each sighting caught up in a viscous 'linguicity' that makes it incompatible with the one that precedes it – or follows. 'And sir Leopold that was the goodliest guest that ever sat in scholars' hall and that was the meekest man and the kindest that ever laid husbandly hand under hen and that was the very truest knight of the world one that ever did minion service to lady gentle' (14.182–5) becomes, after various transformations, 'Calmer' explaining thunder to 'Young Boasthard' (Stephen) as 'a hubbub of Phenomenon' (14.436), and 'Leop. Bloom of Crawford's journal sitting snug with a covey of wags' (14.504–5). Later he stands accused as 'this traitor to his kind ... [who] trembled for the security of his four per cents ... [A] deluder of others ... [A] censor of morals, a very pelican in his piety, who did not scruple, oblivious of the ties of nature, to attempt illicit intercourse with a female domestic drawn from the lowest strata of society!' (14.910–23). The indictment goes on. He 'is at his best an exotic tree which, when rooted in its native orient, throve and flourished ... but, transplanted to a clime more temperate, its roots have lost their quondam vigour while the stuff that comes away from it is stagnant, acid and inoperative' (14.937–41). But then, 'No longer is Leopold ... that staid agent of publicity and holder of a modest substance in the funds ... He is young Leopold ... That young figure of then is seen, pre-cociously manly, walking ... to the high school, his booksatchel on him ban-dolierwise' (14.1041–7). And so it goes, in constant flux, until the 'dear sir' invited to have a drink in Burke's ('Yous join uz?'), asks for 'ginger cordial', and is described by a medley of voices in terms that cast him as Hamlet's mur-dered and heartsick father. (The conversation recalls a bee-sting for which Dixon, one of the medical students, had treated him.) 'Got a pectoral trauma, eh, Dix? Pos fact. Got bet be a boomblebee whenever he wus settin sleepin in hes bit garten' (14.1472–3). Between the brackets of patriarch and baby, he is documented as Jew, self-employed, father of Milly, and bereaved friend: 'no fake, old man Leo ... Vel ... if that aint a sheeny nachez, vel, I vil get misha mishinnah ... [T]he Bloom toff ... Bloo? Cadges ads. Photo's papli, by all that's gorgeous . . . Pold veg! Did ums blubble bigsplash crytears cos fren Padney was took off in black bag?' (14.1524–56). The last sighting is posed as a question (possibly Stephen's): 'Whisper, who the sooty hell's the Johnny in the black duds?' (14.1575). The answer given is no more conclusive, not only because it casts Bloom inappropriately as the arch-sinner/Jew but also because it identifies him with a wrathful God in a single ambivalent pronoun: 'Hush! Sinned against the light and even now that day is at hand when he shall come to judge the world by fire' (14.1575–7). Who is the (lower-case) 'he' who shall 'judge the world'? Surely not 'that man mildhearted' 'that was the meekest man and the kindest that ever laid husbandly hand under hen'.

I have quoted at great length to recall the peculiarities of this episode. By the time you reach 'Oxen of the Sun' you are more than halfway through *Ulysses*. You might even be inured to the lack of a consistent style or even a 'base' style from which the writing digresses and to which it returns. Still, this episode ups the ante very considerably, for it shifts from one style to another at a disconcerting pace. Every paragraph or two a new voice makes itself heard. In doing so, and more particularly in linking its formal preoccupations (the growth of a literary tradition) with the sequence of events I have outlined, it performs 'textually' in interesting ways.

However, 'Oxen of the Sun' has often been explained in terms strikingly opposed to those of 'text'. Not insignificantly, it has also been the episode that readers have been most likely to resist and to resent.

The first temptation is to argue that the formal obsessions of 'Oxen of the Sun' are brilliantly adapted to its subject matter. Month by month in the womb a foetus develops to maturity. Century by century, beginning in a murky chaos (for what could be more opaque than the Saxon and Latinate constructions of the opening pages) the styles of English prose move ever forward into the present. The metaphor is profoundly organic, suggesting that the development of writing is like the gestation and birth of a human being and, implicitly, that the logic of *Ulysses* is similarly and inexorably 'natural'.

One of the most remarkable documents in Joyce criticism, partly because its author was himself a distinguished poet, partly because it was the last thing he wrote before lapsing into schizophrenia and silence, and partly because it pursues its hypothesis of perfect mimetic form with such inexorable and unrelieved passion, is A. M. Klein's 1949 essay, 'The Oxen of the Sun'.[17] For Klein, even the number of clauses in a section, or the numerical position of words in a sentence, add up (quite literally) to the hidden numbers of embryological and evolutionary life. Other readers have been more temperate, but Klein's passion speaks to something important in *Ulysses*: the sheer power of its will to order – or rather the seductive force with which it invites readers to pursue correspondences, coincidences, metaphors of all kinds. In the case of 'Oxen of the Sun' the analogy between language and biology can be so persuasive that what might otherwise seem erratic is taken to confirm and even to refine the paradigm. Thus, for instance, Stuart Gilbert takes care of certain deviations from strict literary chronology with the assurance that the growth of an embryo is not uniform either – that an eye, for example, 'may develop out of its term'.[18] The question remains of course whether the identification of particular styles with particular stages of foetal development does not push the concept of imitative form over the brink, into absurdity. As another of Joyce's early readers puts it: 'For what organic reason, if any, must Lyly represent the foetus in the third month, and Goldsmith in the sixth? And what's Bunyan to Mrs Purefoy, or Mrs Purefoy to Junius?'[19]

'Oxen of the Sun' is clearly a bravura performance of some kind. Perhaps what it represents though is not so much a history (whether biological or literary) as a moment of exhilaration and power on the part of its author. In this reading of the episode the argument shifts from a poetic fascination with metaphor to a novelistic focus on point of view, on the site of utterance, if you will, that organizes the pastiche of styles into a straight line with itself at the end: the point above and beyond all the others that is both a culmination and a point of origins. Anthony Burgess speaks with a fellow writer's admiration when he says that of all the episodes in *Ulysses* this is the one he would most like to have written: 'It is an author's chapter, a dazzling and authoritative display of what English can do. Moreover, it is a fulfilment of every author's egotistical desire not merely to *add* to English literature but to *enclose* what is actually there.' 'But', he adds – and it is a significant 'but' – 'it is a pity that Stephen and Bloom have to get lost in the process of glorifying an art that is supposed to be their servant.'[20] Writing as the site of mastery and servitude: is 'Oxen of the Sun' then a misconceived grab at power, as Burgess implies, or a much more deliberate challenge to what is 'supposed' to be? If Joyce is rewriting in the long line of literary history to show that he can more than do it all, that he can be Author of Authors, why are the imitations so uneven? Some scenes bear the master-mimic's touch: the Swiftean account of the Irish bull in an English china shop (14.578–650), or Mulligan as 'le Fécondateur' and a Sterne-like Lynch (coyly tongue in cheek) discussing the French fashion for cloaks that keep 'a lady from wetting' (14.738–98). Other parodies are less convincing. The Dickensian moment, for instance, is so skewed that without the giveaway 'Doady' and the artful naming of all the babies after Dickens's own children you might well think yourself in a pulp-fiction interlude (14.1310–23). Clearly the advantage of privileging a perspective of 'Joyce the Prodigy' is that it organizes the multiple voices of this episode into the line of history that culminates in *Ulysses*. It also situates you, the reader, in a stable (and safe) place of admiration. But if you adopt this perspective you might have to admit, at some point, that Joyce was not quite the prodigy he claims or is claimed to be and that the chapter is an embarrassing lapse.

A textual reading, on the other hand, does not necessarily centre or stabilize the episode – either through an authorial (and loosely novelistic) point of view, or on a metaphor (loosely poetic) of organic life. Instead, it acknowledges that something disturbing is happening to the relationship between writing and the world it aims – perhaps – to represent. The cumulative effect is of seeing things at various removes, rather like the series of translations that renders the cat's 'Mrkrgnao' in 'Calypso' into a reminder of textual displacement and instability. Knowing something about the stages of composition for the chapter reinforces this impression, for Joyce's sources were less often the originals themselves than mediating texts like Peacock's selection of prose excerpts from Mandeville to Ruskin, and Saintsbury's *A History of English Prose Rhythms*, full of useful if unintended pointers to the would-be mimic.[21] Notably, drafts of the first long paragraph changed it from a fairly straight copy of Tacitus to something much closer to pastiche. A textual reading, attuned to the decentring play of languages, aligns itself with a reader in motion: not a fixed and discrete entity but a moving part of the textual machinery. More specifically in 'Oxen of the Sun' it rereads the central metaphor of birth to suggest that the reader is like Mrs Purefoy or like any woman in labour – her identity temporarily suspended and bound up in another's (the unborn child's, the text's), itself also amorphous and incomplete – thrust forward by an irrevocable logic toward 'the utterance of the word' (14.1390).

Paradoxically, but typically for *Ulysses*, the attempt to gain control, to put the various languages in their place, opens a Pandora's box of complicating and destabilizing pressures. Faced with the gaps between each style and the one that follows, you make a bridge by appealing to literary history. But every time you recall a pre-text a new gap opens up, this time between the imitation (which is often deliberately 'off' and keeps you at a distance), and the original it invokes (which draws you in, by memory, to an entire fictional world). But since the degree of parodic distortion changes at every turn, every new quotation makes you lose your footing in a new way. The episode is further complicated because not only the Joycean text shifts ground – so does each pre-text invoked by memory as it inscribes a different distance to the reader and to the fictional world. 'Pepys's' language, for example (14.474–528), might seem the spontaneous expression of reality, rendering words transparent and the reader invisible. 'Swift's' positions you in quite a different way, demanding your intervention as decoder. It makes it obvious that the relationship between words and meanings is not direct – that the story it tells of Lord Harry, farmer Nicholas, and the gelded bull (14.578–646) requires interpretation back into a narrative of Ireland's long love affair with the Church. Reading 'Oxen of the Sun' you are in a kaleidoscopic space where every 'shake' of the writing creates a new cluster of relationships between language and its origins, language and its reference, language and its interpreter.

I have suggested that the episode plays an interesting game with its own authority. It plays, too, with the point of closure toward which every new parody seems to move as the line of literary history comes forward into the present. Play is distinguished from work because it is energy expended for its own sake. There is no ulterior motive. No pay-off is expected. In this sense at least reading 'Oxen of the Sun' can only be playful, for meaning (the hermeneutic pay-off) and closure (the plot's reward) are both promised and denied. Things certainly seem more intelligible as you progress toward the present but you do not simply move out of the murk of early time into a final clarity. At a certain point – ironically after 'the utterance of the Word' – the writing reverts to opacity. The last pages are among the most difficult in *Ulysses*. Obviously the verbal confusion matches the increasing drunkenness of Stephen and his friends. (The fact that Stephen spends so much of his wages on this day on drinks for himself and others carries its own historic and political burden.)[22] But the claim of mimesis does not answer the main question: why plot a history that returns to murky chaos?

The final pages play on the reader's sense of an ending as the call of closure for those in the pub is heard through the raucous blend of voices. 'Keep a watch on the clock. Chuckingout time . . . Ten to . . . Closingtime, gents . . . Time, gents . . . Time all . . . Night. Night' (14.1452–3, 1471, 1534, 1544, 1561–3). The last paragraph, as we have seen, announces the apocalypse: '. . . even now that day is at hand when he shall come to judge the world by fire . . . *Ut implerentur scripturae*' – that the scriptures might be fulfilled (14.1576–7). The hotgospelling diatribe that follows pulls out all the stops, invoking the prophetic entrance of Elijah (Matthew 17:9–11), the blood of the Lamb (Revelation 7:14 and 5:6–8), and the final gathering in of sinners that marks the Day of Judgement:

> Elijah is coming! Washed in the blood of the Lamb. Come on you winefizzling, ginsizzling, booseguzzling existences! Come on, you dog-gone, bullnecked, beetlebrowed, hogjowled, peanutbrained, weaseleyed fourflushers . . .! Come on . . .! Alexander J Christ Dowie, that's my name, that's yanked to glory most half this planet from Frisco beach to Vladivostock. The Deity aint no nickel dime bumshow . . . He's the grandest thing yet and don't you forget it. Shout salvation in King Jesus. (14.1580–8)

But this is a mock apocalypse. The second coming is utterly carnivalized; the revelation at the end is denied. And while the final verses of the Book of Revelation promise the quenching of thirst by the word of God, the Dubliners' indulgence in drink has quite another effect: writing is not so much fulfilled as thrust forward in its opaque materiality.

In its final gesture, the episode moves away from Stephen and Bloom. The closing paragraph says very little about them (except by suggesting that Bloom is the occasion for Elijah's second coming – but then, has he really sinned against the light?). They disappear until some pages later in the next chapter when Stephen, announced as 'the parson' and *'flourishing the ash-plant in his left hand,'* crosses the stage followed by Bloom *'flushed, panting, cramming bread and chocolate into a sidepocket'* (15.67–73, 142–3). Something has happened at Westland Row Station, but neither 'Oxen of the Sun' nor 'Circe' chooses to reveal what it is – just as, in the other major plot of *Ulysses* (the one involving Bloom, Molly, and Boylan), the crucial moments between man and woman are not given. The closest you get to the assignation at four is Bloom's masochistic fantasy in 'Circe' and Molly's partial reprise in 'Penelope'. And as for its repercussions on the marriage, so little is said between husband and wife that readers continue to argue over what it all means. If Molly brings Bloom his breakfast in bed the next morning, does this mean (as some have argued) that she has learned her lesson and is restored to domestic happiness? Or does it rather mean that, like so many of her fellow Dubliners in *Ulysses*, she has misconstrued the words of another and heard only what she was ready to hear: 'breakfast in bed' (18.2) instead of Bloom's 'roc's auk's egg' (17.2328–9) murmured as he slips into sleep?

In 'Oxen of the Sun' the question of meaning is even more radically at issue because it is not simply a case of leaving certain events out of the narrative. Rather, the very possibility of making something present in language is subverted – comically so, for instance, in the account of the bull of Ireland and his seduction of every 'maid, wife, abbess and widow':

> and the end [of the story] was that the men of the island . . . made a wherry raft, loaded themselves and their bundles of chattels on shipboard, set all masts erect, manned the yards, sprang their luff, heaved to, spread three sheets in the wind, put her head between wind and water, weighed anchor, ported her helm, ran up the jolly Roger, gave three times three, let the bullgine run, pushed off in their bumboat and put to sea to recover the main of America. (14.639–46)

There is such sheer exuberance in the writing: but to what effect? Instead of each additional phrase enhancing the mimetic power of language (as each additional brush stroke on a canvas might increase your illusion of 'the real'), the accumulation of phrases is such that language itself is reified, and meaning (i.e. the thing 'out there' that language points to) recedes into the background. Before they even get out of the harbour, the men of Ireland capsize in a full sea of words. You may or may not agree with Burgess's rueful judgement that 'it is a pity that Stephen and Bloom have to get lost in the process of glorifying an art that is supposed to be their servant': he is nevertheless right to see that the expected hierarchy between words and a fictional world has been overturned. Closing time in 'Oxen of the Sun' discloses the loud and empty rhetoric of salvation – a twist on the biblical Elijah who learns that God's rule is established in a 'still, small voice' (I Kings 19:12). Perhaps, after *A Portrait of the Artist*, Joyce no longer sees himself as a kind of God, aloof, detached from his handiwork, paring his fingernails, and capable of revealing the world in all its meaning. The 'author' that seems to speak in 'Oxen of the Sun' is strangely unauthoritative – not so much a Joyce who parodies the past to proclaim his superiority, as a Joyce who involves the reader in the dilemma of language, and who is himself, like his characters and his readers, dispersed in language. Roland Barthes's account of textuality and its strategy of quotation is most appropriate to this episode. A multivalent text, he writes,

> can carry out its basic duplicity only if it subverts the opposition between true and false, if it fails to attribute quotations . . . to explicit authorities, if it flouts all respect for origin, paternity, propriety, if it destroys the voice which could give the text its ('organic') unity . . . For multivalence . . . is a transgression of ownership.[23]

'Oxen of the Sun' speaks for the text/*Ulysses* in a number of ways. It plays on the themes of closure and disclosure but at the end of the line reveals very little, shifting its attention (and that of its readers) from the signified to the signifier. We are refused that moment of clear vision, 'as though face to face', promised by Revelation. The episode tries out style after style, discarding each in turn, never allowing one to take more than temporary precedence over another, and keeping its readers, always, off balance. And because there is no single language that provides and authorizes a meaning (neither one of the voices of the past nor the voice of Joyce standing above his creation), meaning can only be relational, produced in the spaces between languages – in their play. Most pointedly, however, by its impertinent manhandling of other writing (impertinent in the double sense: both cheeky and, variously, inappropriate or inaccurate), 'Oxen of the Sun' transgresses the principle of ownership on which both poetic and novelistic readings depend. The one assumes that all the elements in a literary work – however complex and paradoxical – ultimately cohere in a formal and thematic unity that the reader must discover. The other (in some ways only a more particular version of the first) assumes that the privileged unifying force is the human voice and individual psychology. To read *Ulysses* as a novel is to ask, at every turn, 'who speaks?' and, beyond that, 'what do these words say about the one who "owns" them?' To read *Ulysses* as a text is to be not a little perverse and focus instead on the places where connections come unstuck and the weaving frays, because it is precisely at such points that the playfulness of the text implicates the reader and allows itself to be seen.

'Oxen of the Sun', like *Ulysses*, is a contested terrain on which poetic, novelistic, and textual readings stake their claims. It offers ambitious answers to questions of formal and thematic unity. (Human, linguistic, and aesthetic life are all subsumed under an organic metaphor of growth and birth.) It sheds its kaleidoscopic light on Stephen and Bloom at a key moment in their (unwitting) search for each other, and with a crazy, strobe-light intensity that simultaneously illuminates and distorts, speeds up and slows down, it embeds them in a sharply observed social world. (Part of the fun of the episode is recognizing the players behind the rhetorical veils.) It also turns on itself, like Penelope's web, to unravel those illusions of originality, authority, and authorship, and to jostle those places of identity, upon which 'Literature' traditionally rests.

NOTES

1 '*Ulysses*, Order and Myth', *Dial* 75 (November 1923), 480–3; rpt. *CH I* 268–71.
2 Hugh Kenner makes a similar point in his *Ulysses* (Baltimore: Johns Hopkins University Press, rev. edn, 1987), p. 28. Based on deep absorption and recall of Joyce's work, Kenner's study is full of insight.
3 *James Joyce's Ulysses* (London: Faber, 1930).
4 For a reading that works centrally with Linati's schema, see Richard Ellmann, *Ulysses on the Liffey* (London: Faber, 1970).
5 See, for example, William M. Schutte, *Joyce and Shakespeare: A Study in the Meaning of 'Ulysses'* (New Haven: Yale University Press, 1957), Mary T. Reynolds, *Joyce and Dante: The Shaping Imagination* (Princeton: Princeton University Press, 1981), and Jennifer Fraser, *Rite of Passage in the Narratives of Joyce and Dante* (Gainesville: University Press of Florida, 2002).
6 For a comprehensive guide to Joyce on the web, including discussion groups, electronic journals, websites, library collections, etc., see *Flying by the Net: James Joyce in Cyberspace*: http://publish.uwo.ca/~mgroden/flying1.html. See also Michael Groden's ongoing project to create a hypermedia version of *Ulysses*: http://publish.uwo.ca/~mgroden/ulysses. One of the questions hypermedia models will have to contend with is this: does a technology that potentially bypasses the

delays, frustrations, and mistakes built into the pre-electronic *Ulysses* rob readers of a crucial literary experience: the sense that understanding (and misunderstanding) unfold in real, lived time? Patience may not be 'all', as Hamlet claims, but it might well be a mistake to dismiss it altogether. Sometimes, as *Ulysses* demonstrates, it is good to wait.

7 A convenient and useful reference work is Don Gifford, *'Ulysses' Annotated* (Berkeley: University of California Press, 1989). See also Weldon Thornton's *Allusions in 'Ulysses'* (Chapel Hill: University of North Carolina Press, 1961). (Both works, of course, also refer to literary contexts.)

8 For the full text of the lyrics, see Thornton, pp. 501–3, or Ruth Bauerle, ed., *The James Joyce Songbook* (New York and London: Garland, 1982), pp. 269–70. Bauerle adds a useful note on Joyce's views regarding performance: the singer must give as much weight to the ensnaring British soldier as to his Irish victim.

9 Postcard dated 5 January 1920, from Trieste (*Letters I* 135). Ellmann reports that Joyce 'had asked for the same information in another card a month or two earlier' (*JJ* 785).

10 See, for example, Clive Hart and Leo Knuth, *A Topographical Guide to James Joyce's 'Ulysses'* (Colchester: A Wake Newslitter Press, 1975), and Jack McCarthy, *Joyce's Dublin: A Walking Guide to 'Ulysses'* (Dublin: Wolfhound Press, 1986).

11 For a very useful account of Dublin English, see Anthony Burgess, *Joysprick: An Introduction to the Language of James Joyce* (London: André Deutsch, 1973), in particular ch. 2, 'The Dublin Sound'.

12 The translator is Giulio de Angelis, whose comment, cited by Sidney Alexander, is noted by Fritz Senn in 'Book of Many Turns', in Thomas F. Staley, ed., *'Ulysses': Fifty Years* (Bloomington: Indiana University Press, 1972), p. 46.

13 The difficulties *Ulysses* poses for translators, and the insights that their labours can provide, have been brilliantly explored by Fritz Senn; see chs. 1–3 of his *Joyce's Dislocutions: Essays on Reading as Translation*, ed. John Paul Riquelme (Baltimore: Johns Hopkins University Press, 1984).

14 Robert Boyle, S. J., 'Miracle in Black Ink: A Glance at Joyce's Use of his Eucharistic Image', in Staley, *'Ulysses': Fifty Years*, p. 47.

15 *Collected Essays*, 1 (London: Hogarth Press, 1966), p. 324.

16 For a concise presentation of the notion of 'text', see Roland Barthes, 'From Work to Text', in *Image-Music-Text*, ed. Stephen Heath (Glasgow: Collins/Fontana, 1977), pp. 155–64.

17 *Here and Now* 1, no. 3 (January 1949), 28–48.

18 *James Joyce's 'Ulysses'*, p. 293.

19 Harry Levin, *James Joyce: A Critical Introduction* (London: Faber, 1944; rev. edn, 1960), p. 95.

20 *Re Joyce* (New York: Norton, 1968), p. 156. Published in Britain as *Here Comes Everybody: An Introduction to James Joyce for the Ordinary Reader* (London: Faber, 1965).

21 See J. S. Atherton, 'The Oxen of the Sun', in Clive Hart and David Hayman, eds., *'Ulysses': Critical Essays* (Berkeley: University of California Press, 1974), p. 315.

22 On the relationship between drinking and more general questions of consumption, modernization, and nationalism in Joyce's Dublin, see for example Paul Delany, '"Tailors of Malt, Hot, All Round": Homosocial Consumption in *Dubliners*', *Studies in Short Fiction* 32 (1995), 381–98, and David Lloyd, 'Counterparts: *Dubliners*, masculinity, and temperance nationalism', in *Semicolonial Joyce*, ed. Derek Attridge and Marjorie Howes (Cambridge: Cambridge University Press, 2000), pp. 128–49.

23 *S/Z*, tr. Richard Howard (New York: Hill and Wang, 1974), pp. 44–5.

8

MARGOT NORRIS

Finnegans Wake

The matter of (with) *Finnegans Wake*

riverrun, past Eve and Adam's, from swerve of shore to bend of bay, brings us
by a commodius vicus of recirculation back to Howth Castle and Environs.

Thus begins James Joyce's last work, figuratively and thematically in mid-
stream. The sinuous sentence, the swerving phrase, continues a journey: by
water, by bodily fluid, by verbal fluency. If we, the readers, are encompassed
in the ambiguous 'brings us', then we can begin to understand why the voice
of that opening sounds so like the narration of a tour guide. For we have no
way of knowing where we, as readers, are situated in this opening. Are we
on a boat in the river Liffey in Dublin, or are we inside a human body; are we
at the beginning of time, or in the eternal present of every human utterance?
The opening of *Finnegans Wake* drops us, without map, clock, compass,
glossary, or footnotes, into an unknown verbal country, and the voice of the
tour guide, alas, speaks their language rather than ours, although we catch
enough cognates to keep from drowning altogether in that verbal stream.
The role of that tour guide is, in a sense, duplicated by the enterprise of this
essay. Surely, no other existing literary work needs a 'guide' more sorely than
James Joyce's *Finnegans Wake*, with its strange language, its neologisms, its
generic ambiguity, the obscurity of its allusions, the mysterious status of its
speech.[1]

The most helpful service a guide to *Finnegans Wake* might seem to offer
would be to tell readers what the text is 'about'. But one of the many peculiarities of *Finnegans Wake* is that its content, what it is 'about', is indivisible
from its form, from the language in which it is told. 'His writing is not *about*
something; *it is that something itself*', Samuel Beckett wrote in an early essay
on the unfinished *Finnegans Wake*, then entitled 'Work in Progress' (Beckett,
Our Exagmination, p. 14). By way of analogy, consider the disservice of the
art critic who helps spectators understand a cubist painting by retrieving for
them the residue of visible representation, the guitar and the bunch of grapes

on the table, for example, and then encourages them to speculate on what the guitar, grapes, and table *mean*. Clearly something far more important is at stake in the cubist painting's distortion of representation, its spatial derangement, the play of textures, and the fragmentation of the spectator's point of view, than the significance of the objects that are represented. Cubist painting is not about goods and furniture, but about the relationship between media and the phenomenon of seeing.[2] Likewise, *Finnegans Wake* might be said to be 'about' not being certain what it is about: its subject is the nature of indeterminacy itself.

The indeterminacy of *Finnegans Wake* is created by the strange ontological conditions the work explores, particularly dreaming and dying, conditions that call the being of the self, and self-identity, into radical question. In dreaming, you no longer know who you are because you do not know if you are the self who thinks conscious thoughts, or the self who produces the strange, distorted, alien images of your dreams revealing that you know things you did not know you knew. In dying, you no longer know whether you are a being or a potential nothingness, and you are obliged to consider, while still in existence, what you will be when you cease to exist.

These cosmic indeterminacies of identity take the form in *Finnegans Wake* of an insistent questioning of everything throughout the text. Nearly every major chapter of the *Wake* is organized around an investigation, a trial, a quiz, a riddle, an inquisition, or some other state of uncertain knowing, that the reader must then duplicate in trying to make sense of the text. The questions seem to pursue problems of identity, as though the dreaming mind were trying to understand who or what it is by remembering and reliving what it desired, what it has done, and how it was judged. The quest for identity therefore tends to become a search for origins. The emotional impulses of dreams, while triggered by recent events and thoughts, must be sought, according to Freud, in forgotten or repressed childhood memories. The questing in *Finnegans Wake*, tracking identities to their sources, therefore takes on a historical character, both in an individual sense, as a return to childhood curiosity, desire, and games, and in a collective sense, as a 'memory' of historical and cultural events. The sons, for example, search for the secret of their identity in the hidden place in their mother's body that was their infantile home, 'the whome of your eternal geomater' (296.35), while their psychological struggles with their father take on historical form as famous military engagements, for example, the battle between Napoleon and Wellington rendered as a comical tour of the Wellington museum ('the Willingdone Museyroom') – 'This is the triplewon hat of Lipoleum. Tip. Lipoleumhat. This is the

Willingdone on his same white harse, the Cokenhape' (8.15) (Wellington's white horse was named Copenhagen). Because the dreaming mind can tap all the history, mythology, literature, and culture it has ever known, *Finnegans Wake* contains an enormous range of historical and cultural allusion that is disorganized, jumbled, and unimportant in itself, but very interesting for the way it assimilates to personal obsession and recapitulates personal experience.

Something like characters and something like narratives do emerge from the reading of *Finnegans Wake*, but it is difficult to be certain just how we learn about them. This partially reflects the way dream elements tend to be overdetermined. Because a dream is trying to tell the self things it does not want to know – its own guilty desires, for example – the dream's message must be indirect and takes disguised form as a kind of code. The difficulty and obscurity of the *Wake* text is therefore meant to baffle the dreamer rather than the reader. But to make itself understood at all, the text relies on endless repetition of its coded messages. Thus the names of the characters emerge slowly, tentatively, and *literally* in bits and pieces – that is, as initials or abbreviations. The figure of the father, for example, emerges as HCE (Humphrey Chimpden Earwicker, we eventually learn, or perhaps Harold Chimpden Earwicker), embedded in phrases that themselves contribute to our understanding of his place, work, familial functions, and the like: Howth Castle and Environs (3.03), hod, cement, and edifices (4.26), Haroun Childeric Eggeberth (4.32), happinest childher everwere (11.15), homerigh, castle, and earthenhouse (21.13), Humme the Cheapner, Esc (29.18).

Critics over time reduced the confusion of Wakean character identity by using little signs, called sigla (see the footnote about 'The Doodles family, ⫟, △, ⊣, ×, □, ∧, [' on 299 in 11.2), that Joyce used in his working copies of the text in order to keep track of the different figures, to produce a sort of cast of characters. They include members of a family – father HCE, mother (ALP or Anna Livia Plurabelle), the twin sons Shem and Shaun, and the daughter Isabel or Issy – and their immediate society: two old domestic servants, a charwoman named Kate and an older manservant, four old men, and twelve pub customers. These figures are associated with certain recurring functions in the works: the father is fallen; the mother tries to save him; the twin sons fight each other, and, united, fight the father; the daughter, when not self-absorbed, comments wryly on the antics of the family; the four old men dispense wisdom; and the twelve customers in the pub criticize and gossip. But these identities are difficult to sustain during the actual reading of the text because the figures have many associative identities and functions, including mythical analogues from the Bible, Irish mythology, classical mythology, political history, opera, and literature. They are also identified with the geography of Ireland – HCE is the land of Dublin, ALP is the river Liffey that runs through it – and features of nature and landscape: Shem is tree, Shaun is stone, and Issy is a little cloud that has not yet become a river like her mother. Their relationships nonetheless appear to be dramatic: the father may desire the daughter, the sons may have caused the father's downfall, the mother may procure younger women for the father in an effort to restore his potency, the family and customers may have produced the father's fall purely with rumours and gossip.

But the story of this family does not unfold in an orderly, linear plot. Instead, there are family 'plots', as it were, dispersed among hundreds of little scenes, stories, fables, dialogues, anecdotes, songs, rumours, and plays, that are often versions of one another, and that are all versions of the same family conflicts. The wild incongruity of these vignettes and the sense of narrative excess they produce – as though we get too many stories with too many versions ('There extand by now one thousand and one stories, all told, of the same' (5.28)) – give the text much of its rollicking humour. They include, among many others, the tale of the prankquean who kidnaps Jarl van Hoother's children because he fails to guess her riddle; the writing of a funny but scurrilous ballad about improprieties HCE supposedly committed in Phoenix Park; an analysis of a smudged letter ALP, as a hen, apparently found in the dump; the triangle of Anthony, Caesar, and Cleopatra retold as the story of butter, cheese, and margarine; the image of Shem, the artist, as a stinking lowlife holed up in a house called 'The Haunted Inkbottle'; children's sexual games at twilight told in the trope of flower pollination; the story of how Buckley shot the Russian General in the Crimean war; four old men watching the lovemaking first of Tristan and Isolde, and later of HCE and ALP in their marriage bed; a hilariously sacrilegious version of the *via crucis* (Christ's stations of the cross as he wends his way to his crucifixion), enacted by an obese, lecherous, and hypocritical Shaun; and the haunting swan song of ALP as, dying, she flows out to sea to rejoin her father, the wild ocean.

Each of these stories or tales or vignettes has its own narrative functions and stylistic charms. For example, one of the most delightful versions of the brothers' quarrel, the fable of the Ondt and the Gracehoper, is meant to function like a gospel parable excoriating the happy-go-lucky, feckless artist in favor of his thrifty, industrious twin. As the starving Gracehoper approaches the Ondt, presumably hoping for grace and money, he finds the fat, happy insect opulently esconced amid a ministering harem of female insects (Floh = flea, Luse = louse, Bieni = bee, Vespatilla = wasp):

Behailed His Gross the Ondt, prostrandvorous upon his dhrone, in his Papylonian babooshkees, smolking a spatial brunt of Hosana cigals, . . . as appi as a oneysucker or a baskerboy on the Libido, with Floh biting his leg thigh and Luse lugging his luff leg and Bieni bussing him under his bonnet and Vespatilla blowing cosy fond tutties up the allabroad length of the large of his smalls. (417.10–20)

No wonder this insect intimacy ('As entomate as intimate could pinchably be') makes the Gracehoper 'aguepe with ptschjelasys', or agape with jealousy. The passage illustrates how Joyce effects overdetermination with 'portmanteau' words (introduced in Lewis Carroll's 'Jabberwocky') – for example, 'dhrone' as a throne for a drone. It also includes clever literary and musical allusions: for example, to the hookah-smoking caterpillar of *Alice in Wonderland* (although the Ondt smokes celebratory (Hosana) Havana cigars, or a French *cigale* or cicada); and to the amorous affairs (cosy fond tutties) of Mozart's *Cosi Fan Tutte*. The telling of the fable, then, does not just point a moral; it expresses, subjectively, what the painful lesson feels like by using the very funny sensuality of the scene to sharpen the Gracehoper's sense of deprivation and frustration. It also explores the enmity and grievances of brothers with very different temperaments, making it difficult for critics to resist seeing the fable as a parody of the exasperation of the thrifty and responsible Stanislaus Joyce with his profligate brother James.

The dreaming text: 'Anna Livia Plurabelle'

Before going on to give the production history of *Finnegans Wake*, it might be useful to explore how a *Wake* chapter is created – not textually, how it is written, but imaginatively, how it was conceived. The last chapter of Book I, the 'Anna Livia Plurabelle' chapter, is considered the most beautiful and the most famous section of *Finnegans Wake*. This is a chapter narrated as a conversation between two gossipy washerwomen doing laundry on the banks of the river Liffey, which runs through Dublin. They gossip about Anna Livia Plurabelle and her husband, who has been indicted in some scandal, and as they delve into ALP's past, they also recount the course of the river Liffey, from its origin as a rivulet in the Wicklow Mountains, accumulating freight and debris as the woman accumulates lovers, responsibilities, and junk, until, laden with filth and life's griefs, she widens, at her delta, back out to the sea. Where did Joyce get the idea to write a chapter like this, and how is he able, technically, to give it its effects?

The anecdotal history of this chapter reveals how Joyce created a set of experiential fictions about its genesis that conceal his structural devices in order to promote its reading as poetry, as lyric. Joyce betrayed to an Italian journalist the controlling metaphor of the chapter, the woman as river:

> They say I have immortalized Svevo, but I've also immortalized the tresses of Signora Svevo. These were long and reddish-blond. My sister who used to see them let down told me about them. The river at Dublin passes dye-houses and so has reddish water. So I have playfully compared these two things in the book I'm writing. (*JJ* 561)

But it is worth noting that Joyce's experience is not *seeing* the tresses of Livia (ALP's middle name) Schmitz but rather *hearing* his sister describe them – so that his voyeurism is mediated by the female voice – 'was she marcellewaved or was it weirdly a wig she wore' (204.23). The sister was presumably Eileen Joyce, who lived with the Joyces in Trieste, and who might have described the beauty of Livia Schmitz's hair not to Joyce, but to her sister Eva, thus perhaps creating for him the interlocutory structure of the chapter: that of a male eavesdropping on the gossip of two women discussing another of their sex. 'O tell me all about Anna Livia! I want to hear all about Anna Livia. Well, you know Anna Livia? Yes, of course, we all know Anna Livia. Tell me all. Tell me now. You'll die when you hear' (196.01–6). The gossip of the washerwomen is never allowed to form a coherent story, however, because the red-haired woman they talk about keeps dissolving into the river: the waves of her hair become the waves of the water ('First she let her hair fal and down it flussed to her feet its teviots winding coils' (206.29–30)); her freckles the dappled light on the water surface ('why in the flenders was she frickled' (204.22–3); her dress the topological features of the water and its surrounding land ('a sugarloaf hat with a gaudyquiviry peak and a band of gorse for an arnoment and a hundred streamers dancing off it' (208.7–9); and her possessions and gifts the flotsam and jetsam riding the seafoam (German: Meerschaum) of her tides ('she raabed and reach out her maundy meerschaundize, poor souvenir . . . and wickerpotluck for each of them' (210.1–6)).

In another anecdotal confidence, Joyce once said that the structuring idea for the chapter was inspired by women washing clothes on both banks of the river Eure, whom he saw on a trip to Chartres (*JJ* 563). Joyce was no doubt delighted and moved by the washerwomen doing their laundry on the banks of the Eure. But the anecdote, with its fiction of a spontaneous and experiential source for the writing of 'Anna Livia Plurabelle', nonetheless serves to retard and divert our recollection that Joyce had written about washerwomen before in the *Dubliners* story 'Clay'. And, indeed, if we compare the two representations of washerwomen, in the ALP chapter and in 'Clay', we can see an intricately inverted structural relationship between them. 'Clay' introduces the washerwomen when they are finished with their washing: 'In a few minutes the women began to come in by twos and threes, wiping their steaming hands in their petticoats and pulling down the sleeves of their blouses over their red steaming arms' (*D* 77). All that is left of their laundering is the steam and the red of their arms and hands, before they pull their sleeves down and it is altogether effaced. *Finnegans Wake*, on the other hand, takes us behind the scene, as it were, and shows us what 'Clay' does not let us see and hear: what the washerwomen do and say when they work – literally and figuratively 'washing dirty linen in public'. The *Wake*'s washerwomen 'read' their laundry, drawing unflattering inferences from the stains, spots, and rips of the underwear of their clients, 'Look at the shirt of him! Look at the dirt of it! He has all my water black on me . . . I know by heart the places he likes to saale, duddurty devil!' (196.11–15). The washerwomen of 'Clay' probably talk about Maria behind her back, but because the story's narrator is so determined to put only the best face on Maria's environment, they are quickly dismissed as vulgar and unimportant, 'Mooney meant well though, of course, she had the notions of a common woman' (*D* 77). The washerwomen of 'Clay' are silenced except when quoted as singing Maria's praises.

Finnegans Wake takes what is background – or 'ground', in the way that term is used in visual representation – and transforms it into foreground or 'figure'. The washerwomen of *Finnegans Wake* are the figure that results from such a reversal, as *Finnegans Wake*, in a sense, turns 'Clay' inside out. The washerwomen's speech, repressed and silenced in 'Clay', is restored to the central narrative position as the dominant subjectivity of the ALP chapter. The thoughts, views, and expressiveness of the washerwomen is restored in the homely idiom and vulgar diction of their speech, 'Lordy, lordy, did she so? Well, of all the ones ever I heard! Throwing all the neiss little whores in the world at him!' (200.27–9). Their rhetorical function is reversed as well, as they now ferret out, and 'air', the little woman's secrets. However, ALP in the *Wake* benefits from the way dreams express wish-fulfilment: the virginal, loveless, childless little old maid in 'Clay' is transformed in 'Anna Livia Plurabelle' into the little wife with a generous sexual history and many children, the figurative 'proper mother' of 'Clay' ('– Mamma is mamma but Maria is my proper mother' (*D* 77)) turned into the literal mother of a nearly countless brood in *Finnegans Wake*. It is as though *Finnegans Wake* dramatizes the hidden wishes and fears of Maria in 'Clay', things the text of 'Clay' *knew* but could not tell us. 'Clay' describes Maria's homely little body dressed in chaste, drab garb; 'the diminutive body which she had so often adorned'

(D 78) is ironically quite *unadorned*, the narrative verb notwithstanding. But *Finnegans Wake* reverses this description as if to gratify the woman's hidden desire for adornment in 'Clay', and the diminutive body of ALP is described in the *Wake* as elaborately bathed ('Then, mothernaked, she sampood herself with galawater and fraguant pistania mud' (206.30–1)), bejewelled ('Then she made her bracelets and her anklets and her armlets and a jetty amulet for necklace of clicking cobbles and pattering pebbles' (207.4–6)), and painted, 'a dawk of smut to her airy ey' and 'the lellipos cream to her lippeleens and the pick of the paintbox for her pommettes' (207.8–10). Maria's nondescript garb becomes on ALP the most outlandish costume in the world, as the little woman who, in her mousiness, is nearly invisible in 'Clay' is transformed into a gaudy, ridiculous, but decidedly eye-catching spectacle in *Finnegans Wake*.

The experiential fiction, that Joyce created 'Anna Livia Plurabelle' out of Chartrean washerwomen and Livia Schmitz's hair, lends the text a spontaneity that conceals the way he is manipulating, reversing, and inverting his own earlier textual material. Joyce thereby creates an oneiric verisimilitude, an illusion that the text is, as it were, dreamt, and that Joyce has himself absorbed and dissolved experience into the unconscious linguistic plenitude of his mind and, in a sense, 'dreamt' *Finnegans Wake*. The fiction of a text created spontaneously and in an *ad hoc* fashion, that is, written in the same way dreams are constructed, out of the transmutation of bits and pieces of experience and memory, was actively fostered by Joyce. He argued to Arthur Power that emotional, not intellectual, factors propelled his writing – 'Emotion has dictated the course and detail of my book, and in emotional writing one arrives at the unpredictable which can be of more value, since its sources are deeper, than the products of the intellectual method' (95) – and he described to Jacques Mercanton the serendipitous nature of his method, 'Chance furnishes me with what I need. I'm like a man who stumbles: my foot strikes something, I look down, and there is exactly what I'm in need of' (*JJ* 661). Archival research will no doubt continue to erode this fiction and suggest a far more deliberate procedure, but it will not alter the significance of Joyce's aim to disavow the rational writing, the puzzle-making construction, of his text. Joyce intended *Finnegans Wake*, I believe, to be 'the dream' of his earlier texts, as though his earlier texts contained hidden truths, secret feelings and desires, unconscious knowledge that the language 'contains' as possible interpretations, but that the narration itself, what the text 'says', does not articulate. *Finnegans Wake* in retrospect reveals the earlier text to have had an unconscious life (which we can equate with the potential of language), and which the *Wake* expresses or 'speaks', using the distorting, displacing, punning, poetic techniques of dream itself.

The writing history of *Finnegans Wake*

The enormous strangeness of *Finnegans Wake*, and the difficulty this creates for the reader, have tended to produce two very different responses that have shaped the controversies of its public reception. During the course of its writing as 'Work in Progress', conflicting attitudes towards the *Wake*'s obscurity determined both the defections and the conversions among Joyce's friends. In some readers and critics, *Finnegans Wake*'s difficulty inspires the desire to master its meaning, an impulse that may disguise the wish that *Finnegans Wake* were really tamer and more conventional than it appears to be. But other readers and critics hail *Finnegans Wake*'s experimentalism and are delighted to treat it as an avant-garde work celebrating a revolution in modern language and literature. Such readers are content to accept the *Wake* as impossible to master or fully grasp, and the text's 'unreadability' becomes for them not an obstacle, but a cause for appreciation. In the 1980s, this approach regained some prominence, as *Finnegans Wake* was assimilated to post-modern literature and the theoretical interest it has generated. A brief account of the composition history, and, in the next section, the critical history of *Finnegans Wake*, will reveal the workings of these two tendencies in the way the aims and strategies of *Finnegans Wake* were reconstructed and assessed.

Joyce began writing *Finnegans Wake* early in 1923. His preparatory moves in December of 1922 included sorting out old notes for *Ulysses*, and Joyce claimed that the *unused* notes alone weighed twelve kilos! (*JJ* 545). This suggests, along with the evidence of the Buffalo Notebook VI. A (edited by Thomas E. Connolly as the 'Scribbledehobble' notebook) that *Finnegans Wake* is constructed, among other things, out of the earlier Joycean works, perhaps even with the earlier works serving as rubrics, although there is controversy about the degree of continuity between *Finnegans Wake* and Joyce's previous fictions. At the same time that old materials were being sorted out, Joyce had new ideas in gestation and got new research underway. He became enamoured with the *Book of Kells* at this time, and, as he had done in writing *Ulysses*, he once again used his aunt, Josephine Murray, as a source of domestic Dublin information, asking her to compile a notebook of 'curious types' (*JJ* 545). The first words Joyce wrote of *Finnegans Wake* were penned on 10 March 1923; by 6 June he was prepared to read aloud to friends the first sixty pages of the work. Before the year was over, the outlines for the first eight chapters that comprise Book I of *Finnegans Wake* were sketched out (*JJ* 555). This is the beginning of the *Finnegans Wake* story as Richard Ellmann narrates it in his biography of Joyce, in an account rich in anecdotal material. The labour occupied Joyce almost totally during sixteen years of his life in Paris, years marked by the growing acceptance and fame of *Ulysses*, but plagued also by frequent eye surgeries, increasing blindness, and mounting anxiety over his daughter's illness.

In reconstructing the compositional history of *Finnegans Wake*, one finds a tendency for the anecdotal and the archival evidence to bifurcate into two opposite versions, one stressing the random, *ad hoc*, free associative nature of his note-taking and textual assemblage, the other, Joyce's rational and architectural constructions. Joyce's friends the Nuttings were particular witnesses to his seemingly random methods. Myron Nutting reports greeting Joyce in the clinic during one of his convalescences, only to have Joyce pull out a composition block and write 'carriage sponge' upon it (*JJ* 566). The *non sequitur* is not explained. Joyce tended to learn an unusual word here, exchange an unusual anecdote there. He eavesdropped, like Shem, on conversations, and when he overheard Phyllis Moss tell Nora about her Irish donkey named Aulus Plautus, he put it into the *Wake* (*JJ* 565). He listened with ironic distance to his own conversations with people and reported them as farcical dialogues. To Harriet Shaw Weaver, for example, he reproduced his conversation with his ophthalmologist, Dr Borsch, in the absurd style of a Mutt and Jute dialogue (10 June 1923; *Letters III* 76).

But study of the notebooks and manuscripts themselves leads archival scholar Danis Rose to deduce a considerably more mechanical and logical system of composition from the evidence of the workshop materials (see *James Joyce's 'The Index Manuscript'*, General Introduction). He proposes that the *Finnegans Wake* text corresponds to units of words or phrases in the notebooks, and that these correspond to external sources, such as books and other literary material. But this model creates the image of a highly systematic procedure with a patently architectural result. In contrast to this master-builder model of Joyce's writing, David Hayman argues for considerable variation in Joyce's composition practice, including the following procedures: '1. straight composition, 2. revise-and-complete, 3. episodic, 4. episodic fusion, 5. piecemeal or mosaic, 6. framing' (*First Draft Version*, p. 12). Questions about the compositional implications of the workshop materials will not be settled until the relationship of texts and notebooks is understood more clearly. But Rose's attempt to use composition practice to give the *Wake* an intertextual foundation, to have the text grow out of a web of literary and other textual sources, supports the venerable scholarly tradition begun by Hugh Kenner in *Dublin's Joyce*, and brought to fruition in James Atherton's *The Books at the Wake: A Study of Literary Allusions in James Joyce's 'Finnegans Wake'*. Atherton's valuable study confirmed that for all of its fun and absurdity, *Finnegans Wake* is in some sense a very learned book, a book created out of and referring back to other books.[3]

The creative act that shaped *Finnegans Wake* over such a long period of time was, no doubt, highly heterogeneous in nature. Its polyglossia resulted as much from Joyce's naturally hearing a variety of foreign speech in the several European countries he inhabited, as it did from deliberate research into arcane or exotic languages. His cosmopolitanism was balanced by a growing interest, in later life, for reappropriating Irish culture, tales, legends, and his own family lore, at a time when he was estranged from his native land, and this information (the *Book of Kells*, the legends of Finn MacCool and Dermot and Grania, the hagiography of St Patrick and St Kevin, the Danish occupation of Dublin and the battle of Clontarf, etc.) returned to him in inevitably estranged form. *Finnegans Wake* also reflects not only Joyce's solid, formal, Jesuit education, whose influence is still apparent in the Italian structural sources, orthodox and heretical, that contribute to the philosophical frames of the *Wake* – Dante, Bruno, and Vico, but also the more eclectic and eccentric erudition he accumulated along the way, that lets him dot the *Wake* with references to occult works and popular culture, Marie Corelli's *The Sorrows of Satan*, or the films of D. W. Griffith, for example.[4] He was influenced, I believe, by those of his friends excited by modernist experimentation and iconoclasm, and yet harked back to an older, more canonical tradition of subversive Irish literature, by referring to his countrymen Swift and Sterne, and his controversial contemporary, Oscar Wilde. Finally, Joyce clearly worked out the drafts of the *Wake* with some system and method for keeping track of the enormous body of external data he incorporated, as well as the internal, psychic logic he was developing; yet it seems he was still willing to respond to accidental stimuli and influences to keep the text's spirit fluid and surprising. The variety and range of his procedures and influences appear no less remarkable than the complexity of the text itself.

The critical history of *Finnegans Wake*

As 'Work in Progress', *Finnegans Wake* first appeared in short extracts in a number of periodicals during the years before its ultimate publication in 1939.[5] As with *Ulysses*, Joyce experienced problems of censorship when English printers refused to set *Anna Livia Plurabelle*. But the incomprehensibility of the language created additional problems of the conflictual sort described earlier: as much as the linguistic and poetic strangeness made the text exciting for its experimentalism, its apparent lack of sense, and its failure to accommodate the reader's desire to understand, made Joyce enemies as well as friends for his new project. Many of those frustrated by the text reacted with hostility and destructive criticism. Pound wrote to Joyce of the Shaun episodes, 'Nothing so far as I make out, nothing short of divine vision or a new cure for the clapp can possibly be worth all the circumambient peripherization' (16 November 1926; *Letters III* 145); Joyce retaliated by making one of the titles of the 'mamafesta' in *Finnegans Wake* 'A New Cure for an Old Clap' (104.34). Stanislaus Joyce called the effort 'the beginning of softening of the brain' (7 August 1924; *Letters III* 103), and even Harriet Shaw Weaver, his faithful benefactor and adviser, wavered. In print, Joyce's new work was attacked by Sean O'Faolain and Rebecca West. Other writer friends like H. G. Wells complained more privately: 'You have turned your back on common men, on their elementary needs and restricted time and intelligence and you have elaborated. What is the result? Vast riddles' (23 November 1928; *Letters I* 275).

But, paradoxically, the very strangeness of 'Work in Progress' that so infuriated some people, its uncompromising unconventionality, also made it converts who abetted its promotion. The publication of *Tales Told of Shem and Shaun* by the Black Sun Press resulted from a friendship with Harry and Caresse Crosby, connoisseurs of exoticism who considered themselves 'sun-worshippers'. They delighted in the text's exploration of 'otherness', and introduced Joyce to the Egyptian *Book of the Dead*, a text with great influence on the *Wake*. But Joyce's most important convert and new ally during the early days of writing *Finnegans Wake* was Eugène Jolas, who embraced the nascent text as a major document of his 'Revolution of the word', and published portions of it in *transition*. Jolas's manifesto for the 'Revolution of the word' included such directives as 'Time is a tyranny to be abolished', 'The writer expresses. He does not communicate', and 'The plain reader be damned' (*JJ* 588). Jolas armed Joyce with an aesthetic and intellectual rationale that made *Finnegans Wake* congruent with other avant-garde movements of his day.

This defence comes to fruition in the critical volume putatively commissioned and supervised by Joyce himself: *Our Exagmination Round his Factification for Incamination of 'Work in Progress'*, published by Shakespeare and Company in 1929, in which Jolas put Joyce in the company of Léon-Paul Fargue, Michel Leiris, André Breton, Gertrude Stein, and August Stramm (pp. 84–5). The contributors to this volume included, among others, the writer Samuel Beckett and the poet William Carlos Williams, and they were not insensitive to their inverted order as critics offering criticism of a literary work far in advance (a decade, as it happened) of its publication. Joyce playfully manipulated this perverse chronology along with other elements to give the volume a fictive feeling: he gave it a siglum (o) and a Wakean title that made the number of the twelve critics refer to the twelve customers, themselves versions of the twelve apostles, in the *Wake*'s pub, and included humorous, parodic letters ('Dear Mister Germ's Choice, in gutter dispear I am taking my pen toilet you know that . . . I have been reeding one half ter one other the numboars of "transition" in witch are printed the severeall instorments of your "Work in Progress"' (n.p.)). Joyce seemed to want to incorporate criticism of the work, insofar as he could control it in the work of his friends, as a kind of extra-textual chapter to his 'Work in Progress'.

But this humorous, fictive frame notwithstanding, the essays of *Our Exagmination* have a serious task in turning back the attacks on 'Work in Progress' by writers like Rebecca West, Wyndham Lewis, and Sean O'Faolain. The strategy of Joyce's friends was shrewd, for they refused the premises of the nascent *Wake*'s critics, and refused to supply the explications and explanations that appear to be demanded. Instead, they turn the argument around and attack the assumptions of Joyce's critics, O'Faolain's assertion of the immobility of English (p. 80), for example, or West's notion of Western art and literary history as preserved within a mould into which writers must fit themselves. 'She fails to fit Joyce to it', William Carlos Williams writes: 'She calls him, therefore, "strange", not realizing his compulsions which are outside of her sphere' (p. 185). The tendency of the essays as a whole might now legitimately be called 'deconstructive', for they dismantle notions of linguistic and literary structure. Samuel Beckett, for example, provides philosophical and philological antecedents for 'Work in Progress' in his essay on Dante, Bruno, and Vico, but in forms that announce them as inapplicable and inimicable. Beginning with the caveat, 'The danger is in the neatness of identifications' (p. 3), he proceeds to show how each of these figures modified or destroyed the nature of the 'pigeonholes', the traditional categories, conceptual frames, divisions and oppositions, that are conventionally required to make sense of history, theology, and language.

The bifurcated response Joyce's contemporaries gave 'Work in Progress', dismay at its incomprehensibility and delight at its unconventionality, continued after the formal publication of the finished work as *Finnegans Wake*, but with an important difference. The displeased response to the work's difficulty took on a positive and constructive form, and defection and outrage at the *Wake*'s crossword-puzzling were replaced by scholarly devotion and a commitment to find solutions. The next four decades saw the publication of a skeleton key, reader's guides, a short version, literary source studies, censuses, a gazetteer, a concordance, language lexicons, and foreign word lists and specialized studies of specific material in the text.[6] The underlying premise of this wealth of scholarship shaped a specifically positivistic vision of the textual nature of *Finnegans Wake* which assumed that the *Wake* was a semantic plenum whose excessive meaning would require an excess of philological scholarship to unpack. This approach entailed several problematic consequences for the reading and interpretation of the work. First, it implicitly promoted an indefinite deferral of attempts to read, interpret, and understand the work on the grounds that the scholarly tools were inadequate and incomplete. Second, it created a fiction of the reader's inevitable incompetence in the face of *Finnegans Wake*, an incompetence measured by implicitly postulating a hypothetical ideal reader who was a universal polyglot and polymath. The result has been *Finnegans Wake*'s status as an unreadable master-text whose function is the intimidation and humiliation of the common reader.

Eventually, the positivistic tradition of *Wake* scholarship yielded such helpful studies as John Gordon's *'Finnegans Wake': A Plot Summary* and Michael Begnal's *Narrator and Character in 'Finnegans Wake'* (with Grace Eckley) and *Dreamscheme: Narrative and Voice in 'Finnegans Wake'*. At the same time, beginning in the 1960s, a series of studies developed interesting strategies for tackling the more complex issues of the work's genres, themes, structure, and its purpose. Bernard Benstock's *Joyce-Again's Wake*, for example, reads *Finnegans Wake* as a comic epic, making the genre elastic enough to accommodate the *Wake*'s excesses of meaning, and its many pluralities and shifting relativities. Clive Hart's *Structure and Motif in 'Finnegans Wake'* uses the structure of the baroque to argue for a clarity of outline beneath an excess of ornamental detail. The critics of the 1970s, 1980s, and 1990s were able to relax their domesticating strategies toward the *Wake* even more, with the help of new metaphors for the work's experimental techniques. Patrick McCarthy's *The Riddles of 'Finnegans Wake'* explores the riddle not only as a thematic instance occurring throughout the chapters of the work, but as a philosophical device for exploring confusions of identity and resistance to self-knowledge. David Hayman introduced a useful structural concept in the 'node', a point in the text where one finds 'coherent clusterings of motif-like materials' ('Nodality and the Infra-structure of *Finnegans Wake*', 136). And Fritz Senn uses chiefly verbal and discursive metaphors by speaking of the 'dislocutions' by which the later Joyce texts are destabilized. In *Teller and Tale*, John Paul Riquelme uses the Moebius strip to represent the unorientability that characterizes our difficulty in reading the text. In a different vein, Kimberly Devlin's *Wandering and Return in 'Finnegans Wake'* invokes Freud's concept of the 'uncanny' as a metaphor for the text's ability to be at once strange and familiar, and offers an 'integrative approach' to explore the relationship between the *Wake* and Joyce's earlier works. 'My premise involves the Freudian notion of psychological return: obsessions, scenarios, and images from these earlier texts resurface in Joyce's final dreambook but in uncanny forms, transformed and yet discernible, in the same way that impressions from waking life appear in dream thoughts', she writes (ix). Finally, John Bishop's *Joyce's Book of the Dark* offers the most original metaphor for *Finnegans Wake*'s incomprehensibility by reducing the text, over and over, to all the different perceptions and experiences of the sleeping body. These are only a few of the major works we have to date on *Finnegans Wake*. They are complemented by other recent important studies: the work on the notebooks by Vincent Deane, Daniel Ferrer, and Geert Lernout; the studies of Wakean language by Susan Shaw Sailer, Lucia Boldrini, George Sandulescu, and Peter Myers; Harry Burrell's revelation of the 'simple text' of the *Wake*; Thomas Hofheinz's work on history in relation to *Finnegans Wake*; the more specialized studies of Grace Eckley, William Jenkins, and Eric McLuhan; and the essays collected in John Harty's casebook and in 1990 and 1994 special issues of *European Joyce Studies* on *Finnegans Wake*.

By the 1970s the influence of French post-structuralism, which had been emerging in the journals *Tel Quel* and *Poétique* in the late sixties, was beginning to make itself felt in such Anglo-American assimilations as my own study, *The Decentered Universe of 'Finnegans Wake'*, and the work of Stephen Heath, Colin MacCabe, and Derek Attridge. However, as the appearances of Jacques Lacan and Jacques Derrida at the International Joyce Symposia of 1979 and 1984 made clear, the genetic relationship between *Finnegans Wake* and post-structuralist theory remains complex and ambiguous, with the *Wake* as both producer and product of French theory, and both stimulant and beneficiary of deconstructive thinking. Post-structuralist criticism of *Finnegans Wake* exhibited shadings from various critical orientations – political, psychoanalytical, feminist, and textual. Its most striking contribution was to rethink the position of *Finnegans Wake* in literary history, a resituation perhaps best characterized by Derek Attridge when he argues in *Peculiar Language* that its dramatization of the potentialities of all language should make *Finnegans Wake* central, not eccentric and peripheral, to literary history itself.

The structure of *Finnegans Wake*

The problem of how to construe the organization of *Finnegans Wake* as a whole remains vexing and difficult, although we increasingly realize that probably no Linati scheme, like the one that lent the organization of *Ulysses* such a satisfying sense of order and coherence, was possible for *Finnegans Wake* without falsifying its unconventional literary production. However, Samuel Beckett does produce a scheme for 'Work in Progress' that bears Joyce's imprimatur in the form of privileged information. The 'lovegame of the children', included in Beckett's 1929 essay, was not begun by Joyce until

1930 and not completed until 1932 (*JJ* 796): Beckett could only have had this proleptic information on Joyce's authority. The scheme presents a perfectly viable outline for *Finnegans Wake*:

> Part 1 is a mass of past shadow, corresponding therefore to Vico's first human institution, Religion, or to his Theocratic age, or simply to an abstraction – Birth. Part 2 is the lovegame of the children, corresponding to the second institution, Marriage, or to the Heroic age, or to an abstraction – Maturity. Part 3 is passed in sleep, corresponding to the third institution, Burial, or to the Human age, or to an abstraction – Corruption. Part 4 is the day beginning again, and corresponds to Vico's Providence, or to the transition from the Human to the Theocratic, or to an abstraction – Generation.   (pp. 7–8)

But Beckett's qualifications virtually undo the scheme – 'The consciousness that there is a great deal of the unborn infant in the lifeless octogenarian, and a great deal of both in the man at the apogee of his life's curve, removes all the stiff interexclusiveness that is often the danger in neat construction' (p. 8).

The formulation of theme is less useful for *Finnegans Wake* than for other literary texts because the continual dissolution of narrative, image, and language in the *Wake* prevents the sort of positive representations that we construe as thematic material from taking shape. For example, Beckett's identification of Book 1 with Vico's Theocratic age does not take the form of a representation of God's governance – even though the text is dotted with the hundred-letter thunderwords taken to be the voice of God (or his cough, 'husstenhasstencaffincoffintussemtossemdamandamna-cosaghcusaghhobixhatouxpeswchbechoscashlcarcarcaract' (414.19–20)) – but of a series of psychological and rhetorical effects in the chapter. God's law is indicated not in stories about God's law, but in the fear of transgression, the fear that a great sin has been committed, that shapes the narratives of investigation and persecution. In Joyce's earliest fictions we find the Theocratic age inscribed in the same way, in the authority-ridden ambience that produces the paranoid perceptions of 'The Sisters' and the confessional pressures of *A Portrait of the Artist as a Young Man*. Indeed, the wake motif in the first chapter, the image of the fallen giant ('Fimfim fimfim. With a grand funferall. Fumfum fumfum' (13.15–16)), a Finnegan or Finn or HCE laid out for a wake, can be seen as 'The Sisters' turned inside out, with the occluded perspective – that of the corpse or the stiff – retrieved and represented. This first chapter of the *Wake* is an imaginative recreation of poor paralytic Father Flynn lying in his coffin, listening to his mourners keen ('Macool, Macool, orra whyi deed ye diie?' (6.13)) and speculate about his secret sins, perhaps the suspected syphilis imputed by critics, 'It has been blurtingly bruited by certain wisecrackers . . . that he suffered from a vile disease' (33.15–18). The sensibility that shapes the first book of the *Wake* is governed by dread of the discourse of the other, who may indeed be no more than the self, or the self's language, or the power of language to accuse, intimidate, and destroy. But the fear of what is heard – 'Hush! Caution! Echoland!' (13.5) – engulfs everyone and everything in Book 1, not only the fallen father, hounded by rumours of his sins, but also his family. In chapter 7, Shem, the dreamer's son, or the dreamer himself as young, is vilified by a malicious tongue ('Shem was a sham and a low sham' (170.25)). And the elusive ALP, the dreamer's wife, or the object of his desire, is herself captured, however fleetingly, by the gentler criticisms of the washer-women ('Ah, but she was the queer old skeowsha anyhow' (215.12)). Much of Book 1 of *Finnegans Wake* can be construed as the earlier Joyce fictions, 'The Sisters', 'Clay', 'Grace', and *A Portrait*, for example, turned inside out with the anxieties, fears, and tensions that underlie them foregrounded and magnified.

Beckett's suggestive remark, that Book 1 may explore the similarities between a paralytic ('lifeless'), sleeping, or dying old man and an unborn child (perhaps 'an overgrown babeling' (6.31)), makes even better sense if placed in the larger context of the ending of *Finnegans Wake*, Book iv. This last chapter of *Finnegans Wake* begins at dawn, at breakfast, as a new day beginning; but as the abstraction of 'Generation' announces, it is also about families and books beginning again, as the last page of *Finnegans Wake* might be thought to continue on the first page of *Finnegans Wake*. Book iv creates a curious, paradoxical image of dying not as a going forward into the future, or into nothingness, but rather as a regression into childhood and a return to the womb, a moving backwards in time, a rejuvenation that culminates in the absorption by the parent. This regression is suggested geographically and temporally by a metaphorical reversal of the idiomatic expression 'going west' as a term for dying (and thereby reverses Gabriel's westward journey at the end of 'The Dead'), by depicting dying as 'going east', toward sunrise rather than sunset, toward Egypt in a historical and cultural regression that returns us to the cradle of civilization (and, if we were to see Book iv *continued* in Book 1, as a return to prehistory). Joyce's figure for this dying as a reverse of being born ('behold, he returns; renascenent; fincarnate' (596.3–4)) as a return to the womb and beyond, was prefigured in *Ulysses* by Stephen's image of linked navelcords, connecting each generation to the next by the fluid-carrying canal of the umbilicus, 'a commodius vicus of recirculation', all the way back, 'past Eve and Adam's' (3.1–2). Narratively and emotionally, then, we might picture Book iv as 'Telemachus' reversed: as Stephen's pain at separation and alienation from his mother is turned into its opposite, reconciliation figured as return to the womb by way of the metaphors of the navel and the maternal sea. The last chapter of *Finnegans Wake* depicts the son (in the guise of St Kevin floating on a raft through the waterways of Ireland) as reabsorbed into the fluid of the mother (who is both *mère* and *mer*, mother and sea, in Stephen and Mulligan's talk at the start of *Ulysses*), and ends with the mother's reabsorption into the oceanic semen of her father. This generational regression continues at the beginning of Book I, as that father's dying (perhaps many generations removed, now back at the beginning, at the time of Adam and Eve) is now pictured in reverse as an effort to become born. A more contemporary analogue for this concept of Generation as a process in reverse might be the one provided by Stanley Kubrick in the film *2001: A Space Odyssey*, in which the dying of the ancient astronaut is imagined as a regression into his form as a foetus.

Book II, in contrast to the predominantly ear, sound, and speech governed structure of Book I, continues the paranoiac fear of hearing ('Now promisus as at our requisted you will remain ignorant of all what you hear' (238.14)), but couples it with psychological fears grounded in the eye: in the fear of seeing either too little or too much, in the fear of ocular titillation and frustration on the one hand ('though if whilst disrobing to the edge of risk, . . . draw a veil till we next time' (238.16–18)), and, on the other, ocular shock ('I seen his brichashert offensive and his boortholomas vadnhammaggs vise a vise them scharlot runners and how they gave love to him' (352.4–6)). Because the controlling mode here is sight, the rhetorical structures of the chapters of Book II are very different, since discourse that takes the form of speech that is heard must be replaced with generic models that emphasize visual perception. Thus, the children's games of II.1 are structured around the modes of theatre, ballet, pantomime, and gesture language. The homework chapter, II.2, in which the quest for knowledge is represented as a voyeuristic exercise, the act of seeing forbidden sights, is expressed through modes of visually apprehended language: reading the book rather than hearing the lecture. Even in II.4, the reports of the four evangelists, or the four annalists of Irish history, emphasize a literal version of their role as 'witnesses', as they spy on the lovegames of Tristan and Isolde. But II.3, which presents a curious inversion of the eye-dominated chapter of the 'Cyclops' in *Ulysses*, augments its tales of forbidden and aggressive seeing (the shooting of the Russian General because the sight of him offends) with the aural modes of the radio broadcast, the tale, and the dialogue.

The first two children's chapters of Book II, especially, serve an interesting function in relation to some of Joyce's earlier texts, for they fill in gaps in *A*

Portrait and *Ulysses* that exist because 'what the children saw', the children's perspective, is elided. There are a number of clues, for example, that would allow us to see the 'lovegame of the children' in II.1 as a filling in of what the little Caffrey twins, Tommy and Jacky, saw and felt on Sandymount strand, while Bloom and the older girls carry on their flirtations oblivious to the children's eyes. Likewise, there are clues that the little boy's quest in the 'homework' chapter, II.2, to look at the female genitalia, perhaps the mother's in some displaced form, was the unnamed transgression for which little Stephen was threatened with such brutal ocular punishment in the opening pages of *A Portrait* – 'His mother said: – O, Stephen will apologise. Dante said: – O, if not, the eagles will come and pull out his eyes' (*P* 5–6). In the 'Mime' chapter of the *Wake*, the eagles appear to have become the female eye, or its mirror, ready to retaliate for an unflattering voyeurism – 'If you nude her in her prime, make sure you find her complementary or, on your very first occasion . . . she'll prick you where you're proudest with her unsatt speagle eye. Look sharp' (248.3–6).

   If Book I is the book of paranoid hearing and Book II the book of desirous looking, Book III might be called the book of deconstructive interpretation. The best analogue for the dissolution of divine authority and pretension in these chapters – the subversion of authoritative and didactic language in the form of sermons, epistles, commandments, benedictions and parables (the parable of the 'Ondt and the Gracehoper', discussed earlier, is here used as a sermon against profligacy) – can be found in Bloom's Messianic fantasies, his speeches announcing the New Bloomusalem and their disintegration amid the heckling of the rabble in 'Circe'. An even earlier analogue might be found in the *Dubliners* story 'Grace', with its quincunx configuration of evangelical figures around the bed of the fallen man, and their reappearance in the church retreat, evoking precisely questions of authoritative language, the Pope's *ex cathedra* pronouncements, powerful sermons and preachings, that the story itself subverts by drawing attention to its potential for error and hypocrisy. The *Wake* language of Book III, likewise, continually disintegrates into its opposite, as commandments reveal their libidinal motivations, and Shaun's discourse lapses into the speech of father and mother, as though his corruption were not only moral but also discursive and genetic. The function of Christology in the chapter appears to be the ironic dismantling of theocracy, as the human residue of Christ is exposed as the flawed, the prosaic, the trivial, in a regression to Vico's Human age. The last chapter of Book III, the witnessed lovemaking in the marriage bed of the Earwickers, represents the disintegration of the foundation of the symbolic order, the laws that govern sexuality and marriage in the form of psychological taboos as well as civil laws (see the absurd Roman domestic trial in the chapter), as the son disintegrates back into his genesis in the coitus of the parents. The second half of *Finnegans Wake* represents the undoing, by reversal, of the Oedipus complex: a reversal of the experience responsible not only for personal and social maturation, but also for the institution of law, patriarchy, and the symbolic order. This process of corruption as regression is then continued on an ontological level in the absorption into the mother's body, the return to the womb, that I previously described as the narrative movement of Book IV.

Now that so much of the scholarly apparatus for reading *Finnegans Wake* is in place, an exciting era in *Wake* scholarship and criticism is beginning. International co-operation among *Wake* scholars offers at least the potential for a wedding of philological information, archival research, and a sophisticated theoretical sense of the nature of textuality. The greater familiarity with *Finnegans Wake* of a generation of post-modern readers will yield, perhaps, a more comfortable relationship with a text whose modes of expression depart more drastically than usual from the conventions of realism and mimesis. And a more thorough assimilation of Freudian psychoanalytic premises may have prepared us better to confront an anarchic, unflattering, and alienating portrait of our dreaming selves, limned in the unfamiliar palette and the deranging perspectives of modern art. Whether readers choose to feel rebuffed and humiliated by this difficult text, or excited by its strangeness and stretched by its challenges, *Finnegans Wake* will measure their capacity for intellectual and imaginative adventure.

NOTES

1 Fortunately, there are several excellent guides available, if the reader wants to find out what *Finnegans Wake* is 'about' – how its narrative progresses (or regresses), how its themes exfoliate, how its characters proliferate, and how its language produces multiple meanings. I especially recommend Patrick McCarthy's essay on 'The Structures and Meanings of *Finnegans Wake*' in Bowen and Carens, *A Companion to Joyce Studies*.

2 Ellmann writes of Joyce's preparations for the writing of *Finnegans Wake*, 'He was interested also in variation and sameness in space, in the cubist method of establishing different relations among aspects of a single thing, and he would ask Beckett to do some research for him in the possible permutations of an object' (*JJ* 551).

3 Joyce's notebooks for *Finnegans Wake* are currently being edited in a series of volumes that include facsimiles, transcriptions, information about sources where these have been identified, and specification of destination in those cases where Joyce utilized the note in his drafts and the final text: *The 'Finnegans Wake' Notebooks at Buffalo*, ed. Vincent Deane, Daniel Ferrer, and Geert Lernout (Turnhout: Brepols, 2001–).

4 The title of *Finnegans Wake* is taken from a popular song, the ballad of Tim Finnegan, the hod carrier with 'a tipplin' way', who falls from a ladder while drunk:

> One morning Tim was rather full,
>   His head felt heavy which made him shake,
> He fell from the ladder and broke his skull,
>   So they carried him home his corpse to wake.

A fight breaks out during the wake – ' 'Twas woman to woman and man to man' – and in the process a noggin of whiskey is thrown and strikes the bier, scattering over the corpse and waking him from the dead:

> Bedad he revives, see how he rises,
>   And Timothy rising from the bed,
> Says, 'Whirl your liquor round like blazes,
>   Thanam o'n dhoul, do ye think I'm dead?'
>
>   (JJ 543n)

5 See Jean-Michel Rabaté's summary of the *Wake*'s early publishing history in ch. 4 above (pp. 62–3).
6 Clive Hart and Fritz Senn printed such notes and essays in *The Wake Newslitter* and *The Wake Digest*. For a list of other scholarly tools for explicating *Finnegans Wake* see 'Further reading' (pp. 280–1 below). Most of the material from earlier sources has been collected and collated in Roland McHugh's highly practical and user-friendly *Annotations to 'Finnegans Wake'*.

WORKS CITED

Atherton, James. *The Books at the Wake: A Study of Literary Allusions in James Joyce's 'Finnegans Wake'*. Revised edition, New York: Paul P. Appel, 1974

Attridge, Derek. *Joyce Effects: On Language, Theory, and History*. Cambridge: Cambridge University Press, 2000

Peculiar Language: Literature and Difference from the Renaissance to James Joyce. Ithaca: Cornell University Press, 1988

Attridge, Derek, and Daniel Ferrer, eds. *Post-Structuralist Joyce: Essays from the French*. Cambridge: Cambridge University Press, 1984

Beckett, Samuel, *et al. Our Exagmination Round His Factification for Incamination of Work in Progress* (1929). London: Faber, 1972

Begnal, Michael H., *Dreamscheme: Narrative and Voice in 'Finnegans Wake'*. Syracuse: Syracuse University Press, 1988

Begnal, Michael H., and Grace Eckley. *Narrator and Character in 'Finnegans Wake'*. Lewisburg: Bucknell University Press, 1975

Begnal, Michael H., and Fritz Senn. *A Conceptual Guide to 'Finnegans Wake'*. University Park: Pennsylvania State University Press, 1974

Benstock, Bernard. *Joyce-Again's Wake: An Analysis of 'Finnegans Wake'*. Seattle: University of Washington Press, 1986

Bishop, John. *Joyce's Book of the Dark: 'Finnegans Wake'*. Madison: University of Wisconsin Press, 1986

Boldrini, Lucia. *Joyce, Dante, and the Poetics of Literary Relations: Language and Meaning in 'Finnegans Wake'*. Cambridge: Cambridge University Press, 2001

Bowen, Zack, and James F. Carens. *A Companion to Joyce Studies*. Westport, Connecticut: Greenwood Press, 1984

Brivic, Sheldon. *Joyce's Waking Women: An Introduction to 'Finnegans Wake'*. Madison: University of Wisconsin Press, 1995

Burrell, Harry. *Narrative Design in 'Finnegans Wake'*. Gainesville, University of Florida Press, 1996.

Campbell, Joseph, and Henry Morton Robinson. *A Skeleton Key to 'Finnegans Wake'* (1949). New York: Viking, 1969

Cheng, Vincent J. *Shakespeare and Joyce: A Study of 'Finnegans Wake'*. University Park: Pennsylvania State University Press, 1984

Connolly, Thomas E. *James Joyce's Scribbledehobble: The Ur-Workbook for 'Finnegans Wake'*. Evanston: Northwestern University Press, 1961

Cope, Jackson I. *Joyce's Cities: Archeologies of the Soul*. Baltimore: Johns Hopkins University Press, 1981

Deane, Vincent, Daniel Ferrer, and Geert Lernout, eds. *The 'Finnegans Wake' Notebooks at Buffalo*. Turnhout: Brepols, 2001–.

Devlin, Kimberly J. *Wandering and Return in 'Finnegans Wake': An Integrative Approach to Joyce's Fictions*. Princeton: Princeton University Press, 1991

Eckley, Grace. *Children's Lore in 'Finnegans Wake'*. Syracuse: Syracuse University Press, 1985.

The Steadfast Finnegans Wake: A Textbook. Lanham, Maryland: University Press of America, 1994

Gordon, John. *'Finnegans Wake': A Plot Summary*. Dublin: Gill and Macmillan, 1986

Hart, Clive. *A Concordance to 'Finnegans Wake'*. Corrected edition. Mamaroneck, N.Y.: Paul P. Appel, 1974.

Structure and Motif in 'Finnegans Wake'. London: Faber, 1962

Hart, Clive, and Fritz Senn, eds. *A Wake Digest*. Sydney: Sydney University Press, 1968

Harty III, John,. *James Joyce's 'Finnegans Wake': A Casebook*. New York: Garland Publishing, 1991.

Hayman, David. 'Nodality and the Infra-Structure of *Finnegans Wake'*. *JJQ* 16 (1979): 135–49

The 'Wake' in Transit. Ithaca: Cornell University Press, 1990

Hayman, David, ed. *A First-Draft Version of 'Finnegans Wake'*. Austin: University of Texas Press, 1963

Heath, Stephen. 'Ambiviolences: notes for reading Joyce'. In Attridge and Ferrer, *Post-Structuralist Joyce*, 31–68

Herring, Phillip F. *Joyce's Uncertainty Principle*. Princeton: Princeton University Press, 1987

Hofheinz, Thomas C. *Joyce and the Invention of Irish History: 'Finnegans Wake' in Context*. Cambridge: Cambridge University Press, 1995

Jenkins, William D. *The Adventure of the Detected Detective: Sherlock Holmes in James Joyce's 'Finnegans Wake'*. Westport, Conn.: Greenwood Press, 1998

Kenner, Hugh. *Dublin's Joyce* (1955). New York: Columbia University Press, 1987

Lernout, Geert, ed. *European Joyce Studies 2: 'Finnegans Wake': Fifty Years*. Amsterdam: Rodopi, 1990.

MacCabe, Colin. *James Joyce and the Revolution of the Word* (1978). Revised edition, London: Palgrave, 2003

McCarthy, Patrick A. *The Riddles of 'Finnegans Wake'*. Rutherford: Fairleigh Dickinson University Press, 1980

McCarthy, Patrick A., ed. *Critical Essays on James Joyce's 'Finnegans Wake'*. New York: G. K. Hall, 1992.

McHugh, Roland. *Annotations to 'Finnegans Wake'*. Baltimore: Johns Hopkins University Press, 1980

The *'Finnegans Wake' Experience*. Berkeley: University of California Press, 1981

McLuhan, Eric. *The Role of Thunder in 'Finnegans Wake'*. Toronto: University of Toronto Press, 1997

Myers, Peter. *The Sound of 'Finnegans Wake'*. London: Macmillan, 1992

Norris, Margot. *The Decentered Universe of 'Finnegans Wake': A Structuralist Analysis*. Baltimore: Johns Hopkins University Press, 1976

Riquelme, John Paul. *Teller and Tale in Joyce's Fiction: Oscillating Perspectives*. Baltimore: Johns Hopkins University Press, 1983

Rose, Danis, ed. *James Joyce's 'The Index Manuscript': 'Finnegans Wake' Holograph Workbook VI.B. 46*. Colchester: A Wake Newslitter Press, 1978

Rose, Danis, and John O'Hanlon. *Understanding 'Finnegans Wake': A Guide to the Narrative of James Joyce's Masterpiece*. New York: Garland Publishing, 1982

Sailer, Susan Shaw. *On the Void of to Be: Incoherence and Trope in 'Finnegans Wake'*. Ann Arbor: University of Michigan Press, 1993

Sandulescu, C. George. *The Language of the Devil: Texture and Archetype in 'Finnegans Wake'*. Gerrards Cross: Colin Smythe, 1987

Senn, Fritz. *Joyce's Dislocutions: Essays on Reading as Translation*, ed. John Paul Riquelme. Baltimore: Johns Hopkins University Press, 1984

Treip, Andrew, ed. *European Joyce Studies 4: 'Finnegans Wake': Teems of Times*. Amsterdam: Rodopi, 1994.

A Wake Newslitter, ed. Clive Hart and Fritz Senn. Essex: University of Essex, 1962–84

9

VICKI MAHAFFEY

Joyce's shorter works

At first glance, Joyce's shorter works – his poems and epiphanies, *Giacomo Joyce*, and *Exiles* – seem to bear only the most tenuous relationship to the books for which Joyce has become famous. It is only by an exercise of the imagination that the epiphanies and *Giacomo Joyce* can even be called 'works'; Joyce published neither in its original form, choosing instead to loot them for the more ambitious undertakings that followed, and neither received the painstaking polish that Joyce lavished on his more ambitious productions. Only forty of at least seventy-one epiphanies are extant and their relationship to one another had to be reconstructed from manuscript evidence; the sketches that comprise *Giacomo Joyce* were similarly composed, arranged, and abandoned, but not destroyed. *Chamber Music*, although published in 1907, was orphaned when Joyce delegated the final arrangement of the poems to his brother Stanislaus. *Pomes Penyeach*, as the title suggests, is a modest offering of twelve and a tilly poetic 'fruits'. Only *Exiles* continued to hold Joyce's interest as an autonomous composition not destined for immediate verbal recycling.

The status of the shorter works as successful, original, or even finished compositions has always been in question; even in more subjective terms, however, they seem to offer few of the rewards of their longer and better known counterparts. First, and most damagingly, they are humourless; what humour may be discerned in them is bitter or ironic, inspired by pained defiance (as in 'Gas from a Burner') or jaded cynicism ('In my time the dunghill was so high' – *E* 43). Secondly, they are spare, denuded of the variable styles and elaborate contexts that make *Ulysses* and *Finnegans Wake* seem inexhaustible. Finally, they are easily dismissed as immediately derivative of both Joyce's experiences and his reading.

Although the brevity and earnestness of Joyce's minor pieces put them in opposition to the major ones, the relationship between the shorter and longer productions is much closer when viewed in structural and thematic terms. *Chamber Music*, the *Epiphanies*, and *Giacomo Joyce* are all composed of isolated, artistically rendered moments arranged to form a loose progression; the three acts of *Exiles* loosely divide thirteen unmarked scenes, each an intimate dialogue between two characters, stitched together by the conventions – both social and theatrical – of entrances and exits. The strategy of producing a longer and more complicated text by stringing together a series of formally self-contained units is essential not only to the design of *Dubliners*, where the structural building blocks are short stories, but also to the increasingly complex episodic structures of *A Portrait, Ulysses* and *Finnegans Wake*. In short, the minor works make it much more apparent that Joyce's technique – even in the longer texts – is in large part an imagist one, adapted from poetry to narrative and massively elaborated in the process.

If the shorter texts outline the basic structure of all Joyce's works, they also provide the simplest statement of Joyce's most characteristic themes, which are treated polyphonically in his longer compositions: themes of loss, betrayal, and the interplay of psychological and social experience. Strikingly, all of the shorter works record the experience of some loss: the *Epiphanies* seem to have been arranged to depict the loss of innocence; *Chamber Music* plays out the loss of youthful love, a theme picked up and translated into predominantly visual terms in *Giacomo Joyce*. Many of the poems in *Pomes Penyeach* echo the theme of lost youth, but the collection also includes more anguished treatments of different kinds of loss: in 'Tilly', a figurative loss of limb makes the dead speak; it is the illusion of beauty that is lost in 'A Memory of the Players in a Mirror at Midnight'. The list can be expanded to include loss of sight in 'Bahnhofstrasse', loss of life in 'She Weeps over Rahoon', loss of faith in 'Nightpiece', and loss of peace and security in the nightmarish 'I Hear an Army'; in the words of another 'pome', '*Tutto è sciolto*' (all is lost). *Exiles* is the most complicated of Joyce's briefer treatments of attrition, since it probes the loss of spontaneity in life and love, which the action of the play suggests is irreparable.

A less apparent symmetry between the shorter and longer works is in the careful balancing of subjective and objective experience. As Scholes and Kain point out, Joyce designed not one but two kinds of epiphanies – one narrative, one dramatic – and then interwove them into a single sequence.[1] The careful counterpointing of opposite perspectives – those of dream and observation – constitutes Joyce's earliest attempt to compensate for the distortion of 'parallax', the term for the inadequacy of a single vantage point that sparks Bloom's curiosity in *Ulysses*. The main problem with Joyce's characterization of both kinds of experience in the epiphanies is its *naïveté*: the imagination is always empowering, and outer experience invariably deflating. The narrative epiphanies celebrate the power of the author's mind; the dramatic epiphanies reduce the stature of those around him (*WD* 4). The epiphanies, like the manuscript novel that succeeded and partly incorporated them, present the nascent artist as an inevitable Hero.

As heroism is increasingly displaced by humour in Joyce's maturer works, his treatment of the relationship between fantasy and drama, desire and reality, also grows more complex.[2] *Giacomo Joyce* and *Exiles*, as narrative and dramatic treatments of problems that would later inform *Ulysses*, at first seem to constitute a two-phase attempt to represent the pain of betrayal from an internal and external point of view, respectively: that of the artist's mind and that of a more detached spectator. *Giacomo Joyce*, from such a perspective, resembles the narrative epiphanies in its depiction of the sensitive artist as dreamer, whereas *Exiles*, like the dramatic epiphanies, presents the artist exposing the imprecision and lack of integrity of those around him.[3]

The attempt to define *Giacomo Joyce* and *Exiles* in terms of the similarities and differences between the two kinds of epiphanies works only up to a point, however, since by the end of each text the oppositions between dream and drama, wish-fulfilment and satire, subject and object have begun to break down. *Giacomo Joyce* cannot sustain its status as pure fantasy; outer circumstances begin to impinge on its enclosed world when the object of Giacomo's gaze enigmatically announces her preference for a lesser man – '"Because otherwise I could not see you" . . . *Non hunc sed Barabbam*!' – and the speaker's imaginative superiority lapses into self-criticism: 'It will never be. You know that well. What then? Write it, damn you, write it! What else are you good for?' (*GJ* 16).

Just as the subjective cast of *Giacomo Joyce* dissipates in the strong light of fact, the objective, even clinical mood of *Exiles* yields to self-pity and hallucination. The upsurge of irrational forces begins when Richard Rowan suddenly sees the hypocrisy of his high-toned opposition to any union between his friend and the mother of his child. He recognizes and confesses the hidden desire that prompted him to watch and passively abet their growing mutual attraction, as the play relentlessly pursues the treachery buried in the accusation of betrayal:

> [I]n the very core of my ignoble heart I longed to be betrayed by you and by her – in the dark, in the night – secretly, meanly, craftily. By you, my best friend, and by her. I longed for that passionately and ignobly, to be dishonoured for ever in love and in lust, to be... . . . To be for ever a shameful creature and to build up my soul again out of the ruins of its shame. (*E* 70)

Richard admits that his furtive desire to be betrayed was motivated, paradoxically, by pride, since Bertha has consistently used her faithfulness to shame him: 'She has spoken always of her innocence, as I have spoken always of my guilt, humbling me' (*E* 70). And as Richard is driven towards truth, he is also propelled into a nightmarish world of imagination, the world of *Giacomo Joyce*. Returning from his hour on the strand he tells Beatrice:

> There are demons . . . out there. I heard them jabbering since dawn . . . The isle is full of voices. Yours also. *Otherwise I could not see you*, it said. And her voice. But, I assure you, they are all demons. I made the sign of the cross upside down and that silenced them. (*E* 98)

Once we see that *Giacomo Joyce* and *Exiles* not only represent an opposition between inner and outer reality but also present complementary accounts of how that opposition breaks down, it is only a short step to an appreciation of how the two dovetail into the 'Circe' episode of *Ulysses*, which is both drama and fantasy, an extravagant celebration of the actor/viewer's superhuman dreams *and* subhuman instincts, his generous pride and shameful prejudices, and finally into *Finnegans Wake*.

The shorter works bear a marked resemblance to their longer counterparts in basic theme and structure, but they also reflect Joyce's characteristic readiness to appropriate the styles and voices of other writers. Whereas in his most famous works this appropriative tendency takes the form of parody or emerges through correspondences, in the slighter pieces it has been dismissed as simply derivative, as evidence of the influence exercised upon Joyce by Christian theology, Yeats, the Elizabethans, or Ibsen. All writing, of course, is derivative; the question that presses is whether a work represents a productive or reiterative reading of its sources: does it replicate the most familiar features of its parent texts, or does it reshape our awareness of those texts?

Not only are the shorter works derived (in part) from identifiable sources, but they, in turn, serve as sources themselves; Joyce reinterprets – and re-uses – them as readily as he uses any other material. And just as the dependence of Joyce's shorter works on the writings of his predecessors can easily obscure the extent to which our understanding of those other writings may change in reference to his, the dependence of Joyce's longer experiments on the shorter ones which frequently contribute to them raises a comparable problem of relation: how can we account for the disjunction between what the shorter works lack (humour, complexity, and a self-consciousness that is acutely philosophical rather than painfully self-dramatizing) and what they share with Joyce's other writings (seriatim structure, concern with betrayal, hunger for experience, and the appropriation of other writers' voices)? One solution is to sever any relationship between the slighter works and their famous siblings by asserting that the shorter works, unlike the longer ones, are unsuccessful on their own terms. Such a contention may be true, but its truth is to some extent irrelevant, since it is not purely on their own terms that any of these documents lay claim to our attention; their value stems largely from their incestuous relationship to other writing, their liminal status as threshold productions that mark the interstices between more apparently autonomous experiments. Whatever Joyce's shorter works have to offer they will not offer in isolation; on the other hand, if they are absorbed too completely into the rest of Joyce's writing we lose a vantage point for reinterpreting his other works. Like Joyce's longer texts, the shorter pieces simultaneously depend upon a large written tradition and strain to break free of that tradition by exceeding it.

The shorter works are most fruitfully approached not only as half-realized versions of Joyce's more ambitious productions, but also as stilled frames in an ongoing process of reading and writing, a process that he parodied, practised and refined throughout a lifetime of experimentation with language. Like the manuscripts, the shorter works provide information indispensable for reconstructing the 'continuous manuscript' of Joyce's writing career,[4] an achievement that is both fluid and discontinuous, fragmented and whole. Unlike the manuscripts, though, which give insight into the arrangement of a published text by tracing the genesis of that arrangement and the false starts that help to define the finished shape, the shorter works preserve contextual as well as textual trials and errors: we see Joyce testing, not only phrases, but variant interpretations of problems like fidelity, combining the perspectives of different authors to create complex backdrops for his own treatments.

The most influential critical treatments of the shorter works show how easy it is to upset the fragile balance between a text's individuality and its applicability to larger contexts. In the case of the *Epiphanies*, the prose bits to which Joyce gave that name are too often digested into the general concept of 'epiphany'. In contrast, the critical focus on the poems, *Giacomo Joyce*, and *Exiles* has tended to be too narrowly biographical or literary. Whether the perspective is telescopic or microscopic, the attitude inclusive or dismissive, what is lost is the depth and flexibility that come from a less consistent, and more Joycean, sense of the continuity and discontinuity of relation.

Epiphanies

The main difficulty presented by the *Epiphanies* lies in the broad application of the word itself, which Joyce used not only to designate the slivers of life that he punctiliously preserved in prose and dialogue from 1900–1903, but also as a metaphor, drawn from classical and Christian myth, for the revelation of the spiritual in the actual. In Greek mythology, *epiphany* referred to the unexpected manifestation of the divine, and in Greek drama it was used to describe the sudden appearance of a god on stage. Christianity appropriated the term for liturgical purposes to commemorate the day that the Magi brought gifts to the Christ child (which represents the first manifestation of divinity to foreign travellers).

In the manuscript of *Stephen Hero*, where the term was first discovered, Joyce uses 'epiphany' both to describe his records of moments that blend triviality with significance and to designate the revelatory climax of aesthetic apprehension. He introduces the more local of the two meanings by describing his reaction to a fragment of overheard conversation:

> A young lady was standing on the steps of one of those brown brick houses which seem the very incarnation of Irish paralysis. A young gentleman was leaning on the rusty railings of the area. Stephen as he passed on his quest heard the following fragment of colloquy out of which he received an impression keen enough to afflict his sensitiveness very severely.
>
> The Young Lady – (drawling discreetly)... O, yes... I was... at the... cha... pel...
>
> The Young Gentleman – (inaudibly)... I... (again inaudibly)... I...
>
> The Young Lady – (softly)... O... but you're... ve... ry... wick... ed...
>
> This triviality made him think of collecting many such moments together in a book of epiphanies. By an epiphany he meant a sudden spiritual manifestation, whether in the vulgarity of speech or of gesture or in a memorable phase of the mind itself. He believed that it was for the man of letters to record these epiphanies with extreme care, seeing that they themselves are the most delicate and evanescent of moments. (*SH* 210–11, 216)

The collection of epiphanies receives further mention in *Ulysses*, where Stephen thinks to himself, 'Remember your epiphanies written on green oval leaves, deeply deep, copies to be sent if you died to all the great libraries of the world, including Alexandria? Someone was to read them there after a few thousand years, a mahamanvantara' (*U* 3.141–4). Several of Joyce's own epiphanies turned up among his papers and those of his brother Stanislaus, and it is Scholes and Kain's arrangement of these into a sequence based on manuscript evidence that constitutes what we now refer to as the *Epiphanies*.[5]

In *Stephen Hero*, after the narrator relates an epiphany and reveals Stephen's determination to collect them, Stephen goes on to explain the idea of epiphany in theoretical terms to Cranly. Epiphany, he argues, is the moment when the spiritual eye is able 'to adjust its vision to an exact focus' so as to apprehend 'the third, the supreme quality of beauty' in an object, its 'soul' or 'whatness', which the mind synthesizes from an appreciation of the first two qualities of beauty in the object, its integrity and symmetry:

> After the analysis which discovers the second quality the mind makes the only logically possible synthesis and discovers the third quality. This is the moment which I call epiphany. First we recognise that the object is *one* integral thing, then we recognise that it is an organised composite structure, *a thing* in fact: finally, when the relation of the parts is exquisite, when the parts are adjusted to the special point, we recognise that it is *that* thing which it is. Its soul, its whatness, leaps to us from the vestment of its appearance. The soul of the commonest object, the structure of which is so adjusted, seems to us radiant. The object achieves its epiphany. (*SH* 218, 213)

When Joyce reworked this portion of Stephen's aesthetic theories for *Portrait* (*P* 212–13), he expunged any reference to epiphany, instead describing the moment of aesthetic apprehension as an experience of stasis.[6] The emphasis of Stephen's aesthetic theory is significantly different in *Portrait*; the goal of aesthetic apprehension is no longer presented as a semi-religious celebration of the spirit's ability to manifest itself through matter, but as a rare balance of spirit and matter, imagination and observation, an evenness of apprehension illustrated by the commingling of light and darkness in Shelley's image of a 'fading coal' (*P* 213).[7]

In philosophical and religious terms, epiphany represents an idealistic, even platonic belief in the superiority of the spirit, its ability to transcend materiality.[8] However, as Joyce's brother Stanislaus suggests, Joyce also used epiphany to signify a psychological revelation of repressed or subconscious truth through slips or errors. In his papers, arranged and edited by Richard Ellmann under the title *My Brother's Keeper*, Stanislaus writes:

> Another experimental form which [Joyce's] literary urge took . . . consisted in the noting of what he called 'epiphanies'; – manifestations or revelations. Jim always had a contempt for secrecy, and these notes were in the beginning ironical observations of slips, and little errors and gestures – mere straws in the wind – by which people betrayed the very things they were most careful to conceal . . . The revelation and importance of the subconscious had caught his interest.[9]

According to Stanislaus's account, the epiphanies began as satiric attempts to expose the pretensions of others, and they grew to include brief realizations of unconscious knowledge as it is unexpectedly unlocked by language or dream.

As Joyce matured, he lost the desire to exalt either spirituality or his own authorial privilege, and he increasingly valued more balanced representations of individual with shared realities. The *Epiphanies* fail to preserve such a balance; although they frequently invite us to entertain two opposed perspectives through puns or dialogue, one is always clearly preferred. In epiphany 32, for example, when Joyce juxtaposes the human race with a horse race, thereby foreshadowing the running puns of *Ulysses*, the human race clearly suffers by the comparison: '[H]uman creatures are swarming in the enclosure, moving backwards and forwards through the thick ooze.' In contrast to the vile human race is the distant, idealized horse race: 'A beautiful brown horse, with a yellow rider upon him, flashes far away in the sunlight.'

Criticism has tended to favour the concept of epiphany over the prose sketches that bear the same name. Lacking context themselves, the epiphanies have seemed less attractive in their denuded manuscript state than when decked out in the heavy robes of myth, religion, and aesthetics.[10] However, most critics have agreed that the importance of the manuscript epiphanies may be traced to a few of their most marked features: the absence of authorial commentary that also characterizes Joyce's later work; the division of the epiphanies into two types; their structure, a sequential ordering of fragments which has the effect of submerging 'plot'; the interplay of conscious and subconscious awareness; and their reappearance in the richer contexts of Joyce's subsequent works.[11]

The epiphanies evoke the desire and fear of discovery, but their exposures are all designed to prove the power and authority of the self over the external world. *Chamber Music*, as we shall see, transposes the theme of disclosure into a new key, taking it out of the psychological and mythic realm and into a private chamber, where attitudes of eroticism and morbidity are paramount.

The poetry

The nature of Joyce's poetic accomplishment may be momentarily pinned down only by a pointed definition of what exactly is meant by 'poetry' in the context of his career. If by poetry we mean a composition in verse that manages, paradoxically, to combine richness of applicability with verbal compactness, bridging public and private experience; if we are talking about poems on the order of Yeats's 'The Tower' or 'Among School Children', Joyce wrote no such poetry, although it could be argued that he realized comparably 'poetic' aims in prose. However, Joyce did not restrict himself to prose; his earliest efforts were primarily in verse, and by the end of his career he had written over one hundred poems, parodies, and poetic fragments. What distinguishes Joyce's poetry from that of someone like Yeats is that Joyce never used verse as a comprehensive form; he seldom strives to integrate different levels of meaning in a single metrical stroke. Instead, Joyce uses conventional poetic forms and metres as a way of *simplifying* emotional experience, whether in the form of a musical lyric, a satirical limerick, or an angry broadside. Versification allowed him to pare away complexity in favour of a simpler emotional and verbal expressiveness.

It is appropriate for a writer as contradictory as Joyce that his greatest poetry never assumes poetic form. Nevertheless, Joyce did write – and publish – two collections of verse, *Chamber Music* (1907) and *Pomes Penyeach* (1927), in addition to two earlier collections that he destroyed, and of which only fragments remain, *Moods* and *Shine and Dark*. In addition, he wrote numerous occasional poems, which tend to be comic or satirical – two broadsides, several limericks, regular quatrain poems, and quite a few poems designed to be sung to music.[12] His verses represent a wide variety of moods, from anguished nihilism or stung pride to lyrical wooing, but the range of emotion is not matched by a comparable flexibility in poetic technique. Joyce's verses are deliberately constructed, like everything he wrote, and they do manage to create some unusual local effects, many of which gather around Joyce's use of one particular word to magnetize the meaning of an entire poem, but his poems lack formal complexity or variation. For this reason, several critics have suggested that Joyce's poems are, more accurately, songs.

What differentiates Joyce's poetry most markedly from that of Yeats, and from his own most successful prose, is its paucity of voices and its propensity towards enclosure. *Chamber Music* might not be an inappropriate title for the majority of Joyce's metrical compositions; even the volume that bears that title is fairly representative of what Joyce achieved – and failed to achieve – in verse.[13] First of all, there is only one voice in *Chamber Music*, that of an alternately idealistic and sensual young lover. That voice serenades a conventionally golden-haired young woman who first appears playing the piano in her chamber (ii). The burden of the lover's song is his desire to enter that chamber, which is a room, her heart, and metaphorically, of course, her womb. At first, the enclosed spaces that he longs to enter are depicted as warm and inviting, but after the poem that Joyce identified as the 'climax' of the sequence (xiv), those spaces cool and grow shadowy, increasingly representing the darker allure of sleep, and, ultimately, death.

At the outset of the sequence, the lover's desire for his beloved to 'unclose' herself to his love emerges by means of the analogies he sets up between his love songs and the music of the night wind, and between his beloved's hidden fire and the dawn. In the first poem, an anthropomorphized Love is wandering (like Yeats's 'Wandering Aengus') by the music along the river; in the next poem, it is the young woman's thoughts, eyes and hands 'That wander as they list', 'list' functioning both as an archaic word meaning 'inclination' and as a contraction of 'listen'. (The woman's frequent attitude of 'bending' or 'leaning' seems to figure a quite literal inclination, in this case her inclination to listen to the lover's songs and what they portend.) In poem III, the lover asks her if she has heard the natural and celestial music of 'the night wind and the sighs / Of harps playing unto Love to unclose / The pale gates of sunrise'. The next poem makes it clear that his music is designed to replicate the music of wind and harps, encouraging her to unclose *her* gate, at which he is singing. In v the gate is replaced by a window, which he urges her to lean through; in vI he openly expresses his desire to be 'in that sweet bosom', which, by the structural similarities that link the two stanzas, is also 'that heart' at which he softly 'knock[s]'. Images of enclosure grow brighter and less confining in successive poems: in vII, 'the sky's a pale blue cup'; in vIII, the 'chamber' is a sunny woodland; and in x it is a hollow. In poem xI, the dominant images of enclosure have been reduced in size and domesticated; the constraint of virginity is here represented by the snood that binds her hair and the stays that enclose her 'girlish bosom'. Picking up on the last word of xI, 'maidenhood', xII launches an argument against all 'hooded' or cautious counsel, particularly that of the hooded moon and the hooded Capuchin. Finally, in xIII, attention shifts back to the woman's chamber as the lover urges the 'Wind of spices whose song is ever / Epithalamium' to 'come into her little garden / And sing at her window' (compare Yeats, 'The Cap and Bells').

By poems xIV and xV, Love has indeed unclosed the gates of pale sunrise, thereby unlocking the potential for a son to rise; these dawn poems are also celebrations of consummated love. The speaker's love has shifted along the fault of rhyme to become a dove, image of the holy spirit, whom he bids, like the sun, to 'arise'. Although 'Eastward the gradual dawn prevails / Where softly-burning fires appear' (xV), the main impulse of the poems that follow xV is to escape the heat of the sun, whether into the 'cool and pleasant valley' of xVI (contrast the hollow of x), the 'deep cool shadow' of the dark pine-wood of xX (contrast the green and sunny wood of vIII), the prison of interwoven arms in xXII (contrast xI), the mossy nest of her heart (xXIII; contrast vI), the wasted sun and cloud-wrapped vales of xXV (compare vII), or the grave where 'all love shall sleep' (xXVIII). In xIII, the lover invited 'The wind of spices' into his beloved's garden to sing; in sharp contrast,

XXIX describes 'Desolate winds that assail with cries / The shadowy garden where love is'. As the lover once knocked at the heart of his beloved, a 'rogue in red and yellow dress' is now knocking at a leaving tree (XXXIII) in mocking echo of springtime desire, and in XXXIV, the voice of the winter is at the door, crying to the Macbeth-like dreamer, 'Sleep no more'. This final poem in the sequence proper (Joyce wrote to G. Molyneux Palmer that XXXV and XXXVI are tailpieces, *Letters* 167) is the only one in which voices begin to proliferate, as the voice within the lover's heart clashes with the voice of the winter outside his chamber, one crying 'Sleep now', the other forbidding further sleep. Appropriately, the music of the water has been displaced by 'noise' in XXXV, and choiring by a monotone. XXXVI is a literal image of nightmare that anticipates Joyce's punning treatment of nightmare in *Ulysses* and in *FW* 583.8–9: horses (mares?) come out of the sea – *mer* – at night, ridden by disdainful charioteers in black armour. The Love of the first poem has been supplanted by war, 'An army charging upon the land'; the idealized figure of garlanded peace ('Dark leaves on his hair') replaced with a multitude of embattled, shouting phantoms shaking in triumph their long, green hair.

The most influential treatments of *Chamber Music* have all arranged themselves around the linchpin of the title. William York Tindall reflects back on *Chamber Music* from the perspective of *Ulysses*, where Bloom thinks of chamber music as the music Molly makes when she urinates in a chamberpot (*U* 11.979–84). He connects this with the varying stories about how the title was chosen told by Herbert Gorman and Oliver St John Gogarty, both of which involve chamberpots as well, concluding with a strained interpretation of poems VII and XXVI as representations of micturition.[14] Tindall identified urination as one among many dimensions of the title's meaning, suggesting that it was also a sequence about wantonness – Elizabethan 'chambering'.

Chamber Music sparsely records a seduction and its chilly aftermath, but the main implication of its title is that it explores the musical possibilities of a small enclosed space. Joyce emphasized the musical nature of *Chamber Music* not only through the title but also by setting one of the poems to music himself (XI), and by encouraging Geoffrey Molyneux Palmer to set others: 'I hope you may set all of *Chamber Music* in time. This was indeed partly my idea in writing it. The book is in fact a suite of songs and if I were a musician I suppose I should have set them to music myself' (*Letters* 167). Stress on the music of the poems has recently been offset by Archie K. Loss's attention to its visual spaces – chamber and wood – in the context of Symbolist art, and by Chester Anderson's interest in its rhythmical gestures and rhetorical figures.[15] Such competing perspectives have made it easier to appreciate the economy with which the musical and spatial dimensions of the poems have been integrated. Technically, the stability and smallness of the poems' structure, together with the fact that they are all sung by the same voice, allow Joyce to explore, not the landscapes of Dublin, but a miniaturized interior chamber, which almost imperceptibly transforms itself into an image of the grave ('We were grave lovers', xxx). The external landscapes of the poem are all psychological and sexualized extensions of other inner chambers, a technique that Joyce learned from Yeats's *The Wind Among the Reeds*.

Poetry seems to have remained a slight vessel for Joyce, a vehicle for expressing emotions of isolation, or for preserving isolated moments. As the title suggests, *Pomes Penyeach* are not worth much individually; they are inexpensive offerings of private moments, one protective and delicate ('A Flower Given to my Daughter'), another arming the speaker against nostalgia for the simplicity and trust of childhood ('Simples'), but most agonized or despairing. As Herbert Howarth has suggested, Joyce's poems are the productions of a Henry Flower[16] (although 'A Memory of the Players in a Mirror at Midnight' could have been written by Virag); they are musical, nostalgic, and markedly sentimental – Siren songs, such as the ones Bloom listens to and ultimately rejects in the 'Sirens' episode of *Ulysses*. Joyce betrays an awareness of the danger of such songs in 'Simples', where the speaker prays for an Odyssean sailor's 'waxen ear / To shield me from her childish croon'; the deficiency of his poems is their power to evoke a 'Flood' of nostalgia. Joyce never underestimated the power of simple song to seduce the sense and shipwreck the desire for life, which explains why, perhaps, a song from *Pomes Penyeach*, 'Nightpiece', was once the core of the 'Tristan and Isolde' episode of *Finnegans Wake*.[17] An early draft of the episode began as ironic marginalia that surrounds and eventually subsumes its sentimental centre: the romantic, despairing poem of youth.

Giacomo Joyce

Like *Chamber Music*, *Giacomo Joyce* is a seduction piece. But if the 'Sirens' episode provides a context against which the power and danger of *Chamber Music* can be read, *Giacomo Joyce* is best read against 'Nausicaa', which takes painting rather than music as its technic. And if the danger of the music that seduces is a function of its univocality and its simplicity, *Giacomo Joyce* – against the background of 'Nausicaa' – shows that the danger of voyeurism is comparable to the seductive lure of the lyric. As *Chamber Music* lacks more than one voice, *Giacomo Joyce* lacks a view from more than one perspective:

it is an example of what Joyce would later see as the distortion that results from failing to account for parallax.

Giacomo Joyce is a series of prose sketches formally akin to the narrative epiphanies. A fair-copy manuscript of sixteen pages transcribed onto eight oversized sheets of heavy paper, most probably in the summer of 1914, it is the only one of Joyce's writings to be set in Trieste, which is also where Joyce left it when he moved on to Zurich in 1915 (*GJ* xv, xi). The story – told through disjointed images rather than successive songs – loosely follows the lines of the story in *Chamber Music*, with emphasis falling once again on the waxing and waning of love, a waning that in this case seems to have something to do with the appearance of a rival. Unlike *Chamber Music*, however, *Giacomo Joyce* does not contain any suggestion that the love affair it chronicles – Joyce's relationship with one of the pupils to whom he taught English in Trieste, Amalia Popper – was ever anything more than an 'affair of the eye', and in this respect it anticipates 'Nausicaa'. However, its divergences from 'Nausicaa' are as important as its similarities: 'Nausicaa' provides two perspectives, that of the woman as well as the man, to Giacomo's one. Also in sharp contrast are the two accounts of the affair's climax. Unlike 'Nausicaa', in which Bloom's encounter with Gerty spends itself in a comically onanistic display of fireworks, *Giacomo Joyce* ends more bitterly when the object of the artist's gaze announces her preference for another man, for Barabbas (who is probably Popper's fiancé Michele Risolo) over Christ (Joyce) (*GJ* 16; see Mahaffey, '*Giacomo Joyce*', p. 406).

What is most notably missing in *Giacomo Joyce* is the perspective of the woman, a perspective that is so strategically provided in *Ulysses*.[18] Our first view of her is prefaced by a question – 'Who?' – and she emerges as a montage created by images of a pale face, furs, and quizzing glasses (*GJ* 1). Typical of the speaker's furtive mode of observing her is the sketch where he looks 'upward from night and mud', watching her 'dressing to go to the play' (*GJ* 6). His voyeurism grows more intimate as he pictures himself hooking her black gown, seeing through the opening 'her lithe body sheathed in an orange shift'. The shift shifts to a ship that 'slips its ribbons of moorings at her shoulders' and reveals her silver fishlike body 'shimmering with silvery scales' (*GJ* 7). She edges more closely towards Gerty MacDowell when, 'virgin most prudent', her 'sudden moving knee' catches her skirt back and the viewer sees 'a white lace edging of an underskirt lifted unduly' (*GJ* 9).

The animality or floral delicacy of her body is frequently available to the eyes of the beholder, but what is withheld are her thoughts, her anxieties, her dreams. This is even the case in the most bizarre sketch of the sequence, the interpolated dream scene that depicts her attacking him with a cold lust mingled with aggression:

– I am not convinced that such activities of the mind or body can be called unhealthy –

She speaks. A weak voice from beyond the cold stars. Voice of wisdom. Say on! O, say again, making me wise! This voice I never heard.

She coils towards me along the crumpled lounge. I cannot move or speak. Coiling approach of starborn flesh. Adultery of wisdom. No. I will go. I will.

– Jim, love! –

Soft sucking lips kiss my left armpit: a coiling kiss on myriad veins. I burn! I crumple like a burning leaf! From my right armpit a fang of flame leaps out. A starry snake has kissed me: a cold nightsnake. I am lost!

– Nora! –   (*GJ* 15)

Paradoxically, her coldness inflames and terrifies Joyce; she is portrayed as a snake whose very kiss injects him with venom, producing a fiery 'fang'. Here in active desire as elsewhere in passive reserve, she remains objectified.

Unlike *Chamber Music, Giacomo Joyce* seems to have been composed without any other listener (or viewer) in mind than 'Giacomo' himself. Partly because of its intense self-referentiality, the course of the imagined affair is difficult for a reader to trace without the aid of biographical information to flesh out the details, or without a guide to the use of unexpected literary allusions to string together disjointed patches of narrative. As a result, most accounts of *Giacomo Joyce* focus on biography or allusion, and the political implications of Joyce's project in *Giacomo Joyce* remain largely unexplored. It is not clear, for example, how Joyce's disturbingly ambivalent treatment of the young Jewish woman in *Giacomo Joyce* accords with his later presentations of women and Jews in *Ulysses*. The German graphic artist Paul Wunderlich has interpreted Joyce's interest in his student as erotic desire mingled with prophetic compassion for what would later be done to the Jews in Nazi-controlled Europe.[19] *Giacomo Joyce* plays on the incommensurability of artistic and social power, as well as that of sexual and racial privilege, but it does so in a way that protects Joyce's privilege as a man, a gentile and a writer. In *Exiles*, as well as in his maturer works, Joyce is quick to recognize such imbalances of power, devising a variety of strategies for drawing attention to them, but in *Giacomo Joyce*, as in the *Epiphanies* and *Chamber Music*, such privileges are protected by the fear of their reversal.

Exiles

Chamber Music and *Giacomo Joyce* record the passing of a carefully controlled passion, but reflect little or no compassion for the figure they idealize. In contrast, *Exiles*, like 'The Dead', aims at exposing the lack of compassion that precludes relationship. *Exiles* relentlessly exhumes the self-interest buried in conventions of love and friendship, pursuing its grim and hack-neyed discoveries unrelieved by Joyce's characteristic humour. As padraic Colum asserts in his introduction to the play (reproduced in the Penguin-Viking edition), the revelations of *Exiles* have a ritualistic decorum: 'In its structure, *Exiles* is a series of confessions; the dialogue has the dryness of recitals in the confessional; its end is an act of contrition' (*E* 11).

Interestingly, the only production of the play that has been generally acclaimed as successful, that of Harold Pinter at the Mermaid Theatre in London in 1970 (repeated by the Royal Shakespeare Company at the Ald-wych Theatre in the following year), also stressed the quiet, threateningly conventional seriousness of the play. Bernard Benstock has described the effect: 'All the lines were read with precise politeness at a slow tempo, with little emotion ever allowed to violate the proprieties; an undertone of quiet menace pervaded throughout, giving a certain shape even to the most "inno-cent" lines; and no suggestion of Joycean irony was permitted in the inter-pretation. It was magnificent, but it was not quite Joyce.'[20] Benstock ques-tions the authenticity of Pinter's interpretation because it conflicts with the assumption that a Joycean text is necessarily ironic. It has never been clear, however, whether *Exiles* is ironic, or whether, like the other shorter works, its ironies are earnest ones.

Concerns about the seriousness of *Exiles* lie behind most critical assess-ments of the promise or disappointment of the play. Which way the needle of judgement points depends, in large part, on our expectations. And that is fundamentally what the play itself is about: the discovery that betrayal is only meaningful in response to a prior expectation. Joyce's interest in the egotism of expectation and its relation to treachery is even apparent in the political background of the play. Although Richard disclaims any kinship with Archibald Hamilton Rowan (*E* 45), Richard's son Archie, who repre-sents future possibility, bears his name. Significantly, the historical Rowan's notable distinction was to be labelled a traitor by both the English and the Irish. Both expected him to support their side, but he did not take sides unilaterally: he refused to help Wolfe Tone in his plans for the revolution of 1798 after he saw the Reign of Terror in France, yet when he returned to Ireland in 1803 he supported Catholic emancipation, which brought the wrath of Peel down on him in 1825.[21]

In the play, Joyce's main characters are less aware than Hamilton Rowan of the dependence of 'treachery' upon expectation: Robert Hand expects Richard Rowan to be a patriot and a possessive lover; when Richard vio-lates these expectations, Robert subtly accuses him of treachery, of having left his country (and his beloved) 'in her hour of need'. Similarly, Richard expects Robert to be honest rather than secretive about his desire for

Richard's companion Bertha, an expectation which is as arbitrary, in a sense, as Robert's expectation that Richard will fight for his 'property'. It is Richard, not Robert, who values honesty, and it is Robert, not Richard, who is obsessed with possession; the treachery of both is the assumption that the other should share his own values. Does Bertha desire the freedom that Richard wants for her? Does Richard want to be the proud and scornful iconoclast that Beatrice Justice admires in him? Does Beatrice yearn to be a cold, dead model for an exiled writer's work? Does Bertha want to be the embodiment of Robert's 'dream of love'?

The possibility of love, or connection, remains shadowy in *Exiles* because love is only possible when the expectations that strive to shape it are confronted and dissolved. Joyce writes that Richard's jealousy 'must reveal itself as the very immolation of the pleasure of possession on the altar of love' (*E* 114), an attempt that Joyce seems to take very seriously (at times too seriously for optimum dramatic effect). Although the conclusion of the play is clumsily rhetorical (Richard is – for the first time in the play – seeing himself in a dramatic light, which reinforces his egotism), it takes the form it does partly because of its importance in the veiled contexts that inform Joyce's analysis of love in the play: his reading of Nietzsche, Wagner, and their disciple D'Annunzio, in particular.

Much of Joyce's reading centred on the destructiveness of seeking to possess another person in the name of love, of desiring to recreate the loved one in the creator's own image instead of accepting and appreciating the differences that necessarily divide lovers. In *The Case of Wagner* (which Joyce owned in Trieste), Nietzsche argues that even philosophers misunderstand the nature of love, refusing to see that what we call love is actually mortal hatred between the sexes. He claims that the only conception of love worthy of a philosopher is one that recognizes that people kill what they love by trying to possess it, citing José's destruction of Carmen as an example (see 'Scylla and Charybdis', where Stephen uses the same example to illustrate his theory of Shakespeare (*U* 9.1022–3)). He asserts that people demand a return for loving another person by wanting 'to *possess* the other creature'.[22] The lover insists on being loved in return, even though the demand results in the 'death' of the loved one. In *Exiles*, Robert yearns for such a 'death of the spirit', in sharp contrast to Richard's fear of it. Richard, wielding honesty as the weapon of his will to power, seems to be modelled partly on Nietzsche; Robert, with his equally strong will to illusion, owes many of his most distinctive characteristics to Wagner.[23]

The most obvious allusion to Wagner occurs at the beginning of the second act, when Robert moves to the piano to strum out Wolfram's aria in *Tannhäuser* (*E* 58). Like Wagner, whom Nietzsche characterized as an 'old robber', a 'seducer on a grand scale' (*Case* 42, 39), Robert stealthily tries to seduce Bertha, an attempt that Richard, attentive to the 'robber' in Robert's name, likens to the act of a thief in the night (*E* 61). Both Richard and Nietzsche describe the art of their former associates as the art of lying (*Case* 35, and *E* 39, where Richard calls Robert's leading articles lies). Most notably, Robert's 'dream of love' for Bertha echoes that of Wagner for Mathilde Wesendonck, wife of Wagner's good friend Otto Wesendonck. Mathilde, like Bertha (and like Nora when Prezioso was wooing her), kept her husband informed of everything that happened between herself and her suitor.[24] Like Robert, who puts a pink glass shade on the lamp in his bedroom, telling Bertha, 'It was for you' (*E* 78–9), Wagner gave Mathilde a pink lamp shade in 1858 (*Wagner to Wesendonck*, p. 18). Robert says to Bertha in *Exiles*, 'And that is the truth – a dream? . . . Bertha! . . . In all my life only that dream is real. I forget the rest' (*E* 106). Similarly, Wagner writes to Liszt in December 1854:

> As I never in my life have quaffed the actual delight of love, I mean some day to raise a monument to this most beauteous of all dreams, wherein that love shall glut itself quite royally for once. In my head I've planned a *Tristan and Isolde*. (*Wagner to Wesendonck*, p. li)

In the composition of *Exiles*, Joyce drew not only on Wagner's life – his dream of love for Mathilde Wesendonck – but also on the opera that expressed that dream. Joyce indicates in his notes that the idealized love of Robert and Bertha is indebted to that of Tristan and Isolde (*E* 123), a suggestion reinforced by the fact that in the 'Scribbledehobble' notebook for *Finnegans Wake*, Joyce entered notes on Tristan and Isolde under the heading for *Exiles*.[25] The most important (and least successful) import from Wagner's *Tristan and Isolde* is the wound that Mark claims Tristan has given him, which reappears to mar the conclusion of *Exiles* in the form of Richard's 'wound of doubt'. In Act II, when Mark asks Tristan why he has wounded him, Tristan tells him that he cannot truly tell, that what Mark would know can never have an answer (II: iii), an awareness that Richard already has in *Exiles*. When Bertha offers to tell Richard what has happened between her and Robert, he replies, 'I can never know, never in this world' (*E* 112; also 102).

The plot of *Tristan and Isolde* revolves around betrayal, as that of *Exiles* would later do in its shadow. Isolde accuses Tristan of having betrayed her by carrying her away from Ireland to the land of king Mark (I: iv, I: v); Brangäne betrays her mistress by giving her the love philtre instead of the death potion she requested; Isolde betrays her husband; Tristan betrays his friend and king; Melot betrays his 'truest' friend Tristan; Mark accuses Tristan of having betrayed him a second time by dying when Mark has come to 'prove his perfect trust' in him. In short, every character accuses every other of treachery, a situation duplicated in *Exiles*. Bertha accuses Richard of having left her when they were in Rome; Richard accuses Robert of trying to steal Bertha from him craftily and secretly; Robert accuses Richard of having abandoned those who depend on him in their hour of need.

Tristan and Isolde deliberately choose night-time, secrecy, illusion, and death over daylight, openness, truth, and life. As Brangäne warns them, love has put out the 'light' of their reason (II: i), and they persist in living in the darkness of a dream. Tristan's passionate desire for death, illusion, and night is shared by Robert; the gradual dimming of the lights during the scene in Robert's cottage between Robert and Bertha recalls the longing of both Tristan and Isolde for the torch to be extinguished, for the sudden darkness to envelop them, signalling Tristan to come to his beloved. Hatred of light and longing for death are the main themes of the famous love duet in the second act of Wagner's opera (II: ii). Night is the realm of dreams, and Tristan and Isolde embrace it, insisting that their dreams are the only reality.[26]

As in *Ulysses*, where the allusions to Homer criss-cross with references to Shakespeare's *Hamlet*, *Exiles* positions itself in relation to not one but two strikingly different authors. If the Wagnerian allusions shadow the relationship between Robert and Bertha, a second pattern of allusion serves to illuminate the relationship between Richard and Beatrice, a pattern which, as Beatrice's name suggests, derives from Dante. For Richard, as for Dante, Beatrice represents the story of his young life, his *Vita nuova*.[27] Aside from Beatrice's name, most of the allusions to the *Vita nuova* in *Exiles* are numerological. Dante meets Beatrice when he is nine, he sees her again nine years later, he has a vision of her at the ninth hour of the day, and she dies in June, which is the ninth month of the year by the Syrian calendar, in the year of her century in which the perfect number ten has been completed nine times. Dante's Beatrice dies in June of her twenty-seventh year; *Exiles* is set in June of Beatrice Justice's twenty-seventh year, and it has been nine years since the departure of Richard and Bertha that so changed all their lives (autobiographically, in June of 1912 it had only been eight years since Joyce left Dublin with Nora). The mysterious union between Bertha, now 'nine times more beautiful' (*E* 86), and Robert takes place at nine o'clock at night (*E* 83).[28]

Strikingly, the sensual relationship between Robert and Bertha, like the idealized one that links Richard and Beatrice, has no basis in reality: they are equally delusory. This is what gives the play its power, the gradual realization that there is no essential difference between Dante's Beatrice and Wagner's Isolde, that both are possessed in a way that threatens the life of each. Such a view represents a significant advance upon Joyce's way of thinking in April of 1912, when in answer to an examination question at the University of Padua he set up a weighted contrast between the medieval the-ologian and the modern journalist. In 'L'influenza letteraria universale del rinascimento', Joyce argued that 'The Renaissance . . . has put the journalist in the monk's chair: that is to say, has deposed an acute, limited and formal mentality to give the scepter to a mentality that is facile and wide-ranging.'[29] In this essay, Joyce illustrates the difference between the theologian and the journalist (whom he would later embody as Richard and Robert) with a comparison between Dante and Wagner, *Tristan and Isolde* and the *Inferno*. Joyce expresses a clear preference for Dante, who, he argues, builds the *Inferno* out of a gradually intensifying idea (the idea of hate), in contrast to Wagner, who expresses the opposite sentiment of love by linking it to sensations of the flesh:

> A great modern artist wishing to put the sentiment of love to music reproduces, as far as his art permits, each pulsation, each trembling, the lightest shivering, the lightest sigh; the harmonies intertwine and oppose each other secretly: one loves even as one grows more cruel, suffers when and as much as one enjoys, hate and doubt flash in the lovers' eyes, their bodies become one single flesh. Place *Tristan and Isolde* next to the *Inferno* and you will notice how the poet's hate follows its path from abyss to abyss in the wake of an idea that intensifies; and the more intensely the poet consumes himself in the fire of hate, the more violent becomes the art with which the artist communicates his passion. One is the art of the circumstance, the other is ideational.
>
> (Berrone, *James Joyce in Padua*, pp. 20–1)

Joyce's disdain for an art of the flesh (he goes on to claim that 'modern man has an epidermis rather than a soul' (Berrone, p. 21)) is still apparent in *Exiles*, but it has begun to break down. The ideal figure that once inspired him, as she inspired Dante, is portrayed as cold and dead; as Joyce suggests in the notes, 'Beatrice's mind is an abandoned cold temple in which hymns have risen heavenward in a distant past but where now a doddering priest offers alone and hopelessly prayers to the Most High' (*E* 119). Only Bertha suggests the possibility of life, combining uncommon receptivity with a practical-minded resistance to the desire of others to possess her.[30]

From a criticism of Wagner's sensuality as it contrasts with the ideality of a writer like Dante, Joyce arrived at a more balanced view of the relationship between ideal and real, partly through the writing of *Exiles*. *Exiles* unveils the power of the thinker as comparable to that of the seducer; if Robert has refreshed Bertha's awareness of her loneliness, Richard has confirmed Beatrice's suspicion that she too is isolated. The deadliness of idealization as a more subtle form of possessiveness is brought home in another work that Joyce draws on for *Exiles* that was itself influenced by the work of both Nietzsche and Wagner, Gabriele D'Annunzio's novel *The Triumph of Death*.[31]

The Triumph of Death details the mortal struggle between two lovers to possess one another, a struggle that culminates in murder-suicide of the kind Robert romantically longs for in *Exiles*: 'I want to end it and have done with it . . . To end it all – death. To fall from a great high cliff, down, right down into the sea . . . Listening to music and in the arms of the woman I love – the sea, music and death' (*E* 35). This is how the lovers die in *The Triumph of Death*, but the climax is anything but romantic: Giorgio and Ippolita have been listening to Wagner's *Tristan and Isolde* for two days, which transports them into 'a world of fiction'. He fears that she will enslave him through the power of desire, and he takes her to the edge of the sea: 'There was a brief but savage struggle, as between two mortal foes who had nourished a secret and implacable hatred in their souls up till that hour', and they crash 'down headlong into death, locked in that fierce embrace' (p. 315).

What Giorgio and Ippolita are struggling over is the power to possess – and to create – one another. From the outset, Giorgio is oppressed by the certainty that he can never possess Ippolita wholly (p. 5); like Gabriel in 'The Dead', he is jealous of the very memories that exclude him:

> Suddenly a thought will strike me cold: what if I, unwittingly, should have evoked in her memory the ghost of some sensation felt once before, some pale phantom of the days long past? . . . You become remote, inaccessible; I am left alone in horrible solitude. (pp. 6–7)

To forestall such infidelity, however inadvertent, he remakes her; as Ippolita meditates, 'In these two years he has transformed me – made another woman of me; he has given me new senses, a new soul, a new mind. I am his creature, the work of his hands' (p. 33). (In *Exiles*, Robert says to Richard of Bertha, 'She is yours, your work', *E* 62.) Later Ippolita repeats to him that she is wholly his creation (p. 119), and he succeeds in feeling 'the thrill of a creator': 'Giorgio had witnessed that transformation, so intoxicating to a lover of intellect – the metamorphosis of the woman he loves to his own image' (p. 141).

Giorgio's power to create and recreate Ippolita, his 'thrill' at creation, is a fantasy of possession. She has sacrificed herself to Giorgio's desire to possess her (p. 188), and he comes to see that he can transform her over and over again at will, into a goddess, an animal, a witch, or a snake: 'Her form is moulded by my desire, her shadow cast by my thoughts. Her aspects are protean as the dreams of fever' (p. 229). The narrator warns that 'his intelligence had reduced his mistress to a mere motive force to his imagination, and stripped her person of all value' (p. 235) (as Rubek did to Irene in Ibsen's *When We Dead Awaken*), but just at the point of his greatest triumph he discovers his greatest fear: she has an equal power over him. In his imagination, he hears her telling him that she knows the secret of her metamorphoses in his soul, that she knows all the words and the gestures that have the power to transfigure her in his eyes (p. 237). Both now long to destroy the person they cannot possess, and Wagner's opera serves as the prelude to the destructive consummation that both, in different ways, desire.

Although Ibsen also dramatizes the deadliness of power masked as love in *When We Dead Awaken*, the intensity of Joyce's exploration of the mortal combat between each of the four main characters in *Exiles* makes sense only in a larger intellectual context that includes Wagner, Nietzsche, and D'Annunzio as well as Ibsen. Moreover, *Exiles* celebrates what Ibsen could not, the refusal of lovers to be killed by the people who attempt to possess them; as Joyce writes in his notes, Bertha loves the part of Richard that 'she must try to kill, never be able to kill and rejoice at her impotence' (*E* 118), just as Richard loves and hates the living part of her that is open to experience. The most important aspect of *Exiles* is its implicit celebration of its characters' refusal to be buried in the snowy avalanche of Ibsen's despairing last play. The alternative to death, however, is acceptance, a hard-won acceptance of human difference that was to usher in *Ulysses*.

NOTES

1 Robert Scholes and Richard M. Kain, eds., *The Workshop of Daedalus: James Joyce and the Raw Materials for 'A Portrait of the Artist as a Young Man'* (Evanston: Northwestern University Press, 1965), pp. 3–4. Hereafter referred to as *WD*.

2 A duality also discussed by John Paul Riquelme in ch. 5 of this volume.

3 I have presented such an argument in '*Giacomo Joyce*', in Zack Bowen and James C. Carens, eds., *A Companion to Joyce Studies* (Westport, Connecticut: Greenwood Press, 1984), p. 393.

4 'Continuous manuscript' is Hans Walter Gabler's term for the successive autograph notations that he uses as the copytext for his edition of *Ulysses*. See Gabler's Afterword to '*Ulysses': A Critical and Synoptic Edition* (New York: Garland, 1984), pp. 1894–6.

5 Of the forty extant epiphanies, twenty-two (in Joyce's hand) are housed in the Poetry Collection at the State University of New York at Buffalo; transcriptions of these were published by Oscar Silverman as *Joyce's Epiphanies* (Buffalo: Lockwood Memorial Library, 1956). The twenty-five remaining epiphanies are at Cornell; all but one of these are from Stanislaus Joyce's commonplace book, and the remaining one (concerning Oliver Gogarty) is a rough draft in Joyce's own hand. Seven of the Cornell epiphanies are duplicates of those at Buffalo. When Peter Spielberg

discovered that the Buffalo epiphanies have numbers on the versos that go as high as seventy-one, Robert Scholes and Richard Kain responded by ordering all the extant epiphanies into a sequence, which they transcribed and annotated (*WD*, pp. 3–51). Facsimiles of all of the epiphanies have since been published in *Archive 7, 'A Portrait of the Artist as a Young Man': A Facsimile of Epiphanies, Notes, Manuscripts and Typescripts*, ed. Hans Walter Gabler. The epiphanies are available, together with the poems, the 1904 'Portrait' essay, and *Giacomo Joyce*, in *James Joyce: Poems and Shorter Writings*, ed. Richard Ellmann, A. Walton Litz, and John Whittier-Ferguson (London: Faber, 1991).

6 Both Hugh Kenner and S. L. Goldberg argued that Joyce's omission represents a deliberate attempt on Joyce's part of weaken Stephen's aesthetic theories (see *Dublin's Joyce* (Bloomington: University of Indiana Press, 1966), ch. 9, and *The Classical Temper* (New York: Barnes and Noble, 1961), chs. 2 and 3), which prompted Robert Scholes to contest the meaningfulness of the term epiphany in a controversial article, 'Joyce and the Epiphany: The Key to the Labyrinth?' *Sewanee Review* 72 (1964), 65–77.

7 Morris Beja attempts to get round the difficulty posed by the 'spiritual' nature of epiphany by redefining spirituality; see *Epiphany in the Modern Novel* (London: Peter Owen, 1971), p. 74.

8 Stephen admits as much in *Portrait*, when he tells Lynch that for a long time he thought Aquinas' third stage of apprehension signified 'symbolism or idealism, the supreme quality of beauty being a light from some other world, the idea of which the matter is but the shadow, the reality of which it is but the symbol', so that the goal of apprehension was 'the artistic discovery and representation of the divine purpose in anything' (*P* 213).

9 Stanislaus Joyce, *My Brother's Keeper*, ed. Richard Ellmann (London: Faber, 1958), pp. 134–5.

10 See, for just one example, Florence Walzl, 'The Liturgy of the Epiphany Season and the Epiphanies of Joyce', *PMLA* 80 (1965), 436–50. Even Robert Scholes, who was through the greenness of the concept of epiphany when he transcribed and edited the manuscript epiphanies, asserts that 'the Epiphanies themselves for the most part bear out Stephen's condemnation of them. They are trivial and supercilious or florid and lugubrious, in the main. Their chief significance is in the use Joyce often made of them in his later works' ('Joyce and the Epiphany', p. 73).

11 Morris Beja has found at least thirteen of the extant epiphanies in *Stephen Hero*, twelve in *A Portrait*, four in *Ulysses*, and one in *Finnegans Wake*. See Beja, 'Epiphany and the Epiphanies', in Bowen and Carens, *A Companion to Joyce Studies*, pp. 710–13.

12 Several of Joyce's poems are literally songs, among the most interesting of which is 'Post ulixem scriptum' (to be sung to the tune of 'Molly Brannigan'). Most of the extant poems and poetic fragments are available in facsimile in *Archive* I, ed. A. Walton Litz, and many are listed in Paul Doyle's bibliographical register of 'Joyce's miscellaneous verse' (*JJQ* 2 (1965), 90–6) and his addenda (*JJQ* 4 (1967), 71). One of the most influential arguments about the musical nature of *Chamber Music* is that of Herbert Howarth, '*Chamber Music* and its Place in the Joyce Canon', in Thomas F. Staley, ed., *James Joyce Today* (Bloomington: Indiana University Press, 1966), pp. 11–27. On the similarity between *Chamber Music*

and Elizabethan songs and airs, see Myra Russel, 'The Elizabethan Connection: the Missing Score of James Joyce's *Chamber Music*', *JJQ* 18 (1981), 133–45.

13 *Chamber Music* does however pose uncharacteristic problems of attribution, since Stanislaus Joyce told W. Y. Tindall that both the title and the final arrangement of the poems were his. Joyce's arrangement of the twenty-seven poem sequence is that of the Gilvary manuscript: I, III, II, IV, V, VIII, VII, IX, XVII, XVIII, VI, X, XIII, XIV, XV, XIX, XXIII, XXII, XXIV, XVI, XXXI, XXVIII, XXIX, XXXII, XXX, XXXIII, XXXIV. The arrangement of the Yale manuscript is Stanislaus's: XXI, I, III, II, IV, V, VIII, VII, IX, XVII, XVIII, VI, X, XX, XIII, XI, XIV, XIX, XV, XXIII, XXIV, XVI, XXXI, XXII, XXVI, XII, XXVII, XXVIII, XXV, XXIX, XXXII, XXX, XXIII, XXXIV. See Litz, *Archive* I.

14 William York Tindall, ed., *Chamber Music* by James Joyce (New York: Columbia, 1954), pp. 70–80. For Gorman's story about the title, see his *James Joyce* (New York: Farrar and Rinehart, 1939), p. 116; for Gogarty's, see his *Mourning Became Mrs. Spendlove* (New York: Creative Age Press, 1948), pp. 53–5, 57–60. According to Tindall, Stanislaus denied both stories and recounted a third in a letter to Gorman, arguing that he (Stanislaus) had already chosen the title for the volume by the time the incident took place (Tindall, pp. 72–3).

15 Archie K. Loss, 'Interior and Exterior Imagery in the Earlier Work of Joyce and in Symbolist Art', *Journal of Modern Literature* 8 (1980), 99–117, and Chester Anderson, 'Joyce's Verses', in Bowen and Carens, *A Companion to Joyce Studies*, pp. 129–55.

16 See the reference to this article in note 12.

17 See *A First Draft Version of 'Finnegans Wake'*, ed. David Hayman (Austin: University of Texas Press, 1963), pp. 210–11.

18 In her excellent discussion of *Giacomo Joyce* in 'Shahrazade's Wake: The *Arabian Nights* and the Narrative Dynamics of Charles Dickens and James Joyce' (University of Pennsylvania doctoral dissertation, 1988), Henriette Power presents *Giacomo Joyce* as a power struggle between female physicality and male inscriptions. Power argues that Giacomo's attempt to capture a woman on paper takes the form of an artistic dismemberment, contrasting Giacomo's strategy with that of Bloom in 'Nausicaa' (pp. 162–80).

19 *Giacomo Joyce*, with introduction by Hermann Lenz (Dielsdorf: Matthieu AG, 1976). The edition of ten lithographs was limited to 125 copies.

20 Bernard Benstock, '*Exiles*', in Bowen and Carens, *A Companion to Joyce Studies*, pp. 361–2. See also J. W. Lambert's review of the Mermaid production in *Drama* 100 (Spring 1971), 21–3, and John Spurling's review of the Aldwych production in *Plays and Players* 19 (December 1971), 44–5, 88; a good overview may be found in John MacNicholas, 'The Stage History of *Exiles*', *JJQ* 19 (1981), 9–26.

21 John MacNicholas, *James Joyce's 'Exiles': A Textual Companion* (New York: Garland, 1979), pp. 197–9.

22 Friedrich Nietzsche, *The Case of Wagner*, in *The Complete Works of Friedrich Nietzsche*, trans. A. M. Ludovici, ed. Oscar Levy, VIII (London: Allen and Unwin, 1911), p. 4. Hereafter referred to as *Case*.

23 In 'Joyce contra Wagner', John MacNicholas also suggests that Joyce 'superimposes Wagner upon Robert Hand' (*Comparative Drama* 9 (1975), 29).

24 *Richard Wagner to Mathilde Wesendonck*, trans. and pref. by William Ashton Ellis, 2nd edn. (1905; rpt. New York: Vienna House, 1972), pp. vi–vii.

25 Thomas E. Connolly, *James Joyce's Scribbledehobble: The Ur-Workbook for 'Finnegans Wake'* (Evanston: Northwestern University Press, 1961), pp. 75–85. See David Hayman's treatment of these notes together with some of the parallels between *Exiles* and Wagner's opera in 'Tristan and Isolde in *Finnegans Wake*: a Study of the Sources and Evolution of a Theme', *Comparative Literature Studies* 1 (1964), 95–102.

26 In *Exiles*, Robert, like Tristan, is associated with darkness, unlike Richard who prefers the light; see Sheldon Brivic, 'Structure and Meaning in Joyce's *Exiles*', *JJQ* 6 (1968), 38–9.

27 In Dante Gabriel Rossetti's illustrated edition of Dante's *La vita nuova* (Joyce owned the Italian version in Trieste), Rossetti argues that 'nuova', which means 'new', also connotes youth, which allows him to assert that Dante's *Vita nuova* is an 'autobiography or autopsychology of Dante's youth until about his twenty-seventh year' (*The New Life of Dante Alighieri*, trans. and illus. by Dante Gabriel Rossetti (New York: Russell, 1901), p. 25). See also Mahaffey, '*Giacomo Joyce*', pp. 408–9.

28 In 'Dante in Joyce's *Exiles*', *JJQ* 18 (1980), 35–44, Mary T. Reynolds asserts that the nine years Richard corresponded with Beatrice, in the light of her inspiration of him, constitute a significant reflection of the *Vita nuova*.

29 Louis Berrone, *James Joyce in Padua* (New York: Random House, 1977), p. 21.

30 Ruth Bauerle argues that Bertha is in fact the centre of the play; see 'Bertha's Role in *Exiles*', in Suzette Henke and Elaine Unkeless, eds., *Women in Joyce* (Urbana: University of Illinois Press, 1982), pp. 108–31.

31 Gabriele D'Annunzio, *The Triumph of Death*, trans. Georgina Harding (London: Heinemann, 1898).

10

JERI JOHNSON

Joyce and feminism

Joyce and *feminism*? Very strange bedfellows. Change either term to catch the full effect: Woolf and feminism; Joyce and Ireland. Now these couples were meant to share beds. But Joyce and feminism? What possibly have these two to say to one another? Can the conjunction be anything more than the now obligatory ('politically correct'?) supplementing of every analytical survey of the work of any writer with a critique supplied by 'feminism'? After all, on most of the several thousand websites currently citing 'James Joyce', readymade 'feminist' hatchet jobs wait to be read. *Caveat lector.* Didn't Joyce himself say 'I hate intellectual women'?[1] Did he not, if we believe his close friend Frank Budgen, 'talk bitterly about women . . . [about] woman's invasiveness and in general her perpetual urge to usurp all the functions of the male – all save that one which is biologically pre-empted, and even on that [to] cast jealous threatening eyes'?[2] Where in his work is there a single example of an independent, successful, happily fulfilled woman character? Beyond this, isn't the writing elitist, being, as it is, notoriously and renownedly 'difficult', and isn't such 'difficulty' just another male modernist writer's attempt to elevate his work to the realm of art, above the domain of the popular and populist culture of the newly educated masses or, more pointedly, to 'ward off the onslaughts of women [writers]'[3] who over the course of the nineteenth and early twentieth centuries were entering the profession of literature in ever-increasing – and increasingly successful – numbers?

Well, yes – and no. Against this picture of the quasi-misogynist Joyce, we find in the details of Joyce's early biography at least a few facts to trouble such a reductive reading. When, in 1901, Joyce's second published work – 'The Day of the Rabblement' – appeared, it did so in a pamphlet with 'A Forgotten Aspect of the University Question', an essay by his friend Francis Skeffington advocating that women students be given equal status in the university in which they were both then enrolled.[4] Of course, most Joycean commentators assume that the statement included in the preface of the pamphlet – 'each writer is responsible only for what appears under his own name' – is meant to distance Joyce from Skeffington's feminism as well as Skeffington from Joyce's argument for the necessary independence of art from what Joyce saw as parochialism masquerading as politics (see *JJ* 88). Perhaps. But in Joyce's first published essay, 'Ibsen's New Drama' (1900), we have enough to give us pause. Here in a precocious review of Ibsen's *When We Dead Awaken*, Joyce praises the playwright in terms at least unusual for a young Irish writer: chief among Ibsen's virtues, Joyce claimed, was his 'extraordinary knowledge of women'; 'that he knows women is an incontrovertible fact. He appears to have sounded them to almost unfathomable depths'; chief in this regard, Joyce cites Ibsen's creation of Nora Helmer of *A Doll's House* who 'capture[s] our sympathy' (*OCPW* 35, 46, 47). Years later, he was to return to elucidate this sympathy. While claiming Ibsen's pre-eminence among playwrights, Joyce argued that 'Ibsen has been the greatest influence on the present generation; in fact you can say that he formed it to a great extent. His ideas have become part of our lives even though we may not be aware of it.' Central among these ideas was his 'purpose' in *A Doll's House*: 'The purpose . . . was the emancipation of women, which has caused the greatest revolution in our time in the most important relationship there is – that between men and women; the revolt of women against the idea that they are the mere instruments of men.'[5] With this in mind, one might re-read the scene in *Stephen Hero* where Stephen, astonished by his mother's expressed desire to read Ibsen, gives her 'a few of his plays to read'. She finds 'Nora Helmer a charming character. . . . But the play she preferred to all others was the *Wild Duck*.' In short, she declares 'they're magnificent plays indeed. . . . I think that Ibsen has an extraordinary knowledge of human nature' (*SH* 86–7), a verdict that echoes Joyce's own 'Ibsen's knowledge of humanity is nowhere more obvious than in his portrayal of women' ('Ibsen's New Drama', *OCPW* 45).[6]

That Mrs Daedalus should have singled out *The Wild Duck* signals to the reader another of the young Joyce's justifications for his (and Stephen's) championing of Ibsen: the play concerns itself with the devastating, and deadly, effects on individuals of living lives wrapped in lies, evasions, fantasies, and distortions. Later in *Stephen Hero*, Stephen meets open opposition from the President of the College to his paper on Ibsen, intended to be read at the College Debating Society. The complaint comes as the President's belief that Ibsen is one of those writers who 'openly profess their atheistic doctrines and fill the minds of their readers with all the garbage of modern society'. Stephen's riposte responds to both the explicit complaint and the implicit theory of art underlying it: 'Even admitting the corruption you speak of I see nothing unlawful in an examination of corruption . . . The lack of a specific code of moral conventions does not degrade the poet.' In reply to the President's contention that if they are to 'examine corruption', poets should 'examine and then show men the way to purify themselves', Stephen blurts out 'That is for the Salvationists . . . Ibsen's account of modern society is . . . genuinely ironical . . . and . . . free from any missionary intention' (*SH* 91–2). In short, the poet's duty is to tell the truth, free from cant and evasion; it is not to convert individuals to moral or political programmes. In 'Drama and Life', the paper that the young Joyce himself delivered to the University College Dublin Literary and Historical Society, he makes these claims more openly: Drama must bring 'men and women as we meet them in the real world, not as we apprehend them in the world of faery'; literature's purpose, he maintained, is *not* to 'instruct, elevate and amuse', but rather to portray truth: 'Art is true to itself when it deals with truth.'[7]

A certain evident irony arises here. Joyce repeatedly praises Ibsen for his truthful and 'genuinely ironical' account of modern society, insists that one of Ibsen's 'purposes' was to write truthfully about 'the emancipation of women, which . . . caused the greatest revolution in our time' (a political concern if ever there was one), and at the same time steadfastly maintains that art must remain aloof from political 'instruction'. To make full sense of these claims, it is necessary to put them in their precise context; Joyce was writing these essays in, and against, an Ireland which he saw as attempting to use 'art' to further precise political demands, and of demanding of 'art' that it subscribe to a political programme. As Joyce later complained in 'An Irish Poet', in Ireland at the time 'the region of literature [was] assailed . . . fiercely by the enthusiast and the doctrinaire' (*OCPW* 61). Literature had fallen into the hands of those who would use it to further the emancipation not of women but of Ireland from England. This 'enthusiasm' arose from the movement known as 'the Irish Revival' formed to promote specifically Irish art in the explicit aim of 'de-Anglicizing Ireland', to use Douglas Hyde's famous phrase.[8] In so doing, felt Joyce, it ran the risk of falling prey to a Catholic sectarianism which took the form of a distorting antimodernism. (As Madden maintains to Stephen in *Stephen Hero*, 'the new movement was politic' and would 'work hand in hand with the priests'; '– Do you not see, said Stephen, . . . that [the priests] consider it is an opportunity to withdraw the people into a past of literal, implicit faith?' (*SH* 53–4)). More to the point, it threatened to unite – at the site of art – politics with a certain Catholic puritanism, one which demanded what Joyce decried: 'lying drivel about pure men and pure women and spiritual love and love for ever: blatant lying in the face of the truth' (*Letters II* 191–2). Joyce found justification for his fears in the protests that arose against the Irish Literary Theatre's 1899 production of Yeats's *The Countess Cathleen* in which a beautiful countess offers to exchange her own soul for the salvation of her starving people. At least one denunciation of the play came in response to what was viewed simultaneously as a blasphemy (the Countess's attempted salvation of her people through her bartered soul) and as a slander against the purity of Irish womanhood. When students at University College joined in the fray, Joyce attended the play, 'clapped vigorously' in the face of student booing, and refused to sign the students' petition of protest (*JJ* 67). He also redrew the entire episode twice, first in the realistic mode of *Stephen Hero*, next in the tight, symbolic, modernist mode of *A Portrait of the Artist as a Young Man*, where every detail of plot, of personal or political history, is subjected to the aesthetic economy of the whole. (We shall hear more of this distinction anon.)

By now we seem to have strayed some distance from the question of Joyce and feminism, but crucial to any discussion of this question should be an understanding of the historical context in which Joyce was writing and of the aesthetic project in which he was engaged. From the outset of his writing career, Joyce maintained that 'truth' – not least, truth about the relations between 'men and women as we meet them in the real world' ('Drama and Life', *OCPW* 28) – was the *sine qua non* of literature. This contention he repeated even after the completion of *Ulysses*, the novel which might be thought to have called into doubt any easy, reductive understanding of what the attempt to represent 'truth' in literature might mean. He also rigorously argued that literature should be free from 'missionary intention' (*SH* 92). In this latter, he agreed with at least one 'feminist' novelist, Virginia Woolf, who herself wrote that the purpose of the novel is 'not to preach doctrines, sing songs, or celebrate the glories of the British Empire'.[9] Literature is not propaganda. Anyone going to the work of James Joyce to find the overt or covert advocacy or, indeed, denunciation of feminist politics will search in vain. Anyone finding there what they believe to be such might pause to look again.

But if both Joyce and Woolf (the latter of whom is repeatedly unproblematically asserted to be a feminist novelist) agree that novels are not political tracts, then how might the question of the relation between a body of literature and feminism be addressed? Not, it would seem, as the reduction of the literary text to easily repeatable politically correct 'themes' or to easily recognized 'positive' (female) or 'negative' (male) representations of character, and most certainly not to an aphoristic or sloganeering gyniolatry or gynophobia. Politics and history might be thought to be most clearly and easily presented in, and so extracted from, argued prose (essays) and represented in and through 'realistic' fiction (*Stephen Hero*) (and by implication less clearly and more problematically in fiction which challenges realism such as

A Portrait of the Artist as a Young Man or *Ulysses*). The history of realism itself is bound up with an ideology which suggests that literature should be exemplary, can faithfully represent reality, must be engaged with history, and will inevitably delineate political or ethical concerns. Not surprisingly, then, the form of feminist criticism which finds itself most comfortable with reading themes, positive or negative images of men or women, of discovering celebratory or triumphalist, or even denigratory or tragic, 'exemplary' narratives in literature will turn again and again to such 'realistic' texts, especially to 'realistic' novels which appear to give little-mediated views of the histories of ordinary, recognizably 'human' lives in their social and subjective complexities; they will turn, that is, to novels like *Stephen Hero*. Such criticism will find sympathy with the kind of critique made by Mary Colum when she describes the representation of Molly Bloom as 'an exhibition of the mind of a female gorilla'[10] or, less obviously, with that of Carl Jung's countering comment that Molly's monologue contains a 'string of veritable psychological peaches . . . about the real psychology of a woman'.[11] The implicit blame in the former and praise in the latter arise from a belief that literature represents real men and women and will inevitably do so with greater or lesser degrees of plausibility, accuracy, efficacy and political bias. This kind of feminist criticism worries little about the definitions of terms like 'women' or 'feminism' itself: the former means 'biological female', the latter 'advocacy of equal (political, economic) rights (and opportunities) for women (and a commitment to representing them as worthy of such rights or to documenting the failure of history to accord them such rights)'. Until recently, it has not generally distinguished sex (biology) from gender (the social construction of patterns of sexuality and behaviour through the imposition of cultural and social norms – what we might call the 'feminine'); nor has it, generally, given an account of writing or language as implicated in or actually producing and reinforcing gender. Its strengths come from attending to the specificities of the histories of women's lives; its weaknesses from lack of attention to the effects of language.

A great deal of debate has been conducted in the last thirty years about what feminist literary theory and criticism ought to be doing (political movements always bring their 'oughts' with them, though often these are hotly contested, and so they should be). This is not the place to rehearse – and so inevitably parody – that history. But we might point out that this kind of feminism, tied as it is to the history and ideological project of 'realism', may well have problems not only, but certainly, with Joyce. When the desire of feminist critics has been to find a realist literature which would represent, not what the position of women and men might actually have been in a particular period (or more accurately, have been discursively constructed as being), but rather what they would desire for it to have been, it has been caught out. Too often this criticism, keen to find unblemished tales of women's possible triumph, has failed to see the politically discursive complexities of realism itself. Or, in a related mode, it has seen literature as an un- (or little) mediated expression of experience. In this guise, it assumes that women writers write more directly from, and of, the experience of being women; male writers from, and of, the experience of being men. Since men have had all the advantages, the implicit argument goes, and since their interests are in keeping those at the expense of the subordination of women, men will be unlikely to produce the kind of supposedly 'realist' representation of women which would be in women's liberatory interests; their texts will repeatedly offer, and endorse, only negative representations of women.[12] Needless to say, Joyce falls at both hurdles: he is a man; he is not a realist.

Or rather, Joyce is not just a realist. That he could write in a mode mistaken for realism is attested to by the fact that the early reviews of his stories about the lives of 'real men and women' in Dublin at the turn of the last century, *Dubliners*, repeatedly described them as so realistic as to be 'naturalistic' – 'naturalism' being that brand of realism that has its nose in the gutter usually with political intent. In Joyce's case his intention was, he claimed, to take 'the first step towards the spiritual liberation of [his] country' (*Letters I* 63) by writing 'a chapter of [its] moral history'. He would do so by refusing 'to alter in the presentment, still more to deform, whatever he [had] seen and heard' (*Letters II* 134); in this way, he would create a 'nicely polished looking-glass' in which 'the Irish people [could have] one good look at themselves' (*Letters I* 64). Now this sounds like realism with intent. And if we turn to <u>Dubliners</u> armed with the questions supplied by this feminist criticism, we can find there what look to be efficacious <u>representations of the 'real men and women' of Dublin, circa 1900.</u>

Dubliners' dingy portraits express lives of <u>poverty, of drunkenness, and of exploitation – not merely of women by men,</u> but of children by adults, of workers by bosses, and even of men by women. Often the stories turn on questions of power, a power neither limited to, nor exclusive of, sexual power in all its guises. So in 'Counterparts', Farrington is humiliated by his boss, takes refuge in drink, and beats his son on returning home, an indictment of the abuse of (not simply, but certainly, patriarchal) power if ever there was one. At the centre of the tale, Farrington spies across the room at Mulligan's pub a woman who answers his gaze with 'large dark brown eyes'; when she leaves, brushing against his chair and saying 'O, *pardon!* in a London accent', Farrington 'curse[s] his want of money' (*D* 73). The implication is, of course, that she is a prostitute, or at least willing to go with men for money, and Farrington's lack of the ready (having already spent it all on drink) becomes another occasion of his humiliation. When immediately afterwards he fails to best his (English) opponent at arm-wrestling, his felt indictment of his failed masculinity is complete. But the encounter with the woman most infuriates him: 'when he thought of the woman in the big hat who had brushed against him and said *Pardon!* his fury nearly choked him' (*D* 74). He returns home to beat his son. Now we could read this story as revealing Joyce's too casual regard for women: they appear here only in the metonymy of the prostitute. Or, we could see it as a resounding indictment of the crippling effects of an internalized masculinity bred from malformed ideas of sexual, national, and paternal power. This latter surely more accurately reflects the tale's workings, and its concerns must surely be those of a feminist criticism attentive to historically situated and culturally specific constructions of gender.

From the outset of his writing career, Joyce was acutely attentive to what individuals wanted to be, to the (economic, religious, sexual, political, familial) sources within this society that produced those desires, and to the brutal and brutalizing effects of those desires, to, that is, the distortions of subjectivity that resulted from the attempt to meet and satisfy them. So, in 'A Mother', Mrs Kearney's ambitious desire – not for her daughter's actual artistic achievement but for the accolades, social position and financial remuneration that might accompany such accomplishment – brings not success but mortification. The story censures not woman as woman, but the false ideals of what maternity entails that this mother has adopted. When the manipulative, conniving Mrs Mooney, in 'The Boarding House', corners Bob Doran into a proposal of marriage to her daughter, Polly, it is her pretence of adhering to (what were for Joyce false) ideals of sexual purity while cynically manoeuvring Polly and Doran into sexual compromise in order to trap him that most bitterly indicts her. She pretends to an ideal of feminine purity in order to secure an economic advantage for her daughter (and, of course, herself). Hers is perhaps the most venal exchange in a book riddled with simoniacal bargainings. Again, the charge lies not finally against Mrs Mooney, but against the culture that produces such warped ideals of 'pure men and pure women and spiritual love and love for ever' in the first place; Mrs Mooney might simply be seen to be using to her, and her daughter's, advantage the tools most readily available to her. Similarly, it is not the 'slavey' exploited by Corley and Lenehan who stands accused in 'Two Gallants', but the man who ruthlessly takes her, then gets *her* to pay, a paying we can only imagine she performs under the false pretence of some future relationship. But the society which produces such male sexual brutality as an accompaniment to puritanical denunciations of sexual desire stands most clearly in the dock.

While Joyce's stories provide 'realistic' representations of real men and women, then, they also involve themselves in questioning the social, political, religious, economic structures and discourses that have produced these 'real' men and women. We must take this a step further if we are to do justice to Joyce's writing. He may have claimed that he was insistently telling the truth in *Dubliners* ('he is a very brave man who dares to alter in the presentment, still more to deform, what ever he has seen and heard'), but he also maintained that he had written the book 'in a *style* of scrupulous meanness' (*Letters II* 134; emphasis added); and herein lies Joyce's distinctiveness. He always insisted that the *manner* of his writing, no matter the text in question, was of central importance. Using language, writing, representing, were all always for Joyce a matter of making, of producing, not merely of transcribing. He possessed an acute awareness that language makes us: what it is we are capable of thinking, believing, knowing, seeing is a product of the languages – whether official and institutional or colloquial and seemingly idiolectic – available within and produced by the particular cultures we inhabit at particular moments in history.

Put slightly differently, and from explicitly feminist concerns, what we mean when we say that gender is a discursive and cultural construction (as I implicitly argued above) is that what it is we think we mean when we say 'I am a woman', for example, derives from and is produced by the language (in the fullest sense) of the worlds in which we live. There are other ways of describing this phenomenon. What has been known for some time as French feminist theory, for example, would place the emphasis differently. I mean to include here the work of such theorists and literary analysts as Julia Kristeva, Hélène Cixous and Luce Irigaray, who in contradistinction to the feminist 'realists' described above would see the term 'Woman' as in itself problematic: biological female will not do as a definition, for as Simone de Beauvoir famously stated 'One is not born, but rather becomes, a woman.'[13] Not only would these theorists distinguish between 'females' (biology) and the 'feminine' (gender), but they would give (varying) accounts through (and against) the critiques produced by such post-structuralist and psychoanalytic theorists as Jacques Derrida and Jacques Lacan of language as implicated in the production of gender. In doing so, however, they have been charged with ignoring the specificity of women's position within this psycholinguistic order, the very specificity that the feminist 'realists' sought to recover. Two of these theorists, Kristeva and Cixous, have written directly on Joyce and, however much they might disagree with one another, their analyses invariably carry an at least implicit argument that Joyce's writing practice is acutely and knowingly productive.[14] They see the activity of writing, or the action performed in writing, as central to Joyce's uniqueness and to what might be described as the feminist political project.

But what does all this mean in the precise context of Joyce's writing? What does it mean to say that Joyce exploits the productive aspect of language or that, even more contentiously, his writings not only produce representations (of men and women) but that he goes one step further and lays bare, by dramatizing them, the conditions of such production? Joyce not only represents; he exhibits the very conditions of 'representation' itself. So, for example, in 'Eveline', Joyce presents what readers have been quick to see as a story critical of one young woman's passivity (in her failure to flee with Frank), and therefore critical of, rather than sympathetic to, women trapped in lives of violence and desperation who will not avail themselves of offered escape.

But the story is more complex than that, and its complexities lie in the manner of its telling. 'Eveline' is focalized through Eveline; that is, while clearly a third-person narrative, what the narrator tells derives from Eveline's angle of vision: we see what she sees, and do not see what she fails to see. Further, while not a first-person narrative, the narrator appropriates not only Eveline's view, but her language, her idiolect. And that language is euphemistic and evasive, derived from Irish, Catholic, Victorian 'ideals' of femininity and commercialized images derived from romance. Carefully examined, Joyce's supposed indictment of Eveline as passive victim unfolds into a nuanced depiction of one steeped in competing codes of femininity, both authorized and unlicensed, in this place at this time: dutiful daughter, battered woman, (failed) romance heroine. In representing Eveline, then, Joyce lays bare the constructedness of femininity, its production in individual cases as the confluence of particular combinations of 'ideals' adopted from culture's impoverished and constraining lexicon.

He does this again and with more edge in 'Nausicaa' (that episode of *Ulysses* in which Bloom eyes up Gerty MacDowell on the beach), making it even clearer here that this 'woman' is a derived figure, a 'projected mirage', born of commodified femininity and an opportunistic masculine desire.[15] Again, this emerges from the way the episode proceeds. It divides clearly in two, the break being marked by the shift from the third-person evocation of Gerty (in a language that Joyce describes as 'a namby-pamby jammy marmalady drawersy (alto là!) style with effects of incense, mariolatry, masturbation, stewed cockles, painter's palette, chitchat, circumlocutions, etc., etc.' (*Letters I* 135)) to Bloom's first-person interior monologue (the style which Joyce uses in *Ulysses* to draw the appearance of idiosyncratically unique character). Narrative and stylistic dissymmetry mark the two halves of the episode. Strictly, as 'she' or 'her', Gerty is the object of this narrative. As 'I' Bloom appears the originating subject of 'his'. This third-person narrator draws Gerty just as the narrator of 'Eveline' drew Eveline: through free indirect discourse, and an affected style. What appear to be Gerty's thoughts come through a language with none of the idiolectic distinctness of Bloom's styled thoughts. Instead these 'thoughts' spring once again from the idioms of romance ('a young gentleman . . . was offering a bunch of flowers to his ladylove' (U 13.334–6)), but also from those of women's magazines ('it was expected in the Lady's Pictorial that electric blue would be worn' (13.150–51), magazines which advertise the benefits for women of 'eyebrowleine' (13.111, 640), 'dolly dyes' (13.150), 'queen of ointments' (13.90) and 'iron jelloids' (13.84)), of fairytale ('You are lovely, Gerty,' her mirror says to her (13.192–3)), of folk wisdom (mistakenly putting old 'undies' on inside out 'was for luck and lovers' meetings' (13.184–5)), of euphemism ('she had raised the devil in him' (13.518) or 'had her father only avoided the clutches of the demon drink' (13.290)), even of mariolatry ('holy Mary, holy virgin of virgins' (13.289)). In short, this is the language of those discourses which tell woman what she ought (and ought not) to be, which in one way or another attempt to sell her a bill of goods (to fall for a moment into the game 'Nausicaa' plays) that she may in turn sell it to the man who will bring her ultimate fulfilment ('love [was] a woman's birthright' (13.200); 'The very heart of the girl-woman went out to him, her dreamhusband, because she knew on the instant it was him' (13.430–1)). Evoked as narrative object through a language of mass-produced, commodified femininity, Gerty emerges as little more than a tissue of citations to femininity as performance, as something one has to apply like 'eyebrowleine'.[16] Or as the narrator reveals, Gerty is 'in very truth, as fair a specimen of winsome Irish girlhood as one could wish to see' (13.80–1).

But whose 'wish to see' is she? That Bloom masturbates to the very sight of her might be our first clue. More than this, the shift to Bloom's allotted portion of 'Nausicaa' – the abrupt move from the ventriloquial third-person narrative to Bloom's interior monologue – dramatizes clearly that femininity exists here as the extension of 'masculine' desire. Linguistically the 'subject' of his discourse, Bloom appears the originator of his narrative; his is (the illusion of) mastery. As narrative object, Gerty is derived figure; hers (the seeming admission of the 'desire' to be, coupled with the attempted evasion of the 'truth' of being) mastered. Beyond this, what the episode dramatizes is (a certain parodic representation of) the libidinal economy of masculinity. The centre of the episode brings Bloom's ejaculation at the moment of the explosion of fireworks at the Mirus Bazaar a mile to the south. When in one of his schemata Joyce described the 'Technic' of this episode as 'Tumescence, detumescence' it was to this male somatic dynamic he referred (Ulysses, ed. Johnson, 735). For as Joyce maintained, *Ulysses* in one of its guises presents 'the cycle of the human body . . . every hour, every organ, every art being interconnected in the somatic scheme of the whole' (*SL* 271). And the body in question here is obviously Bloom's, brought to arousal and completion by the 'winsome picture' before him. Joyce's providing 'The Projected Mirage' as the episode's 'Sense' in another schema draws attention directly to the scopic stimulus, and places its agency outside Gerty (*Ulysses*, ed. Johnson, 738). She is the projection, not the projector; the mirage, not the real thing, Bloom's fantasy sufficient to his own masturbatory desire. When asked by Arthur Power what really happened between Bloom and Gerty on the beach, Joyce replied simply, 'Nothing . . . It all took place in Bloom's imagination.'[17] What Joyce stages in 'Nausicaa' is a scene which reveals the vestedness of this representation of femininity, that is, that it springs from masculine desire. We have neither a positive nor a negative representation of woman *per se*, but a representation of representation itself as embedded in a particular culture, at a particular moment, with a particular investment of gendered desire itself discursively constrained and construed within that culture. Joyce's costume drama of sexual desire announces itself as such.

And if 'Nausicaa' stages such a parodic drama of the 'masculine' libido and 'masculine' desire, we might argue that 'Penelope' displays an equivalently parodic drama of 'feminine' libido and 'feminine' desire. Against Gerty as third-person object lies Molly as first-person subject. If 'Nausicaa' structurally echoes male sexual arousal and accomplishment in its bipartite rising and falling action, 'Penelope' narratively masquerades as 'feminine' libido in its waves of statement, counter-statement, approximation, contradiction, and relentlessly ongoing verbal rush (the last of which comes largely as effect of the episode's simple graphic layout, devoid as it is of punctuation). Where the narrator dresses Gerty up as goods on display, Molly camps it up as 'she' stages a dizzying whirl of roles to be played, costumes to be changed, and reversals to be enacted by her and by the men and women whose encounters with her she figures, re-figures, masks and unmasks, in her nocturnal re-memory.[18] 'Femininity' becomes performance staged *as* performance in 'Penelope'. So does 'masculinity'. Joyce's final display of the vertiginous, polymorphous possibilities of such gender performance comes, of course, in *Finnegans Wake* where the answer to Molly's own question 'Who's [s/]he when [s/]he's at home?' (*U* 4.340) comes as 'anything or anyone that he or she imagines, desires, or that history conspires to provide as imagined fulfilment (or impoverishment) of those desires'.

Joyce mastered early the art of revealing what was at stake in the business of, particularly masculine, desire. The last story of *Dubliners*, 'The

Dead', culminates with Gabriel's realization that his relationship with his wife Gretta has been anchored in his fantasy of what he would have her be, rather than in a full knowledge of what she is. He discovers that she has had a previous suitor, Michael Furey, about whom he knew nothing and that she has been thinking not of him but of Furey at the very moment that he has been anticipating sex with her, assuming in his arrogance that she wishes for the same. The discovery undoes him. But this story, too, comes with its *mise en scène* of masculine desire born of projection rather than objective observation. At the end of the party, Bartell D'Arcy sings 'The Lass of Aughrim'; Gretta stands in a shadow on the staircase, listening; Gabriel 'gaze[s] up' at her whom he at first fails to recognize: 'A woman was standing near the top of the first flight, in the shadow' (D 165). Joyce deftly turns the scene to an imagined scene of representation: Gabriel sees Gretta 'as if she were a symbol of something', asks himself 'what is a woman standing on the stairs in the shadow, listening to distant music, a symbol of', imagines himself a painter who 'would paint her in that attitude' and decides '*Distant Music* he would call the picture if he were a painter' (D 165). The cliché of his imagined title, the kitsch aspect of the whole, reveal the limitations of Gabriel's aesthetic abilities. The fact of his turning or troping this sight into artifice displays the framing and fashioning of the object of desire that his desire requires. The resounding irony that Gretta thinks of someone else, not him, at the moment of his enraptured leap to art is Joyce's final cruel twist: Gretta refuses to align her own desire with Gabriel's. In 'The Dead', Joyce represents while staging (this 'masculine') representation itself as fantasy, as an act of projection (of an ideal of 'femininity') born of ('masculine') ego and ('masculine') desire.

Such stagings recur repeatedly in Joyce's works, the most sustained perhaps that in A Portrait of the Artist as a Young Man, the novel most overtly concerned with aesthetic representation. In the penultimate sentence of the novel, Stephen Dedalus provides the final statement of his artistic intentions: 'Welcome, O life! I go to encounter for the millionth time the reality of experience and to forge in the smithy of my soul the uncreated conscience of my race' (P 213). Here Stephen expresses his desire that he will become not only a conduit for carrying the cultural memory of Ireland, but its creator. An ambitious goal. The conception of art he here articulates resembles very closely that which he first formulated in his encounter with the 'bird girl' at the end of chapter 4: art 'recreate[s] life out of life' (P 145). The artist is, for Stephen, 'a priest of the eternal imagination, [who] transmut[es] the daily bread of experience into the radiant body of everliving life' (P 186). In both these latter instances, Stephen's aesthetic inspiration has come in the

contemplation of 'angel[s] of mortal youth and beauty' (*P* 145), contemplation of, that is, young women. Indeed, Stephen's aesthetic practice consistently and inextricably entwines itself in his relations with women.

At the end of chapter 2, Stephen visited not the 'bird girl' but a different
woman, a prostitute. The scene, mirrored in reverse at the end of chapter 4,
presents the young artist-to-be as becoming 'occupied territory'. Before meeting the prostitute, in a scene proleptic of the actual sexual act, Stephen
encounters 'some dark presence' which 'fill[s] him wholly with itself', and
he 'suffer[s] the agony of its penetration', 'hands clenched convulsively',
'teeth set together' (*P* 83–4). Result? '[T]he cry that he had strangled for so
long . . . issued from his lips', 'a cry which was but the echo of an obscene
scrawl which he had read on the oozing wall of a urinal' (*P* 84). Here language and the body mutually implicate one another: the encounter is prefaced by 'verses pass[ing] from his lips' and 'inarticulate cries' and 'unspoken
brutal words rush[ing] forth from his brain to force a passage' (*P* 83). In
this narrative, it becomes difficult to distinguish bodily orifices from linguistic excurses. Which 'passage' is being forced? one might ask. Stephen here
has become the passive body acted upon by another, not by a person, but
by something represented in *linguistic* terms: it seems he is being brutally
occupied by language itself. The prostitute's taking control of the sexual scenario slightly later merely echoes what has already occurred, for here too she
invades him: he 'trie[s] to bid his tongue speak' but instead stands 'silent'
as 'she embrace[s] him', holds 'him firmly to her' and he 'all but burst[s]
into hysterical weeping'. All that is left to him is somatic response, 'tears of
joy . . . [as] his lips parted though they would not speak' (*P* 84). He cannot
master words, but his body nevertheless expresses itself. Lest we have missed
the point of Stephen's having been invaded by another's tongue, the passage
concludes:

> It was too much for him. He closed his eyes, surrendering himself to her, body
> and mind, conscious of nothing in the world but the dark pressure of her softly
> parting lips. They pressed upon his brain as upon his lips as though they were
> the *vehicle of a vague speech*; and between them he felt an unknown and timid
> pressure, darker than the swoon of sin, softer than sound or odour.
>
> (*P* 85; emphasis added)

Her tongue invades *his body* with a lingual kiss: a literal enactment which
stands as the metaphorical equivalent of the cultural occupation of Ireland
by the invader's tongue.

This scene stands as primal against the inverted mirroring reflection of
chapter 4's tableau vivant of Stephen and the 'bird girl': this time it is
Stephen's language which invades and occupies her. The narrative follows

Stephen's thoughts closely as he turns her into an aesthetic object, from actual young woman to mythic harbinger of his call to the priesthood of art. The movement of description repeatedly and unfailingly swerves from empirical observation to aesthetic figuration. 'Her long slender bare *legs* [are] delicate *as a crane's*', for example; 'her drawers . . . *like featherings* of soft white down', 'her slateblue skirts . . . *dovetailed* behind her' (P 144). The narrative stages Stephen's act of poetic creation as he insistently overwrites this actual woman with the metaphors of a symbolism derived from his own aesthetic fantasy: that life provide corroborating evidence of his own belief in his 'calling' as an artist, as at least the inheritor of the mantle of the 'birdman', the 'old artificer' Daedalus. She becomes the ground against which what he actually draws is a figure of himself as artist. Having himself been occupied by the (literal) tongue of another female, he now occupies this one with (a metaphoric) tongue of his own. Stephen, a son displaced and resentful in this colonially occupied Ireland, repeats just such an act of colonization and makes it central to his own fantasy figuration of himself as artist. For Stephen, the female body is *terra incognita*, the 'dark continent' (as Freud describes female sexuality[19]), there to be figured, to find its meaning, in and through the language of the one-who-would-be-artist.[20]

But not surprisingly, there is another story going on here. The very movement above described is one which, yes, stages this drama, but allows us to see it *as a staging* because of the care with which the movement from observation to aesthetic refiguration is drawn. Put slightly differently, we watch Stephen figure this young woman in and through his own fantasy. Stephen, on the other hand, deludes himself into thinking, not that he has produced her status as 'bird girl' out of his own fantasy, but that she arrives as independent verification that he will be an artist. The scene refuses to be completely swallowed up by Stephen, to accord itself completely with his metaphors. Read it again. It can as easily be read as a scene of exhibitionism and voyeurism, and of the adolescent male body responding physically to the woman's 'shameless' returning of his lustful gaze, as it can as a scene of a spiritualized, poetic, even mythic vision. What else but a description of the post-ejaculatory (in both senses of the word) male body is this: 'His cheeks were aflame; his body was aglow; his limbs were trembling' (P 144–5)?

Let us be even more explicit for a moment. Two things are happening at once in this scene. In the first, Stephen sees the young woman and interprets her as a symbol of his future as an artist: he 'reads' or 'interprets' her, that is, through his own language derived from his desire to be an artist. In the second, the narrative itself shows Stephen doing this and makes it clear that what he is doing is creating a picture of something ('the bird girl') rather than merely observing something (the young woman on the beach). At this second level, then, the narrative stages an act of artistic representation *as* an act of artistic representation, one which *for Stephen* involves the figuration of woman as object of his desire and testimony to his genius. And that act is shown to be one in which figurative language swerves away (into metaphor, symbol, trope) from the thing itself. This second level narrative also depicts Stephen as either unaware of what he is doing or as repressing that awareness (so the language 'he' produces (of symbolic 'bird girls' visiting future artists) overwrites or swerves away from other more mundane considerations (like the physical arousal of the adolescent male body resulting from his voyeurism and her exhibitionism)). In short, Stephen acts and the narrative stages this *as act*. Stephen thinks he's seeing a girl whose significance for the future course of his life is evident. The narrator, on the one hand, presents him as a young man who thinks this about himself and, on the other, shows him to be naive, not least about the processes of aesthetic representation. The narrative knows things that Stephen does not. And what it knows is that 'masculine' desire construes 'femininity' to its own ends and that both are cultural (social, yes, but also political) products.

Finally, then, there is no simple answer to the conundrum, what possibly might Joyce and feminism have to say to one another. But one thing is certain. Feminist criticism has long passed the point of holding yardsticks up to texts and authors to measure their (un)acceptability to 'the Cause'. And that it should have done so is due in no small part to a coming to awareness of what is at stake in the very act of representation, an awareness Joyce's texts display at every turn.

NOTES

1 Joyce to Mary Colum, quoted in *JJ* 529; this is probably the single most often quoted Joyce comment about women; cf. Mary and Padraic Colum, *Our Friend James Joyce* (Garden City, NJ: Doubleday, 1958), p. 132.

2 Joyce to Frank Budgen, quoted in Frank Budgen, *James Joyce and the Making of 'Ulysses'* (Bloomington: Indiana University Press, 1960), pp. 318–19.

3 Sandra M. Gilbert and Susan Gubar, *No Man's Land: The Place of the Woman Writer in the Twentieth Century*, vol. 1: *The War of the Words* (New Haven and London: Yale University Press, 1988), p. 131.

4 *Two Essays: 'A Forgotten Aspect of the University Question' by F. J. C. Skeffington and 'The Day of the Rabblement' by James Joyce* (Dublin: Gerrard Bros., 1901), the latter reprinted in *OCPW* 50–2, 295–6. Francis Skeffington, renowned 'vegetarian, feminist, pacifist, agnostic' and model for McCann/MacCann in *Stephen Hero/A Portrait*, took the name Sheehy-Skeffington when he married Hanna Sheehy.

5 Joyce in conversation with Arthur Power, quoted in Arthur Power, *Conversations with James Joyce*, ed. Clive Hart (1974) (Chicago: Chicago University Press, 1982), p. 35.

6 For a reading of the comment on the circumstances of Mrs Daedalus's own life that Joyce makes through his use of Ibsen here, see Margot Norris, *Joyce's Web: The Social Unraveling of Modernism* (Austin: University of Texas Press, 1992), pp. 15–17.

7 'Drama and Life' (written 10 January 1900; delivered on 20 January 1900; first published 1959), *OCPW* 28, 26, 27.

8 Douglas Hyde, 'The Necessity for De-Anglicizing Ireland', in Charles Gavan Duffy, *The Revival of Irish Literature: Addresses by Sir C. G. Duffy, George Sigerson, Douglas Hyde* (London: 1894), pp. 119–59; the speech was delivered by Hyde to the Irish Literary Society in November 1892, from which the Irish Revival is most often cited as dating; within a year the Gaelic League had been formed with the express purpose of preserving Irish (and all things Irish). See further, Willard Potts, *Joyce and the Two Irelands* (Austin: University of Texas Press, 2000) and Declan Kiberd, *Inventing Ireland: The Literature of the Modern Nation* (London: Jonathan Cape, 1995).

9 Virginia Woolf, 'Character in Fiction' (1924), in *The Essays of Virginia Woolf*, III: 1919–1924, ed. Andrew McNeillie (London: Hogarth, 1988), p. 425.

10 Mary Colum to Joyce in conversation, quoted in Marvin Magalaner and Richard M. Kain, eds., *Joyce: The Man, the Work, the Reputation* (New York: Little Brown, 1962), p. 185.

11 Carl G. Jung, letter to James Joyce, August 1932 (*Letters III* 253).

12 See, in this regard, Kate Millet's early, groundbreaking text, *Sexual Politics* (1969) (London: Virago, 1977).

13 Simone de Beauvoir, *Le Deuxième sexe* (1949), trans. H. M. Parshley (Harmondsworth: Penguin, 1979), p. 295.

14 See, for example, Julia Kristeva, 'Joyce "The Gracehoper" or the Return of Orpheus', in Bernard Benstock, ed., *James Joyce: The Augmented Ninth* (Syracuse: Syracuse University Press, 1988), pp. 167–80; Hélène Cixous, *The Exile of James Joyce*, tr. Sally A. J. Purcell (New York: David Lewis, 1972); Cixous, *Prénoms de personne* (Paris: Editions de Seuil, 1974); Cixous, 'Joyce: The (r)use of Writing', in Derek Attridge and Daniel Ferrer, eds., *Post-Structuralist Joyce* (Cambridge: Cambridge University Press, 1984), pp. 15–30. For a polemical survey and account of the differences between the two kinds of feminist criticism I have outlined, see Toril Moi, *Sexual/Textual Politics: Feminist Literary Theory* (London: Methuen, 1985). In Joyce studies Margot Norris, in *Joyce's Web*, makes a similar argument to that which I put forward here, though she lays greater stress than I on the performative, or dramatic, element of Joyce's writing.

15 The prase 'projected mirage' comes from Joyce, who in the Linati schema (one of two 'tables of correspondence' for *Ulysses*), described the 'Sense (Meaning)' of this episode thus. See Joyce, *Ulysses: The 1922 Text*, ed. Jeri Johnson (Oxford: Oxford University Press, 1993), Appendix A, 'The Gilbert and Linati Schemata: Table of Correspondences: The Linati Schema', pp. 736–9, 738.

16 On gender as 'performance' that is socially, politically, culturally mandated but never completed, see Judith Butler, *Gender Trouble: Feminism and the Subversion of Identity* (New York and London: Routledge, 1990) and *Bodies that Matter: On the Discursive Limits of 'Sex'* (New York and London: Routledge, 1993).

17 Joyce to Power, in Power, *Conversations*, p. 32.

18 For a full articulation of this argument, see Kimberly J. Devlin, 'Pretending in "Penelope": Masquerade, Mimicry, and Molly Bloom', in Richard Pearce, ed., *Molly Blooms: A Polylogue on 'Penelope' and Cultural Studies* (Madison: University of Wisconsin Press, 1994), pp. 80–102. And for a cornucopia of arguments about the stagings of gender in *Ulysses*, see Kimberly J. Devlin and Marilyn Reizbaum, eds., *Ulysses – En-Gendered Perspectives: Eighteen New Essays on the Episodes* (Columbia, SC: University of South Carolina Press, 1999).

19 Sigmund Freud, *The Question of Lay Analysis* (1926), trans. James Strachey, Penguin Freud Library, vol. 15, *Historical and Expository Works* (Harmondsworth: Penguin, 1986), p. 313.

20 In Stephen's fantasy (itself created in the elaborate self-figuration of the artist re-enacting in its form the very colonial occupation he seeks to evade), cultural memory can be created, mastered and deployed like troops in a battle for (Irish or masculine) identity. This, I would argue, arises out of the particular circumstances of his own history in relation not only to individual women but to those particular figurations of women he has encountered in Ireland, in Catholicism, in the poetry of late nineteenth-century aestheticism with which his mind has been saturated.

11

JOSEPH VALENTE

Joyce and sexuality

The early life and career of James Joyce unfolded during a turbulent period in the history of sexuality in the United Kingdom. A cluster of sometimes competing cultural and scientific discourses emerged to catalogue, diagnose, and explain a broad spectrum of human sexual expression. At the same time, a series of explosive events (the Dublin Castle Affair, the Cleveland Street Scandal, the trials of Oscar Wilde, the rise of the New Woman) turned certain less approved elements of that spectrum into matters of mass spectacle and contention.[1] A fundamental if contradictory mutation in the enlightened sexual attitudes of the time occurred in response to these developments. There was an increased awareness of the irrepressible varieties in sexual practices and preferences among individuals and across cultures. But there also arose a closely related desire to limit such variation, manifest in a concerted effort to establish traditional standards of sexual practice as interiorized norms of sexual desire and identity. With its long-standing cultural privilege newly enhanced by its importance to nation and empire building, reproductive heterosexuality became a truly 'compulsory' touchstone in this regard: other erotic modalities were not only treated as deviations from but distorted replicas of this libidinal regime.[2] To take the most salient example, the widely accepted 'inversion' model of homosexuality – the notion of a woman's soul trapped in a man's body or vice versa – referred all same-sex desire not to the bodily sex of its bearer, but to the 'opposite' gender of the mind, thereby framing it as cross-sex desire at a remove.

The double-edged ideological dynamic sketched here informed and was informed by the landmark texts of psychoanalysis. Freud's *Three Essays on the Theory of Sexuality* completely detaches the libidinal drive from any proper bodily aim. On the contrary, it pronounces humankind subject to an innate 'polymorphous' perversity, concentrated in infancy, and imperfectly amenable to civilizing discipline.[3] Freud thus finds the very fulfilment of the reproductive heterosexual norm, the newborn, to be the privileged site of a fundamental and ineradicable resistance to it.

But Freud had also already begun, in *The Interpretation of Dreams*, to elaborate the most powerful modern theory of how such polymorphous perversity grows subject to rule, of how cross-gendered psychosexual identities come to be activated and domesticated within the nuclear family structure. Indeed, the psychologizing of *sexual* identity itself can be seen as an innovation of Freud's theory of the Oedipus complex. It was precisely the triangulated path of oedipal desire that enabled Freud to conceive the twin processes of gender formation and sexual desire as deeply entangled in operation, yet neatly opposed in destination. Under the law of castration, vested in the father, the oedipal subject comes into individual being through an identification with one parental figure that involves aligning him or herself with that parent's sexual desire for the gendered characteristics of the other. At its very inception, then, the oedipal subject is not only sexed but *heterosexed*, and far from disturbing this regulatory configuration, homosexuality consolidates it by 'inverse' repetition, merely transposing the normative coordinates of gender identification and erotic object-choice dictated by the sex (male or female) of the body.

Joyce's major fictions are characterized by the same dialectical interplay between highly labile erotic currents and stabilizing sexual convention, between affective anarchy and normative constraint. In this respect, the structuring principles of Joyce's treatment of eroticism, and the eroticism of that treatment, seem entirely consonant with the historical and intellectual context of his literary production. But his art embodies more than the sum or the symptom of his cultural determinations. From the self-betraying lyricism of *A Portrait of the Artist*, to the psychic transcription of *Ulysses* and the impacted dream-script of *Finnegans Wake*, Joyce's experiments in writing the psychosexual, in the sense of both narrative and stylistic enactment, intervened decisively in the discursive milieu that shaped them. Bridging the gap between literary adaptation and theoretical invention, Joyce's work succeeded in reshaping the sexological accounts with which he began and from which he never entirely departed.

Sex as perversion

The distinctive contribution that Joyce made to the modern anatomy of sexuality lay in his reversal of the received order of genetic priority between sexual impulse and sexual interdiction, his rebuttal of the widespread assumption that erotic desire takes shape prior to and independently of the social restraints laid upon it. In certain respects, his vision anticipates Michel Foucault's much celebrated post-modern interrogation of 'the repressive hypothesis'.[4] According to Foucault, the Victorian prohibitions on sex were far from finalities in themselves. Sexual desire did not simply fall prey to secrecy and prohibition; it was aroused by prohibition and exploited by secrecy as a renewable resource for social management. Joyce's analysis of the late Victorian strictures on homosexuality proceeds on these lines. In his essay, 'Oscar Wilde: The Poet of Salome', written just as he undertook the revision of *Stephen Hero* into *A Portrait of the Artist*, he pronounces Wilde's notorious sexual errancy to be 'the logical and inevitable product' of the sexual 'secrecy and restrictions' endemic to British public schools (*OCPW* 150). The narrative structure of his more finished *Bildungsroman* follows up on this insight. The Clongowes smugging scandal retroactively triggers Stephen's disavowed homoerotic impulses, transfiguring previously charged signifiers ('suck', 'hot and cold cocks', Mooney's 'creamy sweets') into subliminal foretokens of the protagonist's maturing sexual ambivalence. Through this temporal kink in the linear *Bildung* plot, Joyce underlines the systematic tendency of social proscriptions to engender the internal states and even the outward expressions that they propose to eliminate.

Unlike Foucault, however, Joyce found the seductive effects of sexual sanction to be an essential condition of eroticism itself. The initial thunderclap of *Finnegans Wake* registers this lesson in the cosmic dimension. Established Irish-Catholic folklore associated the roar of thunder with the voice of God calling man to account for the Fall, which was typically assumed to be a violation of a sexual injunction. But the first thunderclap in *Finnegans Wake* induces the fall of the hero rather than indicting the offender: 'The fall (bababadalgharaghtakamminarronnkonnbronnton-nerronntuonnthunntrovarrhounawnskawntoohoohoordenenthurnuk!) of a once wallstrait oldparr is retaled early in bed and later on life down through all christian minstrelsy. The great fall of the offwall entailed at such short notice the pftjschute of Finnegan, erse solid man' (3.15–20). In terms of the physical comedy, the fall of Tim Finnegan, who also figures as Humpty Dumpty, appears consequent to the 'great fall' of the 'offwall' he is building, a calamity wrought by the thunderword itself. So far as the moral allegory goes, the destroyed wall is a sign of Finnegan's own rectitude, the 'wallstrait' character of an 'erse solid man,' now reduced, by the explosive voice of God's law, to an embodiment of incontinence ('oldparr').[5] Just as the thunder brings about the fall, so the moral tenor of the thunder brings about the weakness of the flesh.

The implications of Joyce's conception of the law as original sin, as primary stimulus to lapsed sexual desire, has a number of striking, politically momentous implications both for the means of erotic production and the nature of the feelings so produced. Whereas Foucault saw historically specific proscriptions inciting the perversions they named, Joyce's more comprehensive model preserves in altered form the Irish Catholic equation of sex and sin, revealing all erotic desire and enjoyment to be irreducibly perverse. Far from conducing to the reinforcement of positive sexual norms, mobilizing such libidinal energy cannot but corrode them from the inside.

Joycean sexual desire is rooted in a law that manifests itself as an indefinite, historically variable series of normative sanctions – for example, on concupiscence, onanism, masochism, voyeurism, necrophilia, exhibitionism, homosexuality, etc. – and charts an endless detour toward a radically censored *jouissance* that is nothing other than the retroactive excitation of that law itself.[6] As such, desire can have *no* proper or authentic aim, being split in its emergence between an object-relation, what seems to be wanted, and a relation with the mandate that has created the condition of want. Each of these relations is correspondingly split in turn. On the object side, the fulfilment of a desire thus engendered is inevitably coterminous with its frustration; satisfaction is inhibited by the very prohibition, the internalized prohibition, that conditions its possibility. On the side of the law, the dual message of its mandate opens up supplementary strains of gratification (the bliss of submission, the *frisson* of violation) that are not cognate with the object desired but are part of the experience of the law's operation. Under this dispensation, in other words, enjoyment no less than desire is fundamentally perverse: divided and doubled by prohibition, it is ambivalent and yet supercharged, a compressed site of disappointment and surplus pleasure. Whereas psychoanalysis, in the words of Slavoj Žižek holds that 'sexuality strives outward and overflows the adjoining domains precisely because it cannot find satisfaction in itself',[7] Joyce's major novels broach the more difficult counterproposal that sexuality cannot find satisfaction precisely because it does not exist 'in-itself' but only 'other-in-itself'. Instead of a proper substance, sexuality possesses only a fractured syntax; it lives in structural antagonism with the variable laws and limits that animate it. Accordingly, the tendency of sexuality to 'overflow the adjoining domains' is no more and no less essential than its tendency to invest or 'cathect' those domains as sites of definition and regulation. It lives 'in excess' of the normative frameworks on which it continues to depend.

This paradoxical structure helps to answer a central question pertaining to Joyce's critical heritage: *how can Joyce's sexual politics be judged as fundamentally conservative and positively revolutionary with equal persuasiveness?* Joycean sexuality emerges as a dual investment in a control structure and in the violation of its boundaries or, to use Joyce's metaphor, in the net and the flight. The normative framework creates this dual investment, dividing sexual desire between itself and what it forbids, while the dual investment overwhelms the framework, reducing it to a moment in a larger economy. Joyce's literary project is accordingly preoccupied with the dominant conventions of psychosexual constitution and expression, not as fundamentals to be assumed, nor as simple excrescences to be dismissed, but as symptomatic elements in a dynamic of contested enjoyment.

A number of normative frameworks come in for such treatment in Joyce's works, and the most salient bear a close relation to his own erotic singularities, preferences, conflicts, and obsessions. We shall be examining these in turn: (1) the proscription of juvenile eroticism, which bears on both Joyce's youthful experience and his extraordinarily close relation with his daughter, Lucia; (2) the myth of the monogamous couple, which bears on Joyce's jealous interest in sexual betrayal; (3) the myth of the heterosexual family romance, which bears on Joyce's uneasy interest in his own homoerotic feelings. I point up these connections not to introduce a reading of Joyce's sexual representation as confessional, but to indicate that he took that life as a launching point for the literary exploration of sexuality in general. For Joyce, errancy, like error, opened 'portals of discovery' (U 9.229).

The myth of childhood innocence

Joyce's fiction contrives to counter the myth of childhood innocence while at the same time implicating adult proscriptions of childhood sexuality in the germination and development of that myth. How is this done? Repeatedly in Joyce's fiction, adult intervention converts the *ambiguously* sexualized stirrings and scenarios of juvenile life into *explicitly* sexual investments and fantasies. We have already noted how the crackdown on 'smugging' at Clongowes retroactively prompts phobically coloured homoerotic feelings in Stephen, infusing several perceptual cues with unwonted libidinal force. But even earlier, Dante's strictures on his nursery-wish to marry Eileen serve to sexualize that relationship in Stephen's memory, which isolates newly eroticized gestures of friendliness, such as when she 'put her [long, white] hands over his eyes' (P 29).

Along similar lines, Bloom's decision to send Milly away to shield her from Molly's affair with Boylan seems to galvanize her sexual initiation by analogy. She writes to Bloom to introduce her new beau in a manner calculated to imply a parallelism between her mother's unmentioned peccadilloes and her present entanglement: 'he [Bannon] sings Boylan's (I was on the pop of writing Blazes Boylan's) song about those seaside girls. Tell him silly Milly sends my best respects' (U 4.408–9). Milly represents the medium of amorous commerce between Bannon and herself and between Molly, a diva, and Boylan, her manager, to be the very medium connecting the two couples, so that the 'best respects' she sends Boylan betokens a sense of fellowship with him. Noting, in effect, that Bannon now sings Boylan's love songs to her, Milly slyly responds to her exile with the coded warning, 'Like mother, like daughter'. Bloom's reading of the letter confirms her identification of the two cases and thus the effect of his prophylactic strategy in stimulating Milly's sexual appetite.

Parental surveillance and proscription of childhood sexuality activate the youthful libido they aim to curb precisely by introducing and transmitting the dialectical split between sexual desires or practices and the normative regulations they are called upon to observe. That is to say, the sexuality realized through parental restrictions in Joyce is a profoundly riven and so inevitably perverse sexuality. Thus, in A Portrait, Dante ostensibly places Eileen off limits to Stephen because her tribe, the Protestants, ridicule the litany of the Blessed Virgin. But Dante's explanation only imbues the phrases 'Tower of Ivory, House of Gold' with sexual energy for Stephen in the context of their association with his now taboo friend. Those liturgical signifiers, in turn, form the site of a dialectical split in his sexual investment between the sacred and profane, the forbidding and the forbidden, sex-denying law and law-defying sex, a split crystallized in his 'shameful' thrill at prefecting the sodality of the Blessed Virgin while 'the savour . . . of a lewd kiss', bestowed by a prostitute, still 'lingered' on his lips (P 88).

At different points in his work, Joyce indicates that this generative fissure not only results from parental interdiction, but may have its start in the parental unconscious. Joyce understood parental interdictions on sexuality to possess an inherently self-referential structure, to recall and repeat, in reverse order, the parents' childhood experience of having sexual energies communicated, reprobated and censored by the adult world, only to be preserved in their own unconscious representations. As such, the parental bans on childhood sexuality are likely to be ambiguously countered in and by their mode of enunciation, which may well resonate with: (a) the parents' subliminal resistance to the law they are laying down, (b) the parents' own censored desires, likewise forged in a parental-filial bond. More than proposing a concrete, interpersonal mechanism whereby sexual prohibition is received as sexual incitement, Joyce's account shows this fantasy-effect to be highly overdetermined. Not only does a repressive sexual law create the underlying condition of desirability, possible deprivation; not only does it generate supplementary sources of potential pleasure involving the subject's double-edged relation to the law and the outlawed object; the law itself proves double-voiced in its parental transmission, expressing forbidden sexual impulses in the act of forbidding sexual expression.

The palimpsestic method of *Finnegans Wake*, because it allows a kind of narrative multitasking, the invocation of simultaneous and contradictory symbolic actions, seems designed to accommodate the complex role of the parental unconscious in what is, after all, one of the book's main concerns, the development of child sexuality. Let us look at the second version of the Fall, the 'museyroom' (museum/nursery room) episode (*FW* 8–10). We have passed from a mythic hero, Finnegan, the subject of a thunderous divine law, to the already fallen bearer of the paternal law, Earwicker. His properly Victorian surveillance of the nursery for sexual misconduct occasions incestuous misconduct of his own. Having displayed a disciplinary zeal so vehement that the mother, Anna Livia, has attempted to hide her boys behind her skirt (a strategy likewise freighted with sexual overtones), he spies on his schizoid daughter Issy peeing and sets off an antagonistic family romance which, centring on the urinary pun, water-loo, unfolds in a scrambled version of the battle between Wellington and Napoleon. Earwicker himself figures the interdependency of repressive authority and illicit desire: his dress is at once august and carnivalesque ('grand and magentic [magnetic/magenta] in his goldtin spurs and his ironed dux and his quarterbrass woodyshoes and his magnate's gharters and his bangkok's best and goliar's goloshes and his pulluponeasyan wartrews'); his name 'Willingdone' evokes both the omnipotence of divine power and the inexorability of overmastering passion; his means of commanding the familial space, his 'mormorial tallowscoop', condenses references to the Wellington memorial, the telescope, news scoops and waxworks and so can be construed as an instrument of detection in the service of law and tradition and as an instrument identifying the paternal gaze with the erect phallus. The 'tallowscoop' is also denominated a 'Wounderworker', an instrument of phallic sexuality, punishment and (patented rectal) cure all in one,[8] and it is named 'Sexcaliber hrosspower' after the mythical sword of divinely sanctioned sovereignty and the equally mythic power of the paternal phallus.

Willingdone's signature action in this episode reflects this abrasive doubling. While the 'jinnies' (Issy) are 'making their war undisides the Willingdone', he 'git the band up'. Commonly read as a pun on the French *bander*, to have an erection, the formula can just as easily signify raising a brigade or posse of soldiers, particularly given the operative historical conceit. Willingdone responds *both* lecherously and repressively to what are ambiguously sexual signals from his daughter: whether the jinnies are making water ('war') on the side ('undisides') of Willingdone or 'making war' on his 'side', in the sense of assaulting his sexual authority, is very much undecided ('undisides'). The effect of Willingdone's policing is to *decide* the jinnies on the sexual expressiveness he seeks to check – from this point on, they are 'making war' in earnest – and to polarize their sexual impulses in obverse proportion to his own conflicting motives.

On one side, during the remainder of the episode, the jinnies resist Willingdone's proscriptive surveillance of their erotic stirrings by mounting a seductive appeal to his voyeuristic predilections. They send him a 'hastings dispatch', the stated purpose of which is 'to irrigate the Willingdone' (9.3), that is, to irritate him, to lubricate and fertilize him, a plainly erotic proposition, and to arrogate him, to seize his volition (the Willing-done). Here, the thrill of transgressing the paternal law, expressed in the cheer 'Yaw, yaw, yaw!' is at once doubled and adulterated by the *jouissance* of surrendering to paternal desire. On the other side, the jinnies resist the Willingdone's prurient, voyeuristic 'advance' by appealing to patriarchal norms of sexual attachment. Their dispatch tells Willingdone to 'Fieldgaze thy tiny frow!' (9.5). Their admonition might be unpacked as 'look *to* your little wife', 'look *at* your little wife', 'take your pleasure gazing at her, not us' – in sum, behave in accordance with the canons of sexual propriety that you would implement. 'That', the text continues, 'was the tictacs of the jinnies for to fontannoy the Willingdone' (9.6–7), that is, their *reverse* tactics for playing his authority off against his passion. They anger him as a subject of desire while arousing him as a defender of law. Here the thrill of defying the sexual will of the father, expressed in the proto-feminist war cry 'Shee, shee, shee!' is at once enhanced and tempered by the more modest pleasure of taking up the mantle of the sexual norm. The jinnies' final manoeuvre in this sequence, 'jillous agincourting [of] all the lipoleums' (Shem and Shaun as Napoleon particles (9.7–8)), neatly combines the two earlier movements: it defies the father's repressive surveillance, goads him to jealousy, provokes his voyeuristic ardour, and presents a generationally appropriate alternative to his incestuous designs. It is truly a strategy for 'making war' as romance and romance as war, agon-courting, and it originates not with the jinnies themselves but with the ambivalent force of the parental unconscious.

The myth of the monogamous, self-enclosed couple

The triangular cast of the jinnies' erotic alliances merely narrativizes the triangulation at work in the genesis of their sexual affections. Their conflicting libidinal investments in Willingdone's legitimate authority and illicit desire are merely reapportioned in their 'agincourting [of] all the lipoleums', who in different respects constitute both forbidden and relatively legitimate object choices by comparison with the father. The reconfiguration continues in later episodes, in which the brothers themselves occupy the opposed vertices of Issy's romantic triangle, Shem exerting the attraction of a rarefied social ideal, Shem the fascination of the socially abject and unacceptable.

In this regard, Issy's developing psychosexual economy forms an infantile prototype of the structure of sexual affinity in Joyce's fiction. The erotics of Joyce's narratives seem entirely absorbed in the vicissitudes of the compulsory heterosexual romance; the figure of the cross-gender couple bestrides each of his texts from *Chamber Music* through *Finnegans Wake*. But this law of the couple, upon which Joyce's reputation for traditionalist sexual politics resides, proves notoriously unstable, always opening out upon its own subversion, through the introduction of a third term. Indeed, in Joyce's major works, the featured romantic and sexual affiliations take on an almost exclusively triadic cast. The pattern takes hold quite emphatically with the final three stories composed for *Dubliners*: 'Two Gallants' (Corley, Lenahan, the girl), 'A Little Cloud' (Chandler, Gallaher, Annie), and 'The Dead' (Gabriel, Gretta, Michael). It proceeds through *A Portrait* (Stephen, Emma, Cranly), *Giacomo Joyce* (Giacomo, the student, Nora), *Exiles* (Richard, Bertha, Robert), into *Ulysses* (Molly, Bloom, Boylan; Molly, Bloom, Milly) and explodes in multiple variations throughout *Finnegans Wake*. In every case, the triad disposes itself into a protagonist of desire, a figure of social legitimacy or entitlement, and a some way problematic object of erotic attraction.

The figure of legitimacy may function simultaneously as rival and gender ideal, for example, Cranly for Stephen, Richard for Robert or Boylan for Bloom. In such instances, the official but contested heterosexual romance facilitates and disguises a flow of homoerotic desire, establishing the sort of transferential relation between the two sexual preferences that Eve Sedgwick has theorized as homosociality.[9] Due in some measure to the influence of her conception, the triangular sexual relations prevalent in Joyce's fictions have commonly been taken to have as their primary purpose the subversion of the culturally sacrosanct homosexual–heterosexual opposition. But as we observed, there is another side to troilism in Joyce. The figure of legitimacy can also embody the socially preferred love-object (Shaun) by contrast to another (Shem), whose appeal derives from the social defiance he enables. Taking the two sides together, we can see that the primary function of troilism in Joyce consists rather in its reproduction, within the domain of adult relations, of the originary fissure on which human sexuality is founded, its rehearsal of the perverse conditions of desire and enjoyment as such: their simultaneous captivation by and transgression of the normative constraints that incite them.

The myth of the heterosexualizing family romance

That being said, Joyce does tend to interlink and superimpose such homosocial triangles onto oedipal triangles anchored by his juvenile protagonists. The logic of this manoeuvre clearly implies that in mediating the flow of same-sex desire, mature heterosexual competition merely continues the work of the primal scenario of normative heterosexual development, the Oedipus complex. Thus, more than kinship, the relationships that Joyce ultimately proposes between homo- and heteroeroticism is a profound immixture, a mutual adulteration constitutive of their joint possibility.

The primordial bond of hetero- and homoeroticism, in turn, hinges upon a structural anomaly in the Oedipus complex, a crosswiring of its supposedly bipolar components, gender identification and sexual object-choice. As Joyce emphasizes in his representations of children, assuming a gender position involves a libidinal investment in the images, codes, and archetypes of that position. In 'The Sisters', for example, the boy-narrator's identification with the dead 'Father' culminates in his dream of hearing the priest's confession and thereby putting on his institutional authority, expertise and prestige, qualities the boy emulated in the living man. But the dream suddenly changes tone and takes on the furnishings of an Oriental fantasy, something persistently associated in Joyce's Dublin with fervid, forbidden and 'deviant' sexuality. Conversely, a child's oedipal attachment to a parental figure, because it aims so directly at bodily and/or psychic reunification, inevitably comprises a strong element of (cross) gender identification as well. Thus, as Stephen Dedalus moves from *A Portrait* to *Ulysses*, his development increasingly centres on his coming to grips not just with the erotic attachment to his mother that her death has italicized, but with the maternal identification that attachment has left behind. The ghost of his mother precisely objectifies this haunting identification.

Stephen's anxiety on this score arises largely from the previously cited association, among sexual scientists and others, of cross-gender identification with same-sex desire. Freud strengthened the currency of this inversion model by assimilating it to his newly dominant theory of sexual development. His theory appends the Oedipus complex as an explanatory clause of the heterosexual contract and, by the same token, maintains homosexuality as a carbon copy of this document – its reversed negative facsimile. Even as Joyce recirculates the inversion paradigm as a dramatic basis for the anxieties he wishes to anatomize, he maps the originary split of law and desire onto the nexus of gender identification and sexual preference, and thus offers a critique of Freud's oedipal model. On one side, as with the boy's emulation of the priest in 'The Sisters', Joyce shows how normative gender identification entails an inescapable eroticizing of the gender position itself, hence a certain deviation from the norms of object-preference. On the other, as in Stephen's fixation on his mother, alignment with the law of desire or object-choice entails an internalization of the lost parental image of the opposite sex and so a certain departure from the norm of gender identification. Here again, Joycean sexuality comprises an antagonistic interdependency between impulses to submission and transgression, both of which find always compromised satisfaction at different levels of the libidinal structure.

Finnegans Wake offers the most comprehensive rendition of this dynamic as well, again owing to its hypertextual capacity to elaborate the densely layered communication of the parental and filial unconscious. In the museyroom episode, Willingdone's dual embodiment of legitimate patriarchal authority and illicit paternal desire has significant consequences for his children's negotiation of the gender/sexuality bind. 'Making war' upon their father, the jinnies not only come into their feminine sexuality, they engage a martial, implicitly masculine gender identification with him. They sign their dispatch 'Nap', short for Napoleon, indicating that at a certain level they take themselves to be 'little men'. And they begin 'agincourting' their *fellow* Napoleons ('the lipoleums') partly on this basis.

For their part, in identifying with the gender law of the father, the lipoleums come into conflict with him as a subject of desire. This is the classic oedipal scenario: the Willingdone and the lipoleums wrangle over rights of (sexual) access to the family women: ALP and the jinnies. To press their claim, 'the lipoleums is gonn boycottoncrezy onto the one Willingdone' (9.8). Needless to say, this militant assault admits another, sexualized construction, immediately endorsed by Willingdone, who once again 'git the band up' (has an erection, raises a posse). In identifying with the father that is, the lipoleums register a libidinal investment in his gender position – go 'boycottoncrezy' – which arouses his censored homoerotic interest in them no less than his heteroerotic rivalry with them. The remainder of the episode unfolds in a contest and confusion of oedipal aggression ('the lipoleums in the rowdy howses', 9.22) and Greek love ('the lipoleums is nice hung bushellors', 10.3–4), climaxing when 'the dooforhim seeboy blow the whole of the half of the hat of lipoleums off of the top of the tail on the back of his big wide harse' (10. 19–21). This action conjoins

(a) military reconnaissance with a kind of reverse voyeurism; the boys subject Willingdone to the kind of doubly motivated surveillance that he conducts on the jinnies;

(b) a conspicuously violent ambush with an implicitly homoerotic anal penetration – undertaken at much greater length in the 'Buckley Shot the Russian General' episode.

Taking these two aspects together, we may think of the lipoleums as aligned with the father's spatial position, trained competitively with him upon the jinnies, and for that very reason, aligned with the homoerogenous zone of his rear end. The violence of the oedipal aggression, as elsewhere the violence of heterosexual passion, conceals as it admits the expression of homoerotic desire.

Even more than Freud, then, Joyce insisted on the proximity of the oedipal family romance and the inversion model of homosexuality. Freud put the two in a metaphorical relationship, where inversion stood as a negative analogue to oedipal desire. Joyce places them in a metonymical relationship, where they remain fundamentally imbricated in their nonetheless incompatible manifestations. In this manner, Joyce reveals homosexuality, in its dominant construction, to be interior to the law proscribing it, and thus reveals the heterosexual norm, understood as a univocal proposition, to be impossible to fulfil and thus perverse on its face. This move, in turn, goes a long way toward dismantling the foundation of sexual science in his time and our own, the notion of sexual identity, and clearly anticipates the counterdiscourse of queer theory.[10]

Perversion as sex

Masochism, it seems fair to say, is the characteristically Joycean mode of perversion: it lends focus to the notorious 'fuckbird' letters to Nora, and it takes pride of place in *Ulysses*, not just as an enduring facet of Bloom's personality, but as the central fantasy-form in the novel's crowning episode, 'Circe'. But masochism was not only Joyce's impulsive fetish, it was also his self-regarding fascination, his way of interrogating the mystery of sexual enjoyment. The reason behind masochism's saliency for Joyce is that the signature rhetoric of the perversion – wherein Masoch's own male hero/victims enlist, prompt, direct, and contract with dominating women to commit acts of cruelty – serves to epitomize and theatricalize the precise, ambivalent logic that Joyce discerned in erotic experience generally. It is important to note, in this regard, that if Joyce 'participated in Masoch's own space of . . .

masochism',[11] he seems to have done so strictly in writing, not in bodily performance. The distinction suggests a consistently *reflective* interest in the ritualized exchange of control and abandon.

In his letters to Nora, Joyce constructs a fantasy scene wherein she is to play both his torturer and his ultimate moral authority, and so in sum, his disciplinarian. At the same time, his prose brims with non-masochistic, but otherwise perverse fantasies about their shared sexual activity. By regularly situating Nora as both 'whorish' object-choice and maternal lawgiver, Joyce is able to unfold the permutations of a libidinal energy conflictually invested in and unevenly inflected by normative boundaries and their anticipated transgression. The masochistic delirium, its 'madness', to use Joyce's term, forms Nora herself, her embodied participation in the erotic scenario, as a taboo object, towards which every express desire is necessarily 'dirtier [and] dirtier' (*SL* 185). The *frisson* of violating the norms of sexual propriety in this wholesale fashion, however, is bound up with and inhibited, even undercut by Joyce's attachment to these norms. At one point, he specifically reminds Nora, 'As you know, dearest, I never use obscene phrases in speaking. You have never heard me, have you, utter an unfit word before others. When men tell me . . . filthy or lecherous stories I hardly smile' (*SL* 182). His Catholic sense of guilt, itself deeply eroticized, at having deviated from the canons of sexual virtue typically expresses itself in a discomfort that in so doing he has violated the object of his desire. His letters reflect with contrite insistence upon his own characteristically masochistic strategy of conscripting Nora into salacious fantasies which, by his own lights, tend to degrade her, and they thereby labour to refute and remove the thrillingly taboo associations that he has himself imposed. To further this end, Joyce adorns her image in a compensatory beatific aura, but by then qualifying her as a 'saint' and an 'angel', he implicitly proclaims her eligibility and even her responsibility to play the part his fantasy most requires of her, moral sovereign and taskmaster. We find Joyce repeatedly apologizing to Nora and demanding chastisement at her hands for the sin of defiling her image in masochistic binges, of which his repentance is but the nominally hygienic continuation.

In this instance, the classic patriarchal splitting of the female love-object into 'whorish' and divine image is put in the service of elaborating the corresponding split in the relationship of sexual desire to the law, i.e. to the moralizing and normalizing limitations placed upon it. Herein lies the enabling paradox of Joyce's masochism. It establishes a fantasy frame of outrage upon respectable sexual morality that is predicated upon utter submission to that morality as embodied, *within the frame*, by the authoritarian woman. As such, masochism not only makes available the joy of abandoning oneself simultaneously to the electricity of the illicit and to the compelling power of law, but gives rise to each precisely by way of the other and to something else besides, a kind of surplus *jouissance*, in their combination. At the experiential level, the masochistic dynamic results in a self-perpetuating erotic machinery: the imagined punishment reproduces for Joyce the perverse sort of pleasure to be punished and so itself requires still further orgasmic discipline *ad infinitum*. Joyce's missives to Nora not only represent but in a sense perform this cycle, accelerating erotic intensity in inflated, recursive prose interlaced with references to the author's sexual exhaustion. At the hermeneutic level, Joyce's self-reflexive brand of masochism stages and illuminates the core logic of interdependency binding transgressive desire and the desire to comply as they attach themselves to various social sites, registers, and relationships.

That Joyce conceived the analytical potential of masochism in this light seems evident from his delineation of Leopold Bloom's hallucinatory bout of erotic torment in the Nighttown episode of *Ulysses*. In the first instalment of this masochistic revel, Bloom conjures up a bevy of high society ladies whom he has offended with a series of notes exhorting them to commit 'depraved' sexual acts and to punish him for making the suggestion. While the erotic trajectory of his fantasy letters approximates that of Joyce's letters to Nora, class distinction and aspirations contour the terrain on which that trajectory unfolds. This is not to suggest that sexuality in this segment 'overflows' its 'adjoining domains', as Žižek has it, into the register of class politics, but, to the contrary, that sexuality takes class politics as the site of its own complex self-mediation. Thus, in an unconscious recognition of the class determinants of erotic regulation, Bloom's fantasy explicitly identifies sexual with social propriety.

In positioning socially elite women as prospectively willing participants in disreputable sexual activities, from adultery to coprophilia, the letters ventilate a mixture of gender and class aggression redolent of Bloom's earlier comments on the well-heeled lady standing outside the Grosvenor Hotel: 'Careless stand of her . . . Like that haughty creature at the polo match. Women all for caste till you touch the spot . . . Reserved about to yield . . . Possess her once take the starch out of her' (*U* 5.102–6). But Bloom's own respect for caste enters into the fantasy as a successively inhibiting and intensifying factor. He envisions the women's disdain of his prurient advances as resting upon contempt for his class status. Thus Mrs Yelverton Barry snickeringly remarks his 'prentice backhand' script and makes a point of observing that he first saw her in 'a box of the *Theatre Royal*' from the cheap seats or 'gods' (*U* 15.1017–20); the Honourable Mrs Mervyn Talboys simply refers to him as 'a plebeian Don Juan' (*U* 15.1064); Mrs Bellingham claims that

Bloom wrote of envying her coachman his attire and his 'fortunate proximity to my person' (*U* 15.1048). That is to say, just as Bloom's transgressive pleasure in violating the sexual norm is supplemented by an aggressive pleasure at overstepping class boundaries, so his residual shame at his sexual infractions manifests itself in a sense of class abjection. By the same token, his eager submission to the genteel judgements and rigorous physical discipline of these ladies evinces his respect for the paired canons of social and sexual propriety and thus serves to expiate and even to license his perverse infringements of those canons. But more than that, his act of submission actually *extends* those infringements and their attendant enjoyment as well, requiring – or is it entitling – him to undergo a regimen of flagellation, whose own naughty pleasures invite continuing punishment. Here again we see the enjoyment of transgression and the enjoyment of submission collapse together in a sort of perpetual motion machine, perfectly captured in Bloom's plea for leniency while he '*offers the other cheek*' of his bum for flogging (*U* 15.1109).

Bloom's masochistic surrender, finally, proves a way of recreating the class fantasy that shaped it. Insofar as within the middle classes, social status answers as much to cultural as to economic capital, Bloom's accession to the society ladies' strictures on sexual 'misconduct' represents an indirect means of furthering his own social promotion, for it suggests his full appreciation of the strictures of aesthetic taste and moral judgement that characterizes the social elite. Bloom's stated preference for 'refined birching' (*U* 15.1096) not only acts to dissociate himself from the lowly image the ladies have of him, it evokes the hopeful fantasy that his chastisement amounts to a form of participation in their circle. What that participation reveals in turn is that the bourgeois sexual code itself functions as class aggression, forbidding to the lower orders, in the name of morality, the indulgences of their 'betters'. In a mirror image of Bloom's class attitudes, his fantasy ladies identify his sexual perversions with his social pretensions and they scourge the latter with a gleeful ferocity that bespeaks their own perverse inclinations:

> Tan his breech well, the upstart! (*U* 15.1091)
> Thrash the mongrel within an inch of his life. The cat-o'-nine tails. Geld him. Vivisect him. (*U* 15.1104–5)
> To dare address me! I'll flog him black and blue in the public streets. I'll dig my spurs in him up to the rowel . . . (*she swishes her hunting crop savagely in the air*) (*U* 15.1115–18)

Here at the culmination of Bloom's fantasy, the scene of violent correction, its sexual energies bring their class-coding into spectacular visibility even as their intensity overwhelms all disciplinary control.

A similar dynamic unfolds in the second instalment of Bloom's self-demeaning odyssey – his encounter with Bella Cohen – only in this case the gender system forcefully returns to centre stage as the primary articulation of sexual norms. In Deleuze's now standard reading of masochism as gender politics, the male protagonist-victim confers ultimate authority upon the figure of woman in order to expiate his inborn or ingrained complicity in the patriarchal order of sex/gender regulation or, as Deleuze phrases it, 'his resemblance to the father and the father's likeness to him'.[12] But, as a theoretical matter, the Deleuzian analysis of masochism possesses flaws fatal to a reading of the Bella interlude. It fails to acknowledge how in the psychic economy of masochism, the pain inflicted upon a subservient man by a domineering woman as a reversal of patriarchal hierarchies always also counts as a pain suffered by a man for the act of voluntarily subjecting himself to a woman, for consenting to the disturbance of patriarchal mandates. For this reason, masochism must be seen as a means of paying respect, and therefore reinscribing, the gender law that it exceeds, and the most distinctive features of Bloom's masochistic ordeal in the brothel serve to accentuate and anatomize this double itinerary.

The first of these features is that the dominatrix is not selected, encouraged, instructed or stage-managed by the hero-victim. Within the fantasy, Bloom is constrained, often physically, to obey the inimical figure of Bella and to suffer at her hands. Bloom's fantasy here is one of *enforced submission to the law*. But of course the fantasy of enforced submission is not itself enforced, and Joyce emphasizes as much by having Bloom enter the space of sexual captivity voluntarily: '(*cowed*) Exuberant female. Enormously I desiderate your domination' (*U* 15.2777). In this way, Joyce ensures that the subsequent hallucination of violent subjugation will be interpreted as belonging to Bloom, in the sense of being the expression of his erotic proclivities and identifications. The female enforcer, accordingly, is no less the embodiment of Bloom's internalized sexual and social norms than the society ladies are, or than Nora was for Joyce. The difference in this case is that Bloom's object choice is not the dominatrix empowered but rather *himself abased*, from which he extracts the perverse *jouissance* of zero-degree powerlessness, a kind of pure self-abandon, and the corresponding norm that he must honour and so receive psychic licence from is none other than force itself. To put it in psychoanalytic terms, in this masochistic fantasy, Bloom's 'imaginary' ego-identification is *as* pathetic wretch; his symbolic superego identification is with the empowered perspective that sees him and treats him as such. The text makes the last point clear from the start –

BLOOM

(*infatuated*) Empress!

BELLO

(*his heavy cheekchops sagging*) Adorer of the adulterous rump!

BLOOM

(*plaintively*) Hugeness!

BELLO

Dungdevourer!

BLOOM

(*with sinews semiflexed*) Magmagnificence!   (*U* 15.2836–45)

Throughout the remainder of this episode, Bloom punctuates his captive ordeal not with signifiers of consent, which would tend to abrogate the coercion involved, but with signifiers of obeisance, which tend to approve it.

What makes authoritarian force a paramount sexual norm for Bloom and what makes his embrace of sexual enslavement a correspondingly perverse pleasure is of course the patriarchal sex/gender system, which assigns the traits of physical strength and social mastery to masculinity, and the traits of physical delicacy and social docility to femininity. In putting himself at the absolute disposal of anyone, let alone an empowered female, Bloom courts a *jouissance* profoundly identified with the position of woman. Bloom's fantasy thus contravenes the specifically gendered sexual norms upon which it in part depends. Although he continues to worship the historically masculine fetish of irresistible force, he forfeits on his own behalf the masculine possession and privilege thereof.

But this brings us to the second, more conspicuously distinctive aspect of Bloom's fantasy. As it takes on a more violent coloration, there occurs an hallucinatory gender reversal. Bella Cohen morphs into the brutally hypermasculine Bello, who degrades and tortures Bloom, now transformed into a timorous, dependent specimen of girlhood. The virtual transgendering proves a perfect exemplar of Joyce's use of masochism to ratchet the relationship of sexual desire and sexual proscription to a clarifying extreme. On the one hand, the fantasized gender switch is radical and all encompassing; it runs the gamut from an interchange of stereotyped interests and attitudes (for example, Bloom becomes preoccupied with appearance while Bello adopts Bloom's business concerns, evincing a passion for stock investment) to dress and deportment (e.g. Bello wears '*mountaineers puttees*' and smokes a cigar while Bloom dons a 'frock' and '*bangle bracelets*') to the sex of the body itself (e.g. Bloom sports a '*vulva*', which Bello penetrates with his fist). On the other hand, however, operating at the heart of a masochistic fantasy, the gender translation functions to restore the patriarchal identification of physical prowess, social aggressiveness, and sexual dominion exclusively with the man or, rather, with the attribute of masculinity, while reaffirming the conventional misogynist imputation of a natural dependence, sexual and otherwise, to the feminine, a need to be governed and subordinated. For the cultural imaginary staged in Bloom's fantasy, a sexually masterful woman is a phallic woman, and a sexually submissive man is a girly-man. It is only insofar as she is overtaken, and taken over, by Bloom's projected image of robust masculinity that Bella exercises the requisite authoritarian control to bring Bloom to heel. And it is only in losing his manhood, in introjecting a self-image of shrinking femininity, that Bloom comes to acquiesce in a humiliating *jouissance*. In this fashion, Bloom subscribes to his culture's normative gender typology in the very act of breaking with it.

But I would go further still. Consider the dramatic timing of the gender reversal. Firstly, it occurs just at the moment that the masochistic fantasy intensifies from menacing flirtation to flagellation. Bloom, we might infer, can *only* sustain the perverse enjoyment of his 'crimes against gender' if he expresses, in the unconscious plotting of his fantasy, a psychic fidelity to the patriarchal law of gender in its fundamental sexual aspect. For Bloom, the materialization of sexual dominance entails its masculinization. Secondly, the gender reversal occurs at just the moment when Bloom shifts from participating in the masochistic scenario to feeling himself overwhelmed by the tyrannical power of his tormentor, i.e. when the fantasy becomes one of enforced submission. Paradoxically, no greater respect can be paid to power than *involuntary* respect, respect born of the belief in and a secret identification with its invincibility. That Bloom should evince this summary respect in concert with this mutual transgendering implies a still deeper assent to the primary system of sexual constraint, the patriarchal law of gender identity and difference.

By the affective logics we have been sketching in this essay, abject obedience to a figure of sexual regulation within the masochistic fantasy affords compensatory latitude or cover for the perversions at stake in the fantasy itself. Bloom's fealty to Bella-Bello, both as lawgiver and symbolic avatar of patriarchy's law, is virtually absolute: he fantasizes himself obeying under a compulsion whose inexorability his own half-hearted pleas for clemency are meant to adduce. The licence that he garners is correspondingly absolute; indeed, it is mandatory. And since on the terms of the fantasy, Bloom has no choice but to indulge in perverse appetites, he is free to enjoy without responsibility. The licence taken is, accordingly, encyclopaedic as well. As part of the scenario of total duress, he is enabled to recall, imagine, imitate or abide most of the perversions catalogued in the works of contemporary sexologists like

Krafft-Ebing, including exhibitionism, voyeurism, coprophilia, pederasty, fisting, bestiality, cannibalism, various forms of fetishism (leather, lingerie, foot), transvestism, transsexuality, anal sodomy, and the 'Gomorrhan vices' of lesbianism.

Among these enforced perversions, pride of place goes to troilism, for this practice answers to the trying centrepiece of Bloom's entire day, Molly's tryst with Boylan. Throughout the narrative, Bloom connives at the affair and by the conclusion of the novel, Molly even opines that he had arranged it. The Bello encounter reveals the logic whereby what may have been a traumatic betrayal for Bloom was also the fulfilment of an obscure longing. First, Bloom is reminded of how 'in five public conveniences he wrote pencilled messages offering his nuptial partner to all strongmembered males' (*U* 15.3034–5). In light of this graffiti advertisement, Molly's new admirer appears something of an unconscious dream come true. As Bello remarks, 'I wouldn't hurt your feelings for the world but there's a man of brawn in possession there . . . He is something like a fullgrown outdoor man. Well for you, you muff, if you had that weapon with knobs and lumps and warts all over it . . . He's no eunuch' (*U* 15.3136–41). The structure of Bloom's masochistic transactions with Bella/o uncannily repeats itself in relation to his wife's infidelity. His fantasy enthrones Boylan as a phallic exemplar and, like the ad itself, this paean to the ideal of virility serves to validate Bloom's departure from the patriarchal norm: his indulgence in the 'feminine' *jouissance* of powerlessness and abjection does not defy so much as indirectly affirm that norm, by professing his own incapacity to satisfy its demands.

In Bloom's subsequent hallucination of the affair itself, which brings the masochistic extravaganza of 'Circe' to a climax (in every sense of the word), Boylan bears a certain authority connected with his successful *parade virile*; he stands for something like the law of manhood. Bloom serves Boylan and, by extension, the phallic principle he embodies, acting as his '*flunkey*' (*U* 15.3760) and pander ('menagerer' is Bloom's term (*U* 15.325)), giving him the run of both his house and his wife. For his part, Bloom is repaid with instructions from Boylan to take the tryst as an opportunity for vicarious, voyeuristic satisfaction, orders with which Bloom gratefully complies

BOYLAN
. . . You can apply your eye to the keyhole and play with yourself while I just go through her a few times.
BLOOM
Thank you, sir. I will, sir.   (*U* 15.3788–91)

The interchange epitomizes the logic of Bloom's masochism: cringing homage to a figure of phallic gender norms and the sexual performance they underwrite not only affords permission to deviate from those norms but is already, in effect, that deviation. The remainder of Bloom's fantasy sustains this logic by counterpointing the lionization of Boylan's masculinity (the whores cheer his olympian sexual prowess) with the denigration of Bloom's (Molly reviles him as a 'pishogue' (U 15.3778)), which converge in a moment of intense sexual arousal and release:

BLOOM

(his eyes wildly dilated, clasps himself) Show! Hide! Show!
Plough her! More! Shoot!   (*U* 15.3814–16)

Joyce thus stages Bloom's masochistic extravaganza as a kind of meta-perversion, which in summarizing the principles of the perverse, brings along the other perversions in its wake. The capaciousness of masochism as a perversion is linked to its status as a microcosm of sexuality *tout court*. Joycean masochism unfolds in what Žižek has called 'the logic of the exception,' whereby marginal or excluded manifestations of a reality can turn out to crystallize the secret of the whole.[13] Here, a highly non-normative type of sexuality discloses in the form of its enactment the function of normativity within the larger economy of sexuality, its articulation with the desire it pretends to circumscribe. In this light, the indignation that greeted the sexuality in and of Joyce's fiction seem more understandable if no less regrettable. Whereas Freudian theory outraged polite society by situating perversion *within* the structure of the sexual norm, Joyce undertook the still more threatening project of situating the norm within a structure of perversion coextensive with sexuality itself.

NOTES

1 The Dublin Castle saw several prominent colonial officials implicated in a homosexual 'ring', and at least one was subsequently convicted. This scandal in turn facilitated passage of the Criminal Law Amendment Act of 1885, with its notorious section 11, which criminalized all homosexual activity. The Cleveland Street Scandal of 1889, in which prominent London aristocrats were convicted of prostituting West End messenger boys, provided the first major test of the Act. The subsequent trials of Oscar Wilde are still perhaps the most famous prosecution of homosexuality in the modern era.

2 See Adrienne Rich, *Compulsory Heterosexuality and Lesbian Existence* (London: Onlywomen, 1981).

3 Sigmund Freud, *Three Essays on the Theory of Sexuality* (1905) (New York: BasicBooks, 1975), p. 57.

4 Michel Foucault, *The History of Sexuality: An Introduction*, vol. 1 (New York: Vintage, 1978), pp. 36–49.

5 Old Parr was an English centenarian accused of incontinence. See Roland McHugh, *Annotations to Finnegans Wake* (Baltimore: Johns Hopkins University Press, 1991), p. 3.

6 *Jouissance* signifies intense sexual enjoyment that in shattering the coherence of the ego comprises suffering as well as orgasmic ecstasy; it is a form of pleasure that exceeds itself as pleasure.

7 Slavoj Žižek, *The Metastases of Enjoyment* (New York: Verso, 1994), p. 126.

8 For the Wonderworker, 'the world's greatest remedy for rectal complaints', see *Ulysses*, 17.1819–21.

9 Eve Sedgwick, *Between Men* (New York: Columbia University Press, 1985).

10 Since Richard Brown's landmark *James Joyce and Sexuality* (Cambridge: Cambridge University Press, 1985), much of the innovative work on sexuality in Joyce has been done in the area of queer or non-normative sexuality. I would refer the reader to the following collections: *Joyce and Homosexuality*, ed. Joseph Valente, a special issue of the *James Joyce Quarterly* 31.3 (1994); *Quare Joyce*, ed. Joseph Valente (Ann Arbor: University of Michigan Press, 1998); *Joyce: The Return of the Repressed*, ed. Susan Friedman (Ithaca: Cornell University Press, 1993); *'Ulysses': En-Gendered Perspectives*, ed. K. Devlin and M. Reizbaum (Columbia: University of South Carolina Press, 1999). I would refer the reader to the following books: Derek Attridge, *Joyce Effects: On Language, Theory, and History* (Cambridge: Cambridge University Press, 2000), pp. 59–77; Suzette Henke, *James Joyce and the Politics of Desire* (New York: Routledge, 1990); Sheldon Brivic, *Joyce's Waking Women* (Urbana: University of Illinois Press, 1994); Garry Leonard, *Re-Reading Dubliners* (Syracuse: Syracuse University Press, 1991). Finally, I would refer the reader to the following articles: Joseph Valente, 'A Child is Being Eaten: Mourning, Transvestism, and the Incorporation of the Daughter in *Ulysses*', *James Joyce Quarterly* 34 (1997), 21–64; Kevin Dettmar, 'Vocation, Vacation, Perversion', in *James Joyce and the Fabrication of Irish Identity*, ed. Michael Gillespie (Amsterdam: Rodopi, 2001), pp. 132–50; Katherine Mullin, '"Don't Cry for Me Argentina": "Eveline" and the Seduction of Emigration Propaganda', in *Semicolonial Joyce*, ed. Derek Attridge and Marjorie Howes (Cambridge: Cambridge University Press, 2000), pp. 172–200; Roberta Jackson, 'The Open Closet in *Dubliners*: James Duffy's Painful Case', *James Joyce Quarterly* 37 (1999), 83–98; Margot Norris, 'Shocking the Reader in James Joyce's "A Painful Case"', *James Joyce Quarterly* 37 (1999), 63–81.

11 Frances Restuccia, *Joyce and the Law of the Father* (New Haven: Yale University Press, 1989), p. 128.

12 Gilles Deleuze, *Masochism: an Interpretation of Coldness and Cruelty* (New York: George Braziller, 1971), p. 35.

13 Slavoj Žižek, *The Sublime Object of Ideology* (New York: Verso, 1989), pp. 22–31.

12

JENNIFER WICKE

Joyce and consumer culture

'My consumers are they not my producers?'
James Joyce, *Finnegans Wake*

James Joyce's writing is famously, notoriously difficult, especially his two epic works, *Ulysses*, sometimes described as the book everyone claims to have read but no one actually has, and *Finnegans Wake*, whose difficulties have led to innumerable reading groups formed for the sometimes lifelong task of reading and puzzling over the book, a page or two at a time. A famous photograph of Marilyn Monroe exhibits the paradox of Joyce's fame as a writer, coupled with the complexities of his writing: Monroe, wearing a swimsuit, sits in a park absorbed in *Ulysses*. The contradictory conjunction of movie star with great book in the picture is worth, as they say, at least a thousand words – how could the icon of mass celebrity culture, and a supposed 'dumb blonde' to boot, undertake the reading of the twentieth century's supreme work of high literature? It turns out that Marilyn Monroe did succeed in reading at least parts of the book, and the fact that she wanted to make the effort says as much for the celebrity of Joyce and his novel as it does for the intellectual aspirations of the star. In fact, the paradox of the photograph lies not its seeming encounter between opposite poles of modern culture, but in its proof that James Joyce's rarefied literary works are also themselves artifacts of mass culture. Any reader or student approaching them for the first time has Marilyn Monroe as an inspiration, and as quirky evidence that Joyce's writing, like Joyce the author, is as much a part of mass culture or consumer culture as we all are.

The many invaluable skeleton keys to the allusions and literary references in *Ulysses*, to take Joyce's major work of mass culture as an example, imply that an encyclopaedic knowledge of Western literary culture is a prerequisite for reading and even dimly understanding this great novel and totemic book. The intimidation factor in approaching any of Joyce's writing, except perhaps the stories that make up *Dubliners*, is extremely high. But it is just as true to say that fresh readers (or re-readers) of *Ulysses* go into the book's world with a skeleton key already in hand – their knowledge of the rhythms, the media, the forces, the pleasures, and the pains of mass culture and consumer society. Before even cracking open the book, its modern readers are already connoisseurs and critics of Joyce's primary world of allusion, the wide nets his book tosses out to draw in the flotsam and jetsam of modern mass culture, of an everyday life comprised of shopping, ads, mass entertainment, posters, fashion, spectacle, news, and the information bombarding us from multiple public sources. Joyce's consuming subject, or in other words the subject matter that consumed him as a writer, was the replication in the very words of his art of this new modern world of mass culture. His task is to render it visible in all its energies, its splendours, and its miseries, too. A famous character in a Molière play is surprised and delighted to discover that just by talking in ordinary sentences all his life, he has been speaking 'prose' – he had thought prose was a rhetorical genre as mystified as 'poetry', and as beyond his grasp. While no one would deny the complexity of James Joyce's literary universe, it is also true that in a sense we know how to speak its language, or at least one of its major tongues – the mass cultural language of consumer subjects – because we have been speaking it all our lives. Joyce's textual world is not hermetic, elitist, arcane, or removed from everyday life: it draws from it and transforms it, without ever abandoning it. In another context, responding to criticism of the circus as a no more than tawdry example of mass culture and the epitome of its false spectacle, the writer Jean Genet replied 'its sawdust is gold dust'. Joyce's writing translates the textures or sawdust of mass culture in an alchemy whereby its gold dust becomes literary coinage. In this sense, Joyce is not the Olympian modernist writer paring his fingernails atop a mountain of literary complexity: he is instead one of us, a bread and circus man *par excellence*.

That mass, commodity culture is one of Joyce's major subjects has come to be critically acknowledged, as our own critical awareness of and obsession with consumption has increased. The imbrication of *Dubliners* and *A Portrait*, of *Ulysses* and even *Finnegans Wake* in a material world awash in the detritus of consumer objects and the subjectivity of the everyday universe of consumption is now evident. Many things follow from this recasting of our regard, and the decision to take it as important that these texts are extravagantly interlaced with consumer minutiae – not the least what critical paths we then choose to take through Joyce's texts. At this stage of discovery, however, the approach to consumption is still inevitably filtered through long-standing theories of consumer culture, the status of the commodity, and commodity consciousness, or recent theories of those now pressing issues. It will be all the more useful to look at Joyce's texts not just as sites for the application of currently interesting rubrics like 'commodity fetish' but as spaces with privileged access to mass culture. In other words, new things can be learned about the matrix of consumer society by reading Joyce, if these texts are seriously held to have the issue of consumption at their root. Joyce and by extension his writings understand things about the mysteries of mass culture and of how consuming works that we still haven't completely figured out. If we think of consumer culture as simply 'popular', or 'fun', or even more strongly, as 'junk' or 'trash' to be feared, we will be blind to the rich weaving of the mass cultural Joyce's writing makes. The topics of consumption and mass culture must be framed as philosophically, aesthetically, and politically grand and significant enough to warrant such attention: after all, the culture of consumption *is* the culture of modernity.

What consumers consume in modern society are commodities – that's why 'commodity culture' is often a substitute phrase for mass culture. Commodity is a word that describes something bought and sold in a market economy, but the 'commodity form', as Karl Marx delineated it in a definition that has stood the test of time and history, what makes commodities different from ordinary objects, is their arbitrary relationship to one another. Commodities are exchanged on the market for a value determined by their relationship to other commodities, not to any intrinsic worth or 'usefulness'. The commodity system allows for the exchange of goods, services, and money interchangeably, with all of these pegged to their market value, not to any inherent value each may have. Marx also noted that this commodification process extends, in a capitalist economy, to human beings as well. The value of the work that people could do would need, in a mass society, to be turned into a commodity also, an abstraction that covers over the human element in the exchange of commodities. To take one small example from Joyce, in *Ulysses* Leopold Bloom's daughter Milly takes a brand-new kind of job in the entertainment industry, working in a photographic shack at a seaside resort where her prettiness is a commodity used to lure young men on vacation to have a snapshot made of themselves standing on the beach with her, Milly, in a daring bathing costume. Everyone in a consumer society to some extent turns their labour power – even if it consists in having a cute face and a good figure – into a commodity they then exchange for a wage or payment. As will be discussed below, Joyce by no means deplores commodity culture, just as he does not repudiate mass culture (which is a subset of the former), in part because the personal and economic alternatives to be found in past and recent Irish history are in many cases worse: feudalism, slavery, colonial oppression, or underdevelopment. Nonetheless, Joyce is among the first modern writers to link the commodity form with modernity, and to give it a face and a name.

Mass media forms such as journalism, lithography, photography, advertising, film, audio-recording, and ultimately radio distributed the knowledge of what and how to consume to the mass public, so much so that all the new industries of media technology, entertainment and information were intimately bound up in the formation of modern culture. Every aspect of mass culture and media technology makes an appearance across the spectrum of Joyce's writing, from newspapers, magazines, gramophones, silent films, newsreels, telephones, telegraphy, and photo studios in the earlier works to radio and even an intimation of television in *Finnegans Wake*. More so than any other modernist writer, Joyce not only acknowledged that modern literature was intertwined with mass culture and mass media, but saw that the older media technology of the book was capable of encompassing newer media within its covers – not by ignoring mass culture or shutting it out, or worse, repudiating it, but by exploring its furthest reaches.

What may be called the 'GPI' factor in Joyce's writing, his emphasis on the insanely general paralysis of Ireland as a simultaneously underdeveloped and overdeveloped (culturally exploited) country, finds some of its thrust in the attempt to render Ireland modern, linguistically if in no other way. Joyce's story 'Eveline', in *Dubliners*, makes explicit the ways that mass culture and a consumer society were among the few wedges of potential freedom or at least self-transformation available in turn-of-the-century Dublin. Eveline turns away at the last moment from her only chance to escape the grim realities of her life for what might, presumably, be a better and happier life across the ocean – in Buenos Aires, no less, where she has been invited by the sailor she loves. Tickets purchased, waiting in line for departure, Eveline famously lets Frank go; as he implores her to board the ship, she ceases to see him, and turns back. Throughout the short story Eveline has been rehearsing her escape, essentially grasping at the modern, by her intersections with the version of mass culture on offer in Dublin. All these rehearsals occur within the spaces of mass culture – in the department store, at the amusement grounds, in the popular theatre, listening to gramophone music and to popular songs. These exposures to the wider world are filtered in every case through media, consumption, and commodities. The alternatives for Eveline are the horrors of her homelife, her work as an unpaid slavey and possibly sexual slave for her father, and the blighted demographics of a Dublin where it was almost impossible to expect to find a man to marry. What holds Eveline back at the ship's railing is the deathly psychic grip of her domestic tomb, cretonned with dust, where her father holds sway over the encroachments of mass culture as modernity – he even found the low-tech organ grinder's music playing outside the windows of his wife's death-bed an occasion for a xenophobic slur against 'foreign' music. Eveline's entry into the mass cultural with both feet would figure her modernity and her escape, not just from her father and her loneliness, but as a figure for, almost a ship's figurehead for, the vanishing potential for an Irish modernity and an escape from colonization.

Eveline's vanishing horizon of expectations is cruelly gendered by the demands on her for endless housekeeping, for accepting patriarchal violence without a murmur, and for having her only hope of earthly salvation come floating in to her in the form of a possible husband. All of these strictures are connected, though, with either the limitations a colonial violence has imposed, or with the exacerbations of religious proscription it has induced. The irony in Eveline's miniature tragedy is that her desires and hopes are channelled to her through mass cultural, in other words metropolitan, and ultimately British colonial, means. But this is partly what Joyce thinks are the contradictions of Irish history, and its mixed hopes for independence. For Ireland to become a modern nation, it will have to decolonize its mind, in the phrase made famous by the Kenyan writer Ngugi wa-Thiong'o. Eveline is an example of how hard that will be to accomplish: through no fault of her own, her mind can barely find any uncolonized surface. Many readers of Joyce's *Dubliners* and of 'Eveline' in particular adopt an anti-consumer mentality that is foreign to Joyce's writing, and propose a moralistic interpretation of the story that faults Eveline for her pathetic romantic notions, brought to her courtesy of the demon mass culture. To look at mass culture and consumer society in the more complex and richly interwoven way Joyce does, however, is to see that Eveline's mind, and also that of the Irish public, will need to deploy the techniques, tactics, and textures of modernity most often supplied to the society by mass culture. It is possible to claim that the sailor Frank in Joyce's story doesn't exist, except in Eveline's fevered mind, or it is possible to believe he exists but that his intentions are evil, that perhaps he intends to ship off Eveline to Buenos Aires not to marry him but to work in a brothel, the same form of 'white slavery' now experienced by untold thousands of Eastern European women. Buenos Aires was historically a centre for the importation of Irish women and girls whose poverty made them vulnerable to sexual exploitation, and Eveline's shrinking back at the end of the tale may be a *frisson* of terror that is fully justified by historical precedent. She might have been on the verge of a commodity exchange much more serious than Milly's stint as a 'photo girl'. No matter which interpretation of the ending we prefer, or both, since the ending is indeterminate, Eveline's poising on the cusp of escape and falling back is not a moral failure on her part. What she shares with her fellow Dubliners is a failure of imagination, a direct result of an entombing culture. For Eveline, for Ireland at the time, the siren songs of mass culture can never be played too loudly. They make the familiar strange, and raise the imagination quotient necessary to throw off the mental shackles of GPI.

As critical fashions alter, and as other modes of inquiry arrive at a perhaps temporary exhaustion, increasing attention to the material concerns so evident in Joyce's work have emerged, and it has served to shift the perception of *Ulysses*, for example, from a monument of aesthetic erudition to a dynamically social text. In line with these preoccupations a new concentration on what could loosely be called the features of the marketplace, or modernity under the sign of capitalism, or of the forces of social exchange, has also been discernible. Among the facets of the critical diamond are advertising, fashion, and consumption as a practice and a state of mind. Whether issuing from the right or the left, the primary tenor of theories of consumption is distinctly negative. On the one, that is, the right, hand, consumption is a fallen if eminently necessary social process, which is mercifully refined out of existence in the rarefied circles of art and culture – *Ulysses*, for example, can be held up as an artifact impervious to the depradations of mass culture and rigorously defiant of consumption, having made itself unconsumable, the veritable proof of its artistic merit. The left hand of this argument doesn't require that texts attain a purity unsullied by signs of traffic with social relations, since the assumption is that texts arise from social contexts, or are social contexts themselves, but consumption arrives equally tainted in this arena, because it is the very marker of ideological control and the very symbol of capitalism's incursions into art and culture.

With advertising, the scenario is even worse, since the suspicion that ads originate out of commodity exchange is essentially correct. Ads are not, however, individually responsible as artifacts for the social arrangements of late capitalism. Ads do not cause barter, cottage industries, or pastoral communities to vanish; their existence certainly does bear witness to and furthers the inexorable encroachments of a capitalist social process, but ads are also a human creation subject to manifold private and collective uses. The horror of social inequity and violent hegemony is to some extent writ small in ads; when they are read as singular artifacts, as individual texts, their 'messages' can indeed be nightmarishly negative – misogynist, racist, imperialist, domestic, corporate, and so on. That isn't, however, how ads are read in social reading, where they are invariably multiple, intertextual, incomplete, tentative, and provisional as a collective desire mechanism.

No one better understood the social reading of advertisement than James Joyce. *Ulysses* deploys both real ads and invented ads within itself, always with an eye, though, to advertising as a practice, a multi-dimensional space for cultural creation allied, of course, with the goal of market exchange. Ads float free of this rootedness in the commodity, however, as the throwaway ad embodies so well. Joyce sets individual ads floating down the river of his text as if they were bubbles of modernity – inscribing the text with its material

present-ness, as the circulation of ads does in everyday life. Joyce compre-
hends how the implicit 'ideology' of ads necessarily floats freely, becoming
unmoored from its social context and entering the imaginary space of a
potentially altering social reading.

What happens 'between' *Dubliners* and *Ulysses*? The scrupulous meanness
of the realist depiction of Irish modernity in the former collection gives way to
the textual farrago, with actual interpenetration of advertising, mass market
fiction, and the like, in the latter, modernist *Ulysses*. One way to answer the
question is to see *Ulysses* as a species of advertisement in its own right, an
advertisement of the very modernity of under-modernized colonial Ireland
as it moves to a post-colonial status. *Dubliners* makes use of the literary
genre of realism to sequester its allegorical impulses – the stories collected
under the rubric of *Dubliners* may look like strictly realist depictions, but
they are allegories of everyday life in Dublin, using the material details of
description to produce a cumulative effect of repetitive intensity. *Ulysses*
makes use of the emblematic mode of advertisement to produce its historical
and literary effects. This may seem to be an unwelcome revisionary claim –
a bad thing to say about *Ulysses* and a crude way of knocking it off its
high art perch – if advertising is thought of as essentially a label put on
a commodity. Advertising, however, considerably exceeds this role, and in
the abstract sense approaches the auratic power of other discourses Joyce
revered, among them religion and literature.

Take the House of Key(e)s ad that so dominates the 'Aeolus' chapter, at
least in terms of Bloom's peregrinations. Bloom's link to Joyce as an author
should be accepted quite literally in this instance. Bloom after all invents
the political pun on the Isle of Man and its independent parliament he will
try to recapitulate in the ad for Alexander Keyes's wine shop, by wittily
seeing that the emblem for the parliament, the crossed keys, would make
a vivid and politically arousing symbol for a shop named after its owner,
Keyes. Advertising allows for these unexpected cross-over points, because
it uses all the rhetorical facility of language to memorably name human
exchanges. At bottom, the ad will represent the wine shop and will try, of
course, to stimulate people to come into said wine shop. The new wine in the
old linguistic bottle of Keyes is the reference, slightly veiled, to the crossed
keys and their political symbology. Joyce draws a comparison between the
literary procedures of Bloom as ad man and Joyce's political procedures as
literary man. Ads are constellations of desire; prise them apart, recirculate
them, translate them, and they signal a transubstantation devoutly to be
wished. Wishing is part of the game – decolonizing the mind has to do with
the articulation of wishes, and their creative enactments. Joyce's entire book
works – on only one of its many levels – as if it *were* the Keyes ad.

The shocking conclusion is that Joyce's rewriting of advertising is in some ways also the textual avenue of decolonization, in Joyce's relation to the reading public. Joyce's book is written, as it were, after the fact, or during the fact; it is not a substitute for the complex and violent struggles of individuals and groups, the Easter Rising, the formation of political parties and parliamentary and nationalist parties of several stripes, the historical process of enforcing a partial independence of Ireland. It is asking too much of the book, or any book, to try to make *Ulysses* the harbinger or the instigator of these changes. What *Ulysses* does indubitably participate in, and make, is a material event in Irish culture, in English-language culture, in European culture, whereby high art establishes its modernity by decolonizing mass culture, especially advertisement. *Ulysses* forces us to read our (English-language and European) high art literary heritage through the prism of mass culture, and to read the mass cultural as a transubstantiating discourse exhibiting the aura of the everyday. The book is an advertisement within the precincts of modernist European writing for the astonishing and unexpected modernity of Ireland, for the triumph of the colony, the periphery, as supremely modern, most fashionable, the apogee of the 'mass cultural'. What we also have to read in *Ulysses* is a relation to mass culture, and not just any mass culture, but this specific mass culture, of the city of Dublin, Ireland, colony of Great Britain, circa 1904, and the social readings it produces. To the extent that *Ulysses* advertises the modern, it places us as readers in the position of the public reading: 'Of some one sole unique advertisement to cause passers to stop in wonder, a poster novelty, with all extraneous accretions excluded, reduced to its simplest and most efficient terms not exceeding the span of casual vision and congruous with the velocity of modern life' (*U* 17.1770–3).

Ulysses has continued to be the very best advertisement for modernism extant, the colony's perfect revenge. What it advertises is not the glory of British literature, but the velocity of decolonization brought about by the literary imagination, tunnelling from within the English language, and the very wide span a casual vision – or a social reading – can take in.

The antipathy toward consumption at all levels, and the consequent celebration of what is difficult, avant-garde, or modernist as its counterpoint is a prevailing, one might even say the distinctive, feature of contemporary critical thinking in a variety of guises. Often this animus crystallizes in the valorizing of a more authentic, original, or folk culture now eradicated by consumption, or of a working-class culture thought to have more authenticity, or by extolling avant-garde practices precisely for their repudiation of consumptive strategies, in the quite stereotyped vision of what those strategies are thought to be. Even more ironically there is an attempt to recuperate aspects of mass culture as sites of resistance or struggle, with the hidden assumption that those participating in the consumption in the first place are entirely victimized by their contact with a hegemonic cultural industry enforcing its hierarchies in and through mass cultural schemes. The problems arise when the social analysis proceeds from such a reductive view of consumption, which then obscures consumption's manifold possibilities, political and otherwise. Not the least of the results of this oversight, if perhaps less immediately relevant to many people, is the inability to locate the really majestic foresight of *Ulysses* in its understanding of consumption.

Consumption is a mode of work, that, in contrast to its reputation as the passive, effeminate and mindless side of consciousness and modern social being, is in fact a highly complex social and psychic labour, whose results are often contradictory or ambiguous, but never simply foregone conclusions. Work in this sense is not necessarily the physical labour involved in procuring the object of consumption – which, of course, can be a symbolic object as readily as it is a can of beans on the supermarket shelf or a new lipstick from the department store cosmetics counter – nor only the labour sometimes required to physically transform the objects which enter our lives. Instead, this work may signify the time of possession, a particular context of presentation as a gift or as memorabilia, or the incorporation of a single object into a stylistic array that is used then to express the creator's place in relation to others similarly accoutred. The object is transformed by its intimate association with a particular individual or social group, or by the relationship between these, and such transformations are the work of consumption. This is not to say, of course, that all objects are or can be consumed in some transformational way; without question, there are networks of commodities deployed in powerfully oppressive ways, and the estrangements and refractions occasioned by that oppression are only too evident as the backdrop and even the substance of daily life. However, assigning an intrinsic negativity to the commodity, and an equally mordant and inescapable pathos to consumption, has highly reductive effects on how we gauge the social world and the possibilities inherent in it.

To move back to textual terrain is to find *Ulysses* in some senses anticipating this quest for another means of qualifying the social relations of consumption, which are, in modern times, essentially what we call culture. A common approach to *Ulysses'* greatness, or to its quintessential modernism, depending on the style of the critics involved, is to valorize *Ulysses* for its 'dialectic with mass culture', a debate the book wins as it relentlessly reasserts its own imponderable difficulty, its avant-garde or modernist critical edge, and defies consumability. If we consider *Ulysses* to be engaged in another kind of encounter with consumption, however, the boundary lines are not so tidy. *Ulysses* enacts the contradictions of consumption – as a work meant for consumption that is also about the work consumption entails. *Ulysses* sets up a space, both a physical space (the book) and a temporal space (the time involved in traversing the book), for the consideration of this problem. The either/or insistence so embedded in the high art/mass culture debates which swirl around *Ulysses* is alien to this text, which parades itself as an exemplary work of consumption instead.

Gerty MacDowell is a paradigm text for seeing these two senses of 'work' in action. The circumstances of Gerty's life are pitifully catalogued in 'Nausicaa' – a drunken father, a dead mother, too much household labour to accomplish with too little money, a physical disability exacerbating the dearth of marriageable males, a violent male society surrounding her. Against these limitations she posits a work of consumption that is her own salvation, as much as it is the voice of her nation struggling to be born. Gerty is a national 'heroine' in a certain sense, a heroine of everyday life who keeps going in the face of domestic violence, social invisibility, and colonial repression.

The 'Nausicaa' chapter in which she appears as a character is proving to be as rich as a plum pudding for those who have discovered the relation of Joyce's writing to mass cultural texts, ads, and images. Gerty looks particularly smart in the emperor's new clothes she is allotted – many analyses of her character disdain her or pity her for her so-called entrapment in what they see as an inevitably oppressive web of consumerist images of female beauty, fashion, and romantic fantasy. Gerty's interest in the twilight world of beauty culture is criticized as bad faith or false consciousness; Gerty has succumbed to enslavement by beauty ads, has become a victim of feminine objectification, and, even worse, is seen as allowing her own transformation into a commodity, used and abused by the gazing Leopold Bloom. The logic of this analysis depends on the castigation of consumption as passive enthralment, as feminine false-consciousness run amok; Gerty's perceived predicament is thought to follow as much from her subtle use of 'eyebrowleine' as it does from her unmarriageable state. This is not the place to go into all the theoretical problems with accounts of the gaze and of the female as object; they become very serious, though, when adherence to a particular notion of the female as commodity and consumption as feminine thraldom intersect to give us a Gerty who is either passive sexual victim to Bloom, removing every grain of her own sexual desire, or the passive victim of a capitalism which foists its cosmetics and its shirtwaists and its unattainable desires off on an equally blank slate of a young woman. These questions are not meant for a moment to evade the harsh omnipresence of gender inequality or the rigid sexual hierarchy obtaining in Dublin then and to some degree now; they are meant to point to the chapter's own vastly more sophisticated treatment of the gendering of the work of consumption and the forces which come into play in the ambiguities of performing that work. Gerty may be 'penetrated' by an advertising lexicon superimposed on *The Lamplighter*'s domesticating prose, but Gerty refashions these items into her own treasured collection. An ungainly term for what happens in consumption, the personal meanings that are invested in an array of consumables that then give them personal, as opposed to exchange, value, is 'recontextualization'. A new context for the array of consumed items or images or experiences is found. The 're-' in recontextualize is the same as the 're-' in representation, the complicated process by which literature reconfigures what it presents. Joyce's practices as an author are not that far off from those of his character Gerty MacDowell: he takes bits and pieces of little value to others and by placing them within an ensemble, renders not only the whole but the parts much greater than their sum. The new context is akin to a florist's wire that allows for a design of blossoms which hides the structure underneath, as if the flowers were floating in air.

The collection of items in her drawer is Gerty's inventory of transformed objects: 'It was there she kept her girlish treasure trove, the tortoiseshell combs, her child of Mary badge, the whiterose scent, the eyebrowleine, her alabaster pouncetbox and the ribbons to change when her things came home from the wash and there were some beautiful thoughts written in it in violet ink that she bought in Hely's of Dame Street for she felt that she too could write poetry if she could only express herself like that poem that appealed to her so deeply that she had copied out of the newspaper she found one evening round the potherbs'(*U* 13.638–45). Even the contingency of her having found this evocative poem, in its mass cultural garb, accidentally wrapped around the vegetables is an instance of the unpredictable and self-creating aspects of consumption: Gerty is not merely the frozen victim of an insistent interpellation. The fantasy currents running through her life do not mean pure vicariousness, nor does the mythological world suggested by her chosen reading imply pure illusion. The danger in holding out such a revisionist reading is that it gets emptied of any dialectical complexities, and seems to insinuate that all is well in Gerty's world, or that sexism is not an operant element of Gerty's everyday life, which it clearly is as depicted in the chapter. Gerty is shown recontextualizing the objects of her consumer world, not in order to be objectified as a sexual commodity by Bloom, but to let her world open out into a fantasy scripted by her, and for her, in the cosmetic vocabulary of eyebrowleine. She is not taken advantage of by a misogynist Bloom across the strand, she takes advantage of the possibilities for escape and fulfilment, meagre as they are, categorized for her by the allure of the consumer goods she both incorporates and also rearranges.

'Come what might she would be wild, untrammelled, free' (13.673). To deny that Gerty has a tiny moment of liberation, of transcending her limitations in a moment of shared fantasy brought about by mass culture, fashion, and mass fantasy is to impose a sentimentality of our own on the more embracing investigations of the book, where Gerty attains a remarkable persona out of the dribs and drabs of commodities, purple prose, and the desires which animate them. Out of the mere 'stuff' of clothing styles, advice on manners, and romantic dreams, Gerty creates a lexicon for overcoming – one that parallels Bloom's own private lexicon.

Joyce's writing participates in this unusual evisceration of print culture, makes an end run around advertising as modern language, by incorporating its modernity, and then sucking that modernity out, vampirically extracting the essence of modernity and postulating modernities that supersede or exceed this: the modern-ized text of *Ulysses*. We are most accustomed to this process in the vagaries of fashion, for instance as fashion style is used or deployed by women and/or marginal social groups. In the latter case, a fashion trend might be altered or displaced enough to signal both that the ultra-modernity of that fashion is recognized, but is also superseded by being manipulated for new, striking effects that then surpass its former fashion message, upping the ante of fashionability. Joyce's *Ulysses* could be said to be a book obsessed with fashion. It has not been sufficiently appreciated as a minute registration of the beating pulse of fashionability, circa 1904. There is a peculiar contradiction involved in claiming this; since Joyce completed *Ulysses* in 1922, the fashions charted so carefully in the book are, by definition, no longer fashionable. What Joyce brings off in the book is a kind of retrieval or exhumation of a vanished fashionability, the dynamic of fashion preserved in the amber of the book. The concern for fashion in the text is neither off-hand nor insignificant; it is a crucial strand of the book, and its invisibility for many critics and readers speaks to our own discomfort with both fashion and consumption. Joyce does not relegate fashion to some benighted level, and *Ulysses* contains more on-the-money descriptions of fashions in clothes, shoes, ties, hats and underwear than any ten realist novels – down to the prices for many of the goods. If Joyce fetishizes fashion, what can be the reasons for this? The lovingly rendered details of an entire fashion realm are central to *Ulysses*, and to fix for a critical moment on the figure of lingerie, or lingerie as figure, may be a helpful entry into fashionability as a literary and material problematic, certainly integral to Joyce's textual modalities.

Lingerie is a small zone or subset of the immense world of fashionability, one that comes highly charged in our culture, in Joyce, and in our contemporary debates over gender and feminism, and in addressing it one can uncover some of the processes of fashion and of consumption which intersect it, while at the same time respecting the material forces behind Joyce's *Ulysses* which cause it to engage lingerie with such passion and exactitude. The dynamics of lingerie in the book are a carefully orchestrated element in the work's passionate engagement with fashion as a performance of historical (and political) transformation. There is a crucial dovetailing here around the line of gender, since consumption has been articulated most prominently as an analogy to female being, and modern fashion has been coded as the province of female vanity. There is no need to adopt a utopian vision of fashion as entirely liberating in every instance to see that as a cultural dynamic fashion is infinitely more complicated than its assignment to strict sexual hierarchy would allow. The interplay of the fashion pulse with the complexities of consuming styles, of gender creativity, and of historical nuance, bears down upon Joyce's work with signal complication.

'*Lingerie* does it', Bloom opines, on the beach in the 'Nausicaa' chapter (13.797). He is using a fashion term here, since the word was not in common use at all prior to the turn of the century and the sudden upheaval in women's undergarments, in trying to account for the desirability of women in the very new cultural form of the Mutoscope pictures. 'Do they snapshot those girls or is it all a fake?' Bloom wonders (13.796–7). Here we see lingerie on the precipice of eroticized fashion, as a complexly overdetermined shift in the nature of what women wear underneath their clothes comes to have resonances in a set of new representations. Musing on women in the philosophical aftermath of his climax on the shore, Bloom determines telegraphically that 'fashion part of their charm'. He then delivers a formulation which gets at the heart of a mystery: 'Just changes when you're on the track of the secret' (13.804–5).

The secret is certainly not women's bodies; instead, it is the evanescent logic of fashion, which has an internal 'secret' to reveal, or seems to hold out the possibility of one, just as the fashion transforms and alters. That sense of being forever poised on the edge, on the verge of a revelation, is a fashion dynamic Joyce's text wants to explore, because it is also a mystery of contemporary culture, and a key to the representation of history. Walter Benjamin states in the *Theses on the Philosophy of History*: 'History is the subject of a structure whose site is not homogeneous, empty time, but time filled by the presence of the now [*Jetztzeit*].'[1] Benjamin's emphasis on the 'now', as opposed to the mere present, is emblematized in concrete form by references to fashion: 'Thus, to Robespierre ancient Rome was a

past charged with the time of the now which he blasted out of the continuum of history. The French revolution viewed itself as Rome reincarnate. It
evoked ancient Rome the way fashion evokes costumes of the past. Fashion
has a flair for the topical, no matter where it stirs in the thickets of long
ago . . .'

The flair for the topical is a historical force Joyce also aligns to fashion.
Once one becomes alert to it, fashion intelligence is sprayed all over *Ulysses*,
a fashionability mediated by the location of Dublin as a metropolitan back-
water and a colonially underdeveloped nation. In spite of this, or perhaps
precisely because of that impetus, fashion is important to the text and to
the world of its language. Dublin and its citizens cannot hope to compete
in any fashion sweepstakes, where the acknowledged centre would be Paris
and the runner up would be London. Still, the absence of fashion would in
some sense mean the absence of modernity, the absence of time, the absence
of urban life. Fashion in this reading supplies some of the dynamic that the
straitened political and social conditions of colonization and abject poverty
would otherwise militate against. Moreover, fashion encodes a 'now-ness'
with special resonance in a colonized setting, as that now summons up both
a pressing past and a horizon of futurity, a future with the explosive potential
of transformation. Is fashion in *Ulysses* a form of resistance? That would
be too univocal a reading in many respects, and would ignore the temporal
complexities of a book whose 'now' is a shifting one; nonetheless, scenting
fashion on the wind is an activity Joyce's text shares with its depiction of the
denizens of Dublin, most of them women, who care about fashion and make
sacrifices to be fashionable, not out of mere 'vanity', but because fashion is
a kind of compact with modernity.

Gerty's underwear occupies a significant amount of her time, since it has
passed over from the limbo of pure necessity to the more articulated world
of fashion; Gerty's adoption of a chaste form of lingerie is one of the many
fashion choices with which she makes a world.

> As for undies they were Gerty's chief care and who that knows the fluttering
> hopes and fears of sweet seventeen (though Gerty would never see seventeen
> again) can find it in his heart to blame her? She had four dinky sets with
> awfully pretty stitchery, three garments and nighties extra, and each set slotted
> with different coloured ribbons, rosepink, pale blue, mauve and peagreen,
> and she aired them herself and blued them when they came home from the
> wash and ironed them and she had a brickbat to keep the iron on because
> she wouldn't trust those washerwomen as far as she'd see them scorching
> the things. She was wearing the blue for luck, hoping against hope, her own
> colour and the lucky colour too for a bride to have a bit of blue somewhere on
> her . . .   (13.171–9)

These are items of clothing never seen by anyone but Gerty, if we discount the sighting made by Bloom of an edge of knicker, but they set up a force field which invests Gerty's entire world. So powerful is the underlying sense of lingerie, and having the right lingerie, that Gerty even attributes her aborted love affair with the boy next door to her having worn the green-ribboned ones and having failed to put a pair of old underwear on over them inside out, a superstitious practice she knows works 'so long as it wasn't of a Friday' (13.186–7).

We can stand back from this and say with hindsight that Gerty was wasting her time, rinsing out those undies with bluing and bad faith, as they led her to overestimate her chances in the iffy Dublin marriage market. On the other hand, to sweep away the meaning quotient of Gerty's consumption is to do equal violence to her world and her strategies. Her consumption of this narrow array of goods is enlarged and deepened by her fantasy activity surrounding it. Were the chapter simply denigrating Gerty as lingerie consumer its own fastidious accuracy about the fashion items available, their colours and prices and so on, would be inexplicable. Instead, Gerty emblematizes the transformation of even so seemingly recherché a consumer choice. For Gerty is a 'votary of Dame Fashion', as the coy prose of 'Nausicaa' describes her (13.148–9). In her electric blue blouse, a colour possible only with the advent of aniline dyes in the late nineteenth century, responsible for giving us magenta and chartreuse as well, she channels some of the vitality electricity was beginning to bring to the cityscape into her own person. This blouse has a 'smart vee opening', another bit of fashion precision, since the inching downward of the female neckline was just barely underway, and the shape of the vee itself thought to be particularly troubling for its failure to hug the neck. Her shoes are 'the newest thing in footwear' (13.164–5), and her skirt a navy one 'cut to the stride' (13.154–5) – a fashion newly instituted to favour the daring athletic walk adopted by female bicyclists. Gerty is also described as having hunted avidly for just the right elements to trim her straw hat; bought slightly shop-soiled, Gerty is able nonetheless to transform the elements into the 'very it' (13.159).

What the chapter calls, deploying a cliché for new purposes, the 'fashion intelligence' (13.197–8) refers to the situation of human beings, women above all, receiving a constant flow of social messages to be translated and rearticulated in the form of fashion. The nascent field of social sciences was interestingly enough already fascinated by the enigma of fashion; so too Joyce registers the pervasiveness of fashion in his modernism. Gerty and her circle of friends Cissy Caffery and Edy Boardman interrogate one another and display to one another on the strength of their fashionability. Cissy has a flashing moment of transvestism fondly recalled by Gerty, when she dressed in her father's clothing and drew on a burned cork moustache, walking up Tritonville road smoking a cigarette. Another friend wants to dress according to the costumes of her favourite play. Everywhere dress, or fashion, is an ensemble in the broadest sense, a circle of relations both social and personal, enveloping the past, as in the 'halcyon days' costume card Gerty looks longingly at, or projecting into a future, any future not as grim and potentially doomed as that of Dublin. The temptation may exist to judge all this activity as a waste of time, without considering that if this consumption is a waste of time we need to ask how the meta-consumption of Joyce's own text is to be justified, and then, cutting closer to the bone, how our own strategies of consumption are implicated too.

Gerty MacDowell's case perfectly characterizes consumption as an activity, a means of living through the necessary contradictions of subject and object modern culture demands. Of course her case is a gendered one as well, an issue discussed by Jeri Johnson in this volume, but she is not correspondingly stripped of her power to employ objects in rich fabrications of her own making. Moreover, we may have to confront the 'embarrassment' of the woman's magazine as our own; for Gerty, it is a far more productive and educative object relation than anything else she is likely to be exposed to, infinitely surpassing the literature of Mariolatry, the worship of the Virgin Mary, as an attractive cultural force. To borrow from Georg Simmel's study of fashion and consumption, fashion provides a surface which is partly expressive of social being, but which also in part protects individuals from having to expose their private world of taste to the public eye.[2] In that oscillation between individuality and social definition the complexities of consumption are strongly at play. Gerty should not be seen as locked on one side of the specular looking glass of culture, nor as a utopian traveler between the two realms; instead, she is left with all the perplexities and dead ends and also pleasures of her consuming subjects.

The uncanny moment in the chapter when consciousness shifts from Gerty to Bloom takes place, it should be recalled, at a moment of fashion engineering, when lingerie is being invoked. As fireworks unfurl around them and Gerty throws her head back in ecstasy 'the garters were blue to match on account of the transparent and they all saw it and shouted to look, look there it was' (13.716–17). 'The transparent' is a reference both to the transparent stockings very newly in vogue to replace either wool or flannel ones, and also to the transparency of the erotic veil covering the Virgin Mary and cloaking Gerty too. As her face is suffused with a 'divine, entrancing blush' suddenly Bloom is there as a subject: 'he could see her other things too, nainsook knickers, the fabric that caresses the skin, better than those other pettiwidth, the green, four and eleven, on account of being white and she let him and she saw that he saw and then it went so high . . .' (13.724–7). The nexus of desire here is not possible to unpack fully – it involves divinity and erotic transcendence as well as the humble litany of undergarment fabrics and their costs. The rapture Gerty feels and Bloom feels does not get conveyed without that echo of advertising language in 'the fabric that caresses the skin'. All these levels are intertwined, intermeshed, underpinned. Just such a rhetorical admixture ends Bloom's own reverie as twilight falls. 'O sweety all your little girlwhite up I saw dirty bracegirdle made me do love sticky we two naughty Grace darling she him half past the bed met him pike hoses frillies for Raoul de perfume your wife black hair heave under embon *señorita* young eyes . . . showed me her next year in drawers return next in her next her next' (13.1279–85). Frillies – or lingerie – have achieved their own erotic calculus in Bloom's cascading chain of desiring language, lodging there with a vocabulary simultaneously commercial, technical, and eroticized. It should be pointed out that the reverie is also historicized, leaping from past to present to an ecstatic future of return – 'next year . . . in her next'.

And what does Bloom want? Bloom wants the dream of the mass public, the dreams of mass culture, the goods and experiences to consume he knows he will never have. We are told, in excruciatingly fine consumer detail, in the wild inventories characterizing 'Ithaca': from Bloom's dream of his cottage, with every possession in it, to the lifestyle he will be able to acquire as a result. 'In what ultimate ambition had all concurrent and consecutive ambitions now coalesced?' (17.1497–8) is how the question is phrased, and Bloom's internal answer, much truncated here:

> to purchase by private treaty in fee simple a thatched bungalowshaped 2 storey dwellinghouse of southerly aspect, surmounted by vane and lightning conductor, connected with the earth, with porch covered by parasitic plants (ivy or Virginia creeper), halldoor, olive green, with smart carriage finish and neat doorbrasses, stucco front with gilt tracery at eaves and gable, rising, if possible, upon a gentle eminence with agreeable prospect from balcony with stone pillar parapet over unoccupied and unoccupyable interjacent pastures
>
> (17.1504–11)

Every element of home furnishing and even upkeep is plotted out, from Axminster carpets with 'cream ground and trellised border' to corner 'fitments, upholstered in ruby plush', administered by a 'cook, general and betweenmaid', with 'carbon monoxide gas supply throughout' (17.1526–50). No more perfect articulation of what Bourdieu, the social anthropologist, might mean by 'habitus' could exist, because this is no mere wish list of things. Every object is also a relation, implies a work of consumption, a transforming recontextualization of the sort that goes on even with the more mundane goods of actual purchase: in Bloom Cottage, Saint Leopold's, Flowerville, for such are its potential names, a whole range of philosophical and leisure activities are also suddenly possible.

'What syllabus of intellectual pursuits was simultaneously possible? Snapshot photography, comparative study of religions, folklore relative to various amatory and superstitious practices, contemplation of the celestial constellations' (17.1587–91). And in the pendulum swings of contemplation, Bloom, or the text constructing him here, moves from the consumer delights of Flowerville, which also transform his intellectual pursuits, to a cataloguing of his most feared economic trajectory: 'Nadir of misery: the aged impotent disfranchised ratesupported moribund lunatic pauper' (17.1946–7). This ground zero of misery is also the negativity of consumption, the emptying out of consuming possibilities which constellate Bloom's world. The immense cognitive work Bloom performs on the objects of everyday life is attested to on nearly every page of *Ulysses* where he appears; this epistemology of consumption is not restricted to Bloom as a character, however, since it is also the hallmark of the textual style of the book as a whole. It may seem counterintuitive to consider this book in any kind of relation to the books we deem eminently consumable, examples of which dot the text like candy – *Sweets of Sin* will do as well as any other. Its quasi-pornographic status would seem to put it at farthest remove from the Joycean text, since we are convinced that pornography completely bypasses intellection. In fact, *Sweets of Sin* is a nice title for the prevailing view of consumption, since like candy its objects are presumed to go down easily and to vanish into nothingness (death by chocolate, for example), while the appetite for more vacuous consumption is ever whetted by the sinful temptations of those who produce the objects. The book, though, is an incredibly rich text as consumed by Bloom, who takes it up into his own psychosexual, class, and national orbit and gets extraordinary mileage from rearrangements of its fantasy components, not always for erotic purposes – the book can hint to him of mortal thoughts or of philosophical speculations.

Joyce's statement that in *Ulysses* he wanted to render Dublin so materially that, if destroyed, it could be reconstituted from the book gives us additional access into the freeze-dried consumption process this text involves. The quote cunningly evades the fact that the Dublin whose destruction he predicted would, anyway, lie many years beyond 1904. *That* Dublin had already been destroyed, to some extent, by the forces of time and the pressures of modernity, when *Ulysses* was published in 1922. The book never forgets the evanescence of the consumer world, and yet is equally aware of its perdurability as it becomes social relation, or material and intellectual culture. We know biographically that Joyce was very interested in marketing strategies for *Ulysses*, and by no means assumed that he would have no readership. Most commentaries are so convinced of the credentials of this experimental text and its tremendous difficulty that to seriously consider *Ulysses* in the light of consumption seems risible. Without making Joyce a prophet of any kind, the consumer success *Ulysses* has enjoyed is not incidental, and not coincidental. We are so accustomed to extracting our own activities and our scholarly venues from the milieu of consumption that it is jarring to acknowledge that these, too, are sites of consumption and we are a targeted consumer group. Joyce anticipated the work of consumption following in his wake. *Ulysses* is a consistent academic best-seller, and its various involvements in the legal fracas of obscenity trials and political censorship heighten its allure as a text to be taught in the schools. The book is bound up in a literary tradition and a literary education unavailable to most people, that much is clear, but the erudition and allusion-hunting are indissolubly yoked to the objectified material world. My experience as a teacher of and a writer about Joyce, and a reader of others who write about him, is that there is an extraordinary arena of active consumption built up around the book, where lore is exchanged with the passion of baseball card trading and the deepest satisfaction is to quote well-known lines (and they are almost all now 'well-known' in some context or other) to one another in a vast consumptive relay. We eat Joyce like candy, and we do things with the text, we enact the work of consumption, with the same relish. There is immense satisfaction in negotiating the corridors of *Ulysses* with familiarity, having parts of the text become as comfortably known as the contours of an easy chair, coming upon a line with the poignant tug of a treasured song lyric – 'Mr Leopold Bloom ate with relish the inner organs of beast and fowls.' The manifold possibilities inherent in consumption, the consumption of language, of symbolic capital, the objectification of objects which then take up a place in a private universe, do a certain violence to the positive features of the proliferating universe of material objects, whether these be books, ideas, violet garters, or *Sweets of Sin*, in the increasingly differentiated universe of modernity. *Ulysses* takes up the philosophical and political and aesthetic implications of the universe of consumption, and the strong divide we are ready to make between consumable goods and rarefied literature is a distinction *Ulysses* does not want to make. In so saliently replicating the intricate mechanisms of consumption in its own construction and its own reading process, to say nothing of its material orbit, *Ulysses* prompts us to see the potential so rarely glimpsed or acknowledged in our attitudes toward consumption. Given that this is our cultural state, which *Ulysses* accepts with equanimity and realism, Joyce can teach us how we have been performing the work of consumption all our lives.

NOTES

1 Walter Benjamin, *Illuminations*, ed. Hannah Arendt, trans. Harry Zohn (London: Collins, 1973), p. 263.
2 Georg Simmel, 'Fashion', *International Quarterly* 10.1 (October 1904), 130–55, reprinted in *American Journal of Sociology* 62 (1957), 541–58.

13

MARJORIE HOWES

Joyce, colonialism, and nationalism

Joyce's life spans a period in history in which material conditions, political structures, and intellectual life throughout the world were profoundly shaped by the growth and decline of European empires and the flourishing of various nationalisms, both imperialist and anti-imperialist. When Joyce was born in 1882 the 'scramble for Africa', and the era that one historian has called the 'age of empire', had just begun.[1] When he died in 1941 the world was engulfed in the Second World War, a conflict that would fundamentally alter the balance of global power, and the age of decolonization was under way. A good deal of recent Joyce scholarship has explored Joyce's relation to this historical trajectory.[2] Much of this scholarship is informed by debates in post-colonial studies, the academic field most explicitly committed to examining the complex set of issues we can group under the headings of 'colonialism'[3] and 'nationalism'.[4] Colonialism and nationalism were among the period's most visible and important sources of conflict and change, and were the subjects of much discussion and debate. At the same time, they were so important and pervasive – both as realities and as ideologies – that they became part of contemporary conceptions of 'reality' and 'common sense' and supplied many of the unspoken rules and assumptions of the time. Post-colonial scholars study colonialism and nationalism in their visibility, as the subjects of explicit discussion and struggle, and in their invisibility, as the secret structures that underlie much of Western intellectual and political life. Ireland's double status – as both an agent and a victim of British imperialism – is important to any investigation of how Joyce's works engage with these issues. Equally important is Joyce's interest in the international and global dimensions of colonialism and nationalism, and his insistence on the many internal divisions and local variations within Ireland. To grasp the full significance of colonialism and nationalism in Joyce's writing, we must examine the methods he uses to traverse and connect these different horizons and contexts.

One of these methods operates on the level of the individual word. For Joyce, language itself – the medium of his art – was inescapably structured by colonialism and nationalism, and he consistently embedded the complexities of colonialism and nationalism in particular words. We can see an example of this practice by tracking the word 'ivory' which, by Joyce's time, had acquired a number of overt imperial connotations; Joseph Conrad exploited them effectively in *Heart of Darkness*. In *A Portrait*, the young Stephen first thinks about ivory in the context of sectarian animosities between Protestants and Catholics and the strict sexual morality of the anti-Parnellite Dante: 'And she did not like him to play with Eileen because Eileen was a protestant and when she was young she knew children that used to play with protestants and the protestants used to make fun of the litany of the Blessed Virgin. *Tower of Ivory*, they used to say, *House of Gold!*' (P 29). Next, in a passage set in Stephen's first school, Clongowes Wood College, the novel introduces ivory's source in the colonies and continues to associate it with forbidden sexuality: 'And one day Boyle had said that an elephant had two tuskers instead of two tusks and that was why he was called Tusker Boyle but some fellows called him Lady Boyle because he was always at his nails, paring them. Eileen had long thin cool white hands too because she was a girl. They were like ivory; only soft' (P 35). Later, when Stephen walks to university feeling oppressed by the sense that his own creativity is faltering and that he is surrounded by 'heaps of dead language' (P 150), his thoughts return to ivory: 'The word now shone in his brain, clearer and brighter than any ivory sawn from the mottled tusks of elephants. *Ivory, ivoire, avorio, ebur*. One of the first examples that he had learnt in Latin had run: *India mittit ebur*' (P 150).

Joyce uses the apparently idiosyncratic twists and turns of Stephen's mind to make a series of points. Following the associative logic of *A Portrait*, the first two references to ivory establish a continuum between Protestant Ascendancy in Ireland and imperialism elsewhere, suggesting that the origins of Irish sectarianism lie within a larger British colonial project. They also record a common Joycean protest against anti-Parnellite nationalism's commitment to sectarian thinking and to a conservative sexual morality. With the addition of Tusker Boyle, who has been caught engaging in homosexual 'smugging' (P 35), ivory draws one of Joyce's favourite parallels between the two empires – the Roman Catholic Church and the British Empire – that he thought dominated Ireland. Elsewhere in *A Portrait*, Joyce emphasizes that the patron Saint of Clongowes, St Francis Xavier, was an imperialist. Xavier was a sixteenth-century Spanish missionary who travelled to India and Southeast Asia, and the rector describes him in explicitly militaristic terms as 'a great soldier of God' and 'a true conqueror' (*P* 91).

Colonialism, nationalism, and the sexual policing they share are among the foundations of Stephen's Jesuit education. For Stephen, this education is both an obstacle and a resource: ivory also embodies the possibility that Stephen can appropriate or change the languages and histories he has inherited, as he translates the English word into French, Italian, and Latin. Such a translation briefly invokes a European context, rather than a British one. But by the time *A Portrait* was published in 1916, Great Britain had become the world's largest empire and its richest nation. Accordingly, the word's imperial provenance reasserts itself in the reference to India, whose massive economic importance made it the 'crown jewel' of the Empire. During this period, Indians were resisting the British Empire in increasingly visible ways. When Joyce was born, Mohandas K. (later Mahatma) Gandhi, the great Indian nationalist leader, was thirteen years old; India would achieve independence in 1947, just six years after Joyce's death. These historical developments, however, are erased by the Latin phrase '*India mittit ebur*', which means 'India sends ivory'. Imperial ideology assumed that colonialism was benign because it brought Western civilization, Christianity, and/or a modern economic system to the colonies. India, the phrase misleadingly suggests, 'sends' ivory voluntarily, rather than being forced to do so. Thus the mundane details of Stephen's grammar lesson in Dublin are shaped by an ideological grammar – a set of assumptions and principles so widely shared that they were often unspoken – about colonialism in India.

In the 'Wandering Rocks' episode of *Ulysses*, Father Conmee's 'ivory bookmark' (*U* 10.190) establishes further links between Jesuit missionary work and British imperialism, and Conmee thinks of 'the souls of black and brown and yellow men and of his sermon on saint Peter Claver S. J. and the African mission and of the propagation of the faith' (*U* 10.143–5). Earlier in the novel, Bloom thinks about the same sermon, but in terms that reject the claims of the British and Roman imperialisms. He wonders wryly 'how they explain it to the heathen Chinee' who, he speculates, would 'Prefer an ounce of opium' to Christianity (*U* 5.326–7), and he notes that missionary zeal is not peculiar to Catholics: 'The protestants are the same' (*U* 5.325). Joyce's references to ivory illustrate the global connections and the varied local effects of colonialism and nationalism. Colonialism and nationalism are the topics of overt thought and discussion; they also function as underlying grammars that structure sectarianism, education, missionary work, and sexuality. Joyce uses the word to connect different contexts or horizons: Stephen's alienated, individual subjectivity, the British-style public school culture of Clongowes, misunderstandings between religious communities, the conflicts of the Dublin political world in the years after Parnell's fall, and the global reach of the British empire. 'Ivory' becomes a node in a web that is at once linguistic, political, and historical. This web shows how far-reaching colonialism and nationalism are, but, as the counter-example of Bloom suggests, it also shows that they are subject to limitation and resistance. It is a short step from this to the 'intimologies' (FW 101.17) of Finnegans Wake, which use etymologies (and other linguistic forms) to assert surprising intimacies.

A well-known passage in A Portrait takes up linguistic issues in their relation to colonialism and nationalism more directly. At university, Stephen talks to the English Dean of Studies and thinks, 'The language in which we are speaking is his before it is mine . . . His language, so familiar and so foreign, will always be for me an acquired speech' (P 159). Stephen's estrangement from the language in which he writes marks a classic colonial condition, in which the colonizers try to force their language and culture upon the colonized. That condition has several components: Stephen recognizes his identity as Irish, conceives of that Irish identity in opposition to Englishness, and recognizes his Irishness as a divided condition, so that English is both 'familiar' and 'foreign'. The sense of dispossession and resentment generated is a catalyst for the period's Irish nationalism. Critics have often suggested that Joyce's linguistic virtuosity constitutes a project to re-colonize the English language, to take it away from the imperial masters. This is a particularly persuasive way of reading Finnegans Wake, with its deformations of English, its repeated send-ups of various kinds of authority, and its levelling, encyclopaedic drive to appropriate everything and privilege nothing. As early as 1989, critics were finding that, as Colin MacCabe put it, 'Finnegans Wake, with its sustained dismemberment of the English linguistic and literary heritage, is perhaps best understood in relation to the struggle against imperialism.'[5]

This does not mean, however, that Joyce's writings register the complexities of colonialism and nationalism in ways that add up to what Joyce 'believed' about them. For the most part, it would be a fruitless exercise to search through Joyce's works in the hopes of extracting a steady, coherent set of views on those subjects. Joyce made polemical statements that are clear in themselves, particularly in some of his prose writings, but once we begin to combine them they are often contradictory. For example, in 1907 Joyce gave a public lecture in Trieste entitled 'Ireland, Island of Saints and Sages'. The lecture begins with ancient Irish history, when Ireland was 'a true centre of intellectualism and sanctity' (OCPW 108), and argues that when the 'foreign occupation' began, Ireland 'ceased to be an intellectual force in Europe' (OCPW 114). Joyce castigates the English for their brutality and materialism, something he did quite consistently, and speaks sympathetically of Irish nationalism: 'If a victorious country tyrannizes over another, it cannot logically take it amiss if the latter reacts. Men are made that way: and no one, unless he were blinded by self-interest or ingenuity, can still believe that a colonizing country is prompted by purely Christian motives' (*OCPW* 116). For Joyce, colonialism was above all a matter of economic exploitation, and the essay blames English rule for the impoverished state of the country, asserting that 'Ireland is poor because English laws ruined the industries of the country, notably the woollen one; because, in the years in which the potato crop failed, the negligence of the English government left the flower of the people to die of hunger . . .' (*OCPW* 119).

However, elsewhere in the lecture Joyce says that it is pointless to castigate the English: 'I find it a bit naive to heap insults on the Englishman for his misdeeds in Ireland. A conqueror cannot be amateurish, and what England did in Ireland over the centuries is no different from what the Belgians are doing today in the Congo Free State, and what the Nipponese dwarfs will be doing tomorrow in some other lands' (*OCPW* 119). And, having characterized British rule as tyranny, he then offers this further thought: 'I confess that I do not see what good it does to fulminate against English tyranny while the tyranny of Rome still holds the dwelling place of the soul' (*OCPW* 125). Although the essay began by outlining the glories of ancient Ireland, he concludes by rejecting the notion put forth by members of the Irish Literary Revival that contemporary Ireland could make claims to cultural superiority and political independence based on those glories: 'If it were valid to appeal to the past in this fashion, the fellahins of Cairo would have every right in the world proudly to refuse to act as porters for English tourists. Just as ancient Egypt is dead, so is ancient Ireland' (*OCPW* 125). This last remark locates Ireland as part of a global colonial project, like Egypt, but it also suggests that the Egyptians do not, in fact, have the right to disdain serving English tourists. Joyce would live to see them claim that right; the British replaced an unpopular system of direct rule in Egypt with a more indirect system in 1922, and Egypt gained its independence in 1936.

If Joyce's views here appear to lack internal consistency, the picture becomes even murkier when we place them in various relevant contexts. Joyce gave this lecture at a time when he was feeling more positive towards Ireland than usual; having decided that the stories in *Dubliners* presented an overly harsh portrait of Ireland, he had just written 'The Dead' in a mood of reconciliation and affection. In addition, Trieste was an Italian-speaking, Catholic city under Austrian rule. The parallels with Ireland were obvious, and Joyce knew that his audience would welcome nationalist sentiments. Certainly he made other statements at other times that were markedly less sympathetic to Irish nationalism. After the Easter Rising in 1916, Joyce was asked if he was looking forward to the emergence of an independent Ireland, and replied, 'So that I might declare myself its first enemy?' (*JJ* 399).

In *Ulysses*, the arguments of the stridently nationalist Citizen owe a good deal to 'Ireland, Island of Saints and Sages'. The Citizen blames the English for Irish emigration and for ruining the Irish economy, asking, 'Where are our missing twenty millions of Irish should be here today instead of four, our lost tribes? And our potteries and textiles, the finest in the whole world! And our wool that was sold in Rome in the time of Juvenal and our flax and our damask from the looms of Antrim and our Limerick lace . . .' (*U* 12.1240–4). The men in the pub conduct an extensive critique of colonialism that echoes Joyce's lecture at a number of points. They make fun of Britain's pretensions to a Christian civilizing mission (*U* 12.1514–37) and expose the economic motives for colonialism in places like the Belgian Congo: 'Raping the women and girls and flogging the natives on the belly to squeeze all the red rubber they can out of them' (*U* 12.1546–7). They also comment sardonically on the violent excesses of racism in the United States (*U* 12.1324–8) and point out that British imperialism is an effective tool for quelling working class unrest over economic injustice at home: 'That's the great empire they boast about of drudges and whipped serfs . . . – And the tragedy of it is, says the citizen, they believe it. The unfortunate yahoos believe it' (*U* 12.1349–53). The Citizen abuses Bloom, who responds by criticizing injustice and advocating love (*U* 12.1485). In the past, this led critics to assume that all the Citizen's views were completely discredited by the text, and that Bloom's were validated. Recent books by Enda Duffy and Emer Nolan, however, suggest otherwise.[6]

The fact that similar anti-colonial critiques occur in these two different Joycean contexts does not prove that Joyce endorsed them; as always with Joyce, questions of irony and parody haunt every interpretive exercise bent on uncovering sincerity or ideological consistency. But much evidence suggests that Joyce was hostile to most forms of colonialism, and that his works invite us to read them in relation to the histories of colonization and decolonization. His engagement with various nationalisms, on the other hand, was more ambivalent; the Citizen is an acute and funny critic of colonialism, but he is also a bigoted nationalist, rather than an enlightened one, and a land-grabber (*U* 12.1312–16). Joyce's interest in socialism forms an equally important element in his engagement with decolonization. As he wrote to Stanislaus in 1906, 'If the Irish question exists, it exists for the Irish proletariat chiefly' (*JJ* 237). In Joyce's works, colonialism and nationalism appear as historical and political realities, subjects for debate, underlying intellectual structures, materials for creativity and fantasy, and matters of language.

Similarly, scholars working in post-colonial studies investigate the workings of colonialism and nationalism in a wide range of arenas with very different horizons: language, individual subjectivity, group identity and activity, literature and culture, public policy and political structures, and large historical forces.[7] Rather than survey the field as a whole, I will briefly outline some of the arguments and procedures within it that are most useful for readers of Joyce. Despite the name, most scholars in post-colonial studies do not confine their attention to nations in the aftermath of colonial rule. Instead, much post-colonial studies examines the processes and structures of colonization, the various methods through which colonized people resist, adapt to, and exploit imperialism, and the new departures and lingering legacies involved in the transition from colonial to post-colonial status.

Although the nation-state often has a privileged position in studies of colonialism and nationalism, post-colonial studies offers sustained critiques of nationalism, pointing out that nationalism often enforces conformity, and that it often articulates the aspirations of elite classes while suppressing the interests of women, urban workers, and agricultural labourers. Post-colonial scholars frequently seek to uncover the subjugated knowledges and buried histories of such groups. Scholars in post-colonial studies also attend carefully to the forces that reach beyond and break up the nation-state, forces that we can briefly describe as 'globalization' and 'internal division'. The migration of populations, improvements in transportation and communications systems, the movement of money, cultural artifacts and political ideas across national borders were all important features of the age of European empires. At the same time, both colonizing and colonized nations were internally differentiated; factors like religion, economic status, gender, and region influenced what colonialism or nationalism might mean for a given situation, population, or individual. Internal differentiation is also a useful idea for thinking about individuals, who were often divided or ambivalent, in one way or another, in their relations with colonialism and nationalism.

Ireland's place in the global history of the 'age of empire' is complex and has been the subject of some controversy.[8] Before the establishment of the Irish Free State in 1922, Ireland was obviously part of the British Empire, but what *kind* of part? Was it simply a region of an imperial power, or was it England's oldest colony? Joyce found both ways of thinking congenial. He consistently thought of Dublin as an ancient, important, imperial European city, writing in somewhat exaggerated terms to Stanislaus in 1905, 'When you remember that Dublin has been a capital for thousands of years, that it is the "second" city of the British Empire, that it is nearly three times as big as Venice it seems strange that no artist has given it to the world' (*JJ* 208). Just as consistently, Joyce also thought of Ireland as a colonized territory, and the Irish as a colonized people, as Stephen's conversation with the Dean of Studies indicates.

Such dual thinking may appear confusing, but it offers an excellent way to approach the particular, historically determined features of colonialism in Ireland, and Ireland in colonialism. The Ireland Joyce was born into was in several respects a British settler colony. Ireland was dominated by the Protestant Ascendancy, which was both a state of affairs and a sociological group. By Joyce's time, their power was beginning to crumble, but Protestants still controlled much political and economic life, maintained some institutionalized discrimination against Catholics, and owned most of the land. They were descended from sixteenth and seventeenth-century settlers who had displaced earlier inhabitants, and were separated from the majority of Ireland's population by religion, culture, and, to some extent, language.

Unlike the populations of India or Africa, however, the native Irish were white, Christian, and anglicized in substantial ways. They were the victims of British imperialism in Ireland – but they were also the agents of the British colonial enterprise elsewhere. Irish emigrants helped populate the white settler colonies overseas, and numerous colonial soldiers and civil servants in places like India came from Ireland; many, but by no means all, were Protestant.[9] Even Irish nationalists who criticized Great Britain's dominance of Ireland were perfectly capable of wanting to share in its imperial adventures, and the wealth they generated, elsewhere. And, as Bloom observes, both Catholic and Protestant Ireland participated in the civilizing and missionary projects that were part of European imperialism. Ireland, then, was both a colonized territory and part of a colonizing nation. This proposition does not represent a contradiction, nor does it make Ireland unique.[10]

Dubliners is permeated by the sense that Dublin is too close to England and also too far from it, a city damaged by colonial power and by distance from the metropolitan centres of that power. 'After the Race', for example, allegorizes the dilemmas of a particular kind of colonial subject, one who is willingly co-opted by the colonial power. Like the Irish spectators at the race, Jimmy Doyle is 'gratefully oppressed' (*D* 30) by several interlocking forces: economic exploitation, British cultural hegemony, and his own economic and social aspirations. These forces are masked as economic opportunity, egalitarian cosmopolitanism, and upward mobility, false appearances that help ensure Jimmy's enthusiastic participation in his own ruin. The story is obsessed with such masking, and Joyce emphasizes that the other men skilfully manipulate appearances: 'Ségouin had managed to give the impression that it was by a favour of friendship the mite of Irish money was to be included in the capital of the concern' (*D* 32). Joyce uses 'capital' to tie Jimmy's aspirations to the predicament of colonized Ireland. Dublin had not been the effective capital of Ireland since the Act of Union in 1800. Under British rule, the city can only wear 'the mask of a capital' (*D* 33), and Jimmy can only wear the mask of a cultured Cambridge gentleman with capital to invest.

Finnegans Wake also satirizes the idea of a prosperous Irish capital city. The 'question and answer' section of Book I exposes this idea as a combination of grandiose pretensions and actual poverty: 'What Irish capitol city (a dea o dea!) of two syllables and six letters, with a deltic origin and a nuinous end, (ah dust oh dust!) can boost of having (a) the most extensive public park in the world, (b) the most expensive brewing industry in the world, (c) the most expansive peopling thoroughfare in the world, (d) the most phillohippuc theobibbous paùpulation in the world' (*FW* 140.8–13). Here the city with Celtic origins declines to a ruinous end, as the 'extensive' gives way to the merely 'expensive', the strength of the brewing industry results in excessive love, even worship, of drinking (in 'phillohippuc theobibbous'), and the population of Dublin (the apparently correct answer to the riddle) is also a collection of paupers (in 'paùpulation').

In 'After the Race', Jimmy's family history includes a commitment to Irish nationalism, but his father 'had modified his views early' (*D* 30) in order to pursue material prosperity. When 'the buried zeal of his father' surfaces in Jimmy and he gets into an argument with the Englishman Routh, Ségouin diffuses the conflict by appealing to a trans-national, universal concept: he proposes a toast 'to Humanity' (*D* 33). The 'continentals'' exploitation of Jimmy is concealed by an empty cosmopolitan ideology that denies the differences in power and wealth among the participants, masking the group as a fellowship of equals: 'They drank Ireland, England, France, Hungary, the United States of America' (*D* 34). The outcome of the card game, which may have been set up specifically to fleece Jimmy, reinforces the inequality of the Irish and English members of the party; Jimmy loses the money he had planned to invest in Ségouin's business, and Routh is the big winner. Given his many critiques of Irish nationalism, it may seem perverse for Joyce to suggest here that Jimmy would have done better had he retained a livelier sense of nationalist grievance and Irish distinctiveness. But in this story Joyce shows that cosmopolitanism and universalist ideals can function as a covert European nationalism, and can help to sustain imperialism rather than to dismantle it.

Joyce's work is full of similar insights. During the age of high colonialism, and then, even more, during the age of decolonization, Western thinkers were impelled to confront the Eurocentric nature of their intellectual traditions, and post-colonial studies pursues this line of thinking.[11] Enlightenment concepts like Reason, Humanity, History, and Justice were supposed to be universal, but were in fact based on various exclusions: women, slaves, proscribed religions, and non-Europeans were not part of their 'universality'.

As thinkers in the colonies (and in metropolitan centres) began to articulate critiques of colonialism and its ideologies, this contradiction, and its place in the history of colonialism, became increasingly apparent. In the 'Nestor' chapter of *Ulysses*, the imperialist Mr Deasy asserts that the English 'are a generous people but we must also be just' and Stephen replies, 'I fear those big words, . . . which make us so unhappy' (*U* 2.263–4). Stephen thinks about justice again in 'Proteus', this time in conjunction with the state-sponsored injustice of wrongful conviction: 'Yes, used to carry punched tickets to prove an alibi if they arrested you for murder somewhere. Justice. On the night of the seventeenth of February 1904 the prisoner was seen by two witnesses' (*U* 3.179–82). Bloom also raises the possibility that the word 'justice' may not be what it appears when he thinks about a chant that closes the second Seder at Passover: 'Justice it means but it's everybody eating everybody else' (*U* 7.13–4). By the time Bloom counters the Citizen's nationalist hostility with the assertion that he too belongs to a persecuted race – 'I'm talking about injustice' (*U* 12.1474) – the attentive reader will both admire Bloom for his benevolent universalism and understand that this universalism's 'big words' have an historical, troubling, and often hidden relationship to violence, both imperialist and nationalist. *Finnegans Wake* pursues this theme. In one version of the conflict between Shem and Shaun, Shaun, as 'Justius', prosecutes Shem 'with the empirative of my vendettative' (*FW* 187.31) in order to prove that he is mad. 'Empiratives' – supposedly impartial imperatives or principles that actually enable the piracies and exploitations of empire – are precisely what Joyce traces through his investigations of words like Justice, Humanity, and History.

For Joyce, the Enlightenment concepts and the nationalist formulations the Irish could employ to articulate their political aspirations were marked by important debts to colonialism, as was the Catholic educational system that could help them to knowledge and prosperity. Stephen turns from these to the English literary tradition, and Joyce reveals that it too is marked by those debts. In 'Scylla and Charybdis', for example, in the midst of his discussion of Shakespeare, long considered one of the greatest writers in that tradition, Stephen comments on Shakespeare's participation in the ideology of Renaissance imperialism: 'His pageants, the histories, sail fullbellied on a tide of Mafeking enthusiasm' (*U* 9.754–5). Mafeking was a small town in South Africa that was half-heartedly besieged by the Boers during the Boer War. When it was liberated (without having been in much danger), celebrations in London were quite excessive in comparison with the actual military significance of the event. As Don Gifford observes, thereafter, 'Mafeking' became 'a term for extravagant (and essentially unwarranted) display of enthusiasm for the British Empire and expansionist policy.'[12] Stephen also contemplates the imperialist tendencies of a more contemporary literary giant, Matthew Arnold, whose influential *Culture and Anarchy* proposed culture as a means of educating, and therefore controlling, the elements that threatened society with anarchy, particularly the working classes. Arnold was also a committed liberal imperialist, and published a series of lectures promoting the mutual benefits of Ireland's absorption into the British Empire.[13] Stephen envisions the students, and their abusive hazing rituals, at an institution like Oxford, as if he were a Native American viewing white European invaders. He calls them 'Palefaces' (*U* 1.166), a term he also applies to some English tourists later (*U* 10.341), and then imagines 'A deaf gardener, aproned, masked with Matthew Arnold's face' (*U* 1.173–4). Stephen wilfully embraces the position of the barbarous, anarchic 'native', and reduces Arnold's civilizing culture to the inconsequential pursuits of the gardener, weeding the hedges and mowing the lawns of Empire, unable or unwilling to hear the voices of the colonized.

For Joyce, the fact that the available languages, traditions, and institutions were shaped, sometimes overtly and sometimes covertly, by colonialism and nationalism was not a matter of merely individual import. It was a central issue facing any community, and, indeed, raised questions about the meaning, composition, and scope of community. During Joyce's time, such questions, and their relation to literature, were being taken up and debated, most famously by the writers of the Irish Literary Revival. Joyce discerned what a good deal of current scholarship on the Revival also sees (though not without disagreement and controversy): that this form of cultural nationalism derived some of its important assumptions, procedures, and claims from colonialism. Joyce rejected most of the Revival's projects, and felt more in sympathy with the rioters who objected to Synge's *The Playboy of the Western World* in 1907 than with Synge and Yeats. In 'A Little Cloud' Little Chandler's vague poetic aspirations organize themselves around the idea of becoming a poet of the Celtic Twilight. Little Chandler is 'not sure what idea he wished to express' (*D* 55); in his 'revery' (a deliberately Yeatsian word) he concentrates on inventing reviews from English critics and on crafting a more Irish-looking pen name. This encapsulates Joyce's view of the Revival as a movement that often lacked real intellectual content and manufactured clichéd versions of Irishness for condescending English audiences.

In *Ulysses*, Haines is both a Revivalist ethnographer and a British imperialist. Haines speaks Irish to the uncomprehending milkwoman in a scene that Vincent Cheng has read persuasively as a parody of an ethnographic encounter.[14] He goes to the National Library to do folkloric research, buys Douglas Hyde's Revivalist classic, *Lovesongs of Connacht*, and appears to be working on a book about Irish folklore (*U* 1.365). Haines also refuses to acknowledge England's responsibility for colonialism in Ireland: 'We feel in England that we have treated you rather unfairly. It seems history is to blame' (*U* 1.648–9). Like Deasy, who claims that 'All human history moves towards one great goal, the manifestation of God' (*U* 2.380–1), he subscribes to a providential view of history in which what occurs is inevitable, and, like Deasy, Haines is 'The seas' ruler' (*U* 1.574, 2.246). With people, as with words, origins matter to Joyce. Haines' wealthy father was an imperialist adventurer who 'made his tin by selling jalap to Zulus or some bloody swindle or other' (*U* 1.156–7). Haines dreams about 'shooting a black panther' (*U* 1.61–2); his dream invokes the violence of colonialism and the leisured, sporting life of the Indian Raj. Accordingly, Stephen scornfully casts him as a 'panthersahib' (*U* 3.277). Buck Mulligan, who is fond of quoting Matthew Arnold, deliberately and humorously plays, and plays up, the role of native informant for Haines, and encourages Stephen to do the same (*U* 1.506). But, for Joyce, the threat that Haines represents cannot be neutralized by sheer parody and mimicry; it must be countered by alternative collective visions of the Irish.

As this suggests, despite his scathing criticisms of the Revival, Joyce had much in common with its writers. Seamus Deane observes in his contribution to this volume that Joyce 'is himself a dominant figure in that movement' (p. 34). Despite his stance on the *Playboy* riots, he promoted the works of Yeats and Synge in Trieste, collaborating on Italian translations of *Riders to the Sea* and *The Countess Cathleen*.[15] He did not so much reject the Revival's efforts to renovate Irish culture and community as transform them. Stephen's quest for freedom and individuality is also a quest for a satisfactory form of community. At the end of *A Portrait*, he sets out to 'forge in the smithy of my soul the uncreated conscience of my race' (*P* 213). Like the thinkers of the Revival, Stephen embraces the notion of the representative Irish individual. In a common nationalist trope, the story of the individual becomes, at the same time, the story of the nation. Characteristically, however, in the double meaning of 'forge', Joyce leaves open the possibility that such a transformation is just fakery.

Throughout chapter 5 of *A Portrait*, Stephen inhabits the intellectual structures of the Revival, even as he rejects that movement. He wants to fly by the 'nets' of 'nationality, language, religion' (*P* 171) and rejects the prevailing forms of cultural nationalism. But he continues to think of the 'nation' in precisely the terms those forms would offer him. Cultural nationalism tended to define the Irish nation through concepts of Irishness, rather than as a conglomeration of all the people who lived in Ireland or who considered themselves Irish. In most formulations, Irishness was an essence that appeared to a greater or lesser degree in various regions, populations, and cultural artefacts. Stephen, too, is fascinated by the idea that there is a distinctive Irish 'race' with a secret essence that could be embodied by particular individuals. He seeks access to 'the hidden ways of Irish life' (P 152) through Davin, casts the woman in Davin's story as 'a type of her race and his own' (P 154), and wonders if a female acquaintance harbours the 'secret of her race' behind her 'dark eyes' (P 185–6). That Stephen should accede to some of the basic assumptions of the Literary Revival while vociferously rejecting the cultural nationalism it promotes should not surprise us. It fits one of the major patterns through which Joyce charts the non-linear vagaries of Stephen's development. In a related instance, Cranly tells him, 'your mind is supersaturated with the religion in which you say you disbelieve' (P 202). We can say the same thing of Stephen's relation to the Revival – his mind is supersaturated with the cultural nationalism he claims to reject.

Joyce, of course, treats Stephen with a good deal of irony, but the same observation holds true for Joyce himself, who was fascinated by the idea of national traits (JJ 382, 395, 515). His works offer many different ideas about what kinds of community or collectivity might exist or be possible. Most of them involve the Irish, or some portion of them, but they rarely coincide neatly with the borders of the whole island or of the twenty-six counties of the Irish Free State. Here again, Joyce is most interested in an Irish nation characterized by global connections and internal divisions. In *Dubliners*, he diagnoses the condition of the Dublin Irish – more specifically, the Dublin Irish of the middle and lower middle classes. No one in this world is rich, and no one is destitute; they represent a fairly specific portion of Dublin's population. All, as critics routinely observe, are paralysed in some way. It is less often observed that this population is also shaped by Ireland's history of massive emigration in significant respects. Joyce's Dubliners have what we might call diasporic imaginations. For them, emigration offers ambiguous but real avenues of escape; it also offers numerous fantasies, including nostalgic fantasies of Ireland as a lost home. 'Real adventures' reflects the narrator of 'An Encounter', 'do not happen to people who remain at home: they must be sought abroad' (D 12). In 'Eveline', a young woman finds herself unable to leave her home and seek the adventure of eloping with a sailor whose intentions may or may not be honourable. Little Chandler thinks 'There was no doubt about it: if you wanted to succeed you had to go away' (D 55), and Gabriel Conroy follows European fashions and takes his vacations on the Continent. In *Dubliners*, Joyce depicts a community through its collective pathology. But does this pathology manifest itself as a provincial and false idealization of places outside Ireland, or as an inability to break local ties and seek one's fortune in the wider world? The characteristic Joycean answer is 'both'.

In *Ulysses*, Joyce contemplates a wider range of Irish collectivities. The Citizen asserts a nationalist reading of emigration as a loss to the national body of 'our missing twenty millions', while Bloom proposes a definition of the nation that includes the possibility of migration in less polemical fashion: 'A nation is the same people living in the same place . . . or also living in different places' (*U* 12.1422–3, 1428). Gossip, rumour, and the oral tradition provide another model for community. Stories are told and re-told, rumours circulate, and much of the book's action revolves around various kinds of speech: conversations, political speeches, sermons, and so forth. Such speech embodies a traditional community based on the face-to-face interaction of its members. Other forms of community are more anonymous. 'Wandering Rocks', for example, uses the principle of coincidence to suggest that all the characters it depicts are part of the same community. Further examples of circulation and connection, some local, some national, and some international, include the opening section of 'Aeolus', which describes the operation of the Dublin tramline route and the British mail system (*U* 7.1–19) and the scene in 'Ithaca' when Bloom turns on the tap (*U* 17.163–228). One influential theorist of the nation, Benedict Anderson, has suggested that the novel form itself, which often depicts members of the same community going about their lives simultaneously, but without necessarily being aware of one another as individuals, is ideally suited to the 'community-in-anonymity' of the modern nation.[16] Following this insight, we could suggest that *Ulysses* as a whole embodies the vision of Irish collectivity capable of countering the imperialist narratives of Haines and Deasy, while avoiding the nationalist chauvinism of the Citizen. Above all, however, *Ulysses* offers, not a portrait of 'a' community, or even portraits of several communities, but different ways of conceptualizing community.

Joyce's versions of Irish community were not defined through appeals to a shared Irish culture; this remained a major difference between his works and those of the Irish Literary Revival. Joyce rejected the idea of cultural insularity or purity; his interest in culture included the ways in which Irish culture changed in response to its contacts with other cultures. Like Joyce, scholars in post-colonial studies often explore such cultural mixing or hybridity. Joyce was fascinated by the popular culture of his day, collecting scraps of it assiduously, and including them in his works. Much Irish popular culture in Joyce's time was nationalist, like the sentimental ballad 'The Croppy Boy' that moves its listeners in 'Sirens'. A good deal of it also came from Great Britain, and was saturated with references to colonialism. Advertising, for example, persistently constructed images of the ideal domestic home by invoking the civilizing mission of empire. An 1899 ad for Pears' Soap ran: 'The first step towards lightening THE WHITE MAN'S BURDEN is through teaching the virtues of cleanliness. PEARS' SOAP is a potent factor in bright-ening the dark corners of the earth as civilization advances, while amongst the cultured of all nations it holds the highest place – it is the ideal toilet soap.'[17] Bloom, the ad canvasser, is both sceptical of advertising's blandish-ments and committed to their efficacy. He is both an architect and a critic of the processes that commodify the memory of nationalist heroes like Robert Emmet, the 'gallant pictured hero in Lionel Marks's window' (U 11.1274), or enable a cake of soap to generate consumer demand by appropriating the ideology of colonialism. He rejects Father Conmee's missionary project to 'brighten the dark corners of the earth' in 'Lotus-Eaters', but uses the racialist language of that project to defend himself in 'Circe': 'I did all a white man could' (U 15.797).[18] Perhaps Joyce had seen the Pears' Soap ad; Bloom's animated soap implicates him further in the colonial project, claiming: 'He brightens the earth. I polish the sky' (U 15.339).

Britain's dependence on its colonial possessions was both obvious and hid-den, everywhere and nowhere, exotic and mundane. When Deasy prompts Stephen to guess 'the proudest word you will ever hear from an Englishman's mouth', Stephen's first answer, that 'on his empire . . . the sun never sets', is a clichéd claim to the perpetual visibility of an enormous territorial empire. But this answer is wrong. According to Deasy, the real answer is '*I paid my way . . . I owe nothing*' (U 25). By refusing to define colonialism as the military conquest of foreign territories and by defining it instead as an eco-nomic project, Deasy is pointing to the economic motives that were central to Joyce's view of colonialism. He is also engaging in a particular kind of imperialist fantasy: the fantasy of economic independence. England extracts wealth from the colonies but does not acknowledge its dependence on them, thus rendering them invisible. As a result, the Englishman imagines he paid his way himself, and owes nothing to anyone. Stephen has no access to this kind of fantasy; in response he thinks of everything that he owes to other people: 'Mulligan, nine pounds, three pairs of socks, one pair brogues, ties. Curran, ten guineas. McCann, one guinea. Fred Ryan, two shillings. Temple, two lunches. Russell, one guinea, Cousins, ten shillings, Bob Reynolds, half a guinea, Koehler, three guineas, Mrs. MacKernan, five weeks' board' (U 2.255–9).

If we can approach Joyce's engagement with colonialism and nationalism by locating it on the smallest horizon – that of individual words – we can also locate it on the largest – the formal qualities of each text as a whole. As I suggested above, Anderson's theory enables us to read the novel form in general for clues as to how *Ulysses* registers the complexities of nationalism. On the other hand, Fredric Jameson claims that the form of *Ulysses* inscribes the complexities of colonialism. His argument combines the imperialist un-knowing that Deasy illustrates with the forms of traditional, knowable community Joyce investigated. Under colonialism a significant portion of the metropolitan economy is located elsewhere, in the very different world of the colonies. As a result, it is no longer possible for individuals in the imperial centre, as they go about their daily lives, to grasp how the system functions as a whole: there will always be a piece missing. The formal qualities of modernist literature – its fragmentations, hesitations, and disjunctions – spring from this condition of incomplete knowing or partial invisibility. Jameson invokes Ireland's double status in the global history of the age of empires, characterizing it as 'a kind of exceptional situation, one of overlap and coexistence between these two incommensurable realities which are those of the lord and of the bondsman altogether, those of the metropolis and of the colony simultaneously'.[19] The result is the version of modernism particular to *Ulysses*, in which extreme formal innovation combines with a depiction of Dublin as something like a premodern, face-to-face community, 'still un- or under-developed enough to be representable, thanks to the domination of its foreign masters'.[20]

Post-colonial studies can investigate colonialism and nationalism in Joyce on a number of different levels, from analyses of individual words to discussions of general tendency and overall form. It enables us to see them as much discussed and hotly debated topics, and as a set of overarching and often unarticulated assumptions about the world of Joyce's time. It incorporates their vast global connections and their minute local divisions. In Joyce, colonialism and nationalism constantly carry us inward, to the fantasies, divisions, and traumas of the individual psyche; just as constantly they carry us outward, to the institutions, contending communities, political conflicts, and historical forces of our interconnected world. If we approach Joyce's writings with these points in mind, it becomes clear that some of the apparent paradoxes that structure them – his nationalism versus his internationalism, his obsession with Ireland versus his residence in Europe, his rejection of the Irish Literary Revival versus his participation in it – are not really paradoxes at all. They merely indicate the everyday complexities that surround the topic of this essay.

NOTES

1 Eric Hobsbawm, *The Age of Empire 1875–1914* (New York: Vintage Books, 1987).
2 See Derek Attridge and Marjorie Howes, eds., *Semicolonial Joyce* (Cambridge: Cambridge University Press, 2000); Vincent Cheng, *Joyce, Race, and Empire* (Cambridge: Cambridge University Press, 1995); Enda Duffy, *The Subaltern 'Ulysses'* (Minneapolis: University of Minnesota Press, 1994); Ellen Carol Jones,

Joyce: Feminism / Post / Colonialism, European Joyce Studies 8 (Amsterdam: Rodopi, 1998); Declan Kiberd, 'James Joyce and Mythic Realism', in *Inventing Ireland* (Cambridge, Mass.: Harvard University Press, 1996), pp. 327–55; David Lloyd, 'Adulteration and the Nation', in *Anomalous States: Irish Writing and the Post-Colonial Moment* (Durham: Duke University Press, 1993); Emer Nolan, *James Joyce and Nationalism* (London: Routledge, 1995); Joseph Valente, *James Joyce and the Problem of Justice: Negotiating Sexual and Colonial Difference* (Cambridge: Cambridge University Press, 1995).

3 Because I am concerned with the broad spectrum of arrangements, formal and informal, old and new, through which states pursued their imperialist ambitions at this time, in this essay I will use 'colonialism' and 'imperialism' more or less interchangeably.

4 Edward Said's *Orientalism* is often considered a foundational text for this field (New York: Vintage, 1978); so are the works of Frantz Fanon, including *Black Skin, White Masks* (1952) (New York: Grove Weidenfeld, 1967), *A Dying Colonialism* (1959) (New York: Grove Press, 1967), and *The Wretched of the Earth* (1961) (New York: Grove Weidenfeld, 1963).

5 Colin MacCabe, 'Finnegans Wake at Fifty', *Critical Quarterly* 31:4 (Winter 1989), 4.

6 See Duffy, ch. 3, and Nolan, ch. 3.

7 There are several anthologies and introductions to post-colonial studies, including Bill Ashcroft *et al.*, eds., *The Post-Colonial Studies Reader* (London and New York: Routledge, 1995), Gregory Castle, ed., *Post-Colonial Discourses: An Anthology* (Oxford: Blackwell, 2001), Patrick Williams and Laura Chrisman, eds., *Colonial Discourse and Post-Colonial Theory: A Reader* (New York: Columbia University Press, 1994), Bill Ashcroft, *et al.*, *The Empire Writes Back: Theory and Practice in Post-Colonial Literatures* (London and New York: Routledge, 1989), and Leela Gandhi, *Post-Colonial Theory: A Critical Introduction* (New York: Columbia University Press, 1998).

8 Studies that assert the relevance of post-colonial perspectives include David Lloyd, *Anomalous States: Irish Writing and the Post-Colonial Moment* (Durham: Duke University Press, 1993) and Gerry Smyth, *Decolonisation and Criticism* (London: Pluto Press, 1998). Those who are largely critical of such perspectives include Stephen Howe, *Ireland and Empire* (Oxford: Oxford University Press, 2000) and Liam Kennedy, 'Modern Ireland: Post-Colonial Society of Post-Colonial Pretensions?' *Irish Review* 13 (Winter 1992/3): 107–21.

9 See Scott B. Cook, 'The Irish Raj: Social Origins and Careers of Irishmen in the Indian Civil Service, 1855–1914', *Journal of Social History* 20 (Spring 1987), 520.

10 For an extended discussion of Irish participation in the Empire which refutes the notion that this involves a contradiction, see Kevin Kenny, 'The Irish in the Empire', *Ireland and the British Empire*, ed. Kevin Kenny (Oxford: Oxford University Press, forthcoming).

11 For an excellent treatment of decolonization and the critique of Eurocentrism, see Robert Young, *White Mythologies: Writing History and the West* (London and New York: Routledge, 1990).

12 Don Gifford, *Ulysses Annotated* (Berkeley: University of California Press, 1988), p. 235.

13 Published as *On the Study of Celtic Literature* (1867) (London: Macmillan, 1893).

14 Cheng, pp. 151–62.

15 See Willard Potts, *Joyce and the Two Irelands* (Austin: University of Texas Press, 2000), p. 57.

16 Benedict Anderson, *Imagined Communities: Reflections on the Origin and Spread of Nationalism* (London: Verso, 1983; rev. edn 1991).

17 Quoted in Anne McClintock, *Imperial Leather: Race, Gender and Sexuality in the Colonial Contest* (New York and London: Routledge, 1995), p. 32. For an extended discussion of advertising, commodity culture, and colonialism, see pp. 207–31. See also Jennifer Wicke's essay in this volume.

18 See also 15.876 and 980.

19 Fredric Jameson, 'Modernism and Imperialism', in *Nationalism, Colonialism and Literature*, intro. by Seamus Deane (Minnesota: University of Minneapolis Press, 1990), pp. 43–68. The quotation is from p. 60.

20 Fredric Jameson, '*Ulysses* in History', in *James Joyce and Modern Literature*, ed. W. J. McCormack and Alistair Stead (London: Routledge, 1982), p. 35.

FURTHER READING

The number of books and articles about Joyce is enormous and ever-increasing; the quantity of secondary material not directly concerned with Joyce but relevant to his work is even greater. None of these publications is without value, but none of them needs be regarded as essential. The bibliographies mentioned below give comprehensive lists, and the chapters of this volume refer to specialized works of particular relevance to their topics. What follows is a highly selective set of suggestions for the interested reader, with an emphasis on works that will provide useful information or critical stimulation (or, in the case of Joyce's own works, editions with the most reliable texts and helpful annotations). The arrangement within sections is chronological.

Texts

Dubliners (1914)

Terence Brown, ed. London: Penguin Books, 1992. Introduction, appendices, and notes; text edited by Robert Scholes, Richard Ellmann, and A. Walton Litz.

John Wyse Jackson and Bernard McGinley, eds. London: Sinclair-Stevenson, 1993. Large-format edition with illustrations and copious notes.

Hans Walter Gabler with Walter Hettche, eds. New York: Vintage, 1993. Fully re-edited text; Afterword by John S. Kelly. Includes 'A Curious History' (Joyce's open letter to the press on the saga of getting *Dubliners* published) and the *Irish Homestead* versions of 'The Sisters', 'Eveline', and 'After the Race'.

Jeri Johnson, ed. Oxford: Oxford University Press, 2000. World's Classics edition. Introduction and notes; text edited by Scholes, with variants noted. Includes 'A Curious History' and the *Irish Homestead* version of 'The Sisters'.

A Portrait of the Artist as a Young Man (1914/15; 1916)

Seamus Deane, ed. London: Penguin, 1992. Introduction and notes; text edited by Chester Anderson.

R. B. Kershner, ed. Boston: Bedford Books, 1993. A volume in the Case Studies in Contemporary Criticism series; text edited by Anderson, with new corrections (including the restoration of '*geen*' in Stephen's song on p. 1).

Hans Walter Gabler, with Walter Hettche, eds. New York: Garland, 1993. Fully re-edited text; Afterword by Richard Brown.

Jeri Johnson, ed. Oxford: Oxford University Press, 2000. World's Classics edition. Introduction and notes; text edited by Anderson, with variants noted.

Exiles (1918)

Joyce's one surviving play has not been re-edited. Several reprints based on the 1951/2 edition published in the USA by Viking and the UK by Cape, 'with the author's own notes and an introduction by Padraic Colum'. See also *Poems and 'Exiles'* under 'Collections'.

Ulysses (1922)

Hans Walter Gabler, with Wolfhard Steppe and Claus Melchior, eds. *Ulysses: A Critical and Synoptic Edition*, 3 volumes. New York: Garland, 1984. Right-hand pages give the 'reading text' available in the one-volume edition (see below); left-hand pages show how Joyce added to and revised manuscripts and proofs up to publication (as revealed in the manuscripts that had come to light by 1984). Includes a historical collation of the variants in editions prior to 1984.

Hans Walter Gabler, with Wolfhard Steppe and Claus Melchior, eds. New York: Random House; London: Bodley Head, 1986. The standard edition of *Ulysses*, with the line-numbering used in almost all Joyce criticism. Some of the editorial details have been questioned, but this is the most error-free text available.

Jeri Johnson, ed. *Ulysses: The 1922 Text*. Oxford: Oxford University Press, 1993. World's Classics edition. Introduction and notes. Reprints the text as originally published, which is historically interesting but not recommended for reading. The extensive explanatory notes are this edition's strong point.

Jacques Aubert, ed. *Oeuvres*, vol. II. Paris: Gallimard, 1995. The second volume of the Pléiade edition of Joyce's works reprints the authorized translation of *Ulysses* together with some 800 pages of notes by Aubert, Michel Cusin, Daniel Ferrer, Jean-Michel Rabaté, André Topia, and Marie-Danièle Vors. It also includes maps and a useful index to the text.

Finnegans Wake (1939)

Finnegans Wake has never been re-edited or reset; this means that all printings follow the same pagination and lineation as the original Faber edition, with only very minor discrepancies arising from corrections. It also means that the current text has many errors (but the notion of 'error' is even more problematic in the case of the *Wake* than in the case of *Ulysses*). Some reprints are set more spaciously on the page; these are better for reading and annotating. The following are currently available:

Deane, Seamus, introd. London: Penguin, 1992. Introduction, outline of chapter contents.

Bishop, John, introd. New York: Penguin, 1999. Introduction, outline of chapter contents.

Stephen Hero (posthumous, 1944)

Theodore Spencer, ed.; revised by John J. Slocum and Herbert Cahoon. New York: New Directions, 1955; London: Cape, 1956. Several reprints.

Giacomo Joyce (posthumous, 1968)

Richard Ellmann, ed. London: Faber; New York: Viking, 1968.
See also *Poems and Shorter Writings* under 'Collections'.

Collections

Jacques Aubert, ed. *Oeuvres*, vol. I. Paris: Gallimard, 1982. French translations of *Dubliners, Stephen Hero, A Portrait, Exiles*, all the poems and epiphanies, the critical writings, a selection of letters, and other manuscript materials. The texts are comprehensively annotated by Aubert.

Richard Ellmann, A. Walton Litz, and John Whittier-Ferguson, eds. *Poems and Shorter Writings*. London: Faber, 1991. Introduction and notes. This volume includes *Giacomo Joyce*, Joyce's collections of poems, *Chamber Music* (1907) and *Pomes Penyeach* (1927), as well as all his other poems; the early epiphanies; and the essay 'A Portrait of the Artist' (1904).

J. C. C. Mays, ed. *Poems and 'Exiles'*. London: Penguin, 1992. Introduction and notes. The collected poems and Joyce's one surviving play.

Kevin Barry, ed. *Occasional, Critical, and Political Writing*. Oxford: Oxford University Press, 2000. Introduction and notes. Some fifty non-fiction pieces, many of the most important ones newly translated from the Italian by Conor Deane.

The James Joyce Archive

Michael Groden, Hans Walter Gabler, David Hayman, and Danis Rose with John O'Hanlon, eds. 63 volumes. New York: Garland, 1977–9. This massive set of facsimiles collects most of the surviving pre-publication material relating to Joyce's works.

Letters

Stuart Gilbert and Richard Ellmann, eds. *Letters*. 3 volumes. New York: Viking; London: Faber, 1957, 1966. These volumes also contain some useful supplementary material, including (in vol. II) a list of Joyce's addresses and a detailed chronology of his writings, and are well indexed.

Richard Ellmann, ed. *Selected Letters*. New York: Viking; London: Faber, 1975. The *Selected Letters* contain some correspondence not printed in the three volumes of the letters. (A large number of Joyce's letters remain unpublished.)

Bibliographies

John J. Slocum and Herbert Cahoon. *A Bibliography of James Joyce, 1882–1941.* New Haven: Yale University Press, 1953; reprinted Westport, CN: Greenwood, 1971. A comprehensive bibliography of Joyce's own writings.

Robert H. Deming. *A Bibliography of James Joyce Studies.* 2nd edn, Boston: G. K. Hall, 1977. A full listing of earlier works on Joyce.

Thomas Jackson Rice. *James Joyce: A Guide to Research.* New York: Garland, 1982. A detailed annotated bibliography up to 1981.

Thomas F. Staley. *An Annotated Bibliography of James Joyce.* Brighton: Harvester, 1989. A brief guide through Joyce criticism up to the 1980s.

William S. Brockman. 'Current JJ Checklist'. List of recent primary and secondary material (including reviews), published quarterly in *JJQ*.

General works

Introductions to Joyce

Harry Levin. *James Joyce: A Critical Introduction* (1941). Rev. edn, New York: New Directions Press, 1960. A pioneering but still valuable study.

Patrick Parrinder. *James Joyce.* Cambridge: Cambridge University Press, 1984.

Zack Bowen and James F. Carens, eds. *A Companion to Joyce Studies.* Westport, CN: Greenwood, 1984. A full survey of Joyce's life and works by eighteen Joyceans.

Richard Brown. *James Joyce: A Post-Culturalist Perspective.* London: Macmillan, 1992.

Steven Connor. *James Joyce.* Plymouth: Northcote House, 1996.

Michael Seidel. *James Joyce: A Short Introduction.* Oxford: Blackwell, 2002.

For reference

Matthew J. C. Hodgart and Mabel Worthington. *Song in the Works of James Joyce.* New York: Columbia University Press, 1959. Includes *Finnegans Wake*, which Bowen's more detailed study does not.

Robert H. Deming, ed. *James Joyce: The Critical Heritage.* 2 vols. London: Routledge, 1970. A selection of reviews and critical writings from 1902 to 1941.

Zack Bowen. *Musical Allusions in the Works of James Joyce: Early Poetry through 'Ulysses'.* Albany: State University of New York Press; Dublin: Gill and Macmillan, 1975.

Shari and Bernard Benstock. *Who's He When He's at Home: A James Joyce Directory.* Urbana: University of Illinois Press, 1980. A directory of the named individuals in Joyce's work other than *Finnegans Wake* (for which see Glasheen, below).

A. Nicholas Fargnoli and Michael P. Gillespie. *James Joyce A–Z.* New York: Oxford University Press, 1995. A convenient reference work in encyclopaedia form.

Critical studies

Hugh Kenner. *Dublin's Joyce* (1955). Reprinted New York: Columbia University Press, 1987. A kaleidoscopically rich book both tendentious and illuminating; the chapter on *A Portrait* – 'The *Portrait* in Perspective' – has been particularly influential.

The Stoic Comedians: Flaubert, Joyce, Beckett. Berkeley: University of California Press, 1962. Joyce in a tradition of writers who wrest comedy from the limitations of discourse.

A. Walton Litz. *The Art of James Joyce: Method and Design in 'Ulysses' and 'Finnegans Wake'*. London: Oxford University Press, 1969, rev. 1964. A useful guide to Joyce's working methods.

Hugh Kenner. *Joyce's Voices*. London: Faber, 1978. A readable study of the indeterminacies of narrative voice.

Colin MacCabe. *James Joyce and the Revolution of the Word*. London: Macmillan; New York: Barnes and Noble, 1979. One of the first studies to bring post-structuralist theory to bear on Joyce's work.

Colin MacCabe, ed. *James Joyce: New Perspectives*. Brighton: Harvester; Bloomington, Indiana University Press, 1982. Reflects some of the new directions taken in Joyce studies during the 1970s.

John Paul Riquelme. *Teller and Tale in Joyce's Fiction: Oscillating Perspectives*. Baltimore: Johns Hopkins University Press, 1983.

Fritz Senn. *Joyce's Dislocations: Essays on Reading as Translation*, ed. John Paul Riquelme. Baltimore: Johns Hopkins University Press, 1984.

Inductive Scrutinies: Focus on Joyce, ed. Christine O'Neill. Baltimore: Johns Hopkins University Press, 1995. These two collections of Senn's essays (covering between them the period 1969–92) show why he is in many ways a model reader of Joyce: subtle engagements with the text that raise, freshly and undogmatically, large questions.

Derek Attridge and Daniel Ferrer, eds. *Post-Structuralist Joyce: Essays from the French*. Cambridge: Cambridge University Press, 1984. Includes essays by Hélène Cixous, Jean-Michel Rabaté, Stephen Heath, and Jacques Derrida.

Vicki Mahaffey. *Reauthorizing Joyce*. Cambridge: Cambridge University Press, 1988.

Bernard Benstock, ed. *The Augmented Ninth: Papers from the Ninth Joyce Symposium*. Syracuse: Syracuse University Press, 1988. Includes essays by Jacques Derrida and Julia Kristeva.

Derek Attridge. *Peculiar Language: Literature as Difference from the Renaissance to James Joyce*. Ithaca: Cornell University Press; London: Methuen, 1988. Two chapters on *Ulysses* and two on *Finnegans Wake*.

Jean-Michel Rabaté. *James Joyce: Authorized Reader*. Baltimore: Johns Hopkins University Press, 1991.

Joyce upon the Void: The Genesis of Doubt. New York: St Martin's Press, 1991.

Margot Norris. *Joyce's Web: The Social Unraveling of Modernism*. Austin: University of Texas Press, 1992.

Katie Wales. *The Language of James Joyce*. London: Macmillan, 1992.

Vincent J. Cheng. *Joyce, Race, and Empire*. Cambridge: Cambridge University Press, 1995.

Emer Nolan. *James Joyce and Nationalism*. London: Routledge, 1995.

Joseph Valente. *James Joyce and the Problem of Justice: Negotiating Sexual and Colonial Difference*. Cambridge: Cambridge University Press, 1995.

Christine Froula. *Modernism's Body: Sex, Culture, and Joyce*. New York: Columbia University Press, 1996.

Joseph Valente, ed. *Quare Joyce*. Ann Arbor: University of Michigan Press, 1998. A collection of essays on the place of homosexuality in Joyce's writing.

Garry Leonard. *Advertising and Commodity Culture in Joyce*. Gainesville: University of Florida Press, 1998.

Derek Attridge. *Joyce Effects: On Language, Theory, and History*. Cambridge: Cambridge University Press, 2000.

Derek Attridge and Marjorie Howes, eds. *Semicolonial Joyce*. Cambridge: Cambridge University Press, 2000. A collection of essays on the importance for Joyce of Ireland's situation within the British Empire.

Jean-Michel Rabaté. *James Joyce and the Politics of Egoism*. Cambridge: Cambridge University Press, 2001.

Katherine Mullin. *James Joyce, Sexuality and Social Purity*. Cambridge: Cambridge University Press, 2003. Joyce's response to the anti-vice movements of his time.

Joycean contexts

Forrest Read, ed. *Pound/Joyce*. New York: New Directions, 1967. Over sixty letters from Pound to Joyce, together with Pound's critical essays on Joyce: an entertaining insight into one of modernism's most significant relationships.

Dominic Manganiello. *Joyce's Politics*. Routledge: London, 1980. A study of Joyce's attitudes towards and involvement in the political movements of his time.

Bonnie Kime Scott. *Joyce and Feminism*. Bloomington: Indiana University Press, 1984.

Richard Brown. *James Joyce and Sexuality*. Cambridge: Cambridge University Press, 1985. A thorough discussion of the sexual discourses that informed Joyce's treatments of the subject.

Seamus Deane. *Celtic Revivals: Essays in Modern Irish Literature*. London: Faber, 1985.

A Short History of Irish Literature. London: Hutchinson, 1986.

Cheryl Herr. *Joyce's Anatomy of Culture*. Urbana: University of Illinois Press, 1986. Joyce's relation to Dublin working-class culture, with special attention to newspapers, pantomime, and sermons.

Jennifer Wicke. *Advertising Fictions: Literature, Advertisement, and Social Reading*. New York: Columbia University Press, 1988.

David Lloyd. *Anomalous States: Irish Writing and the Post-Colonial Moment*. Dublin: Lilliput, 1993.

Seamus Deane. *Strange Country: Modernity and Nationhood in Irish Writing since 1790*. Oxford: Oxford University Press, 1997.

Lawrence S. Rainey. *Institutions of Modernism: Literary Elites and Public Culture*. New Haven: Yale University Press, 1998.

Michael North. *Reading 1922: A Return to the Scene of the Modern*. New York: Oxford University Press, 1999. A study of the cultural scene in the year in which *Ulysses* appeared.

Dubliners and *A Portrait*

For reference

Don Gifford. *Joyce Annotated: Notes for 'Dubliners' and 'A Portrait of the Artist as a Young Man'*. 2nd edn, Berkeley: University of California Press, 1982.

Bruce Bidwell and Linda Heffer. *The Joycean Way: A Topographic Guide to 'Dubliners' and 'A Portrait of the Artist as a Young Man'*. Dublin: Wolfhound Press; Baltimore: Johns Hopkins University Press, 1982. Maps and photographs as well as descriptions.

Donald Torchiana. *Backgrounds for Joyce's 'Dubliners'*. Winchester, Mass.: Allen and Unwin, 1986.

The making of *A Portrait*

Robert Scholes and Richard M. Kain. *The Workshop of Dedalus: James Joyce and the Raw Materials for 'A Portrait of the Artist as a Young Man'*. Evanston: Northwestern University Press, 1965. Manuscript materials and analysis.

Critical studies

Morris Beja, ed. *'Dubliners' and 'A Portrait of the Artist as a Young Man': A Casebook*. London: Macmillan, 1973.

Thomas Staley and Bernard Benstock, eds. *Approaches to Joyce's 'Portrait': Ten Essays*. Pittsburgh: University of Pittsburgh Press, 1976.

Garry Leonard. *Reading 'Dubliners' Again: A Lacanian Perspective*. Syracuse: Syracuse University Press, 1993.

Mark Wollaeger, ed. *James Joyce's 'A Portrait of the Artist as a Young Man': A Casebook*. New York: Oxford University Press, 2003.

Margot Norris. *Suspicious Readings of Joyce's 'Dubliners'*. Philadelphia: University of Pennsylvania Press, 2003.

Ulysses

For reference

Don Gifford. *'Ulysses' Annotated*. Berkeley: University of California Press, 1989. Page-by-page annotations; not always reliable.

Weldon Thornton. *Allusions in 'Ulysses': An Annotated List*. Chapel Hill: University of North Carolina Press, 1968.

John Henry Raleigh. *The Chronicle of Leopold and Molly Bloom: 'Ulysses' as Narrative*. Berkeley: University of California Press, 1977. Converts the scattered information about the lives of the Bloom family into a chronological sequence.

Clive Hart and Leo Knuth. *A Topographical Guide to James Joyce's 'Ulysses'*. Colchester: A Wake Newslitter Press, 1975, rev. 1986. Maps, commentary, list of addresses.

William M. Schutte. *Index of Recurrent Elements in James Joyce's 'Ulysses'*. Carbondale: Southern Illinois University Press, 1982. A useful tool for tracing the web of cross-references and repetitions in *Ulysses*.

Wolfhard Steppe with Hans Walter Gabler. *A Handlist to James Joyce's 'Ulysses'.* A computer-generated concordance, produced in conjunction with the 1984 edition of *Ulysses*.

The making of *Ulysses*

Frank Budgen. *James Joyce and the Making of 'Ulysses'* (1934). Bloomington: Indiana University Press, 1960; London: Oxford University Press, 1972 (with additional articles). An anecdotal account of the years of *Ulysses'* construction by a friend of Joyce's, incorporating many of Joyce's own suggestions.

Philip F. Herring, ed. *Joyce's 'Ulysses' Notesheets in the British Museum.* Charlottesville: University Press of Virginia, 1972.

Joyce's Notes and Early Drafts for 'Ulysses': Selections from the Buffalo Collection. Charlottesville: University Press of Virginia, 1977.

Michael Groden. *'Ulysses' in Progress.* Princeton: Princeton University Press, 1977. A study of Joyce's work on *Ulysses* and his shifting conception of the book.

Critical studies

Stuart Gilbert. *James Joyce's 'Ulysses'* (1930). Rev. edn, London: Faber, 1952; New York: Random House, 1955. An influential study whose interest lies partly in the fact that Joyce assisted in its composition; since it was designed to gain acceptance for *Ulysses* among a sceptical audience it emphasizes the book's learned allusiveness.

Clive Hart and David Hayman, eds. *James Joyce's 'Ulysses': Critical Essays.* Berkeley: University of California Press, 1974. Eighteen critics discuss one chapter apiece; a mixed bag.

Hugh Kenner. *'Ulysses'* (1980). Rev. edn, Baltimore: Johns Hopkins University Press, 1987. Sharp observations and strong opinions make this a lively and illuminating short study.

Karen Lawrence. *The Odyssey of Style in 'Ulysses'.* Princeton: Princeton University Press, 1981. Focuses on the striking shifts in the book's style and their implications.

Christine van Boheemen. *The Novel as Family Romance: Language, Gender, and Authority from Fielding to Joyce.* Ithaca: Cornell University Press, 1987. *Ulysses* discussed in relation to the English novel's perennial exclusion of 'woman'.

Bernard Benstock, ed. *Critical Studies on James Joyce's 'Ulysses'.* Boston: G. K. Hall, 1989.

Richard Pearce, ed. *Molly Blooms: A Polylogue on 'Penelope' and Cultural Studies.* Madison: University of Wisconsin Press, 1994.

Vincent Sherry. *James Joyce: 'Ulysses'.* Cambridge: Cambridge University Press, 1994. A short introduction, giving a good sense of the historical context of Joyce's work.

Enda Duffy. *The Subaltern 'Ulysses'.* Minneapolis: University of Minnesota Press, 1994. *Ulysses* as a guerilla text.

Margot Norris, ed. *A Companion to James Joyce's 'Ulysses'.* Boston: Bedford Books, 1998. A volume in the Case Studies in Contemporary Criticism series; it includes Norris's own essay on the critical history of *Ulysses* and others on different critical approaches.

Kimberly J. Devlin and Marilyn Reizbaum, eds. *Ulysses: En-Gendered Perspectives.* Columbia: University of South Carolina Press, 1999. One essay on each episode, raising questions of gender.

Andrew Gibson. *Joyce's Revenge: History, Politics, and Aesthetics in 'Ulysses'*. Oxford: Oxford University Press, 2002.

Derek Attridge, ed. *James Joyce's 'Ulysses': A Casebook*. New York: Oxford University Press, 2003.

Finnegans Wake

For reference

James S. Atherton. *The Books at the Wake: A Study of Literary Allusions in James Joyce's 'Finnegans Wake'* (1959). Rev. edn, Mamaroneck, NY: Paul P. Appel, 1973. A pioneering and still useful guide to the major books and authors exploited in the *Wake*.

Clive Hart. *A Concordance to 'Finnegans Wake'* (1963). Reprinted Mamaroneck, NY: Paul P. Appel, 1974. An invaluable tool, which lists not only all the 'words' of *Finnegans Wake* but also meaningful parts of those 'words' and other words suggested by those 'words'.

Adeline Glasheen. *Third Census of 'Finnegans Wake': An Index of Characters and Their Roles*. Berkeley: University of California Press, 1977. A remarkably full and lively directory of people's names in the *Wake*.

Louis O. Mink. *A 'Finnegans Wake' Gazetteer*. Bloomington: Indiana University Press, 1978. A detailed guide to place-names in the *Wake*.

Roland McHugh. *Annotations to 'Finnegans Wake'* (1980). Baltimore: Johns Hopkins University Press, rev. edn., 1991. McHugh's highly convenient handbook gathers together the work of many scholars, including those (not listed here) who have produced lexicons of a number of languages used in the *Wake*.

The making of the *Wake*

Fred H. Higginson. *Anna Livia Plurabelle: The Making of a Chapter*. Minneapolis: University of Minnesota Press, 1960. Six draft versions of the 'ALP' chapter of the *Wake*.

Thomas E. Connolly, ed. *James Joyce's Scribbledehobble: The Ur-Workbook for 'Finnegans Wake'*. Evanston: Northwestern University Press, 1961. This transcription will doubtless eventually be superseded by the Brepols volume (see below), but in the meantime it provides a fascinating glimpse of Joyce's early preparations for the composition of the *Wake*.

Vincent Deane, Daniel Ferrer, and Geert Lernout, eds. *The 'Finnegans Wake' Notebooks at Buffalo*. Turnhout: Brepols, 2001–. Transcriptions of the notebooks Joyce kept as he wrote *Finnegans Wake*, with reproductions of each page, together with identification of each note's source (where this has been discovered) and details of later usage. A prodigious work of scholarship.

Luca Crispi and Sam Slote, eds. *A Genetic Guide to 'Finnegans Wake'*. Madison: University of Wisconsin Press, 2004. A chapter-by-chapter account of the genesis of the *Wake*, making full use of the notebooks.

Critical studies

Samuel Beckett *et al*. *Our Exagmination Round His Factification for Incamination of Work in Progress* (1929). Reprinted London: Faber; New York: New Directions, 1972. A collection of pieces on the earlier parts of the *Wake*; orchestrated by Joyce, it is of considerable historical interest and continuing critical value – especially the essay by Beckett.

Clive Hart. *Structure and Motif in 'Finnegans Wake'.* London: Faber, 1962. Especially useful on repeated motifs.

Margot Norris. *The Decentered Universe of 'Finnegans Wake': A Structuralist Analysis*. Baltimore: Johns Hopkins University Press, 1976. An important early use of French theoretical models in discussing the *Wake*'s matter and method.

Roland McHugh. *The Sigla of 'Finnegans Wake'*. London: Arnold; Austin: University of Texas Press, 1976. Raises interesting questions about the 'characters' of the *Wake*.

The 'Finnegans Wake' Experience. Dublin: Irish Academic Press, 1981. A down-to-earth account of one person's encounter with the *Wake*.

Danis Rose and John O'Hanlon. *Understanding 'Finnegans Wake': A Guide to the Narrative of James Joyce's Masterpiece*. New York: Garland, 1982. Based on a somewhat rigid theory of the relationship between the notebooks and the final texts, but useful if used critically.

John Bishop. *Joyce's Book of the Dark: 'Finnegans Wake'*. Madison: University of Wisconsin Press, 1986. Particularly good on Joyce's use of Vico and the Egyptian *Book of the Dead*.

Kimberly J. Devlin. *Wandering and Return in 'Finnegans Wake': An Integrative Approach to Joyce's Fictions*. Princeton: Princeton University Press, 1991.

Patrick A. McCarthy, ed. *Critical Essays on James Joyce's 'Finnegans Wake'*. Boston: G. K. Hall, 1992.

Lucia Boldrini. *Joyce, Dante, and the Poetics of Literary Relations*. Cambridge: Cambridge University Press, 2001.

Biography

Stanislaus Joyce. *My Brother's Keeper: James Joyce's Early Years*, ed. Richard Ellmann. New York: Viking; London: Faber, 1958. A vivid account of Joyce by a brother three years younger.

The Complete Dublin Diary, ed. George Healey. Ithaca: Cornell University Press, 1971. James figures significantly in this diary kept by Stanislaus.

Arthur Power. *Conversations with James Joyce*, ed. Clive Hart. London: Millington; New York: Columbia University Press, 1974.

Willard Potts, ed. *Portraits of the Artist in Exile: Recollections of James Joyce by Europeans*. Seattle: University of Washington Press, 1979.

Richard Ellmann. *James Joyce* (1959). Rev. edn, New York: Oxford University Press, 1982. A mass of raw material transmuted into a magisterial biography; inevitably, the portrait that emerges is a reflection of Ellmann's as well as Joyce's views, and it has been challenged in matters both of detail and of general bias.

Bruce Bradley. *James Joyce's Schooldays*. Dublin: Gill and Macmillan, 1982.

Brenda Maddox. *Nora: A Biography of Nora Joyce*. London: Hamish Hamilton; Boston: Houghton Mifflin, 1988. (The American edition bears the misleading subtitle *The Real Life of Molly Bloom*.) An important complement and corrective to Ellmann's biography of Joyce.

E. H. Mikhail, ed. *James Joyce: Interviews and Recollections*. London: Macmillan, 1990.

Morris Beja. *James Joyce: A Literary Life*. Columbus: Ohio State University Press, 1992. A brief and critically astute biography.

John McCourt. *The Years of Bloom: James Joyce in Trieste, 1904–1920*. Dublin: Lilliput, 2000. A full account of the time Joyce spent in Trieste, from the completion of *Dubliners* to the writing of much of *Ulysses*.

Current journals

James Joyce 'Newestlatter'. A newsletter sent to members of the International James Joyce Foundation, which also organizes a symposium every two years. Department of English, Ohio State University, 164 W. 17th Avenue, Columbus, Ohio 43210, USA.

James Joyce Quarterly. Scholarly articles on Joyce, with book reviews, notes, and lists of recent publications. University of Tulsa, Tulsa, OK 74104, USA.

James Joyce Broadsheet. Reviews, illustration, and comment; published three times a year. The School of English, University of Leeds, Leeds LS2 9JT, UK.

James Joyce Literary Supplement. Twice a year. Reviews and features. Department of English, P.O. Box 248145, University of Miami, Coral Gables, FL 33124, USA.

Joyce Studies Annual. A yearly collection of essays on Joyce. P.O. Box 7219, University Station, The University of Texas, Austin TX 78713, USA.

European Joyce Studies. A series of themed essay collections, averaging one issue a year. Amsterdam: Rodopi.

World wide web

There are numerous websites devoted to Joyce and Joyceana; inevitably, some are more up-to-date than others. Most provide links to other sites. Three of the most useful are:

www.cohums.ohio-state.edu/english/organizations/ijjf/ The website of the International James Joyce Foundation.
www.robotwisdom.com/jaj/portal.html The James Joyce Portal.
www.libyrinth.com/joyce/ The Brazen Head.

Audio

Dubliners, *A Portrait*, *Ulysses*, and *Finnegans Wake* have all been released by Naxos AudioBooks, featuring superb readings by Jim Norton and Marcella Riordan. *Dubliners* and *Ulysses* are complete, *A Portrait* is abridged; an abridged version of *Ulysses* is also available.

INDEX

Abbey Theatre 35
Adams, R. M. 74
'After the Race' see *Dubliners*, stories of
ALP (in *Finnegans Wake*) 81, 151, 152, 219, 223; see also *Finnegans Wake*, 'Anna Livia Plurabelle' chapter
Anderson, Benedict 267, 268
Anderson, Chester 182
Anglo-Boer War 263
Anna Livia Plurabelle 55, 159
Antheil, George 52
Apollinaire, Guillaume 56, 73, 75, 76, 77, 81
Aquinas, St Thomas 62–4, 72, 193
'Araby' see *Dubliners*, stories of
Aristotle 32, 50, 72
Arnold, Matthew 68, 69–70, 264, 265
'Art and Life' see essays and lectures by Joyce
Artaud, Antonin 57
Attridge, Derek 96, 98, 101, 163
Austen, Jane 26, 121

Banim, Michael and John 38
Barnacle, Nora see Joyce, Nora Barnacle
Barthes, Roland 145, 147, 151
Barzun, Henri-Martin 77
Baudelaire, Charles 76
Beach, Sylvia xvi, 55–6, 57, 58
Beauvoir, Simone de 203
Beckett, Samuel xvi, 82, 83, 141, 149, 160, 161, 163–4, 165
Begnal, Michael 162
Belvedere College xiv
Benjamin, Walter 246–7
Benn, Gottfried 76, 81
Benstock, Bernard 162, 186
Bérard, Victor 58, 75
Berg, Alban 82

Bergson, Henri 75, 80–1
Berlitz School xv
betrayal 29–30, 34, 40–1, 43–4, 45, 47, 186–9
Bishop, John 163
Björnson, Björnstjerne 68
Blake, William 84, 115, 128
Bloch-Savitsky, Ludmila 54
Bloom, Leopold (in *Ulysses*) 42, 80, 106, 129–34, 138–40, 144, 182, 226–32, 240, 246, 249–51
as Odysseus 123–4
Bloom, Molly (in *Ulysses*) 81, 144, 200, 206, 231–2
as Penelope 123, 124
Bloomsday 50, 56
'Boarding House, The' see *Dubliners*, stories of
Bohemian Girl, The (Balfe) 7, 8
Boldrini, Lucia 163
Book of Kells, The 157, 159
Book of the Dead, The 20, 160
Bourget, Paul 80
Boyd, Ernest 76
Brandes, Georg 68
Breton, André 57, 160
Brion, Marcel 82
British Broadcasting Corporation 17
British Empire 36, 37, 40, 52, 90, 93, 199, 241; see also colonialism
Broch, Hermann 74
Brown, Richard 69
Bruno, Giordano 159, 161
Budgen, Frank 75–6, 196
Burgess, Anthony 73, 141, 149
Burrell, Harry 163
Bush, Ronald 74
Butler, Samuel 75, 80

CAMBRIDGE COMPANIONS TO LITERATURE